PENGUIN BOOKS

AMERICAN DREAM

Jason DeParle is a senior writer for *The New York Times* and a frequent contributor to *The New York Times Magazine*. A graduate of Duke University, DeParle won a George Polk Award and was a two-time finalist for the Pulitzer Prize for his reporting on the welfare system. He lives in Washington, D.C., with his wife, Nancy-Ann, and their two sons.

Praise for *American Dream*

New York Public Library Helen Bernstein Award Winner
Sidney Hillman Award Winner
Washington Monthly **Political Book Award Winner**

"Masterful . . . every bit the exhaustive and authoritative account we might expect from a *New York Times* reporter whose welfare coverage during the Clinton years twice made him a finalist for the Pulitzer Prize. What's startling is the gripping read DeParle provides along the way—an alchemy wrought by the fusion of his encyclopedic knowledge with his mischievous prose. The story of welfare reform turns out to be suspenseful, emotionally rich, rife with dramatic reversals and packed with enough ironies to keep Don DeLillo busy for several years. Who knew?"
—*The Nation*

"Fascinating . . . one of the best books on the American underclass ever written, a compelling account that is disturbing, yet hopeful."
—*National Review*

"Journalism doesn't get any better than this."
—Ellen Goodman, *The Boston Globe*

"DeParle connects the personal and the political . . . with a keen eye and an even more remarkable pen." —*American Prospect*

"Jason DeParle's *American Dream* is a singular achievement. He interweaves a fascinating discussion of the politics of the welfare reform movement with a poignant portrayal of the lives of three women in one extended family who move on and off the welfare rolls in a struggle to survive. This is must reading for anyone concerned about the limitations of American social policy in addressing the problems of the urban poor."
—William Julius Wilson, author of *The Truly Disadvantaged*, Lewis P. and Linda L. Geyser University Professor, Harvard University

"Beautifully written . . . important . . . the narrative really crackles." —*The New Republic*

"A significant book—clear-headed, deeply sensitive, and richly informative." —*San Jose Mercury News*

"DeParle . . . opens up the lives of his subjects in a way that . . . challenges easy left and right assumptions about them. . . . It's DeParle's achievement to detail all these impolite truths while catching you up in these women's lives and revealing their underlying strength. It helps that he's picked an appealing central character in Angie, the nurse's aide, who has a hilarious, no-B.S. mouth on her. . . . DeParle does a brilliant job."
—Mickey Kaus, *Slate*

"A panoramic view . . . starkly honest . . . a humorous, emotional story that is exhaustive in detail and scope."
—*The Boston Globe*

"A powerful bracing antidote ... masterful detail."
—*Los Angeles Times*

"DeParle ... shuns sentimentality and middle-class moralizing. His women are tough, profane and sad. They make wrong decisions, and you cringe. They hustle the system, and you shake your head. Then they surprise you by climbing out of bed in the middle of a frigid Wisconsin night to catch the van to suburban nursing homes in order to work double shifts. ... It might even become an instant classic along the lines of Anthony Lukas' *Common Ground.*" —*The Times-Picayune*

"Reads like an epic novel." —*New York Post*

"With equal measure of compassion and dispassion, Jason DeParle confronts us inescapably with the reality of poverty in America. You cannot read this book and remain indifferent to those who are being left behind. This is one of the great works on social policy of this generation."
—Daniel Schorr, NPR senior news analyst

"A brilliant exercise that combines an honest but sensitive portrait of the women and their families with a larger look at the policy and the politics of welfare reform." —*The Economist*

"Superb and affecting ... debunks many myths surrounding the old system." —*BusinessWeek*

"In this beautifully written, heartfelt book, Jason DeParle has pulled off a stunning feat of journalistic storytelling. Equally at home in the West Wing as he is on the inner-city streets of Milwaukee, DeParle chronicles the story behind the most important piece of social policy to come along in decades, and its impact on real lives. With a novelist's eye for irony and detail, he is unflinching in his reporting. What he finds will surprise you. It did me." —Alex Kotlowitz, author of *There Are No Children Here*

"Richly researched, beautifully written." —*Mother Jones*

"A superb book—honest, richly observed, and artfully written."
—*Commentary*

"A superb piece of reporting and narrative . . . his stories simmer on the page." —*Dissent*

"A dramatic and moving journey . . . told through three amazing women." —Townhall.com

"Convictions and prejudices of the left and the right all fall before this meticulously researched book; it will become a classic account of the lives of the American poor."
—Nathan Glazer, professor of sociology, Harvard University

"This is a book that will break your heart and open your mind. In the vividness of its characters and the sweep of its ambition, *American Dream* is the *Les Miserables* of our day. This book teems with humor, surprise, paradox, and redemption."
—Sister Helen Prejean, author of *Dead Man Walking*

American Dream

THREE WOMEN, TEN KIDS, AND A NATION'S DRIVE TO END WELFARE

Jason DeParle

PENGUIN BOOKS

To Nancy-Ann, Nicholas, and Zachary

PENGUIN BOOKS

Published by the Penguin Group

Penguin Group (USA) Inc., 375 Hudson Street, New York, New York 10014, U.S.A.

Penguin Group (Canada), 90 Eglinton Avenue East, Suite 700, Toronto,
   Ontario, Canada M4P 2Y3 (a division of Pearson Penguin Canada Inc.)

Penguin Books Ltd, 80 Strand, London WC2R 0RL, England

Penguin Ireland, 25 St Stephen's Green, Dublin 2, Ireland (a division of Penguin Books Ltd)

Penguin Group (Australia), 250 Camberwell Road, Camberwell,
   Victoria 3124, Australia (a division of Pearson Australia Group Pty Ltd)

Penguin Books India Pvt Ltd, 11 Community Centre, Panchsheel Park, New Delhi – 110 017, India

Penguin Group (NZ), cnr Airborne and Rosedale Roads, Albany,
   Auckland, New Zealand (a division of Pearson New Zealand Ltd)

Penguin Books (South Africa) (Pty) Ltd, 24 Sturdee Avenue, Rosebank, Johannesburg 2196, South Africa

Penguin Books Ltd, Registered Offices:
80 Strand, London WC2R 0RL, England

First published in the United States of America by Viking Penguin,
a member of Penguin Group (USA) Inc. 2004
Published in Penguin Books 2005

10 9 8 7 6 5 4 3 2 1

Excerpt from "What Does the Political Scientist Know" by Artur Miedzyrzecki from *Spoiling Cannibals' Fun: Polish Poetry from the Last Two Decades of Communist Rule*, edited and translated by Stanislaw Baranczak and Clare Cavanagh (Northwestern University Press). Used by permission.

LIBRARY OF CONGRESS HAS CATALOGED THE HARDCOVER EDITION AS FOLLOWS:
DeParle, Jason.
American dream : three women, ten kids, and a nation's drive to end welfare / Jason DeParle.
p. cm.
Includes index.
ISBN 0-670-89275-0 (hc.)
ISBN 0 14 30.3437 5 (pbk.)
   1. Public welfare—United States—Case studies.   2. Welfare recipients—Employment—United
   States—Case studies.   3. Public welfare administration—United States—Case studies.   I. Title.
HV95.D26 2004
362.5'568'0973—dc22   2004049494

Printed in the United States of America
Designed by Nancy Resnick

I think all of us know in our heart of hearts America's biggest problem today is that too many of our people never got a shot at the American Dream.

—BILL CLINTON
FEBRUARY 2, 1993

I am born of black color
Descendant of slaves,
Who worked and cried so I can see better days
Who fought and ran
So I can be free to see better days.
Better days are here, so they say
So why am I still working, running, fighting and crying?
For my better days?
Or is it so my descendants can know of the work I'm putting in
For their better days?

—ANGELA JOBE
2003

CONTENTS

x | Contents

PART I

Welfare

ONE

The Pledge:
Washington and Milwaukee, 1991

Bruce Reed needed a better line.

A little-known speechwriter in a long-shot campaign, he was trapped in the office on a Saturday afternoon, staring at a flat phrase. A few weeks earlier, his boss, Bill Clinton, had stood on the steps of the Arkansas Capitol to announce he was running for president. One of the things Clinton had criticized that day was welfare. "We should insist that people move off the welfare rolls and onto the work rolls," he said. It wasn't the kind of thing most Democrats said, which was one reason Reed liked it; he thought the party carried too much liberal baggage, especially in its defense of the dole. But the phrase wasn't particularly memorable, either. With Clinton planning a big speech at Georgetown University, Reed tried again.

"If you can work, you'll have to do so," he wrote.

Mmmmm . . . still not right.

At thirty-one, Reed had a quick grin and an unlined face, but he was less of an innocent than he seemed. Five months earlier, when Clinton was still weighing the race, Reed had struck a hard-boiled pose. "A message has to fit on a bumpersticker," he wrote. "Sharpen those lines and you'll get noticed. Fuzz them and you'll disappear." Now the welfare rolls hit new highs with every passing month. And Reed lacked bumper-sticker stuff. At 5:00 p.m. he joined a conference call with a half-dozen other operatives in the fledgling campaign. Clinton wasn't on the line. He was in such a bad mood he wanted to cancel the speech. His voice was weak; he didn't feel ready. He wanted Mario Cuomo, the rival he most feared, to define his vision first. He was angry to hear that invitations had gone out and it was too late to turn back.

The group reviewed the latest draft, which outlined Clinton's domestic plans, and agreed the welfare section needed work. How about calling for an "end to permanent welfare"? Reed asked. That was better. Not quite right, but better. They swapped a few more lines, and the following morning Reed sent out a draft with a catchy new phrase. If Clinton spotted the change, he didn't say. On October 23, 1991, he delivered the words as drafted: "In a Clinton administration we're going to put an end to welfare as we know it." By the time it was clear the slogan mattered, no one could say who had coined it.

At first, no one noticed. *The New York Times* didn't cover the speech, and *The Washington Post* highlighted Clinton's promise to create a "New Covenant." But soon the power of the phrase made itself known. *End welfare as we know it.* "Pure heroin," one of the pollsters called it. When Reed reached the White House, he taped the words to his wall and called them his "guiding star." In time, they would send 9 million women and children streaming from the rolls.

One of those women was Angela Jobe. The month Bill Clinton announced that he was running for president, she stepped off a Greyhound bus in Milwaukee to start a new life. She was twenty-five years old and arrived from Chicago towing two large duffel bags and three young kids. Angie had a pretty milk-chocolate face and a fireplug build—her four-foot-eleven-inch frame carried 150 pounds—and the combination could make her look tender or tough, depending on her mood. She had never seen Milwaukee before and pronounced herself unimpressed. "Why they got all these old-ass houses!" she groused. "Where the brick at?" Irreverence was Angie's religion. She arrived in Milwaukee as she moved through the world, a short, stout fountain of exclamation points, half of them capping sentences that would peel paint from the bus station walls. Absent her animating humor, the transcript may sound off-putting. But up close her habit of excitable swearing, about her "cheap-ass jobs" and "crazy-ass friends" and her "too-cool, too-slick motherfucker" men, came off as something akin to charm. "I just express myself so accurately!" she laughed.

The cascade of off-color commentary, flowing alongside the late-night cans of Colt 45, could make Angie seem like a jaded veteran of ghetto life. Certainly she had plenty to feel jaded about. She grew up on the borders of Chicago's gangland. Her father was a drunk. She had her first baby at seventeen, dropped out of high school, and had two more in quick succession. She didn't have a diploma or a job, and the man she loved was in jail. By the time she arrived in Milwaukee, she had been on welfare for nearly eight years, the sum of her adult life. The hard face was real but also a mask. Her mother had worked two jobs to send her to parochial school, and though Angie tried to hide it, she still bore traces of the English student from Aquinas High. Lots of women came to Milwaukee looking for welfare checks. Not many then felt the need to start a poem about their efforts to discern God's will:

> *I'm tired*
> *Of trying to understand*
> *What God wants of me*

Worried that was *too* irreverent, Angie substituted "the world" for "God" and stored the unfinished page in a bag so high in her closet she couldn't reach it with a chair. The old red nylon bag was filled with her yellowing treasures: love letters, journals, poems by Gwendolyn Brooks, the hospital bracelets that each of her kids had worn in the nursery. Stories of street fights Angie was happy to share, but the bag was so private that hardly anyone knew it existed. "Don't you know I like looking mean?" she said one day. While it sounded like one of her self-mocking jokes, Angie segued into a quiet confession. "If people think you're nice, they'll take your kindness for weakness. That's a side of me I don't want anybody to see. That way I don't have to worry about nobody hurting me." In welfare terms, Angie could pass as a paragon of "dependency": unmarried, uneducated, and unemployed. But Angie never thought of herself as depending on anything. She saw herself as a strong, self-reliant woman who did what it took to get by. She saw herself as a survivor.

No one survived on welfare alone, especially in Chicago, where benefits were modest but rents were not. Sometimes Angie worked, without telling welfare, at fast-food restaurants. Stints at Popeye's,

Church's, and KFC had marked her as a chicken-joint triathlete, a minimum-wage workhorse steeped in grease. She also relied on her children's father, Greg, a tall, soft-spoken man in braids who looked out at the world with seductive eyes. Greg, not welfare, marked the major border in Angie's life. Before Greg, she wore a plaid jumper and went to parochial school. After Greg, *right* after Greg, Angie was a teenage mother. Their relationship hadn't completely passed as a portrait of harmony. Once, when he went without feeding the kids, she tried to shoot him. But unlike most teen parents, they stayed together, and by the time their oldest child was entering school, Greg was making "beaucoup money" in the industry employing most men Angie knew. Greg was selling cocaine. His arrest, in the summer of 1991, hit her with the force of a sudden death. She had never even lived alone, never mind raised kids by herself. Without Greg, she couldn't pay the bills: rent was more than her entire welfare check. Ninety miles away, the economics were reversed. You could sign up for welfare, get an apartment, and have money left over. So many poor families were fleeing Chicago that taxpayers in southern Wisconsin griped about "Greyhound therapy." Higher welfare, lower rent— that's all Angie knew about Milwaukee when she stepped off the bus.

A few days later, Greg's sister arrived. Since Angie and Greg were all but married, Jewell was her all but sister-in-law. She was also Angie's closest friend. Jewell's boyfriend, Tony, had been caught in the same arrest, so Jewell faced a similar problem: she was twenty-two, with a three-year-old son, and unless she moved to the projects she couldn't live on welfare in Chicago. Plus she was six months pregnant. On the outside, they formed a study in contrasts. While Angie groomed herself for durability, Jewell arrived in cover-girl style. She was a half foot taller, with a curl in her hair, perfect teeth, and art gallery nails; with a gleaming pair of tennis shoes, she could turn sweatpants into high couture. She wasn't married, but Tony's letters from jail came addressed to "my sexy wife." Still, there was nothing brittle about her beauty or soft behind her reserve. While Angie swore away her frustrations and cried after too many beers, Jewell treated pain as a weakness best locked inside. Jewell was a survivor, too.

They went about settling down. Piling in with Angie's cousin for a week, they signed up for welfare at a three-story fortress of local fame known by its address, "Twelfth and Vliet." Like the shuttered homes around it, the building had traced the parabolic journey of American industrial life; launched as a department store near the century's start, it had sparkled with the city's blue-collar prosperity before being padlocked in 1961 and sold off to the county. By the time Angie and Jewell arrived, the building overlooked an eight-lane gash that funneled the prosperity to the suburbs north and west, and there was nothing left inside but long forms and hard chairs. The thirty-one-page application asked if they owned any stocks, bonds, trust funds, life insurance, farm equipment, livestock, snowmobiles, or boats. It asked nothing about the tragedy that had brought them to the county's door. Welfare dispensed money, not advice.

A few days later, they had their checks and started the apartment hunt. Jewell got a tip from a neighbor. If they moved into a homeless shelter first, the Red Cross would pay their security deposit and first month's rent. ("Getting your Red Cross" it was called.) "Homeless shelter" may conjure a vision of winos in a barracks, but the Family Crisis Center, in a converted monastery in the heart of the ghetto, had a cheerful air. It offered private rooms, a play area for the kids, and a chance to meet new people. From the shelter, they resumed the search for housing, and Angie found the perfect solution: adjacent apartments in a renovated Victorian complex on First Street, owned by an old woman who soon grew too senile to collect the rent.

On October 23, 1991—the day Clinton pledged to "end welfare"—two welfare mothers and four welfare kids awoke on a wooden floor. The apartment didn't have a refrigerator or stove, so they fashioned three meals from lunch meat. At five, Angie's middle child, Redd, still cried for his father. He was having a harder time accepting the arrest than Kesha, an openhearted, adaptable girl of seven, or Von, who, even at four, coolly distanced himself from family trouble; Redd was as hot as his name. Angie ached for Greg, too, but she was relieved to finish the move. There's something to having a place of your own, even when it's empty and hard.

As soon as he pledged to end welfare, Clinton had second thoughts. He needed the liberals, who turn out in primaries, but Cuomo, the liberals' philosopher-king, struck back by calling dependency a myth. Clinton feared his enemies might compare him to another white southerner who was criticizing welfare in the fall of 1991, the ex-Klansman David Duke. (Cuomo tried to do just that.) Looking ahead to the Super Tuesday ballot, Clinton chided his staff that "half this election is about winning the southern black vote." A black governor, Doug Wilder, was running, and Clinton feared Wilder might call him a racist. "This is a major, major deal," Clinton warned.

To protect himself, Clinton launched an attack against Duke even before the Georgetown speech. He also put out feelers to Jesse Jackson, who kept his guns quiet. But the best reassurance came from black voters themselves. In a focus group in North Carolina in the fall of 1991, they said they were all for cutting welfare, as long as they sensed an equal commitment to education and jobs. A campaign aide, Celinda Lake, flew home amazed. "The welfare message, worded correctly, plays extremely well in the black community," she reported. Indeed, far from alienating anyone, Clinton's welfare pledge roused voters everywhere. Clinton's main pollster, Stan Greenberg, was startled by the emotions it raised. Three-quarters of the people he probed in New Hampshire were impressed by Clinton's stance on welfare, while just a quarter cared he was a Rhodes Scholar. It was "by far, the single most important component of Clinton's biography," Greenberg wrote in a campaign memo. Voters were "stunned to hear a Democrat saying . . . 'Hey, you on the lower end can't abuse the welfare system any more.'"

As the scandal-a-day campaign rolled on, welfare emerged as its all-purpose elixir, there to cure what ailed. It reassured ethnic voters in Illinois, who found Clinton too slick. (They "were taken aback when Clinton talked about welfare," Greenberg wrote.) It soothed the reflexive distrust among Florida conservatives. ("The strongest media message was introduced by the 'welfare spot.'") It won Clinton a fresh look in Pennsylvania, where more than half the voters had character doubts. ("No other message comes close to this one on intensity and breadth of interest.") It was a values message, an economic message, and a policy message in one. It supplied his second-most popular line at the Democratic convention, and his most effective answer to the GOP's post-convention attacks. While the pledge to "end welfare" featured prominently in the barrage of late-season ads, the only mystery, given its force, was that Clinton didn't stress it even more.

The Republicans felt robbed—welfare was *their* issue. Sagging in the polls, President George H. W. Bush tried to copy the tune but sounded painfully off-key. "Get a job or get off the dole!" he screeched. On November 3, 1992, Clinton, the "end-welfare" candidate, became the end-welfare president-elect.

By then, Angie had spent another year in the system Clinton was pledging to end. When she arrived in the fall of 1991, the country already had a small welfare-to-work program called JOBS, and soon she got a letter. "Angela Jobe is a mandatory work program registrant," it began. "Work" was a bit of a euphemism, since the program mostly sent people to study for their high school diplomas, not to sweep the streets. "Mandatory" was euphemistic, too: Angie could have ignored the summons and kept more than 90 percent of her food stamps and cash. Still, she was happy to go. "I always worked!" Angie said. "What—I'm supposed to move up here and get lazy?" As a statement of fact, "I always worked" ignored some large résumé gaps. But as an assertion of identity it was revealing. Despite nearly eight years of welfare checks, Angie saw herself as a worker.

Arriving for the program, Angie discovered that six weeks of training could turn her into a certified nursing assistant. *Nursing assistant*: now that had a ring. She didn't know what nursing assistants did, but she figured they made good money. And it sounded better than frying chickens, "'cause 'chicken place' just ain't a nice career." She pictured her abridged frame draped in nursing whites and started to play with the words. "Nursing assistant . . . assisting a nurse . . . working in a hospital." Until the class began, Angie didn't realize that most nursing aides did scut work in nursing homes, a revelation that stole some of her excitement. ("Wiping butts" is how lots of welfare recipients described it.) She also felt intimidated to be back in a classroom, a place where she had known only failure. The bus stop was frigid in the depths of December. The blood pressure cuff gave her grief. More than half her classmates gave up. But if stubbornness was the stuff of many of her problems, it was also the start of her solutions. She forced herself to show up every day, and she was so proud at her graduation she had Jewell bring the kids. She went out that night to celebrate at a bar and started talking with the deejay.

Angie liked the class more than the work. She had understood, in a theoretical way, the physical strain involved: the lifting and pulling, the washing and feeding, the business of bedpans. But once she started at a nursing home, the sadness of it all set in. "I don't want to find no dead person!" was all she could think. She lasted eight days. Angie stayed home for a few months, then caught another break. She had thrown in an application at the post office, and an offer came through. The post office! A job for life! People look at you with respect when you work at the post office! It wasn't what she thought. She wasn't a full-fledged unionized worker, but a temporary employee at $6 an hour with no benefits or security. She didn't even work in the main post office. She caught a van to an airport annex, where she spent her time double-checking the presorted mail. All the same, it was a foot in the door, and she liked the routine. Since it was second-shift work, she could stay out late with the deejay and still have time to sleep. The welfare office didn't know she was working, so she kept her full benefits. Two more friends from Chicago had moved into the compound, which felt like a cross between a kibbutz and a sorority house; there was always someone to talk to or babysit the kids. Angie felt sufficiently good about herself to enroll in a GED class. A year after she arrived in Milwaukee, indigent and effectively widowed, she was reassembling a life.

The first sign of trouble was the Vienna sausage. The second was the naps. She'd drag herself to class, then stop by her girlfriend's house to munch potted pork and sleep on the couch. As the mound of empty weenie tins grew, so did her girlfriend's suspicions. "You need a pregnancy test," her friend said. Angie knew she wasn't pregnant. She had ditched the deejay months ago. She couldn't be pregnant. She had just had her period and she was taking birth control pills. She better not be pregnant. Von, her youngest child, just started school, and she wasn't going back to diapers. "I ain't," she said. "You is," said her friend. "You crazy!" Angie said. In November 1992, just after Clinton won the election, her friend ran an errand at a clinic. Along for the ride, Angie took a pregnancy test just to prove her wrong. "Miss Jobe, I need to speak with you," the nurse began. *Unh-uh,*

Angie thought. *Unh-uhhh!* She drank for a week and cried for a month. Then she quit the postal job. When you're too depressed to get out of bed, there's no sorting the mail.

Sorting the mail didn't cross Jewell's mind when she arrived in Milwaukee, no longer a girl yet not quite grown. Neither did making beds, mopping floors, frying chickens, or any of the other jobs she could land. Her adult work history consisted of a few months locked in the cashier's booth at an all-night Amoco station. Jobs weren't something that Jewell thought much about. Babies were.

Unlike Angie, Jewell was delighted to be pregnant. It didn't matter that her first son's father was long gone or that the new baby's father was in jail. Babies made Jewell feel alive. Like lots of girls who have a baby in high school, Jewell had gotten pregnant on purpose, thinking a child would bring her something to love. Unlike most, Jewell had found the theory worked. She loved everything about her first son, Terrell, from the moment he was born. His new baby smell. His miniature clothes. Even his middle-of-the-night cries. Ghetto life requires a hard face, but babies let Jewell smile. She went into labor in December 1991, two months after she arrived in Milwaukee. It was the middle of the night, but soon everyone in the compound was shouting. Angie stayed behind to watch the kids, while another friend rode with Jewell in the ambulance. By breakfast, Jewell had a second son, Tremmell. A few weeks later, Jewell swathed him against the Lake Michigan wind, got back on the bus, and carried him into the Cook County Jail, where father and son caught their first glimpse of each other through a partition of bulletproof glass. Jewell enjoyed showing Tony his son, but it was starting to sink in that Tony wasn't coming home.

Thrown into troubled waters, Angie and Jewell navigated in contrasting ways. Angie chugged ahead like a rusty tug, forming a wake of jettisoned plans: she was going to be a nurse or a postal clerk; she was going to get her high school degree; she was going to figure out what God wants of her; she was going to stop crying about Greg. Jewell was a sailboat without a sail, adrift with no plan at all. Passivity offered protection; when you don't get your hopes up, there's less to let you down. The new baby was almost four months old when one of her younger brother's friends floated into town—a wild, wiry street kid, barely out of his teens, whom everyone knew as Lucky. Or as one of the gang later said, "His name is Lucky but he's not." Lucky liked to drink, and drinking made him talk. He covered Jewell in verbal rainbows—Technicolor pledges of devotion, mixed with white lies and purple jokes. "Jewell! You want me to rob a bank? I'll rob it for you, Jewell!" "Jewell! I been wanting to talk to you ever since we was in grammar school! Man, you had a *big* ol' butt!" "Jewell! Can you be my lady?" They danced. She wasn't so much smitten as amused and lonelier than she knew. In Lucky, the court found its inebriated jester, and Jewell found a man.

Communal living got to Jewell—the noise, the gossip, the lack of privacy. She and Lucky moved away for a few months, but Lucky had problems with the neighborhood gang and they raced back after he got shot in the hand. Bored, restless, putting on weight, Jewell did something wildly out of character. She volunteered for JOBS, the same welfare-to-work program that had summoned Angie. "Dear Jewell M Reed," came the reply. "Please read the rights and responsibilities pamphlet." The dour bureaucratic response set the tone for what followed. Her case got handed to an inner-city group, the Opportunities Industrialization Center, whose renown lay more in winning state contracts than in finding poor people jobs. First she got parked in a motivation class. Then a caseworker urged her to forget about work and pursue her GED, though Jewell insisted that she wanted to make money. Finally she got herself referred to a course for nursing assistants, like the one that Angie had taken. She waited for two months, then learned that it was canceled. "They don't ever do much of nothing except take you through a lot of hassles," Jewell said. It was the last time she asked the welfare office for anything but a check.

Home soon after to visit Chicago, Jewell was catching up on family news when she learned that one of her favorite cousins was having problems. She had had another baby, split up with her husband, and moved in with her mother. Nearly a decade had passed since Jewell had seen Opal Caples, though as kids in the projects the two had been close. Even the big-city names chosen by their rural-born mothers had framed them as natural friends: Ruthie Mae and Hattie Mae had Opal and Jewell. Jewell wasn't one to act on impulse, but something made her pick up the phone, and the conversation clicked. Opal said she had three young daughters with rhyming names: Sierra, Kierra, and Tierra. *"F'real?"* Jewell said. "Yup!" Jewell had two preschool sons with rhyming names: Terrell and Tremmell. *"F'real?"* Opal said. "Yup!" Opal was drawing welfare, too, and her dilemma was the same one Jewell had faced: without help, she couldn't afford a place of her own in Chicago. Living with her churchy mother left Opal feeling caged. Jewell said her landlady had an empty apartment for $325, and welfare would pay more than $600. "Yahoo!" Opal said. "I'm coming."

Jewell didn't take her seriously—no one makes a decision like that in a few minutes on the phone. Yet something about Opal had always set her apart. She was probably the smartest of Jewell's childhood friends and definitely the wildest. Expelled from not one but two public schools, Opal, unlike Angie and Jewell, went on to graduate and even did a semester of community college. While Jewell didn't spend much time mulling life beyond the ghetto, Opal worked worldly allusions into her conversation. Her husband was so stuck on himself "he thinks he's the Prince of Wales." When their mothers made them go job hunting as teens, Opal got all the offers. "I have a personality that attracts people to me—I do!" she said. "Lotta people tell me that." With education, experience, and a gift for making friends, Opal could leave a welfare office voted most likely to succeed. But there was something that neither her caseworkers nor cousins knew. Opal had been smoking cocaine. A little at first, then a lot—off and on during her second pregnancy and constantly during her third. One reason she was living at home is that she had smoked up the rent money and fled before her husband found his stuff on the street. Opal's mother didn't want the extended family to know, and Opal wasn't about to tell. Among the hopes she held for Milwaukee was the hope of getting clean.

When she and Jewell met at the station there was no time for a reunion scene. They piled the kids and suitcases aboard and headed off for the two-hour ride up I-94. When Angie got home from work that night, she found a new resident of the compound—a short, dark, beguiling woman who told riotous stories of her life's escapades and was quick to swap Newports, insults, and beer. "That's my cousin!" Angie and Opal each would insist from then on. Biologically, they're not related (though through Greg their kids are), but that's a technicality that Angie indignantly dismissed. "What you mean?" she said. "We 'bout as biological as it gets!"

A few days later, a book of Jewell's food stamps disappeared. Soon Opal disappeared, too. "Damn, she must a met somebody already," Jewell thought. Her mother had heard a rumor that Opal was using drugs, but Jewell paid her no mind. Her mother said all kinds of crazy things. For years, her mother had said that the government was going to take welfare away. Jewell figured that was just something mothers liked to say.

Now and then at a social event, someone asks me what I do. If I don't feel like talking, I tell the truth. I say I cover "social policy" for *The New York Times,* and the conversation moves on. In a more adventurous mood, I tell the truth in a different way. I say I cover "welfare." That keeps the table boiling: say the word *welfare,* and there's no telling what might bubble up. Bill Clinton started one of those conversations on the fly in a campaign season, and what bubbled up was a free-for-all—and an "end" to welfare—more radical than anyone had imagined. This book represents a seven-year effort to find out what happened next.

Though I had spent years watching the welfare bill evolve, I realized why I found the subject so compelling as I listened, in the summer of 1996, to the final hours of Senate debate. The senators were talking about welfare the way people talk of it at dinner tables, in terms so ideological as to be virtually religious. They were talking of how their parents and grandparents had made it. (Or hadn't. Or couldn't.) They were talking of how their communities would care for the poor. (Or didn't. Or wouldn't.) At times, it seemed that the very idea of America was on trial. We live in a country rich beyond measure, yet one with unconscionable ghettos. We live in a country where anyone can make it; yet generation after generation, some families don't. To argue about welfare is to argue about why. I'll be pleased if this story challenges, and informs, the assumptions on both sides as much as it has challenged my own. "Ideas are interesting—people are boring," a welfare expert once told me. Ideas *are* interesting. But I proceeded on a broader faith, that what has occurred in the lives of the welfare poor is more interesting than either camp has assumed.

The story focuses on three women in one extended family, inseparable at the start but launched on differing arcs. Perhaps no three people can stand for 9 million. But with Angie's gumption, Jewell's reticence, and Opal's manipulative charm, the threesome cover a great deal of ground. A catalog of their collective lives would include everything from crack house to 401(k), with results that roughly reflect the experiences of welfare families nationwide. Two grabbed a toehold on the bottom of the employment ladder. One wound up with a journey through the new welfare system more tragic than I would have guessed possible.

Since welfare is a subject filled with biases, the reader may welcome a word about mine. At the time the president signed the law— the Personal Responsibility and Work Opportunity Reconciliation Act of 1996—I had been writing about inner-city life for more than a decade. Inevitably, I had opinions. I thought the harshness of the low-wage economy and the turmoil of poor people's lives required a federal safety net, not one torn by arbitrary time limits and handed to the states. I also thought the most constructive thing to do as a reporter was to clean my mental slate. With the welfare system starting over, I tried to do the same. To my relief, the first years brought reassurance: more work, less welfare, falling poverty rates. No signs of children "sleeping on grates," as Senator Daniel Patrick Moynihan had famously warned. Surely the vibrant economy helped, and tougher tests awaited. Still, after years on the poverty beat, there was something truly exotic to report: good news.

At the same time, I felt uneasy with the triumphal claims ringing through public life. The "greatest social policy change in this nation in sixty years," is how Tommy Thompson put it, after leaving his job as governor of Wisconsin to become the secretary of Health and Human Services. *The Wall Street Journal* did him one better: "the greatest advance for America's poor since the rise of capitalism." The very phrase "welfare-to-work" brims with implication: rising incomes, inspired kids, more hopeful lives. But the successes I witnessed were never so clear. Paradoxically, the closer I got to the welfare story, the less central welfare appeared. "Did it *work*?" people would ask about the landmark law. "That's your crazy stuff," Angie said, insisting the law was no landmark to her. "We don't be thinking 'bout that!"

In assembling this account, I have relied on years of discussions with the main characters. With their permission, I have also examined a decade's worth of welfare and earnings records and talked with others in their lives: relatives, boyfriends, caseworkers, bosses, and friends. Court records, tax returns, school transcripts, and letters have enhanced my understanding, and a trail of genealogical material extends the family history back six generations. In launching the project, I imagined, if only half-consciously, that it would follow a sleek narrative line of underdogs against the world. It is that story, but also a more complicated one—of adversity variously overcome, compounded, or merely endured. In that way, too, it embodies the story of welfare writ large.

Some readers may wonder why I focused on an African American family when nationally blacks and whites each accounted for about 40 percent of the rolls. I first chose to focus on Milwaukee, the epicenter of the antiwelfare crusade, and, as it happened, nearly 70 percent of the city's caseload was black. As the drive to end welfare began, the paradigmatic Milwaukee recipient was a black woman from Chicago whose mother or grandmother had started life in a Mississippi cotton field, a description that fits Angie, Opal, and Jewell. At the same time, there are advantages to seeing the rise and fall of welfare through African American eyes. Given their share of the national population, black families were more than six times as likely as whites to receive a welfare check. Among long-term recipients, the racial imbalance was even more pronounced: nearly seven of ten long-term recipients were African American. Considering our national history, that shouldn't be a surprise; for more than three centuries blacks were barred by violence and law from the full benefits of American life.

The story that follows is rooted in the racial past, a past much less distant than I first supposed. In understanding where it began, I got help from a regal woman named Hattie Mae Crenshaw. She is Jewell's mother, grandmother to Angie's kids, and an elder cousin whom Opal regards as an aunt. She was born beside a Mississippi bayou in 1937, in a shack without electricity or running water. By the time she reached late middle age, a job as a private nursing aide had carried her by Concorde to Paris. In between, she had lived much of the country's welfare history. Barely sixty when I met her, Hattie Mae wasn't old. But she was old enough to remember chopping cotton to pay the plantation store. She settled into her story from a white-tiger love seat in Jewell's living room. Family history bores Jewell; she left the room to do her nails. Hattie Mae smiled as she began: "I growed up on Senator Jim Eastland's plantation in Doddsville, Mississippi. That's when black peoples was just beginning to come out of slavery." Patient with my puzzled looks, Hattie Mae talked on, pointing me toward welfare's forgotten prequel.

The Caples Family

Generation I
(Mississippi)

Generation II
(Mississippi)

Generation III
(Mississippi)

Ed Caples
Frank Caples
Ola Mae Caples
Jessie Caples
John Caples

Elijah "Lij" Caples —

Samuel Caples
ca. 1785-1868
(slaveholder)

Wiley Caples ———
1912-1998

(other wives) ———
&
Pie Eddie Caples
1876-1930
&
Hattie Caples
1900-1951

Mack Caples
1915-2003

Frank Caples
ca. 1835- ?
(slave)

Mayola Caples ———
1920-1939
Lula Bell Caples
Will Caples
Vidalia Caples
Lewis "Pop" Caples

Generation IV
(Mississippi/Chicago)

Generation V
(Chicago)

Generation VI
(Milwaukee)

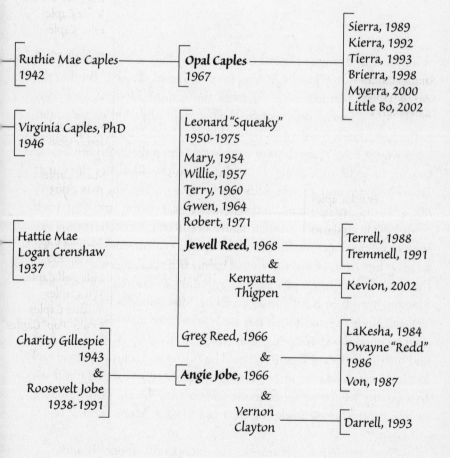

Ruthie Mae Caples
1942

Opal Caples
1967

Sierra, 1989
Kierra, 1992
Tierra, 1993
Brierra, 1998
Myerra, 2000
Little Bo, 2002

Virginia Caples, PhD
1946

Leonard "Squeaky"
1950-1975

Mary, 1954
Willie, 1957
Terry, 1960
Gwen, 1964
Robert, 1971

Hattie Mae
Logan Crenshaw
1937

Jewell Reed, 1968
&
Kenyatta
Thigpen

Terrell, 1988
Tremmell, 1991

Kevion, 2002

Charity Gillespie
1943
&
Roosevelt Jobe
1938-1991

Greg Reed, 1966
&
Angie Jobe, 1966
&
Vernon
Clayton

LaKesha, 1984
Dwayne "Redd"
1986
Von, 1987

Darrell, 1993

TWO

The Plantation:
Mississippi, 1840–1960

It may sound strange to hear Hattie Mae say that at her birth in 1937 black people were "just beginning to come out of slavery." But her argument wasn't much different from those most modern historians make. And it was no different from what an improbable visitor found in the same fields a few years before she was born. Hortense Powdermaker must have caused quite a stir when she pulled into Sunflower County in 1932, explaining she had come in the depths of the Great Depression to conduct a scientific study of Negro life. She was a thirty-one-year-old Jewish academic, educated in London and just back from Melanesia—not a familiar figure in the cotton patch. It took the state's leading aristocrat, the poet and planter William Alexander Percy, to keep her from being run out of town. But soon she was traipsing through sharecropper shacks and sweating at church revivals, immersing herself in black life as no white Mississippian would dream. Though she struggled to get her study into print in 1939, *After Freedom* attained the status of a minor classic, praised by W. E. B. DuBois and reissued with each generation. The title is both chronological and ironic: it wasn't so long after slavery, and there wasn't much freedom. In a county where seven of ten residents were black, Powdermaker summarized white attitudes on the eve of Hattie Mae's birth:

> Negroes are innately inferior to white people, mentally and morally. Their place is in manual work.
>
> Any attempt at any kind of social equality would result in

some disaster so overwhelming that it is dangerous even to talk about it. . . .

Because the Whites are so seriously outnumbered, special means must be taken to keep the Negro in his place. . . .

There may be good "niggers," and bad "niggers," but a "nigger" is a "nigger" and cannot escape the taint.

Powdermaker wrote as an optimist. While she didn't foresee anything like the northern migration or the civil rights revolution, two movements that would change the world of Hattie Mae, she did sense an impatience among younger blacks and presciently called it a force "capable of being mobilized." At the same time, she was attuned to an aspect of sharecropper life that would prove cause for less optimism: the widespread social chaos, in particular the fluid family structure. Outside a tiny black elite, formal marriages were rare. Most sharecroppers lived in unsteady common-law arrangements, "easily entered and easily dissolved." Nonmarital births prevailed: "Even if there is a man in the household, he is often not the child's father." Since women had broader access to jobs—they could work as field hands or domestics—black men were doubly marginalized. Domestic violence was epidemic ("It is something for a woman to boast about if her husband does not beat her"), and so were other forms of black-on-black violence, much of it ignored by the law. Among poor blacks, "it is more or less assumed that some member of any family will get into jail." Put differently, Powdermaker was describing many of the conditions later associated with a welfare underclass: single mothers, peripatetic men, an undertow of crime and violence. But welfare—that is, Aid to Families with Dependent Children—could scarcely be blamed. It didn't yet exist.

Charting the rise of the northern ghettos, Nicholas Lemann became the first contemporary writer to stress the ties to sharecropper life. "Every aspect of the underclass culture in the ghettos is directly traceable to roots in the South," he wrote in *The Atlantic* in 1986, "and not the South of slavery but . . . the nascent underclass of the sharecropper South." In the exchanges that followed, critics noted the many positive aspects of sharecropper society: the safety-net functions of the extended family, the vibrancy of the church, the yearning for education on display in the one-room schoolhouse. All true: countless black sharecroppers moved north and prospered, including some of Hattie Mae's kin. But the point as it pertains to welfare is simpler. Many of the problems blamed on "the liberal, welfare plantation" were flourishing decades before, on the not-so-liberal one.

To picture Hattie Mae's childhood, you have to picture the Mississippi Delta—endless, empty, mud-puddle flat, and stretching to the earth's very edge. The Eastland property runs about three miles west from the Sunflower River and three north and south. In other words, it is vast. To cross it on foot, as Hattie Mae used to do, is to be reminded daily of one's humble place in the scheme of things. The Eastlands lived on the eastern border, by the bridge to the wider world, in a house that spoke more of suburban comfort than antebellum grandeur. Across the river sat the crossroads "town" of Doddsville (1940 pop. 262), but with its own gin, shop, and store, the plantation was a town in itself. The commercial buildings clustered toward the front, near the Eastlands' home, while several hundred tenants spread out behind in places marked by informal names like "Sparkman" and "Sandy Ridge." Hattie Mae lived about two miles in, along a bayou behind Bob McLean Curve.

Even in the early 1940s, the plantation had a nineteenth-century feel. There were mules in the fields. Tenants did without electricity or running water. Some shacks barely had walls. "You could set on the inside and look at the outside," Hattie Mae said. With medical care rudimentary at best, anything from a mule kick to childbirth could prove life threatening. In the basic bargain of sharecropper life, the planter provided land, seed, tools, housing, and living expenses, often in the form of credit at an overpriced plantation store; think of it as a proto-welfare system. The tenant provided labor in exchange for half the profits. But since the accounting stayed in the planter's hands, so did the money. As a little girl, Hattie Mae would watch her uncles line up for the annual "settle." "Some would come out crying," she said. "Some would break even. If you came out with two hundred dollars, you were rich." James Eastland took over the plantation from his father, Woods, in 1934, and he ran it with unchecked power; the police were barred from crossing the bridge onto the property. "These are my niggers," Hattie Mae quoted him as saying. "If they keep themselves outta the grave, I'll keep 'em out of jail."

Hattie Mae's grandfather, Pie Eddie Caples, arrived on the plantation in 1927 with the kind of family tree that Hortense Powdermaker would have recognized. The wife he brought to the plantation was at least his fourth, and he had children with all of them. (The law firm handling the divorce was Eastland & Nichols.) One of the children he brought along was a six-year-old girl named Mayola, and a decade later she went into labor in the shack by the bayou and gave birth to Hattie Mae. The following year Mayola Caples got pregnant again, but this time the labor killed her. Not yet two, Hattie Mae was orphaned and not for the last time.

"My grandfather was a slave," Hattie Mae said, passing along the family legend as Jewell tended her nails. Family legend wasn't off by much. A bit of historical probing revealed that Pie Eddie Caples was a slave's son, whose father was first sent to the fields at the start of King Cotton's reign. With the expulsion of the Choctaw from central Mississippi in the early 1830s, 10 million acres of prime cotton land opened up, and a tide of white men rushed in to claim it. Squatters, settlers, gamblers, and thieves, they arrived hatching frontier schemes and dreaming of dollar signs. Among them in about 1843 was an aging Alabama saloonkeeper with a young wife and seven black slaves, including a boy about eight years old. The saloonkeeper's name was Samuel Caples. The boy's name was Frank. He was Pie Eddie's father, Hattie Mae's great-grandfather, and the person with whom the Caples story begins.

When the slaveholder Samuel Caples was young—he was born about 1785—black slaves had labored in American fields for more than 150 years, and it seemed the awful practice might die a natural death. Economically, it threw off shrinking rewards, since the soils of the upper South were spent. Philosophically, it posed discomfiting problems for a generation of Revolutionary leaders demanding their own freedom; they recognized, even though they didn't rectify, their hypocrisy at home. The slaveholder Thomas Jefferson called slavery a "detestable" institution. But by the time Samuel Caples arrived in Mississippi, no white southerner would say such a thing. Tantalized by cotton profits, a new generation embraced slavery not as a necessary evil but an outright social good, the burden a superior race endured to care for a lesser caste. Since the faith in white supremacy would outlive slavery itself, it was a development of some note.

Samuel Caples's life unfolded in eerie sync with the national tragedy. Born in Maryland around the time of the Constitutional Convention, he grew up with the new republic, impatiently pushing west in search of land and human property. By the 1830s, he had abandoned his life in middle Tennessee and settled in northwestern Alabama, where he seems to have prospered. He ran a tavern in the Fayette County courthouse; increased his slaveholdings to seven, from five; and had a son who served as constable. Then he packed up and lit out again. What dislodged a comfortable townsman isn't clear, but when he arrived in Scott County, Mississippi, in the early 1840s, he was a man approaching sixty and toting an eighteen-year-old bride. As a small slaveholder (one with fewer than twenty slaves), Caples was by far the most prevalent kind, though not one easily conjured by modern minds. His life was nothing like those of the grand planters along the Mississippi River, with hundreds of slaves, thousands of acres, and European books and clothes. Caples would have lived in frontier housing, probably a log cabin, and worked in the fields alongside his bondsmen. With virtually no savings—his wealth was tied up in his slaves—he was acutely vulnerable to market busts, a risk for the people he owned, since selling them was his easiest way to get cash. For Frank, bondage to a small slaveholder had some potential advantages; it spared him the mythic overseer, famed for his quick cruelty, and it may have brought a more varied workday. But it also deprived him of the communal life a large plantation afforded, like a broader potential choice in mates and the safety of numbers. What it really did was bind his fate to the whims of Samuel Caples, whose authority over his human possessions was all but absolute. The distance to free soil made escape nearly impossible.

There were two aspects of slavery its defenders preferred not to discuss: the sale and the lash. Whether Caples was quick with the lash is unknown, but he wasn't above the sale. In 1849, with prices for slaves and cotton rising, Caples disposed of "my Negro boy Hyram about fifteen years old" for $818.50, about $20,000 in contemporary terms. Hyram was about Frank's age, possibly his brother, perhaps even a twin. Though able to buy and sell men, Caples couldn't write his name, and he consummated the deal with an X. On the move again within a few years, Caples headed east into Newton County, where he had more kids, bought more land, and needed more cash. On April 16, 1855, he took out a loan of $833, offering as collateral one of the most valuable things he owned: Hattie Mae's great-grandfather. "Caples has this day executed his note," he acknowledged with his X,

> and . . . to secure full and punctual payment of said note . . . doth bargain, sell, and convey a certain negro boy slave for life named Frank in color black aged about twenty years to have and to hold the same unto himself, his heirs and assigns forever.

Amid the reverent "untos" and "doths," the note let Caples keep working his "slave for life" until the debt came due nine months later. But if he failed to repay, the lender was then free to take possession of Frank and sell him to the highest bidder. Whatever terrors he experienced in bondage, Frank Caples was spared that one. Cotton prices ticked up that year, and Samuel Caples repaid the debt.

What a strange sight the homestead must have made on the eve of Civil War—this old man, lord of 100-plus acres, thirteen kids, and nine slaves. At seventy-five, Samuel Caples had pushed his way across a succession of frontiers to an estate worth something like $200,000 in contemporary terms—nearly all in human property—and he lived just long enough to see a terrible war sweep it away. Surrendering to no one in martial fervor, he named his next son Jefferson Davis and joined a local militia formed, its founder proclaimed, "to aid in driving the enemy from our country." But no less an enemy than William T. Sherman entered the county a mile from Caples's farm, burning and looting in a practice run for his more infamous march to the sea. Chasing freedoms they had never known, thousands of slaves ran off to trail the conquering force—"ten miles of negros," "a grotesque crowd," a "remarkable hegira," Sherman and his entourage called them. Nothing if not prolific, Samuel Caples survived long enough to give his wife their sixteenth child, then died by the end of the decade. She lost the homestead in a tax sale, and much of the family left for Arkansas. Frank Caples, now a freedman, stayed.

Given the tragic history that followed, it's easy to forget the brief flowering of freedom that black Mississippians of his era enjoyed. Mississippi sent two black men to the United States Senate; black policemen patrolled the capital; and black letter carriers toted mail. Economically, progress halted with sharecropping, an impossibly rigged system close to slavery itself. Politically, blacks were driven from the polls first by violence and then by the law. As the future governor James Vardaman put it, the 1890 Mississippi constitution, with its poll taxes and literacy tests, was designed "for no other purpose than to eliminate the nigger from politics." With that, the Mississippi of modern legend emerged, in a tumult of lynchings, Jim Crow laws, and race-baiting politicians. No state entered the twentieth century with a larger ratio of black citizens—nearly six in ten Mississippians were black, and one in ten black Americans lived there—and no state went to greater lengths to insure black subjugation. Into this world of lost opportunity, the next three Caples generations were born, down to Hattie Mae. In 1876, Frank had a son, whom everyone called "Pie Eddie."

The red clay hills that Pie Eddie farmed would never yield an easy living. But one of the world's most fertile plains was a few hours away, running beside the Mississippi River for two hundred miles below Memphis. The Mississippi Delta was still mostly wilderness in antebellum days, but with the arrival of railroads and flood control it erupted in a speculative boom. Among those who began buying Delta land was a hill country pharmacist named Oliver Eastland, who in 1888 launched a giant cotton plantation that remains in the family today. He died a decade later and left it to his young sons, Woods and James.

The history of the Delta has only one theme: the need for cheap and abundant (in this case, black) labor. Without it the rich land was worthless, since cotton was an extremely labor-intensive crop. A plantation the size of the Eastlands' would need several hundred field hands, and planters went to extraordinary lengths to recruit and retain them. While *dependency* was a word typically tied to the region's poor blacks, dependency ran both ways; perhaps nowhere was the prosperity of the white elite as dependent on perpetuating a large black underclass. The corollary to the white need for black labor was the fear of black numbers in counties where blacks formed as much as a nine-to-one majority. Socially, an elaborate caste system evolved to underscore who was in charge. Of all the degradations of Hattie Mae's youth, none stung more than the prohibition on drinking from a white person's glass. Where caste failed, violence prevailed. In the first three decades of the twentieth century, the Delta was a national leader in lynchings, dispatching a black man, woman, or child to a mob death every 5.5 months. Whites knew they were guarding an island of privilege in a sea of potential black trouble.

Trouble came to the Eastland brothers early in their tenure as planters, after they recruited a field hand named Luther Holbert, who had worked for them back in the hills. What prompted the dispute with Holbert is unclear, but the outcome is not: on February 3, 1904, Holbert shot James Eastland dead. The murder of a planter by a black worker was no mere crime but a threat to the social and economic order. (The Memphis paper referred to James Eastland as Holbert's "young master.") Woods Eastland joined a rampaging posse that claimed at least three innocent blacks' lives before returning to the plantation with Holbert and his wife. By midday a crowd of a thousand assembled, and the accounts of what happened next, especially that of the *Vicksburg Evening Post*, made the case a touchstone in the literature of lynching:

> The blacks were forced to hold out their hands while one finger at a time was chopped off. The fingers were distributed as souvenirs. . . . one of his eyes, knocked out with a stick, hung by a shred from the socket. . . . The most excruciating form of punishment consisted in the use of a large corkscrew. . . . bored into the flesh of the man and the woman . . . and then pulled out, the spirals tearing out big pieces of raw, quivering flesh.

Holbert and his wife were then thrown on a pyre and burned to death.

Woods Eastland was indicted for murder—burning Holbert at the stake "was the intention of W. C. Eastland from the start," the Memphis paper noted with approval—but the case was thrown out before it reached a jury, and he was swept from the courthouse by a cheering crowd. He moved back to the hills, became the district attorney, and managed the plantation from afar. Nine months after the gruesome execution, his only child was born, and he named him for his slain brother: James Eastland. For much of the country, the younger Eastland would become the very symbol of southern defiance, the cigar-chomping Dixiecrat senator who boasted that he had a special suit pocket where civil rights bills went to die. For Hattie Mae, he was the man who owned all the land and made all the rules.

The two decades after the Holbert affair brought Delta planters their glory days. Rising cotton prices made Woods Eastland wealthy and kept him in need of more workers. One of the men he employed in the hills was Pie Eddie Caples, who was about fifty years old with a young wife and a passel of kids when "Mr. Woods" persuaded him to give the Delta a try. Climbing in the back of Woods Eastland's truck, the Caples clan rode out of the hills and onto the plantation in search of a better life, and when I found him three-quarters of a century later, Pie Eddie Caples's son Mack was still there. A strapping man of eighty-five, he had gnarled hands, bright eyes, and vivid memories of a twelve-year-old's first glimpse of the fertile land. "So much cotton in the field, look like it snowed!" he said. While the next generation, Hattie Mae's, despised plantation life, Mack spoke of it with the kind of vicarious pride a midcentury worker might have shown in GM or GE. The store shimmered with more stuff than he had seen, all offered on easy credit. While some planters plowed every acre, the Eastlands let tenants garden. And as patrons with influence, they could keep favored workers from jail. "Just as much money as Papa wanna borrow, Mr. Woods let him have it," Mack said. "I ain't never heard him cuss none of his hands. Mr. Woods was a mighty fine man!"

One cruelty of sharecropping was that the promise of prosperity almost always proved false. Another, as Nicholas Lemann has noted, was that the failure was subtly marked as the tenant's fault; he was, after all, ostensibly a partner in a profitable enterprise. If the system was meant to breed self-doubt, it also encouraged an ethos of "getting over," exacting your revenge on an unfair system by cheating it in return (an ethos that would reappear in dealings with the welfare system). Hortense Powdermaker found more than eight in ten sharecroppers worked all year, only to break even or sink further into debt. She was startled at how openly planters talked of cheating; they justified it by arguing that "the Negro is congenitally lazy and must be kept in debt in order to be made to work." Whatever disappointments Pie Eddie Caples suffered in the Delta, he didn't suffer them long. Three years after moving, he fell from a roof and injured his head. "Mr. Woods" sent him to a hospital in Jackson, and he died in surgery. Pie Eddie's widow and children stayed on the plantation, where seven years later, Hattie Mae was born to an unmarried teenage mother she would never know.

"I was a gorgeous little black child!" Hattie Mae told me one day. Though she started her life poor and orphaned, she didn't start it unhappily. Her saving grace was Pie Eddie's widow, the thirty-seven-year-old grandmother from whom she drew her home, her resilience, and her name. "I thought the sun rose and set in that old lady," she said. As a cheerful woman who could cook and sew, Mama Hattie had escaped the fields to make her living in white folks' homes, where the benefits to a cute granddaughter included a stream of hand-me-downs and "goo-gobs" of white girls' dolls. Early life had other comforts. With several acres to farm, there were fresh corn and peaches in season, jarred greens in winter, and smoked hogs year-round. The Gilfield Missionary Baptist Church was about a mile's hike across the fields, and the two Hatties regularly made the trek. Rounding out the household were Mama Hattie's kids—Will, Lula Bell, Vidalia, and Pop—who, a half generation ahead of Hattie Mae, were more like older siblings than aunts and uncles. Hattie Mae spent her days making mud pies and waiting for her grandmother to walk up the road. "Those were the happiest days of my life," she said.

Sharecropper society was not monolithic, and the Capleses had a reputation for inhabiting its tougher tiers. If you buy the notion that the social problems of northern ghettos had roots in the Jim Crow

South, the family history is one to explore. Among the children that Pie Eddie left behind, one (Frank) was shot and killed by his girlfriend. Another (Lula Bell) shot and killed her man. A third (Pop) did time in penitentiaries from Parchman to Joliet; among other things, he killed a man dating his ex-wife. Another, Vidalia, got involved with a man whose wife retaliated by torching Vidalia's house. A picture of Opal's grandfather, 'Lij, survives from the day the carnival came to town. Clenching a cigar between his teeth, he stares down the camera and thrusts open a wallet overflowing with bills, a portrait of the bravura that would fill his granddaughter's veins; the quickest way to get a laugh in the family is to ask how many times 'Lij married. Even Wiley, the stable homesteader of the group, kept a still. "They were known as a rough-riding group that stuck together," Hattie Mae said of her uncles and aunts. "If you mess with them you might as well kill them." Hattie Mae's father, Robert Logan, who was fifteen when she was born, came from a more prosperous and lighter-skinned plantation family that didn't approve of the Capleses; he left town for a long army career, and Hattie Mae's visits with him were confined to the occasional furlough.

As a stable, pious, hardworking woman with a bunch of hell-raising kids, Mama Hattie would scarcely be an unfamiliar figure in the contemporary ghetto. Nor would the crime that put an end to Hattie Mae's carefree years, sexual molestation. She was about seven when her grandmother's boyfriend, Clyde, started catching her alone and doing things she didn't want him to do. Afraid of retribution if she told, she kept the secret inside, as a source of confusion and pain. "Men back then didn't allow girls to have much a childhood," she said. Another calamity befell the family at about the same time, when her uncle Will got into a dispute with another plantation hand over a woman. Out playing one day, Hattie Mae ran home to say she had seen some men stuffing Will into a car. But no one listened to an excitable child until his body was found the next day. Bereft over her son's death, Mama Hattie briefly moved the family back to the hills, but Clyde came along, and in an argument he stabbed her. The boys gave him the kind of beating that insured he wouldn't return, and Mama Hattie moved back to the Doddsville plantation. Soon the household was going separate ways. With no one but young Hattie Mae at home, her grandmother landed a job as the Eastlands' cook, a privileged perch but one that required her to live in the cook's quarters near their house with no room for a child. Nine years old, Hattie Mae was effectively orphaned again, left to spend what remained of her childhood with whichever relative might take her in.

The life that followed would have extinguished a spirit less keen. At nine, she was old enough to pick cotton; at twelve, she could "chop," or weed, it. Both tasks took precedence over school, which let out when the cotton needed tending, and Hattie Mae made it no further than the eighth grade. As an abandoned girl whose beauty showed, she attracted more sexual predation. This time she told, but Aunt Vi accused her of lying about Uncle George and administered one of her infamous beatings. If black men were one source of Hattie Mae's grief, white folks were another. Unlike her grandmother, she had a hard time striking the pose of grateful deference that plantation life required. "I was the troublemaker," she said. Tired of snapping stalks in the cold, she led a group of younger cousins, including Opal's mother, Ruthie Mae, out of the field one day. When the overseer rode up on a horse and ordered them back to work, Hattie Mae snapped, "I'm not your child," which brought Uncle 'Lij racing to make peace before things got out of hand. Years later, as Congress debated the welfare bill, its proponents talked about work in transcendent terms, as a source of dignity, order, and hope. But the first thing Hattie Mae noticed about work was the unfairness of it all: "All the black people was out working for nothing." In picking season, she dragged a heavy sack across the field, bent or sometimes crawling, and pulled the fluffy fibers from the lacerating bolls. The bending made her back ache. The bolls made her fingers bleed. It felt like snatching thousands of eggs from nests of angry thorns.

As Hattie Mae took to the fields, James Eastland embarked on a long if accidental career in the United States Senate, one that like the plantation itself was bequeathed to him by his father. It began in 1941 when the incumbent senator died, leaving Mississippi governor Paul Johnson free to appoint a successor. For counsel, the governor turned to his old college roommate; the roommate was Woods Eastland. Declining his own chance to fill the seat, Woods persuaded his friend to send his son, who had served two terms in the state legislature but had been out of politics for nearly a decade. With that, at thirty-six Jim Eastland became the youngest senator in state history. War loomed and the Depression lingered when he arrived in Washington, but Eastland found fame with an issue of more limited interest: the price of cottonseed. The seed was an important byproduct of every farmer's harvest, and a federal official's talk of price controls had prices deeply depressed. With a fiery speech on the Senate floor, Eastland squelched the effort. Prices doubled, and Eastland, an unknown planter with a humorless style, became a statewide hero overnight. He left the Senate after eighty-eight days but went home and won the next year's race for the first of his six full terms.

If locally Eastland made his name with cotton, nationally it rested on race. One of the first battles of the civil rights age erupted midway through his first term, when President Truman sought permanent status for a wartime antidiscrimination agency, the Fair Employment Practices Commission. Segregationists rightly saw the move as a threat, and in the summer of 1945 Eastland helped kill it with a filibuster that marked him as no mean southern bigot but a truly distinctive one. The commission was a "Communist program" to "rape American justice," he said. "I assert that the Negro race is an inferior race. I say quite frankly that I am proud of the white race. I am proud that the purest of white blood flows through my veins. I know that the white race is a superior race. It has ruled the world. . . . It is responsible for all the progress on earth." Of would-be black voters, he later added: "The mental level of those people renders them incapable of suffrage." Reelected with no opposition, Eastland was rewarded with the chairmanship of the subcommittee on civil rights.

Eastland's turn on center stage arrived a few years later, when the Supreme Court decided the most important civil rights case of the century, *Brown vs. Board of Education*. The white South was divided as it groped for a response, with some segregationists seeing no choice but to give in and desegregate the schools. Eastland helped lead the opposite charge, condemning *Brown* as a "pro-Communist" decision and embracing the doctrine of massive resistance. As a prime supporter of the Citizens Council, he allied himself with a movement that all but explicitly endorsed the violence that terrorized the South. (J. W. Milam, one of the men who lynched Emmett Till not far from the Eastland plantation, explained he was acting in part to take a stand against school integration.) In 1956, Eastland's fervor landed him on the cover of *Time*, which argued that his aura of wealth and respectability made him a "far more dismaying phenomenon" than the usual southern demogogue. Amid this assault on Constitutional governance, Eastland got another promotion—to chairman of the full Judiciary Committee, through which all civil rights bills and judicial nominations passed.

To modern ears, he merely sounds cartoonish—a forgotten foil for a civil rights movement whose success in retrospect risks seeming preordained. But for the next twenty-two years, every legislative victory had to find a way around him, and by the 1970s, as Senate president pro tem, he stood third in line to the presidency. Long before that, he was for the Caples family a kind of feudal lord. To understand why there were holes in her roof or an ache in her back; why she couldn't vote or stay in school; why the field hand who shot her uncle Will was beyond the reach of the law, Hattie Mae had to look no farther than the other end of the cotton field. Even now, Ole Miss students study at the James O. Eastland Law Library, and justice is dispensed from the James O. Eastland Federal Courthouse. But one place visitors won't find his name is on the road to the Doddsville plantation, now run by his son, "Little Woods." Instead they find a sign celebrating the county's civil rights pioneer: "Home of Fannie Lou Hamer."

While one revolution was coming to politics, another was coming to the farm. Midway through Hattie Mae's childhood, the Delta greeted the awkward machine that would alter its way of life, the mechanical cotton picker. Rumbling across the heat-baked horizon, each of the pioneering contraptions could pick as much as fifty field hands. And no one would talk of giving them the vote. Suddenly the demographic logic of the Cotton Kingdom was upended. It no longer needed surplus labor; on the contrary, most whites were happy to see the black majority dwindle. Eastland's friends at the Citizens Council offered free tickets out. And with the postwar factories of the North hum-ming, workers had places to go; a field hand could take a train to Chicago and quadruple his wages overnight. The black migration, which had started as a trickle, swelled to a flood. From 1940 to 1970, 5 million black southerners moved, filling the northern cities. Because it happened incrementally and seemed mostly to affect poor blacks, the migration never registered in white America as a momentous event, on par with war or depression. But there are few corners of American politics or culture it left unchanged. It gave rise to the modern black middle class, one of the great success stories of the cen-tury, and also to fearsome new ghettos whose problems would, for much of the public, become synonymous with welfare.

The Caples family split on Chicago. Most of Pie Eddie's kids gave it a try, but the older ones found it too fast; a few, like Mack, returned to the familiar rhythms of plantation life. Most stayed gone, and from Florida to California, their descendants now number in the hundreds, showcasing a level of black achievement that James Eastland couldn't have imagined. They are teachers, preachers, social workers, an air traffic controller, computer technicians, and a career navy man. But scores of others wound up in northern prisons or in long stays on the welfare rolls. As it happened, the family's biggest success grew on southern soil. Opting for the devil he knew, Pie Eddie's son Wiley Caples, the stable householder, gave up on Chicago and returned to the Eastland plantation. He got some ribbing from other field-workers by insisting that his daughter stay in school, but she took his faith in ed-ucation to heart. After graduating from the county's Jim Crow schools, Virginia Caples went on to earn a PhD and became dean, provost, and acting president of Alabama A&M. Opal, who met her once as a child, boasted that her cousin Ginny was the "dean of Mississippi!" Like her father, Virginia Caples argued the family's obstacles only mounted with the transition to urban life. "I have always thanked my parents for mov-ing back to Mississippi," she said. Among relatives who moved north, "You were always hearing about somebody killing and shooting."

For a long time, Hattie Mae shared the fear of Chicago. It sounded like a "big raggedy place that you could get lost in," and she felt lost enough. She was twelve years old and living with her aunt Vidalia when a man named Toot came to call. Toot was two decades older, and with Vidalia gone Hattie Mae had no way to stop him. She was nearly halfway through her pregnancy when Vidalia noticed and tried to beat the baby out with a switch. Four decades later, as Speaker of the House, Newt Gingrich would move to end welfare by citing "twelve-year-olds having babies" as one of its legacies. Hattie Mae is the rare woman who really did get pregnant at twelve. But she didn't know anything about welfare.

When the baby came in December 1950, the sharecropping system was falling apart, and the move to Chicago was well under way. Her grandmother died six months later, leaving Hattie Mae even more alone with the little boy she called Squeaky—Jewell's oldest brother. One of her aunts, Lula Bell, came home for the funeral, and saying, "You ain't nothing but a baby yourself," took the infant back to Chicago. There was a vague plan for Hattie Mae to follow, but she wouldn't catch up for nearly twenty years. She lived here and there until 1953; then, homeless, uneducated, alone, and abused, she sought shelter in her first marriage, to a young man named Willie Reed. He was twenty, she was fifteen.

Poor single mothers had plenty of problems, as welfare would later make clear. But so did reluctant teenage wives. Hattie Mae viewed her husband as little more than a housing program. They had the first of their three children when she was sixteen. She lost her next pregnancy a few days after one of Willie's attacks. She left him, returned, and followed his parents to a plantation in southern Missouri, where after years of Willie's explosive violence Hattie Mae decided to leave. Twenty-three years old, with two kids in her care and another on the way, she was scraping by as a field hand and domestic when someone told her she could get some help—a monthly welfare check. She had heard something about government checks a few years earlier. But it never occurred to her that a black woman could get one. Nervous, curious, she went to an office in Caruthersville, Missouri, in 1960 and enrolled in a small federal program called Aid to Families with Dependent Children. She became a welfare mother.

One thing to notice about Hattie Mae and welfare is that the check gave new powers. Rather than promote "dependency," which was later seen as a major failing, its effect was the opposite: it gave her a degree of independence she had never known. To begin with, it re-duced her reliance on men, so it decreased the predatory violence in her life. It also bolstered her leverage in a rigged labor market de-signed for exploitation. Now she had options besides chopping cotton and washing white people's clothes. She said she didn't agree with friends who argued "the money is due you—your grandparents, they worked as slaves." But she certainly felt no qualms about getting paid for doing nothing. White folks had been doing it for years.

Another thing to notice is that Hattie Mae couldn't live on welfare alone. It reduced her dependence on her twin forms of grief, white folks and black men, but it eliminated neither. From the start, she jug-gled three sources of cash—welfare, boyfriends, and jobs—just as Jewell, Angie, and Opal would do. No single strategy assured a living, but you could survive by mixing all three. The problem was that to keep the welfare you had to hide the men and the jobs: you had to cheat. Fending off her caseworkers' questions made Hattie Mae feel that welfare was a seamy affair—impractical to avoid but a lot of work for a small piece of change. She doubted it had much of a future. Someday, she warned her daughters, the white folks would bring it to an end.

About the time she went on welfare, Hattie Mae met the first man she loved—Jewell's father, Isaac Johnson. He was tall, tough, and hand-some, twenty years her senior, and considerably more prosperous than any black man she had known. He had a plumbing business and a corner store that he ran with a lady friend. When Hattie Mae stopped in to buy some pop, he made a point of driving her home. Af-ter they started going together, she ran into an old boyfriend, who slapped her outside the store; Isaac cut him from head to toe. That was but one of the protections he wrapped her in. He built her a com-fortable house in the hamlet of Hayti, where she lived for seven years. In addition to the four children she had already had, she and Isaac had four more. Greg, her sixth, came in 1966 and grew up to father Angie's kids. Jewell, her seventh, followed in 1968.

Isaac could support the family, but Hattie Mae was in no rush to surrender the added security of her welfare check. Loving Isaac was one thing, but counting on him was another. She knew he had other women, and she never knew when he might leave. This was the age of the midnight raid, when caseworkers arrived unannounced to shine flashlights under the bed. Men and TVs were both forbidden, and Isaac had bought her a big one. When her caseworker knocked, she hid the television under a sheet and stuffed Isaac in a box. The caseworker wasn't fooled. "I know you can't make it on public aid alone," he said afterward. "You know how it is," she answered. That is, she admitted nothing. But when the caseworker didn't turn her in, she came to think of him as her first white friend. In time, he confided the reason for the raids. One of Isaac's other girlfriends kept calling the office to complain he was spending the night.

Hattie Mae never stopped loving Isaac. She just tired of his fooling around. She warned him she would leave, and she did in 1970, a few months before Jewell's second birthday. Thirty-three years old, pregnant with her eighth child, she waited for Isaac to go to work. Then she raced to the bus station, kids in tow, for the five-hundred-mile ride to Chicago. In arriving pregnant by bus in a new city after a problem with a man, Hattie Mae was writing the script that Jewell would follow with uncanny precision two decades later, when she stepped off a bus in Milwaukee. Hattie Mae never saw Isaac again, but he called every now and then. He said if any man raised a hand to her, he would *walk* to Chicago just to whip him. When the news arrived many years later that Isaac had died, Jewell, then a teenager, didn't care. She had never had any interest in meeting her father. But Hattie Mae felt like a piece of her heart had stopped beating.

THREE

The Crossroads: Chicago, 1966–1991

Much as Hattie Mae had feared, Chicago proved a "big raggedy place that you could get lost in," and countless people did. In the three decades before she arrived, Chicago's black population grew by eight hundred thousand. A city-within-a-city sprang up in its midst, and while it fostered a proud black middle class it also bred a destructive new street life, spreading havoc in the ghettos and fears far beyond. Just how it happened is still not fully understood. There had always been chaos in black southern life. But the stabilizing forces of the rural world—church, school, communal networks—carried less weight in the anonymous city, where someone looking to live the wild life could do it on a grander scale. Economics played a role. While the work paid better than picking cotton, many of the best jobs remained off-limits, and by the time Hattie Mae arrived in 1970, the blue-collar economy was dying. In two decades, Chicago would lose 60 percent of its manufacturing jobs, and with them the promise of a decent living on muscle alone. Plus, Chicago had its own segregationist passions, especially in housing and schools. Most tragically, it piled the poorest black migrants into monstrous public-housing towers, whose names would become synonymous with government folly: Henry Horner Homes (1957), Stateway Gardens (1958), Cabrini-Green (1958), the Robert Taylor Homes (1962).

In the early days, the ghetto was an eclectic place, with lawyers and preachers sandwiched beside porters and prostitutes. Fair-housing laws let much of the middle class escape, and those left behind grew not only poorer but socially set apart. Welfare rules loosened in the mid-1960s, and within a generation the nation's rolls quadrupled. From 1964 to 1976, the share of black children born to single mothers doubled to 50 percent. Crime, drugs—likewise up in startling fashion, especially after the mid-1980s onslaught of crack. In Chicago, a vicious gang culture appeared, filling the vacuum left by absent fathers. By the late 1980s, even left-of-center experts had broadened their concerns from poverty per se to self-defeating behaviors—to what William Julius Wilson, the country's preeminent black sociologist, called the "social pathologies of the inner city." That all this was happening after the triumphs in civil rights only lent the tableaux a more tragic cast. When Angie, Opal, and Jewell were born in the mid-1960s, the word *underclass* was obscure and distrusted; its suggestion of intransigence collided with the national faith in class mobility. By the time they reached high school, the word was widely used, however imprecisely, to describe people much like them.

Hattie Mae settled in more easily than she expected; she knew people everywhere. From the bus station, she took a taxi to the southside projects where Aunt Lula Bell had a place. Hattie Mae's grown son, Squeaky, whom Lula Bell had raised, was in and out of the Stateway Gardens apartment, so among the reunions Hattie Mae enjoyed was that of mother and son. Her cousin from the Eastland plantation, Ruthie Mae Caples, lived in Stateway, too, with five kids and a factory job at Zenith. Ruthie's daughter Opal was a mischievous girl of four, two years older than Jewell, and both generations bonded. For all the hard living condensed in her years, Hattie was only thirty-three and still ready for some fun. Three decades later, a Polaroid of her and Ruthie in white go-go boots still crackled with danger. "We thought we was Miss Fine!" Hattie Mae said. Soon she had her own Stateway apartment and a version of her old survival plan: an unreported job, a boyfriend, and a monthly welfare check. The job, at a linens factory, didn't last. The boyfriend, Wesley, did, much to her children's chagrin.

The high-rise was tolerable for the first few years. But as Opal and Jewell were starting school, it was spinning out of control. The gangs frightened even Hattie Mae, who had witnessed more than her share of roughness. Coming home late from work one night, she barely outraced some teenage boys intent, she presumed, on rape. Ruthie moved out first. Hattie Mae stayed, and a year later her son Squeaky was murdered—done in, she was told, by friends in a drug gang who suspected him of stealing their money. Hattie Mae was devastated, maybe all the more so because, as a thirteen-year-old mother, she had given him away. After two of her other sons were assaulted—Willie was shot at, and Greg was hit by a brick from a balcony—Hattie worried the whole family had become a target of gang reprisal. Vowing to salvage something from Squeaky's death, she promised she would get the rest of the kids out, and she found a job waiting tables at a bar.

The job, at the Marcellus Lounge, was a big break. The lounge drew a high-rolling crowd, including the drug baron Flukey Stokes, who would seal his place in Chicago lore (and a song by Stevie Ray Vaughn) by throwing himself a $200,000 anniversary party and burying his son, "Willie the Wimp," in a casket shaped like a Cadillac. Having traveled from Big Jim Eastland's plantation to Flukey Stokes's pool hall, Hattie Mae was living a kind of pulp fiction version of the underclass formation story. Flukey and his sidekicks liked Hattie. They called her "sister," bought clothes for her kids, and put out the word that she wasn't to be hurt. With $100 tips, she could net as much in a night at the lounge as she could in a month on welfare. As for where her friends got their money, she said, "I didn't get into their business, and they didn't get into mine." Hattie Mae kept the job (and since she didn't report it, her welfare check) well into Jewell's teens. She fled the projects when Jewell was eight. By then, the black belt had burst out of its historic confines and spread fifteen miles to the city's southern edge. Hattie Mae and the kids went with it, eventually landing in the far southeastern corner of the city, in a rough-and-tumble place called Jeffrey Manor.

Angie's mother had found her way to Jeffrey Manor, too—with her marriage dead and the neighborhood dying, Charity Jobe was trying to get out as Hattie Mae moved in. It was their children's lives that would converge in the Manor, much to Charity's dismay. Like Hattie Mae, Charity once picked Mississippi cotton. But while Hattie grew up orphaned and abused, Charity's roots were against-the-odds middle class, with her grandfather the rare sharecropper who made it. A son of emancipated slaves, Levi Gillespie was already an old man of sixty-eight in 1941, two years before Charity's birth, when he took out a contract to buy 110 acres in Egypt, Mississippi. He made the payments past the age of eighty, then transferred the mostly paid-for land to Charity's father. Henderson Gillespie retained his father's acreage and will. One family story celebrates the time a white store clerk called him a "nigger." "That'll be *Mister* Nigger," he said, and grabbed him in the groin until he said it. In contrast to Hattie Mae's childhood of violence and dislocation, Charity's was a model of order. She spent mornings in school and afternoons in the field. Meals didn't start without a blessing, and church on Sunday was an all-day affair. Her parents' marriage lasted nearly sixty years. When suitors called on his daughters, Henderson warned that if he saw them with a drink or a cigarette he would knock it down their throat. Walking four miles to the Jim Crow school, six of his eight kids earned high school degrees.

Charity hated the drudgery of fieldwork, and when she graduated in 1961, there was nothing else to do. One brother worked construction in Chicago and another parked cars at O'Hare; a sister ran a South Side bar. Charity followed them north and got an office job at a commercial laundry, where she met Angie's father. Roosevelt Jobe also came from northeastern Mississippi, but from a poorer, more troubled family; he told Charity his father had left when Roosevelt was still a boy and was never heard from again. "My daddy's family is really sometimey," Angie would say. "Sometime they like you, sometime they don't." At five foot three, Roosevelt compensated for size with flash; he talked smooth, dressed well, and courted Charity with candy and flowers. After two years, she went as far as applying for a marriage license, before deciding that a marriage wouldn't work. Then she found out she was pregnant. She couldn't face her father like that. She married Roosevelt on her lunch break in her pastor's living room.

Angie was born in 1966; her brother, Terrance, arrived the next year. Charity got a job as a hospital receptionist. Roosevelt moved to the Handy Button Company, where he made good money on the factory floor. Charity wanted to buy a house, and Jeffrey Manor, a ring of duplex townhomes with modest yards, was a place they could afford; they settled at 9807 South Clyde. Although Angie started first grade in the public system, Charity found the teachers indifferent—one said that she called in sick a lot because she didn't like the kids—and Charity transferred Angie to parochial school. When Charity wasn't at work, she was running to Scouts and Holy Cross Church, where, despite the family's Baptist roots, Angie was baptized as a Catholic and Terrance served as an altar boy. With Roosevelt scarcely around, her life was her kids.

Charity's brand of mothering was devoted but intense, at times overbearing. Loving and lecturing, caring and carping, combined with the force of a pressure hose. "Angela! The Lord don't play!" went one frequent refrain. A portrait of innocence in her plaid jumper, Angie had the kind of sweet streak that mothers prize in daughters, trusting Charity with confidences that others save for best friends. "My mother is the nicest person in my life," Angie wrote in grade school. "My mother's the best, if you ask me." But she also made an early practice of tugging against Charity's leash. While her younger brother feigned obedience and excelled in class, "I was the bad one," Angie said, "'cause I couldn't keep my mouth shut." An indifferent student, she did her homework with a knee in the chair and a foot out the door, convinced a freer, faster world beckoned just beyond. Few of the neighbors shared Charity's strictures, and Angie could look outside at midnight and see kids crowding the stoop. Charity's great fear was that Angie would somehow wind up with them; Angie's great fear was that she wouldn't. Mocking Charity's curfews, the neighborhood kids dubbed her "Mean Mama Lulu," and Mean Mama didn't spare the rod. Once, when some kids chased Angie home, Charity threatened to whip her if she didn't defend herself, a move she came to regret, as Angie found that despite her skinny schoolgirl frame fighting came naturally. A running routine of Angie's childhood involved Angie starting to say something smart, Charity warning her not to, and Angie saying it anyway—feeling empowered early on by her ability to take a blow. "I got slapped in the mouth a whole lot," Angie said. "The slap, sometime it felt good, 'cause I said what I wanted to say."

Years later, deep into a very different life, Angie would affectionately sum up her mother with a kind of spontaneous spoken poem. "My Mama is very different from me," she said.

My Mama don't drink,
My Mama don't smoke,
My Mama don't do nothing.
My Mama go to church.
That's all she do.

When the topic of her father arose, Angie began less lyrically. "My daddy was an asshole," she said. Growing up with Roosevelt Jobe wasn't much different, except in negative ways, than being raised by a single mom. She didn't see him much, and when she did he hardly spoke. His Cadillac had a rhinestone dash, and while Charity talked up the Ten Commandments, Roosevelt issued two: Don't Eat in My Car. Don't Fuck Up My Seats. For the most part, the family ignored him.

"You wanna marry my mama?" Angie asked a city bus driver one day. "I want a daddy!"

"Angela! You have a daddy!" Charity said.

"But he's never home!"

For a girl under her mother's thumb, Roosevelt modeled a looser way of life. Charity's friends warned her that he was messing around. Then a woman checked into the hospital where Charity worked and identified the father of her newborn son as Roosevelt Jobe. Angie wasn't old enough to understand what was going on, but she never forgot that fight. No matter how often Charity changed her unlisted number, the other woman continued to call, and Angie came to realize that her father had a second family. He also drank. Angie knew the extent of it before Charity did. She found vodka bottles hidden everywhere—inside the toilet tank, behind the dresser, underneath the couch. She would drain the bottles and refill them with water, but Roosevelt blamed Charity. As a grade school girl, Angie once rescued her mother by smashing an empty bottle against her father's head. One night when Roosevelt took a swing, Charity knocked him out with a flashlight, sending a terrified Angie racing from the house.

"Angela said you killed her daddy!" the neighbor said.

"I don't know if I killed him or not," Charity said. "If he isn't dead, he should be."

Angie's teachers at Holy Cross knew nothing of the turmoil at home. But they sensed that something was wrong. She was smart, popular, and sensitive; she wrote well. Still, she disliked school, and her grades languished in the low Cs. They couldn't understand why she didn't do better, and they urged Charity to hire a tutor. Although she found a kind one, he came to change Charity's life more than Angie's.

As Angie's family was coming apart, so was the neighborhood around her. The area known as Jeffrey Manor encompassed an eighty-acre subdivision called Merrionette Manor, which was built just after the Second World War and formed the neighborhood's core. The signature of its eponymous developer, Joseph E. Merrion, was the curving, mazelike streets, which isolated the enclave from the urban grid and lent it a leisurely feel. A small playground-park sat in the middle, and a school sprang up on the southern end. For a generation, the neighborhood worked as intended, providing a sheltered spot for raising kids. The 1968 graduates of Luella Elementary were left with so much nostalgia, they kept a Web site of memories three decades later: "pony league games," "the library bus," "Passover shopping at Hilman's." Not even Richard Speck's infamous slaughter of eight nursing students shattered the aura of innocence. But the arrival of black homeowners did. Across Chicago, whites fought housing integration with everything from rocks to full-blown riots; the first black family in Jeffrey Manor encountered a burning cross. A classic wave of panic selling followed, with realtors multiplying their commissions by urging white families to salvage what they could. In 1968, the Luella student body was nearly 90 percent white. Three years later, it was nearly 90 percent black.

Like Charity, who arrived in 1972, the first black families had a middle-class cast; some were more prosperous than the whites they replaced. But with an entire neighborhood up for sale, the Manor fell into disarray. Some of the newcomers came from rougher parts of town, trailing troubled relatives and friends. The labyrinthine streets, built for bikes, proved equally good for peddling drugs, since the police had no easy route in. Still on welfare and working at the bar, Hattie Mae arrived in 1979 with her boyfriend, Wesley, and four of her kids, the youngest of whom, Robert, at eight, was already proving a hellion. By the time Angie finished grade school in 1981, the playground was sprayed with a six-point star, marking the presence of the Gangster Disciples. Angie's first boyfriend, Jay, was shot at on the playground as a teen and later murdered outside a bar. "Our generation was terrible!" Angie said. "Everybody started losing they damn mind."

With its backdrop of gangs, guns, and drugs, the Manor of Angie's adolescence sounds like a familiar story of a big-city ghetto. Or it does until you take a closer look, when the facts of neighborhood life upend expectations. Jeffrey Manor wasn't even poor; the poverty rate of ten percent in Angie's census tract was two points below the national average. Nine of ten families owned their own homes. Seventy-three percent of the adults worked, well above the national average of 62 percent. Household income (about $47,000 in contemporary terms) ran a third higher than the average citywide. It certainly wasn't a welfare neighborhood; Hattie Mae aside, only one household in ten received cash aid. That was a bit more than the national average (8 percent) but much less than the Chicago norm (15 percent). In demographic terms, that is, the Manor defied the theories of decline canonized left and right. If it wasn't poor and jobless (left) or enervated by the dole (right)—then what was it? What made so many kids like Angie, "lose they damn mind"?

Despite decades of study, the honest answer may be that no one really knows. But one theory starts with race: black neighborhoods like Jeffrey Manor just seem like more precarious places to come of age than their white equivalents, even when they have similar incomes. The sociologist Mary Pattillo-McCoy spent three years studying a neighborhood just north of Jeffrey Manor for her book, *Black Picket Fences*. Like the Manor, the neighborhood she gave the pseudonym "Groveland" was filled with lower-middle- to middle-class homeowners and beset by drugs and gangs. She argued that the residents of such neighborhoods were caught in spatial buffer zones, trapped between the ghetto and prosperous white areas beyond. Given the recency of their middle-class status, black families lived in social buffer zones, too; they were more likely than whites to have relatives or friends who were poor or in jail. As a result, their kids grew up at what Pattillo-McCoy called a "crossroads," with as many ties leading back to the ghetto as leading away.

If the story was partly one of exclusion, from established social networks, it may also be one of seduction. Street culture can exert a downward pull even on would-be achievers. (The black student accused of "acting white" is a staple of inner-city life.) Southern black folklore paid special homage to tricksters and badmen, marginal figures skilled at overpowering or deceiving—"getting over" on—their white oppressors. Pattillo-McCoy, who was raised in a buffer-zone neighborhood in Milwaukee, warned that their modern equivalents, gangsta styles that "glamorize the hard life of poverty," carry special peril for buffer-zone teens. The Winnetka kid who wears baggy pants draws a reproving look from his mother; the Groveland kid draws a cop or a real gang. Lots of crossroads kids succeed, but with licit and illicit, gangsta and straight, so deeply intertwined, one Groveland resident could have been speaking for Angie when she said: "You could go any way any day."

There's another lens through which to see the Manor's problems: the abundance of single mothers. By 1980, a third of its children were being raised in female-headed households. That was less than the national average for African Americans (49 percent), but twice the rate for all kids nationwide. Indeed, it's the only piece of demographic data that makes the Manor look like an at-risk neighborhood; statistically the evidence is clear that children raised in single-parent homes face greater risks of educational failure, early pregnancy, unemployment, and crime. ("I wanted to join, 'cause I thought my father didn't love me," one Groveland gang member said.) In most Jeffrey Manor cases, the single moms were *working* moms, which may have meant they set an industrious example but also left their kids with lots of unsupervised time. "When we were in Jeffrey Manor, a lot of those kids out there didn't even have fathers," Charity said. "They were living with the aunties, staying with their grandmothers. They could stay out as late as they want." And Angie yearned to be with them.

While the marriage died nearly as soon as it started, Charity took her vows seriously enough to stay for a dozen years. The beginning of the end arrived one night when the kids ran out of food; Roosevelt told her to feed them bread and water and drove off in his Cadillac. Charity sent the kids to her brother's and went to bed with a butcher knife. This time, if he tried to hit her, she really would try to kill him. ("I had to pray on that, real hard," she said.) Charity enrolled in beauty school, and Angie, in the sixth grade, was old enough to crack the code: her mother was getting ready to leave. Angie was with her mother one night when Charity, exhausted from work and school, fell asleep behind the wheel and plowed into the neighbor's yard. "My mother was tired as hell," Angie said. "She was trying to get her life together; she didn't see ours drifting away."

The divorce hit Angie harder than anyone expected. It just seemed to shatter one of life's basic rules, that mothers and fathers come bundled together, however imperfectly. "He was an asshole, but he was still my daddy," Angie said. When Roosevelt refused to vacate the house, Charity and Angie were forced to move, violating a tenet of divorce management by leaving Angie further uprooted; her brother stayed with her dad. Even her body started to change. "Everything happened so fast," she said. As a young child, Angie had blended a winning innocence ("Wanna marry my mama?") with an insolent streak. Her mother had her pegged as a "follower," willing to abet whatever the worst kids wanted to do. After the divorce, the innocence faded and the insolence grew, to a level that would startle Angie herself.

As Angie finished eighth grade, Charity married Rodger Scott, the Holy Cross teacher she had hired to help Angie a few years earlier. Angie had liked Rodger as a tutor, finding him young, fun, and kind. But as a stepfather, even a mellow one, he inevitably formed a different identity in her mind. "It was like he was taking away my mama," she said. He, too, had been through a bitter divorce, and he brought his two young kids into the house, which left Angie feeling additionally invaded and burdened as a babysitter. Hugette, at six, was manageable enough, but even as a preschooler, Rodger's son, Jay, was beyond-the-pale wild. With Jay storming through the house, Angie was in no mood for her stepfather's discipline, however mild.

"How was school?"

"Where's your homework?"

Angie would mutter under her breath, "Who the hell are you?"

In her first year at Aquinas High, a Catholic girls' school that Charity struggled to afford, Angie still indulged her earnest streak. She joined the pep squad and gave an impassioned debate-team speech calling for temperance. ("Today I will persuade you that being a teenage drinker is not what you want to be.") She carried around four-by-six cards with poems by Jackie Earley ("Got up this morning / Feeling good & Black") and Langston Hughes ("I am the darker brother"). But as the year wore on, so did the tensions at home. She started tongue-lashing Rodger and smoking pot. She ran back to her father's house in Jeffrey Manor, where there were no rules. As her freshman year ended, Angie left to spend the summer with her father—or more to the point, without him, since Roosevelt was never around. In a sense, she never returned. After years of envying the kids on the stoop, Angie was free to join them. "I got a chance to be wild."

As an adolescent child of divorce staging a rebellion, Angie was scarcely an unfamiliar figure. With a caring if overbearing mother and a place in Catholic school, she did have a safety net. But it was thinner than it may seem. She struggled in class and had few close friends, an alcoholic father, and a gangland neighborhood. Charity grew so worried that she scraped up the money to send Angie to a psychologist, who certainly could have found much to explore. A little girl had grown up close to her mother, but close in a complicated way, relishing the attention but resenting the reins. Early on, she had found strength in defiance ("the slap, sometime it felt good"), and then everything had disappeared: her father, her brother, her home. A strange man had stolen her mother, too. Angry and abandoned, Angie responded as she would for decades, hiding her feelings behind a tart lip and quick fists. "Fighting I can deal with," she later said. "Emotions I can't deal with too good." At some level, Angie knew it even then, but she didn't tell the psychologist. Instead she spun fanciful tales of privation until Charity gave up. Her mother had bought her a dime-store journal, and it became the only therapist that Angie would trust. "Everything that bothers me, everything that hurts me, everything that's just not right—I write it down!" she said. "I write it down and I rise above it. That way I don't have to worry about nobody hurting me."

One night in high school, Angie smuggled in a forbidden girlfriend to sleep at the house. Charity confronted Angie. Angie said something smart. The next thing that Charity knew, she had dragged Angie into the kitchen, where she was beating her uncontrollably. "I went temporarily insane," Charity said. "I done grabbed her by the throat. I was banging her head against the refrigerator. I was so scared, I was shaking. I was sure I had killed her." Not long after, when Angie announced she was moving back to the Manor to stay with her father, Rodger and Charity felt powerless to stop her. Just a few years earlier, Angie had written a seventh-grade essay, singing her mother's virtues. "If she didn't love me, she wouldn't be out there working herself half to death trying to give me the best in life." By the end of her sophomore year, Angie was pretty much raising herself.

Angie was sixteen when she returned to Jeffrey Manor, and Hattie Mae was living down the block. Jewell was fourteen. Greg was sixteen. Both were warring with Hattie Mae's boyfriend, Wesley, a scowling presence in the house. The process of neighborhood change was more than a decade old, and the Manor's working-class homeowners contended with a rough street culture in their midst. Socially, the teenagers' world centered on Merrill Park, a small playground where they gathered after dark to smoke weed and get loud. That's what Angie was doing when she met Greg, a six-foot-tall manchild in braids, who towered over her by more than a foot and gazed down with his mother's soft eyes. Angie wasn't consciously focused on his looks. He had a girlfriend. She had a boyfriend. But Angie could tell Greg *anything*—the "crazy shit" her stepfather said, the way the weed made her giggle. Given Greg's feelings toward Wesley, they shared an easy solidarity on the stepfather question; then again, they shared an easy solidarity on everything. On the park benches filled with rowdy kids, Greg was both a leader and loner, a picture of competence. Half a lifetime later, Angie would still describe him as the strongest man she knew.

By the end of her sophomore year, her life swirled around him.

She woke up and went to bed with a joint; in between, she hung out with Greg. "Dear Diary," she confided, after they spent her seventeenth birthday drinking wine. "We got fucked up in the park tonight. But he made sure I got home all right. . . . We talked to each other all night." Not long after: "He seems to knows more about me than I know about myself." And then: "I think I'm falling in love." Over time, Angie's middle would thicken with matronly heft, but at seventeen her precocious build left Greg's older sisters alarmed; beside each other, Angie and Greg looked like they were about to combust. That summer, her father sold the house in Jeffrey Manor and moved a few miles away. Angie ran back to the Manor, where Hattie Mae found her in Greg's room and delivered a lecture about men: "All they want to do is screw ya." Angie brushed it off. She and Greg weren't sleeping together. He was her best friend. They were at his brother's house one night at the start of her junior year when Greg put on Michael Jackson's "Pretty Young Thing": "Where did you come from lady/and ooh won't you take me there." That's when Angie knew. Because her mother worked in a hospital, Angie had a pile of pamphlets about birth control. A month later, she was pregnant.

American life overlooks many things. But having a baby at age seventeen isn't one it overlooks easily. To most of the world, Angie presented a face of studied indifference. She didn't tell her mother for months, and she never did tell her father, who stayed too drunk to notice. But her worries ran deep. "I don't know what I'm going to do," she told her diary. "I just have to change my life. I have another life with me." After she fretted to her diary about how Greg would react, she found his response so comforting it bore recording twice. "He just said we will be all right," she wrote. "We will be all right." The relationship turned "wishy-washy" as the pregnancy advanced—she was moody, and he was tired from a job at Kentucky Fried Chicken—but Greg was with her when her water broke. They shared the ambulance to the hospital, where Greg fell asleep in his KFC clothes and in the early hours of May 7, 1984, Angie wept with relief at the sight of LaKesha Elaine Jobe. "Little tiny feet, little tiny hands," she wrote. "It's my baby girl."

About one American child in five was born outside marriage that year; among black children, the figure was three in five. Many people worried that mothers like Angie were organizing their lives around welfare—having babies to get a check. Angie's life suggests a competing view: it wasn't organized at all. It was rocketing forward on the adolescent fuel of anger, fear, hormones, and pot. Until she got pregnant, welfare was one of many things to which she had given no thought. (Charity, virulently antiwelfare, had briefly gotten food stamps during the divorce but was so embarrassed she gave them away.) Although Angie didn't get pregnant to get a check, a subtler welfare critique may hold more sway. Its easy availability may have played an enabling role, giving her a reason to set aside her appropriate alarm. "If we said how are you going to take care of this child, she could say I'll get on welfare," Rodger said. He and Charity resented it for reducing their leverage. Then again, they had no real leverage. With welfare or without it, chances are the outcome of Angie's teen rebellion would have been much the same. Hattie Mae helped with the forms, and Angie got the first in a string of checks that would last a dozen years.

Charity and Rodger could accept the fact that Angie had a baby. What they couldn't accept was Greg. He wouldn't look them in the eyes or come in the house. "He ain't nothing but a thug," Charity said, insisting that Angie stop seeing him. In Angie's mind, Greg's independence from the real thugs was part of his appeal. She considered him just streetwise enough to be interesting—"thug lite," she once said—and was proud when he bought Kesha diapers and milk. Tired of her father's drunken rages, Angie moved back to Charity's at the start of the school year and enrolled at a public school for teenage mothers. Angie lied and told her mother that she was hardly talking to Greg, a dodge belied by his late-night calls. Rodger would hang up, but Greg would call back and cuss him out. That's another thing Angie liked about Greg; he didn't take any guff. "Why can't they understand that we love each other and we gonna be together," Angie wrote in her diary. A few months into her senior year, Angie dropped out—another move that American life is slow to forgive. She said the school nursery wasn't changing Kesha's diaper. Charity thought she wanted more time with Greg.

One night Rodger found one of Greg's letters and started in again: Greg's no good. . . . You're a mother now. . . . You have to think of the future. When Rodger followed her into her room, Angie went off. "You ain't my daddy! Get away from me!" Greg had given her a switchblade, and she warned she was ready to use it. Amid the threats and accusations, Angie grabbed Kesha and raced back to her father's house. In retrospect, Rodger and Charity would blame themselves: if only they hadn't pushed so hard, maybe they could have retained some influence. Angie would look back and think of the fight as the night she regained her life. She and Greg were together. The sooner everyone accepted it, the better things would be.

Most relationships between teen parents quickly fall apart. Angie discovered why. Raising a child is hard work, even harder when you're poor and still partly a child yourself. Both she and Greg wanted to run the streets, and with a baby to care for they started to fight. After a few months at her father's house, Angie lowered her opinion of freedom and returned home to Charity and Rodger, where there was food in the fridge and a hand when a diaper needed changing. Her mother insisted she get a job, and as part of the truce she found one at Popeye's, working nights while Charity babysat. Angie liked going to work—it got her out of the house—and since she didn't tell the welfare office, she kept her whole welfare check. Greg had a job making pizzas. As Angie turned nineteen, they moved into their first apartment, a one-room kitchenette with a bed that folded out of the wall.

A life with Greg was what she had wanted, but poverty, youth, and a child in Pampers remained a combustible mix. Angie figured Greg saw other women; she saw other men. Popeye's provided an escape but left her muttering in her sleep about biscuits. She put herself out to cook Thanksgiving dinner, only to hear Greg call her potato salad nasty. (Worse, he was right.) By then, Angie was pregnant again, not quite on purpose but not purely by accident. Adding another child—a boy, Dwayne, they nicknamed Redd—did nothing to reduce the tension. At one point, Angie packed up and left, but she knew she wouldn't stay gone. No matter what she and Greg said to each other, they would quickly shrug it off. To others, not least her mother, Angie may have seemed a portrait of failure, another inner-city girl, out of school, coming of age as a welfare mother. But as Angie lived it—greasy biscuits, food stamps, and all—the story felt like one of overcoming the odds. She worked, kept her kids fed, and saw nothing to apologize for. "I was on my own, making it," she said. "I was with the guy I was in love with. We wasn't married by the courts, in God's eyes, but to me we was married. Married people have kids, married people take care of each other, even when they have problems. We was a family."

By the time Angie turned twenty-one, she was pregnant again, and the kitchenette would no longer do. They found a bigger place a few miles east in Chicago's South Shore, where their lives took a new turn. The apartment was in the middle of a drug market, and Greg, who'd had an on-and-off job hanging ceiling fans, discovered a gift for selling cocaine. Until then, Angie's finances had rested on the usual three-legged stool; she had welfare, a sporadic under-the-table job, and whatever money Greg brought in. No single income stream sufficed, but together they provided a living on the borders of just enough. Now Angie still had welfare and in time another job, at Kentucky Fried Chicken. But with the money that Greg brought in, her checks went uncashed for weeks. Chicken paid about $4 an hour, and welfare about $340 a month, but by Angie's guess Greg was pocketing $1,000 a week. He drove a Seville and kept the kids in brand-name clothes. For the first time as an adult (also the last), she didn't have to worry about money.

Crack was just arriving in Chicago, and the demand seemed insatiable. By the time their third child, DeVon, was born in 1987, Greg's customers were banging on the door day and night. One day she woke up with Greg in handcuffs and a cop over her bed, searching the room for drugs. But the only thing he found was Angie's .22. "I need a little protection," she explained, "'cause it's terrible around here!" With no drugs in the house, Greg was back by the afternoon. Sometimes Angie portrays herself as a mere observer of the chaos. In other tellings, she assigns herself a more active role. Once Greg handed her three sacks of cocaine to hide in the apartment; when he returned, there were only two left. With a frantic search, they found the missing parcel lying on the ground, like an unclaimed lottery ticket. One of their worst fights erupted when Angie came home from work to discover the kids hadn't eaten, though Greg was outside with money in his pocket, waiting for his supplier. She went out to get the kids' dinner and returned to see Greg still on the street—feeding himself. She got smart. He got smart. She chased him down the street, shooting. Stop playing, he screamed; you crazy? "You make me crazy!" Angie said.

Angie saw nothing wrong with selling drugs; no one forces anyone to buy, and if "you don't use it, you ain't got to worry about it." But she did sometimes worry about the danger, especially with the kids. As the business grew, Jewell moved in; she had gotten pregnant in her junior year of high school and Wesley had put her out. Until then Angie knew her only as Greg's younger sister, a long-legged teenager whose looks and reserve ran the risk of making her seem soft. Angie discovered that Jewell wasn't as reserved as she seemed, and she certainly wasn't soft. They quickly became best friends. The birth of Jewell's son, Terrell, left four young children in the house, and there was no telling what craziness Greg might attract. He mostly "served" from a nearby smoke house, but Angie dreamed that someone had broken in and killed them all. She couldn't sleep for a week.

Now and then, Angie would tell him to quit. But the money was good, and oh, that man could charm! One morning after a fight, Greg brought Angie roses; he sent them motoring across the floor in the arms of a robot the family named Robbie. A few years later, after Greg was gone, Angie would cry herself to sleep in Milwaukee, staring at the motorized toy and thinking of better times. "He did what he had to do to take care of his family, and I love him for it," she said. Life in Chicago was good.

It didn't strike her mother that way. Chicago had gotten Charity out of the fields, but its streets had stolen her kids. A decade later, the officials revamping the welfare laws would stress the potential of working mothers to serve as role models for their kids. For those with faith in the role-model theory, Charity gives reason to pause. She was the role model from central casting: hardworking, devout, zealously antiwelfare. But of the four kids she helped to raise, three took troubled turns. Angie chose a life with Greg. Angie's book-smart brother, Terrance, got twenty years for selling cocaine. Rodger's rebellious son, Jay, was murdered by his mother's boyfriend. Only Rodger's daughter, Hugette, navigated the passage to a stable adult life, with a four-year college degree and a job as a legal secretary. After a shooting beside the beauty parlor she ran, Charity moved back to Mississippi, where she and Rodger built a house on the land bought with her grandfather's sweat. She took a job at the welfare office and offered a stream of poor single mothers the lectures lost on Angie: stay in school, keep a job, commit yourself to marriage.

Hattie Mae's view of Chicago was more complex. In one light, her life seemed a grand dramatization of the underclass tragedy unfolding nationwide. All three of her daughters had gotten pregnant in high school and gone on welfare; two, including Jewell, would stay there for years. Of her five sons, only one held a steady job. Another was murdered; one would vanish for years at a time; and two were headed for long prison terms. But her life in Chicago didn't *feel* like a defeat, not to someone who started life in a shack by a cotton field. Between welfare and the Marcellus Lounge, her deep freeze had stayed full, and she didn't have to kowtow to white people. Compared to where she came from, her children lived "like millionaires." When Greg and Jewell were nearly grown, Hattie Mae, in her midforties, left welfare, went to school, and got certified as a nursing assistant. Her aura of cheerful kindness and midlife mellowing brought a job with a Chicago banker, who needed help for his mother. Born miles from paved roads, Hattie Mae entered late middle age accompanying the family on a European vacation. Her aunts had said a person could make it in Chicago. In time, she had proved them right.

As for the kids, she told herself to give them back to the Lord. "He can take care of them better than I can," she said. With some of the boys, she had seen trouble coming, but Greg surprised her. She considered him the "gentleman" of the house, the one who gave her no problems. But as he settled into life with Angie, Hattie Mae knew that something was wrong. He had nice cars and clothes but didn't keep a job, so she figured he was selling drugs. Hattie Mae didn't know it, but the police were catching on, too. In the seven months after his twenty-third birthday, Greg was arrested three times on drug-related charges. Two of the cases were dropped. The third earned him eighteen months probation for possessing a small amount of cocaine, which the police had found, along with a gun, after a traffic stop. His probation officer kept notes, warning of "His Tendency to Project Blame For His Action On Others." Still on probation, Greg was soon picked up again, on another drug-possession charge. The case was still pending as Greg and Angie approached their twenty-fifth birthdays in the spring of 1991.

One Sunday that June, Hattie Mae awoke with a start. It was one in the morning, and a spirit was talking: "Go see Greg," it said. "It's the last time you'll see him on the outside world." What a foolish dream, she thought. But as she tried to sleep, the spirit returned: "Get up and go see Greg." She found him the next afternoon and warned him that he was flirting with danger and three young children to feed. Greg assured her nothing was wrong, but that night she woke up again. She lit a cigarette and started to cry. "Lord, what is wrong with me?" she thought.

Angie quarreled with Greg that same night. Not long after Hattie Mae left, his friend George came by, and when George appeared, trouble usually followed. Eavesdropping as they stepped outside, Angie caught bits of the conversation. Some dudes had jumped George. He wanted revenge. He needed Greg's help. Jewell's boyfriend, Tony Nicholas, was in the living room watching the Bulls in the NBA finals. George promised him a new radiator and springs if he lent a hand. Another of Greg's friends, Dave Washington, left and returned with some guns. Angie took Greg aside. "You don't need to be involved!" she said. "Somebody's going to end up going to jail." Angie went to bed angry. George had other friends. Why bother them?

When the police banged on the door the following day, Greg was just waking up. Angie had been asleep when he had returned, so she hadn't yet talked to him. But the cops were talking about a wild shooting: a spray of bullets had wounded three men and killed a fourteen-year-old girl. "I know these motherfuckers ain't shot nobody," Angie told herself. She had seen Greg arrested before, but this time he looked worried, especially when police began to search his dresser drawers. After they left, Angie found what they missed, two guns in the secret compartment where Greg kept his drugs. She called Dave, who hid one in an abandoned house and threw the other in Lake Michigan. By then Greg had started talking, and soon the others fleshed out the story: Tony and Dave had opened fire while Greg had watched their backs. They missed the men they were looking for but hit the crowd out celebrating Michael Jordan's win. Dave led the police to the guns—they fished one from the lake—and a forensics lab identified the murder weapon as the one that Tony had fired.

Jewell was three months pregnant with Tony's baby, their first together, and she thought he would be home soon. He *couldn't* have shot that girl, he told her, and she saw no reason to doubt him. But Angie knew this kind of trouble was different from any that she had seen. While Greg hadn't fired a shot, he could still be charged with first-degree murder. The prosecutors offered a reduced sentence in exchange for his testimony, and Angie begged him to take it. With good behavior, he might be home in time to know his kids. Greg didn't want to testify against his friends, and he didn't consider himself guilty: he hadn't shot anyone. He recanted his statement and placed his bets on a trial. It was the one thing that Greg ever did that Angie would find hard to forgive.

Angie was twenty-five years old, and they had been together for eight years. Life with Greg was the only life she knew. Kesha would start second grade in the fall. Redd was ready for kindergarten, and Von about to turn four. Angie had children to raise, and without Greg she saw no way to support them. Frying chicken wouldn't pay the bills, and her welfare check wouldn't even cover the rent. Apartments in Milwaukee were cheaper and welfare paid more. Neither she nor Jewell knew anything else when they boarded the bus to go.

FOUR

The Survivors:
Milwaukee, 1991–1995

The Milwaukee ghetto didn't look like a ghetto, at least not the kind that Angie had in mind when she stepped off the bus in September 1991. Its central city was strictly a low-rise affair. Tumbledown duplexes lined the streets, and corner stores announced themselves with hand-lettered "We Accept Food Stamps" signs. While ghettos once teemed, Milwaukee's vegetated, its vacant lots making the near north side feel almost pastoral. "Where Have All the Houses Gone?" the *Milwaukee Journal Sentinel* would ask, over an aerial shot of the vernal decay. Toward the ghetto's western edge, the padlocked factories on Thirty-fifth Street formed an industrial mausoleum. Three miles east, Third Street had died in the fifties and burned in the sixties; renamed Martin Luther King Jr. Drive, it now ran past a black holocaust museum. Between the district's rough borders, Thirty-fifth Street to a bit past Third, stretched the state's welfare belt: nine square miles, two shuttered breweries, and about fifteen thousand families drawing checks.

Angie harrumphed at the weedy vista, but it offered something that Chicago did not, an apartment of her own. From the Family Crisis Center, a shelter just off King Drive, she followed a lead to a "raggerly mansion" a few blocks east. The landlady, Rosalie Allen, had nine units in an old Victorian complex that were newly painted and by Chicago standards unbelievably cheap. Angie took one. Jewell took another. A friend from the shelter took a third. In Chicago, rent alone was $250 more than Angie's monthly check. In Milwaukee, Angie's check rose by two-thirds (to $617), while her rent fell in half. Now, she could pay the rent with $250 to spare. Proportionally, Jewell's welfare check rose even more, by almost three-quarters. She was sufficiently impressed that she called Chicago and told her friend Shon, who was pregnant with her third child and chafing at her mother's. Shon brought her cousin Lisa, who had just delivered her third child and was eager to escape the projects. Until Mrs. Allen could get the apartments ready, everyone slept at Jewell's: four women with nine kids and two more on the way. Jewell's brother Robert moved in. Robert's friend Lucky came, too. In time, the de facto economics grew even better than they appeared, since elderly Mrs. Allen forgot to collect the rent. While a strange new city might seem forbidding, the house on First Street felt like a freshman dorm: hardly anyone worked; everyone drank; and there were more people stirring at midnight than noon. "We just partied on First Street," Angie said. "Everybody partied."

Framed in docudrama clarity, this was just what Wisconsin feared: welfare families—*black* welfare families—racing in for higher benefits. The aid givers' fear of attracting aid seekers is a timeless one, or at least as old as the Elizabethan Poor Laws, which greeted migrating paupers with residency requirements nearly four centuries earlier. But the tensions in Wisconsin in the early 1990s were especially pronounced. A run-up in the state's benefits had left a stark imbalance along the Illinois line and roiled Wisconsin politics for decades. Angie and Jewell had no way to know that the very thing that had drawn them to town, larger welfare checks, was about to turn Milwaukee into the world's most famous welfare-eradication zone.

In Milwaukee, as in most American cities, the story of welfare was tangled in the story of race. One reason the city had almost no public housing was the belief, as one opponent put it in 1952, that the lack of affordable shelter was "the only thing that has kept ten thousand— aye, twenty thousand—Negroes from coming up here." A main champion of black interests, the white socialist mayor Frank Zeidler, survived a particularly ugly challenge in 1956 when his critics spread rumors that Zeidler was posting billboards across the South to lure more blacks to town. *Time* dubbed the campaign "the Shame of Milwaukee," and it bore a second distinction: forty years before Congress put time limits on welfare, Zeidler's opponent called for time-limiting stays in public housing, to keep black migrants away.

They came, anyway. As late as 1950, blacks composed as little as 3 percent of the city's population. Their numbers rose fivefold over the next two decades, though welfare was hardly involved. While Wisconsin's benefits were higher than those in the South, they were not much different from neighboring states, and the migrants mostly came for other reasons—for better jobs and schools, to join family, or to flee Jim Crow. Ironically, the racial conflict that ensued brought a liberal ascension—and with it, the rising benefits—that made Wisconsin a welfare magnet, after all. Some of the worst racial confrontations occurred on the city's south side, in blue-collar neighborhoods fiercely opposed to housing integration. After those precincts gave George Wallace his first strong northern showing in his 1964 presidential race, he said if he ever left Alabama he would settle on the south side of Milwaukee. Wallace stayed out, but a few years later the city's home-grown radical priest marched in. Organizing a band of black "youth commandos," Father James Groppi led a series of marches for six months, drawing rock-throwing crowds thousands strong and helping to win the city's first fair-housing laws. Next he turned to welfare.

The battle began in 1969, after conservative Republicans in the legislature pushed through a benefit cut of 15 percent. Groppi led what started as a small protest march and ended as a melee, as thousands of university students joined an impromptu occupation of the Capitol. The day played out like a carnival set piece. Groppi proclaimed a "war on the rich," while protesters flew a red flag and picnicked on the lawmakers' floor. Bloody clashes continued for a week. In the short run, the protest backfired. The moderate Republican governor, Warren Knowles, was trying to restore the cuts, but the trashing of the Capitol only hardened the conservatives' resolve. Yet the welfare cutters also suffered self-inflicted blows. Sneering about "virgin births," Assembly Speaker Harold Froehlich urged that recipients be prosecuted under antifornication laws. His ally, Ken Merkel, a John Bircher from the Milwaukee suburbs, suggested they trim their food budgets to twenty-two cents a meal, and his supporters called recipients "gorillas." The ugly racial subtext, coupled with the bloodied protesters, fed a broader rejection of the political right. In a landslide the following year, the Democrats captured the governorship and two-thirds of the assembly. Throughout the 1970s, the Democrats ruled Wisconsin.

The changes that followed made the state a lodestar of welfare liberalism: benefit increases, eligibility expansions, and streamlined applications. Benefits more than doubled in the 1970s. Caseloads tripled. In 1970, Wisconsin's grants per family ranked twenty-sixth nationwide. Five years later, among the lower forty-eight, only Connecticut paid more. The legislators who championed the benefit expansion saw it as an overdue bit of economic justice (and a hedge against further violence). But among the problems they created was a disparity along the southern border. Before the run-up, benefits in Wisconsin were 21 percent lower than those in Illinois. By 1980, Wisconsin's payments were 54 percent higher. The Chicago ghettos had horrific problems. Milwaukee offered safer streets, cheaper housing, and larger welfare checks—all just ninety miles up the road. Who wouldn't be tempted to move?

The notion that women like Angie and Jewell move for higher benefits has long been discounted by academics, and nationally the evidence was slight. But the Milwaukee-Chicago situation was unique, both in the proximity of the cities and the difference in what their benefits could buy. In 1986, a state-sponsored study concluded that migration played a "relatively small" part in the Wisconsin's caseload growth. Yet it also showed that nearly half the applicants in Milwaukee were newcomers from another state. In 1991, another study found that 21 percent of Milwaukee applicants had arrived in the previous three months. Surveyed by strangers, most migrants cited less stigmatized reasons for a move—family ties, better schools—but with people they knew, Angie and Jewell were blunt. "We came up here because the aid in Chicago wasn't nowhere as much as it was up here," Jewell said. Angie said the same: "We were figuring out how we were gonna pay our bills."

When they arrived in 1991, Milwaukee had the nation's fastest-growing ghetto. The number of high-poverty census tracts (those where two-fifths of the residents were poor) had tripled in just a decade. In 1970, only 1 percent of metro area residents lived in such areas of dense poverty, and nearly half were white; by 1990, 10 percent lived in the expanding poverty zone, and more than two-thirds were black. Half the black population of Milwaukee County was drawing a welfare check. Welfare was by no means the sole cause of the urban transformation; Milwaukee had lost nearly half of its manufacturing jobs in just twenty years (from 1967 to 1987). But welfare, compared to deindustrialization, was an issue politicians could more readily address, and voters were screaming for change. "Go back to Illinois," advised a letter published in the *Kenosha News*. "[A]ll you bring with you are more drugs, gangs, vandalism, murder, muggings, robberies and more rug rats for us to feed."

In 1986, advisers to the Democratic governor, Anthony Earl, approached him with a plan to trim benefits and impose work rules. Earl demurred; for many Democrats, the criticism of welfare still carried a racist taint. Earl's opponent in the fall election, Republican Tommy G. Thompson, made a similar welfare-cutting plan a cornerstone of his campaign. No one took Thompson seriously. Preternaturally ambitious, he had captured his assembly seat straight out of law school but was still stuck there twenty years later—the leader of a powerless minority, so reflexively negative he was known as "Dr. No." His opponent in the Republican primary had dismissed him as a "two-bit hack," and the head of the state Democratic Party declared her bra size larger than Thompson's IQ.

"Tommy Thompson wants to reform welfare and make Wisconsin like Mississippi," Earl complained.

"With you in charge," Thompson answered, "we're attracting all the people from Mississippi up here anyway."

Thompson rode the issue to an upset victory, cut benefits 5 percent, and put the savings in an early work program. Still, benefits remained comparatively high, and the work program weak. When Angie and Jewell arrived four years later, nothing much had changed.

Finding a house came easy for Angie. Living without Greg did not. She had been on her own for four months, so the shock of his arrest hovered in a strange middle distance, as raw as yesterday and as distant as a lifetime ago. She took so many of his collect calls she needed fake names to keep the phone turned on. They spent half their time telling each other he'd be home soon and half secretly wondering

since   what's   5 persent ?   an option?

what to do if he wasn't. A month after Angie got to Milwaukee, her father died, bringing her something new to grieve. With everyone on First Street drinking, Angie drank, too: coolers, daiquiris, Tanqueray, beer. Drinking took her mind off Greg.

By the time Angie arrived, Thompson's early work initiative had been folded into a federal program called Job Opportunities and Basic Skills (JOBS), which for the first time required a part of the caseload to seek work, education, or training. When the appointment notice arrived, Angie met it with an open mind. She wanted to do something to let the kids know—to let herself know—that things would be all right. JOBS sent her to the nursing aides' course where graduation had conferred such pride, but once she quit the nursing home it lost track of her. After a few months, she pressed ahead on her own, finding work at the post office; taking up with the deejay, Vernon; and enrolling in a GED class. Her efforts to scramble onto her feet stood out, not least since she scrambled alone; no one else in the First Street compound was thinking about work or school. After a year in Milwaukee, Angie couldn't say just when her life there had come together. But she knew when it fell apart, the moment the nurse said the pregnancy test had come back positive. She went home and cried for a month.

She was much more upset to be pregnant at twenty-seven than she had been at seventeen. Then she had Greg. Now she had Vernon. Or actually, she didn't—she had already ditched him. Just getting her kids out the door some days was more than Angie could manage. Kesha had arrived in Milwaukee as a cheerful second-grader, surprisingly well-adjusted after what she had been through, but she was absent a third of the school year. Her asthma attacks were part of the problem, but so was everything else: the late-night parties, the winter cold, Angie's sadness over losing Greg. Kesha "tries very hard to do her work, even though all of the work that involves reading is difficult," her teachers wrote. At the end of the year, they called her a "pleasure" but held her back. Redd missed *half* his kindergarten year and struck his teachers as less of a pleasure. "Dwayne has to put forth more effort," one warned the next year, as he failed first grade. Having finally gained some forward momentum, Angie just couldn't see returning to bottles and diapers. Something about abortion made her hesitate, but survival was its own imperative: you do what you have to do. Angie bought a $350 money order and asked her cousin Adolph for a ride.

Adolph started up on the way—abortion's a sin, God don't play that—but Angie wasn't in the mood, particularly from a man. Adolph wouldn't be there to raise this child and neither would Vernon. "Just drive and shut up," she said. One of the protesters outside the clinic called her a "baby killer." A counselor asked if she'd considered other plans. She had considered them night and day. Finally she was in the examining room, with her feet up in stirrups, when a nurse explained what would follow. She would give Angie a pain pill, wait thirty minutes, and return to dilate her cervix. The aspiration would produce uterine cramps. To some women, it feels like labor.

Labor? As the words sank in, Angie couldn't believe what she had heard. "Labor" brought to her mind another word. *Baby.*

"*Un-uhh,*" she thought. "*Un-uhh!*"

"Are you telling me I have to have my baby in order to kill my baby?" she said. "That's murder for real!"

Her legs flew out of the stirrups. Her feet hit the floor. "Gimme my money back," she said. "I'm fittin' to be gone."

To explain how much she wanted that abortion, Angie would later resort to quadruple adverbs; she "really, really, really, really" wanted it. She wanted it, literally, more than she could say. "My conscience just wouldn't let me," she said. In surrendering to biological chance, Angie surrendered more broadly. She quit school. She quit the post office. Too depressed to face the world, she stayed home drinking for months. If she couldn't control what was happening to her body, how could she pretend to control her larger fate? In June 1993, a miserable pregnancy peaked in an excruciating birth—a boy she named Darrell. She had been in Milwaukee for nearly two years, and she was in a deeper hole than when she had arrived.

Angie had summoned enough sentiment to put Darrell's sonogram in her photo album. But the flesh-and-blood presence of an infant did nothing to boost her spirits. Jewell didn't think she was coping very well and took over for a few days. Vernon dropped off some Pampers and clothes, but Angie didn't want to see him, and for years she more or less didn't. Angie sent the older kids to see her mom in Mississippi, and while they were gone, she heard the post office was hiring again. "It was time to get up off my ass," she said. She still had her welfare check, and the baby brought a two-year exemption from JOBS. But "I don't like sitting around no house," she said. "Some people's mind just ain't right for kids."

Angie's second tour at the post office is a story she tells with pride. It lasted a year and a half, long enough to earn her label as the First Street "workaholic." Sent downtown, rather than to the airport, Angie had a shorter commute. And as a handler, rather than a sorter, she could move around and talk with friends. Since no one else in the compound had a regular job, child care wasn't a problem. A romance with Lucky's uncle, Johnny, didn't work out, and Angie was more hurt than she liked to show. But she launched another, with a postal worker named Sherman. She bought her first car. Then she learned to drive. The kids had some good news, too. By the end of his kindergarten year, Von had learned to count to one hundred, and his report card swelled with superlatives: "A very good student and friend!" Kesha scored an even bigger triumph. After struggling through two years of second grade, she gained ground in third, and had a breakthrough year in fourth. Her attendance rate reached 90 percent, and, except for reading, she earned straight As; by the end of the year, even her reading had reached grade level. "Lakesha is a lovely young lady," her teacher wrote. "She has great potential for success."

But maintaining the momentum was hard, for Angie and the kids. Six months into her postal job, Angie found two Chicago police officers at her door, asking for Angela Jobe. "She ain't here," Angie said. The next thing she knew, she was in the back of their car, heading to Greg's trial. It had been nearly three years since Greg's arrest, and they each had reason to feel abandoned. Angie didn't write much anymore or bring the kids to see him; Greg couldn't do anything to help her raise them. Angie knew little about the shooting, and from the stand she shared as little as possible about what she did know. But she got a private visit with Greg before the trial began. The prosecutors were still offering a deal, and Angie urged him to take it. He wound up instead with sixty-five years.

Redd, still in first grade, turned eight the day after his father's sentencing. He still didn't know what his father had done, but among the kids he missed him the most. While Kesha missed Greg in a misty, little girl's way, sending him valentines, Redd missed him with raw fury. He put on weight as he repeated first grade, and classmates started to taunt him. Redd wasn't afraid to fight back, with his lip or with his fists. Academically he didn't meet the promotional requirements to get out of second grade, but at nine he was too old to stay back again, so his teacher passed him on to third. A lackluster student who had missed her own father, Angie identified with Redd. She also felt powerless to help him.

What she did was continue to work. Either from knowledge or canny sixth sense, Angie finally reported the job just before the state computer network probably would have caught her. "I have never had no friends tell them when they was working," she said. "Nobody but my dumb ass!" The fall-off in her benefits explains her reluctance: for every $100 she earned, her package of welfare and food stamps fell by $61, and she paid $7 in payroll taxes. She faced a higher marginal tax rate than Bill Gates did. With her take-home pay running about half the minimum wage, why bother? "'Cause I like working—that's why!" Angie said. "It makes me feel good, like I accomplish something. As long as I'm working, I can say 'I work,' doing what I can for my kids."

Angie's pride was real but hard to sustain, especially when the job left her with so little to show. Angie usually says her postal career ended with a layoff, a version she half believes. In truth, she quit. She quit because her "cool" supervisor was replaced by an autocrat. ("Everything went to hell! We was doing shit somebody else shoulda done.") She quit because the Christmas rush left her so tired, she was ready to go postal herself. ("Not one day off! You wonder why they crazy up in there?") She quit because she resented her temp-worker caste, while veterans could walk into union jobs at twice the pay. ("We ain't got no war—what makes you so special?") That is, she quit because the job market for low-skilled workers is stressful and exploitative. Yet quitting left her stuck at its lowest rungs. "If I was still working at the post office now, I'd be making about $12, $13 an hour," she said years later.

She also quit because she could: she had a welfare check. "I knew if I left the post office, I could still have money," she said. She told her caseworker she had stopped working months before she did, and with her full benefits restored, she bought a new living room set. For all her efforts, Angie was still stuck, and the welfare system let her stay that way.

Unlike Angie, Jewell wasn't thinking about jobs, and the JOBS program wasn't thinking about her. She was seven months pregnant when she got to Milwaukee, and the birth of her second son, Tremmell, left her exempt until he turned two. While Angie found refuge in the First Street parties, Jewell wearied of the commotion and made one of the modest bids for independence that subtly defined her. She moved away. The appearance of the letters *PZ* in her welfare file might have given her pause. In moving to Twentieth and Brown, she and her new boyfriend, Lucky, had moved to a "pickup zone," an area where checks got stolen so often the office made recipients come get them. With gunfire outside the window most nights, Jewell and the kids slept on the floor. Lucky had grown up a Gangster Disciple; Brown Street was Vice Lord ground. He got shot in the hand walking to the corner store, and Jewell raced back to First Street the next day. "I ain't no kicking-it type—I'm a home-bound type," she said. "But I ended up in the same place."

At twenty-four, Jewell had spent her life seeming to travel in circles. It took a second look to see the determination beneath the drift. The seventh of Hattie Mae's eight kids, Jewell was chubby as a little girl and painfully shy; as her oldest sister, Mary, put it, "If you didn't stop and pay attention, you wouldn't even know Jewell was around." She was just starting school when her oldest brother, Squeaky, was murdered. The killing quickened Hattie Mae's resolve to flee the projects but left her working nights at the Marcellus Lounge, with the kids home unsupervised. From the projects they moved to a house that Greg accidentally burned down. Their next apartment, lacking heat, got condemned, and it was from there they left for Jeffrey Manor. For a girl with an instinct to keep to herself, the frequent dislocations—new neighborhoods and schools—did nothing to diminish her reserve. "I didn't have no lotta friends," Jewell said. "Didn't nobody dislike me or anything. . . . I [just] wasn't the type to butt in on somebody's conversation." Reticence became her resilience.

Jewell's shyness never struck her as a problem, and neither did most of the other forces shaping her childhood: the absence of a father, the poverty of the projects, the series of here-and-there moves. What bothered Jewell was Wesley, Hattie Mae's boyfriend of nearly twenty years, and after that her husband. "Living with somebody you hate," is how Jewell describes it, a feeling her siblings shared. You can give the family tree a great shake without unloosing a kind word on his behalf. As a longtime worker at an aluminum factory, Wesley had money. But the kids complained he treated them like strangers in their own house, barring them from eating his food, accusing them of stealing things they hadn't stolen and doing things they hadn't done. For years on end, he and Jewell scarcely spoke.

As she reached her teens, Jewell started to thin out, and by eighth grade she had the kind of figure that made men notice. It was something that a shy girl enjoyed knowing about herself. "Guys would ride up and try to talk to me," she said. She was barely in her teens, and "they were like nineteen or twenty." Having started school late (because of a December birthday) and stayed back a year, Jewell entered high school nearly two years older than most students in her grade. Cutting classes and smoking weed, she failed ninth grade, which left her even farther behind—nearly eighteen by her sophomore year. Jewell had spent years dating her best friend's brother, Johnny. But in tenth grade she left him for a drug dealer named Otha, who ferried her around in an apple-red car with speakers that echoed blocks away. He presented her in public with a silent head-to-toe wave, a king presenting his queen. "Most women like a roughneck—a thug, if you want to call him that," she said. *Thug*, in her mind, meant nothing debased but *stylish* and *strong*, able to survive the ghetto unbowed. "I have a little thug in me," she said.

Soon, a bit of it showed. One day Jewell and Otha pulled up in front of Johnny and his new girlfriend, Dominique. The two men started to fight, and then the women did, too. The next day brought a rematch, and when Jewell bloodied her rival's face, Dominique vowed to raise a posse and exact her revenge. Everyone knew a big fight was coming. By the time Dominique appeared with four of her uncles and aunts, Jewell had smuggled Wesley's switchblade out of the house.

Surrounded as the fight began, she took two wild swings and carved a ravine through Dominique's arm. Jewell's family was stunned. Nice-and-quiet, keep-to-herself Jewell was the last person anyone expected to see arrested for battery. "I'm a nice person," Jewell said. "But I ain't gonna let nobody fuck over me." Including Otha. Tired of the king having too many queens, Jewell went back to Johnny. A few months later, Otha was murdered in a Manor feud, and Jewell was pregnant.

Mary, her oldest sister, urged her to get an abortion. Having been a teen mother herself, she had worked her way through community college and into a halfway decent job in a hospital billing office; she knew the struggles ahead. But Jewell had made up her mind. "I'd been thinking about it a long time," she said. "I just wanted something of my own, something that's mine, that I could love. I just wanted a baby, just *wanted* one. Even though I wasn't working, I didn't have my own place, whatever—I still wanted a baby." Wesley made Hattie Mae put her out, which was part of Jewell's hazy plan. She was tired of living in a habitat of hate. What may seem to others an act of self-destruction was to her one of self-preservation. On October 14, 1988, with the birth of Terrell Reed, Jewell had someone to love. She left school, went on welfare, moved in with Angie and Greg, and was neither surprised nor disturbed when Johnny drifted away. "I didn't feel like I needed anybody to help me take care of my baby," she said.

In Jewell's life, proximity often proved destiny. When Terrell was about six months old, a buddy of Greg's stopped by—a "big, tall chocolate man" named Tony Nicholas. Having had a baby with her best friend's brother, she took up with her brother's best friend. The next two years unfolded as a series of aborted plans. Tony was helping Greg sell drugs and would soon have a drug problem of his own. Jewell got partway through a dental hygienists' course and spent a few months as a gas station cashier. Wanting an apartment of her own, Jewell and Tony moved to Minneapolis, where they had heard welfare was high enough to cover the rent. But they didn't like being so far away and came back after eight months. Jewell had been trying to get pregnant again, and she had just told Tony she was having his baby when he joined the impromptu plot forming in Greg's kitchen. It was Tony's errant bullet that killed fourteen-year-old Kathryn Miles. A few months later, Jewell was back on the bus, this time to Milwaukee. She was a seasoned survivor, a woman half formed, and a prison widow at twenty-three.

It took Jewell two and a half years in Milwaukee just to apply for a job. Some efforts to explain why recipients languish focus on self-esteem. But Jewell liked herself just fine. Her real struggle was with something a psychologist might call self-efficacy: she just didn't think she could do much to shape the course of her life. And why would she? Her whole childhood can be read as a lesson in powerlessness. Shy by nature, often uprooted, subject to a stepfather she loathed, Jewell was raised in a world virtually designed to keep her feelings of self-efficacy low. She had seen nothing to suggest that cause brought effect, work brought results, or that risks would be rewarded. When it came to jobs, even her imagination was crimped. She was as close to Tony's mother as she was to anyone, but the only thing she knew about her work was that she "sat at a front desk." Jewell's only adult job, at the Amoco station, was one that Tony's mother had arranged. "I don't never think I'm going to get a job when I put in an application," she said. Especially if white people were involved. "I don't put myself in a place where there's a whole lotta white people," she said.

All of which makes Jewell's first encounter with the JOBS program especially disheartening. Tired of sitting around, Jewell finally called her caseworker and asked for help. In another context, this might be called a teachable moment. But the lesson it imparted was a familiar one of futility. Jewell sat through a two-week motivation course, signed up to train as a nursing aide, and heard nothing for two months. When she finally called in, she learned the course had been canceled. As bureaucratic runarounds go, this was exceedingly mundane. It just happened to reinforce one of her life's cruelest lessons: that things were the way they were and nothing she did would change them.

In time, she did something, anyway. The following year, Lucky's cousin Tiffany applied for a job at a factory that made airplane seats. Jewell tagged along and was startled when she got hired, too. "I guess they needed help that bad," she said. When Tiffany quit a few weeks

Affirmations important

networking

later, Jewell lost her ride and the job. But not long after, Angie's cousin Adolph introduced her to his boss on an office-cleaning crew. "I didn't think I was going to get hired," Jewell said, though again she proved herself wrong. Since she didn't report the job, she kept her full welfare check. And after a few months, Jewell layered on a second job, as a postal temp for the Christmas season. That left her cleaning offices in the early evening, and sorting mail from midnight to six. About the same time, she started having terrible stomach pains. She was passing blood and making weekly trips to the emergency room, where for years her bleeding ulcers went undiagnosed. Feeling too weak to work two jobs, she left the cleaning crew. But the postal job, which paid better, ended after the holiday rush, and Jewell, now starting her fourth year in Milwaukee, was idle once again.

The JOBS program was supposed to do something about that. But having neglected to help her when she volunteered, it proved equally inept once Tremmell turned two and her exemption expired. It took eight months just to send her an appointment letter. By then she was secretly cleaning offices, so she threw the notice in the trash. Four more letters followed over the next five months, each of which she ignored. Then, about the time Jewell lost her job, the letters from the JOBS program ceased, and she sank back into bureaucratic oblivion. Like Angie, Jewell was stuck.

The taxpayers of Wisconsin, among many others, were wondering why. It's a big prosperous country out there—what kept women like Angie and Jewell from reaping its rewards? Just about everyone has given the subject at least a passing thought, the tragedy of the ghettos looming so large it can cast shadows on the whole national enterprise. One common liberal formulation was that welfare poor were "just like you and me"—generally trying their best—but held back by barriers beyond their control. They faced a shortage of jobs (or good-paying jobs); a lack of child care and transportation; the inability without welfare to get medical care. Parts of the First Street story can be read as vindicating this view. Angie left the post office largely because of its low pay. Jewell lost her job at the seat factory when she lost her ride;

her stomach pain made it harder to work. Still, it's hard to rest comfortably with the view that late-twentieth-century America was bereft of opportunity when so many penniless Ghanaians and Guatemalans were making their way. Years later, Bill Clinton would tell me that one of his aims in signing a welfare bill was to give recipients "the same piss and vinegar these immigrants have got." Another liberal body of thought (in muted conflict with the first) held that the poor weren't like you and me at all but beset by extraordinary problems. They were sick, addicted, depressed, and abused; they were stalked by violent men. This theory fits more easily with the evidence from First Street, where Angie fell into an immobilizing funk and the stacks of empty beer cans grew. But it omits the most prominent feature of Angie and Jewell's lives, their extraordinary resilience. While Jewell's stomach bled, she worked two jobs. From a terrible depression, Angie struggled back to work, while raising four kids. Lots of vastly more successful people would buckle under lighter loads. When I asked how they pictured themselves, Angie and Jewell each began with the same words: "I'm strong."

On the right, theories of the ghetto once began with talk of Easy Street, where happy idlers dined on food-stamp steaks. Ronald Reagan famously conjured the welfare cheat whose "tax-free cash income alone is over one hundred fifty thousand dollars." The Reaganesque talk of Welfare Queens was fading by the 1990s, and it was easy to see why. For all the parties, life on First Street was anything but happy. "We did a lot of crying," Angie said. "Maybe the drinking and the partying was a way just to escape." Another theory had recipients trapped in a subculture utterly isolated from work, in communities where alarm clocks never rang and no one learned the value of an honest day's pay. Though a staple of after-dinner speech, this view hardly described the world of Angie and Jewell. Both grew up with working mothers. And for all his drinking, Angie's father was a steady worker, too. Jewell's loathed quasi-stepfather worked. Angie had worked at three chicken joints, two post offices, and a nursing home. Even Jewell, despite her self-doubts, had found a succession of jobs, and she found them through a network of working ghetto friends. I once asked her if she had thought of her mother—a longtime AFDC recipient who was secretly employed—as a worker or a welfare recipient. The either-or formulation left her puzzled. "Both," she said. The thought that work and welfare were contrasting ways of life—a central premise of the public debate—was to her nonsensical.

The conservative critique that seems more on point concerns the absence of responsible fathers, a condition that had shaped the Caples family for at least three generations and that speaks more directly to the broader underclass dilemma. The lack of a father means the lack of the income, affection, and discipline that a father can provide. Kids can overcome it, and they do so all the time, but for someone growing up poor, having just one parent amounts to a double dose of disadvantage. Not too long ago, a statement like that would have been controversial; a generation of leftist and feminist scholars celebrated the strengths of single mothers and argued their children fared no worse on average than children with both parents at home. Several large-scale data sets have given subsequent scholars an empirical edge, and not many still argue that single parenthood carries no special risks. (They do argue over the risks' magnitude and the underlying causes of the fathers' absence.)

An illustrative figure here is Sara McLanahan of Princeton, a liberal sociologist (and then a single mother herself), who set out in the mid-1980s to disprove what she saw as the prejudice against the single-parent family. Toiling in the fields of multivariate analysis, she found the opposite of what she had expected. Her 1994 book with Gary Sandefur, *Growing Up with a Single Parent*, remains a definitive text.

We have been studying this question for ten years, and in our opinion the evidence is quite clear: *Children who grow up in a household with only one biological parent are worse off, on average, than children who grow up in a household with both of their biological parents, regardless of the parents' race or educational background.* . . . [They] are twice as likely to drop out of high school, twice as likely to have a child before age twenty, and one and a half times as likely to be "idle"—out of school and out of work—in their late teens and early twenties. [italics in original]

They are also more likely to commit crimes. McLanahan didn't argue that all fatherless children would be better off with their *particular* father in the home; were he, say, violent or drunk, things could be worse with him nearby than gone. But on average at all tiers of society, having a father helps. It's true that troubled fathers are often the product of poverty and social disadvantage. But in turn, they become a cause.

Hattie Mae didn't grow up with her father (or, in her case, her mother, either), and she wound up a repeated victim of sexual abuse. Jewell, never knowing her father, despised his stand-in so much that she was relieved when he put her out. Angie did know her father— knew him as a drunk. Neither Greg nor Tony knew his father (they both had working mothers), and as they were serving a combined 150 years, their children faced a fatherless future, too. Among Angie's kids, the longing for a father was palpable. Angie saw Redd's grade-school fights as the product of his smoldering anger over the absence of Greg. Seven when she witnessed her father handcuffed and swept away, Kesha had processed the loss by airbrushing the memory. As she pictured it for the rest of her life, the police returned, removed the shackles, and let a father give his little girl a parting embrace.

The condition of central-city fathers was catastrophic—but was it welfare's doing? Fatherhood was a troubled institution in sharecropper society, too, as Hortense Powdermaker had found. ("Often there is no man in the household at all.") The conservative critique of the ghetto tended to blame welfare for all of its woes: poverty, crime, drugs, nonmarital births. Yet up close welfare's influence didn't seem so pervasive. Angie and Jewell moved just to get it. They received it for years. But that's different from saying they "depended" on it in any soul-altering sense. It was one way, among others, of hustling up some cash.

Angie and Jewell offered no theory about what stood between them and conventional success. But one striking part of the story they told is what they left out. They didn't talk of thwarted aspirations, of things they had sought but couldn't achieve. They certainly didn't talk of subjugation; they had no sense of victimhood. The real theme of their early lives was profound alienation—not of hopes discarded but of hopes that never took shape. In an unnoticed line in the first welfare speech of his presidency, Bill Clinton would say, "America's biggest problem today is that too many of our people never got a shot at the American Dream." He might have added that some people never even get the chance to dream it. The building blocks of middle-class life aren't hard to identify: finish school; keep a job; form a stable marriage. "We didn't think like that!" Angie erupted one day. "You think we just *had* to live in Milwaukee? So many opportunities for us here in Milwaukee? We got a nice job in Milwaukee! Nice home! We didn't come here because of that shit!" I started to ask what might have helped, when Angie cut me off. "If my *man* woulda come home! I just wanted my life to be back the way it was, happy or sad." Training, health insurance, wage subsidies—Angie could have used the programs the Left prescribed, as well as the prod sought by the Right. But she and Jewell also needed something more, something in which to believe. And that's something that any welfare office would find it hard to provide.

Just as no one expected Tommy Thompson to capture the governor's mansion, no one expected to him to keep it. He was a quirk, a fluke, a "two-bit hack"—and he went on to become the longest-serving governor in state history. One reason was his mastery of welfare politics. "It's a fantastic campaign issue," he told me in 1994, when the issue had reached such a boil that even Ted Kennedy ran workfare ads. One observer that year argued that "all the Republican candidates, and a good portion of the Democratic candidates, are copying Tommy Thompson." The observer was Tommy Thompson.

Thompson's early claims of success rested on a single statistic: caseload declines. From 1987 to 1993, the Wisconsin rolls fell 20 percent. Over the same years, caseloads rose in all but two states—nationally, they rose by a third. Thompson liked to say that he had moved more people off welfare than the rest of the country combined. *Res ipsa loquitor.* There was reason to be skeptical and not just because falling caseloads are value-neutral. (The question, of course, is what becomes of those not on the rolls.) Some of the declines simply came from his benefit cut, which also reduced eligibility; some came from the state's strong economy; and caseloads barely budged in Milwaukee, the only place where Thompson's efforts could be measured against the challenge of ghetto poverty.

As programs, Thompson's first efforts had flopped. Learnfare tried to keep kids in school by reducing the checks of families with teenage truants. Thompson said he got the idea while talking to his campaign driver, and it had that kind of commonsense appeal. But it assumed more control over their kids than many parents had, and bureaucratically it proved a nightmare, especially in Milwaukee where the schools were too disorganized to track attendance. In 1992, when researchers at the University of Wisconsin–Milwaukee found that it failed to boost school attendance, Thompson attacked them as liberal ideologues and canceled their contract. Then the new analysts found the same thing: "Learnfare had no detectable effect on school participation." The debate over Thompson's first work program ran a similar course. Work Experience and Job Training sent modest numbers of recipients into work or training programs. But when the evaluators (UW-M, again) found that it did little to move people into jobs, Thompson ended that contract, too, and ordered them to hand over their data to the state. They published their report, anyway, showing the earnings of recipients had risen in just two of twenty-nine counties.

Thompson was done with big messy programs and prominent evaluations. In his second term, he ramped down to pilot projects and focused on the press release. In the early nineties, Gerald Whitburn, Thompson's savvy welfare chief, ran the department like a unit of Procter & Gamble, rolling out a glossy new product each year, with maximum marketing oomph. "Bridefare," a four-county marriage project, won Thompson a Bush White House event. "Two-Tier," an effort to dissuade welfare migrants, staged a competition among prospective sites, a drawn-out process that kept the words *Thompson* and *welfare reform* in local headlines. It says something about Thompson's lens on welfare that Whitburn held a second cabinet portfolio. He was the governor's point man on polling.

Thompson's supporters make two plausible claims for his early record. By highlighting welfare's failures, they say, his programs helped build support for deeper change. "It's what I call the drip theory," Whitburn said. "Over and over, and pound and pound, and out of that comes more and more understanding and fewer and fewer opponents." To his credit, Thompson was also the rare governor who put up enough state matching funds to receive all his federal JOBS money. As a result, the modest percentage of the Wisconsin case-load enrolled in a welfare-to-work activity was two to three times the national average. That gave the bureaucracy some practice and probably helped trim the rolls. At the same time, Thompson had an advantage no other governor enjoyed, a special pipeline to federal aid. In one of his first acts in office, he cut a unique deal with the Reagan administration that eventually brought him a federal windfall of $148 million. Of that, $78 million ostensibly represented money the state had saved the feds by reducing its benefits, though no other state that cut benefits was allowed to make the same claim. The remaining $70 million was an even purer political gift. The embattled administration of George H. W. Bush, needing Thompson's active support, signed off on the figure a few months before the 1992 election, saying that it represented unspecified cost savings. As one White House negotiator explained: "Wisconsin was in play. It was an election year. You don't have to connect too many dots."

The "drip, drip, drip," the special deals, the outsized claims of success—it all made Wisconsin Democrats chafe. In early 1993, as Clinton took office with a pledge to "end welfare" through time limits, Thompson tried to upstage him by announcing his own time-limit plan. It would affect only one thousand people in two rural counties, but it captured national headlines and left the state Democrats an unappealing choice. They could go along and feed the Thompson publicity machine or be tagged as welfare apologists. (When I saw him afterward, Thompson bragged he made liberals feel like "their hearts had been cut out.") One thing that set Milwaukee apart from most big cities is that its leading Democrats were antiwelfare, too. Father Groppi notwithstanding, the idea of paying people *not* to work had never fit comfortably in its blue-collar culture; the focus of its famed socialist mayors had been clean government and rights for workers. As early as 1990, John Norquist, the Democratic mayor, had called for repealing AFDC and replacing it with public jobs. The mayor's chief of staff, David Riemer, a public jobs zealot, had written a book on the subject. Their ally, Representative Shirley Krug, had been pushing a bill to replace welfare with jobs.

In the fall of 1993, Norquist held a backyard picnic. A state legislator named Antonio Riley was there, complaining about Thompson's latest headline grab. Riemer, the mayor's aide, responded with a plea: end it. Answer Thompson's two-county tinkering with a plan to abolish AFDC statewide. Riley had grown up on welfare himself and considered it "a jailer of people." With the mayor's blessing, he and Riemer drafted a one-page bill to scrap AFDC and replace it with a system of public employment. As for the obvious questions—how would it work? what would it cost?—the sketchy bill left five years for future debate. It passed without a Republican vote. Now, in a bizarre inversion of politics, it was the GOP's turn to squirm: the Democrats had become the welfare repealers. The Republicans called it a publicity stunt, and they were largely right. Half the Democrats voted for the bill just to put Thompson in a bind. Whitburn, the welfare secretary, threatened a veto, and the effort seemed dead.

At breakfast the following morning, Thompson chewed him out. *Veto* a death sentence for AFDC? "It was like serving me up a filet mignon when I was only supposed to get a cheese sandwich," he later said. Wisconsin's unique partial veto let him excise the public-job guarantees, and as for the rest of the new system, he had until nearly the end of the decade to figure it out. The feds would have to sign off first. It probably wouldn't come to pass. If it did, no one had more than the vaguest idea of what would take the program's place.

As the backyard plot to end welfare hatched, Jewell recruited another recipient onto the Wisconsin rolls—her cousin Opal. They had been playmates in the projects two decades earlier, but until Jewell made a visit to Chicago and gave her a call, she hadn't heard Opal's voice in years. On the outs with her drug dealer husband and doubled up at her mother's with three young kids, Opal was dying for a place of her own. When Jewell told her she could get a place on First Street, she hung up and started to pack. Coming home from work a few days later, Angie found a kindred spirit in the compound and embraced her as "family." Opal had a knack for winning people over, and after five years of marriage she put it to quick use. She raced though a line of instant boyfriends with street names like "Smoke" and "Man." She fell for a preachy black Muslim named "Dre," whom Angie dubbed

"Me Don't Eat Pork," after she caught him sneaking bites of bacon. Opal seemed crushed when Dre moved on, but recovered to celebrate her twenty-eighth birthday with two suitors in her apartment, each unaware of the other. "Opal was crazy," Angie said. "Opal shoulda been caged!" The duo became a trio—not just real and fictive cousins, but closer than sisters. "We did just about everything together besides taking a bath," Angie said.

At about the time the three women were born in the mid-1960s, the anthropologist Carol Stack went to live among a group of poor black single mothers who, just like the trio's mothers, had migrated from the South to a midwestern city. A generation later, her famous study, *All Our Kin*, still reads as though it could have been written about Opal, Angie, and Jewell. Stack's women survived by creating a domestic network, across multiple households, of real and honorary kin, with few of the boundaries that characterize middle-class life. "They trade food stamps, rent money, a TV, hats, dice, a car, a nickel here, a cigarette there, food, milk, grits, and children." Life is a giant favor bank; letting someone move in with you today insures you can do the same tomorrow. While others had labeled the poor black family "broken" and "disorganized," Stack celebrated this cooperative living as "a profoundly creative adaptation to poverty."

And in part it was. But if the bond among the trio served its functions, it brought dysfunctions, too. Angie said she started to drink when her friend Lisa did; Jewell said she hung out and partied because Angie and Opal did. Even Stack found the networks discouraged work and marriage by casting them as "precarious" alternatives to the coop life. You don't travel very far in the ghetto without hearing a crab-pot story, of someone who tried to get ahead but was dragged down by family and friends—a resentful boyfriend, an addicted sister, a brother headed for jail. Stories of ghetto success often involve a moment of physically breaking away, to school, the army, or merely the asylum of an outside mentor. Stack argued that "survival demands the sacrifice of upward mobility." Maybe in 1968, but a generation later that was a high price to pay. While Angie denied feeling any downward pull, one noteworthy thing about her efforts to work is how little overt encouragement she received. "We ain't like, 'You go, girl!

Good!'" Angie said. "Who do shit like that? I don't need nobody to pat me on the back. I'm a grown woman." Looking back, Jewell would conclude that "everybody was too, too close."

And with Opal they grew closer still. She landed on First Street with charm, guile, a seductive smile, and a secret crack addiction. When Jewell's food stamps disappeared, Jewell suspected her brother Robert. When Opal disappeared, Jewell figured she had met a guy. Angie was clueless, too. But six months after Opal arrived, the child welfare bureau received an anonymous complaint: "Ms. Caples had minimal food, no beds or stove, and the children were sleeping on the floor. The caller indicated that Ms. Caples uses all of her AFDC on drugs." Sierra was four, Kierra was two, and Tierra was about to turn one. An investigator, unable to find Opal, let the matter drop. It wouldn't be the last time a bureaucracy would lose her trail.

Not long after, Opal brought Angie and Jewell along on a shopping trip to Kmart. Opal got into an argument with a security guard, and the three went to jail on shoplifting charges, only to emerge the following morning with another yarn. The case was dropped, but the episode lived on. One of their cellmates spent the night spinning tales about the crack house she ran. All three found Andrea's stories diverting, but Opal seemed especially engaged. She ran into Andrea shortly after her release, and when Andrea showed her where the drug house was, Opal knew all she needed to know. Jewell, by now aware of Opal's problem, began to chide her. "You need to leave that shit alone," she said. "I know what I'm doing," Opal would answer. "You ain't my mama. Shut up!" One thing Opal liked about Andrea is Andrea didn't lecture.

The First Street life sputtered to a close in the spring of 1995, after three and a half years. By then, Mrs. Allen was eighty years old, and she ceded control to her younger brother, who proclaimed himself the new sheriff in town. The metaphor was apt. Felmers O. Chaney had started his career in law enforcement by walking a ghetto beat, then gone on to become the city's first black police sergeant and the head of the local NAACP; soon he would have a Milwaukee prison named after him. Pay up or get out, he said. Jewell's tempestuous brother Robert knocked him to the ground, which sealed the end. Everyone decided to go.

As Angie and Jewell were making plans, Opal disappeared. In the past, she had straggled back after a day or two, fending off the lectures with a weary, "I know." This time, she never returned. Four days later, when the high wore off, Opal was sitting in Andrea's kitchen, too tired and ashamed to go home. She guessed, rightly, that Jewell had called her mother to come and get the kids; that was one lecture she didn't want to hear. Opal picked up a phone.

"Where are you now?" the drug counselor asked.

"In a smoke house," Opal said.

"Get in the car—don't stop, come straight here."

Frightened, crying, filled with dread, Opal did what she was told. Angie and Jewell found new apartments, and life on First Street ended as it began, with everyone still on public aid. At that point, something called the "Personal Responsibility Act" was making its way through Congress, though none of them paid it any mind. For decades, Hattie Mae had warned her kids that the white folks were going to stop giving out welfare checks. "When you're young," Jewell said, "you don't believe stuff like that."

PART II

Ending Welfare

FIVE

The Accidental Program:
Washington, 1935–1991

The people who created Aid to Families with Dependent Children*
weren't thinking about Angie, Opal, and Jewell. They had no idea
their program would become the federal government's answer to
ghetto poverty. They had no idea that ghetto poverty would demand a
federal response. They thought they were excluding the two groups
that came to dominate the rolls: unmarried women and racial minorities. Everything about welfare's trajectory—its size, its longevity, and
the hostility it engendered—would have left them astonished.

The program began during the Depression as part of the Social Security Act. When the law passed in 1935, the main action revolved
around programs of "social insurance" for working men, like unemployment insurance, old-age pensions, and survivors' benefits. With
the whole capitalist system reeling, Edwin Witte, the economist
Franklin Roosevelt tapped to draft the bill, took such little interest in
the welfare provisions he farmed them out to the Children's Bureau
of the Labor Department. Even there, they remained a secondary
concern, behind a program to improve maternal and child health.
AFDC was thrown in as a temporary measure, to tide over widowed
mothers until Social Security matured. Over time, as workers paid
into the system, their widows would qualify for death benefits, and welfare would wither away.

Impossible as it is to imagine now, a welfare check once conferred

---

*The program was originally called Aid to Dependent Children; "Families" was
added in 1962. For simplicity's sake, I refer to AFDC throughout.

an element of prestige. AFDC essentially brought federal support to a system of underfinanced, state-run "Mothers' Pensions." Before the state programs arose in the 1910s, the care of destitute children was often left to charities, which dispatched them to orphanages or even leased them out as indentured servants. As concerns about abuse grew, Mothers' Pensions sought to keep poor children in their homes—but not just any homes. The payments were reserved for a small elite of "fit" mothers with so-called suitable homes. That typically excluded divorced mothers and those with children born outside marriage, and it almost always excluded racial minorities. The screening was so rigorous, those on the rolls were sometimes called "gilt-edged widows." Decades later, welfare would be condemned for encouraging poor women not to work. But that was precisely what it was created to do—in Edwin Witte's words, "to release from the wage-earning role the parent whose task is to raise children." Here's the dewy vision of one Arkansas congressman:

> I can see the careworn and dejected widow shout with joy . . . after having received assurance of financial aid for her children. I see her with the youngest child upon her knee and the others clustered by her, kissing the tears of joy from her pale cheek as she explains they can now obtain clothes and books, go to Sunday school, and attend the public school.

The "pale cheek" is telling: the last thing Congress intended in the thirties was to move black women out of the fields and onto the welfare rolls. The beneficiaries of the Mothers' Pensions were 96 percent white, and AFDC was meant to support the same population. Southern members of Congress controlled the presiding committees and made sure the law did nothing to interfere with the South's supply of cheap field labor. They let states set payments low, kept local discretion high, and rejected language seen as outlawing racial discrimination. The federal government shared in the costs, but states set benefits and many of the rules. As Witte later wrote, "No other federal aid legislation has ever gone to such lengths to deny the federal government supervisory power."

At the outset it worked as intended: black women like Hattie Mae were mostly barred from the rolls, especially in the South. Georgia went as far as establishing Negro quotas. After his tour of the South in the early 1940s, Gunnar Myrdal wondered how welfare discrimination had gone "to such extremes" and blamed state laws requiring "suitable homes." Since "practically all Negroes are believed to be 'immoral,' almost any discrimination against Negroes can be motivated on such grounds," he wrote. Another inspector, Mary S. Larabee, found southern officials approaching poor blacks with the "attitude that 'they have always gotten along' and 'all they'll do is have more children.'" The officials, Larabee wrote, "see no reason why the employable Negro mother should not continue her usually sketchy seasonal labor or indefinite domestic service rather than receive a public assistance grant." Covering about 2 percent of American children, welfare in 1940 was more or less what Congress intended: a small, predominantly white program.

But it didn't wither away. Between 1945 and 1960, caseloads nearly tripled. They grew partly from federal pressure to reduce racial discrimination. The size of the benefits also grew, which extended eligibility a bit farther up the income ladder. And as black families moved North, the racial barriers they faced, though significant, tended to be lower. More significant than the growth of the rolls was the shift in their composition. Congress accelerated the ability of widows to move into the more generous Social Security program. That creamed off the "worthy poor" that AFDC was meant to serve and left welfare with the stigmatized remains: the divorced, abandoned, and never-married mothers of out-of-wedlock children. At the program's start, five-sixths of its beneficiaries were widows. By 1960, when Hattie Mae first enrolled, almost two-thirds came from so-called broken families. By then, 40 percent of the caseload was black, triple the original rate.

Hostility was quick to arise. One of the iron laws of American life is that cash payments to the healthy nonworking poor breed suspicion. Mothers (or at least suitable white ones) were briefly deemed an exception only because society didn't expect them to work—their work was raising children. Yet even the Mothers' Pensions were carefully policed. At the time he created AFDC, Roosevelt himself was deeply concerned about dependency. The 1935 State of the Union

Address, which has been called the "founding document" of the modern welfare state, criticized the cash welfare strategy of the early New Deal and called for replacing it with a giant work program, the Works Progress Administration. In a passage much beloved by welfare's critics, Roosevelt warned that to give away cash "is to administer a narcotic, a subtle destroyer of the human spirit." The antigovernment conservatives who quote him today forget that Roosevelt wasn't just criticizing welfare; as the author Mickey Kaus has noted, he was creating as an alternative more than 3 million government jobs.

At first, the welfare expansion was incremental and bureaucratic—almost accidental. In the next stage, it was anything but. The welfare explosion of the 1960s proceeded from conscious design. Looking to wage a broader fight on poverty, a coterie of activists launched a remarkably successful crusade for something not previously known to exist: "welfare rights." They organized. They demonstrated. And above all they sued. *King vs. Smith* (1968) found in the statute an individual entitlement to benefits, meaning everyone who was eligible had to be served. (There could be no waiting lists.) *Shapiro vs. Thompson* (1969) struck down residency requirements. *Goldberg vs. Kelly* (1970) ruled that benefits couldn't be taken away without due process. From 1960 to 1973, the rolls more than quadrupled.

Though it has been much maligned in retrospect, it is easy to see in the context of the times the appeal of a welfare expansion. At the start of the sixties, poverty rates were twice what they are now; more than half of black Americans were poor. Mississippi had commissioned a study of families dropped from the rolls, and it inspires no nostalgia for the good old days. "Animals shouldn't live in such a place," investigators reported after visiting families left without aid. "There were six or seven little Negro children running freely through the shack and they were half-dressed, dirty and barefooted. . . . The older women seemed to accept their situation as if nothing mattered anymore. They seemed more like shells—defeated." In Sunflower County, where *90 percent* of the black people were poor, the millionaire James Eastland got welfare of a sort; the $170,000 a year he collected in cotton subsidies was nearly twice the county's annual

school-lunch budget. As the civil rights leader Ralph Abernathy used
to ask, if the country could pay Eastland not to grow food, couldn't it
afford to help poor children eat?

As the sharecropping system fell apart, the poor flowed into cities
looking for help, and welfare offices had endless tactics for turning
them away. Some greeted migrants with bus tickets home. Others
menacingly posted police outside their waiting rooms. Applications
could be reclassified as "inquiries" and set aside instead of processed.
Even in New York City, no more than half of the eligible population
was enrolled in the early 1960s. Racial discrimination was rampant.
Of the twenty-three thousand children purged from the Louisiana
rolls, 95 percent were black. Under the famous "man in the house"
rule, recipients also had to open their lives to degrading investigations. *King vs. Smith*, perhaps the most important welfare ruling of
the age, reinstated benefits to a black woman dropped from the Alabama rolls for having sex with a weekend visitor. Under state law the
relationship made the man a "substitute father," and she could regain
her benefits only after two people swore the affair had ceased. The
state offered a curious list of suitable sexual witnesses: "law-enforcement
officials; ministers; neighbors; grocers." If welfare rights meant getting the grocer out of Mrs. Smith's bedroom—well, who could argue
with that?

But a large, rights-oriented program would create problems, too—
for poor people and the politics of poverty. The most audacious campaign for welfare rights occurred in New York City, where it was led
by two Ivy League intellectuals, Richard Cloward and Frances Fox
Piven. The spiraling rolls, the indignant protests, the saturation of
welfare with due process rights—many of the movement's traits can
be traced to the program that Cloward helped found and Piven
helped staff on the Lower East Side of Manhattan, Mobilization for
Youth. Though it quickly became the model for the war on poverty
and the Legal Services program, poverty per se wasn't its focus when
it started in 1962. Juvenile delinquency was. But no sooner did the
program open its doors than it was overrun by families needing
money. "The workers began focusing on getting these families on welfare," Cloward said. "It was something they could do." Their strategy
can be summarized in a word: aggression. "They argued and cajoled;

they bluffed and threatened," Piven and Cloward later wrote. They also sued. By 1966, the city's rolls doubled to half a million, a figure not seen since the end of the Depression.

By then Cloward and Piven had glimpsed something bigger. In a 1966 article in *The Nation*, they called for a "massive drive to recruit the poor onto the rolls" nationwide. Arguing that aid only flows when the poor demand it, they urged "bureaucratic disruption in welfare agencies" and "demonstrations to create a climate of militancy." Requests for reprints ran thirty thousand strong. Soon after, the National Welfare Rights Organization was born, and the age of the welfare radical was officially under way. As Angie was born in the spring of 1966, demonstrations for welfare rights erupted in forty cities. "Harassment, giving ultimatums, overwhelming centers is our greatest tactic," wrote the NWRO. For some recipients, entitlement grew from a legal concept to a social one. In Brooklyn, welfare families jammed a Korvette's store, telling cashiers to "charge the goods to the welfare department." The classic exchange of the era involved Louisiana senator Russell Long, who dismissed the protesters as "brood mares" and "people who lay about all day making love and producing illegitimate babies." Referring to Long's complaint that he couldn't find anyone to iron his shirts, one welfare recipient warned: "We only want the kinds of jobs that pay ten thousand dollars or twenty thousand dollars! We aren't going to do anybody's laundry!" Another recipient pressed the thought to its logical conclusion: "You can't force me to work!"

Just as Cloward and Piven predicted, the bureaucracy responded by opening the tap. With ghetto riots quickening the impulse to placate the poor, New York reduced its application to a single page of self-declared need, and its welfare commissioner became known to detractors as Mitchell "Come and Get It" Ginsberg. Between 1966 and 1972, the New York City caseload doubled again. Nationally, the rolls nearly tripled. The creation of Medicaid in 1966 increased welfare's lure, since signing up for AFDC was the only way most families could enroll in the health insurance program. In pushing cities and states toward bankruptcy, Cloward and Piven had hoped to win local support for a federal bailout—preferably in the form of a guaranteed income. Astonishingly, the strategy nearly worked. Most leaders of the war on poverty embraced the idea, though the chief poverty warrior did not. It's ironic that the words *Lyndon Johnson* and *welfare* remained knotted in national memory, since Johnson hated the very word so much he sometimes called the Department of Health, Education, and Welfare "my department of health and education." Johnson thought the war on poverty would *cut* the rolls and predicted "the days of the dole in this country are numbered." It was Richard Nixon, of all people, who proposed a guaranteed income, after a Democratic adviser, Daniel Patrick Moynihan, helped persuade him of his chance to become a great Tory reformer, the American Disraeli. The Family Assistance Plan cleared the House in 1971, only to fail a year later in the Senate, where conservatives denounced it as a giveaway, and, in the strangest twist of all, liberals called it tight-fisted.

By 1973, when the welfare explosion finally slowed, there were 11 million Americans on the rolls, including one out of every nine kids. The program had reached a size it had never been expected to reach; served groups it hadn't been intended to serve; and armed them with rights it was never meant to confer. Over the next generation, nearly a third of the country's children would spend part of their childhood on welfare. For black children, the figure would approach 80 percent. Welfare had won in the streets and the courts. But it had lost in the broader culture. Even as a million people a year flowed onto the rolls in the late 1960s, Merle Haggard had topped the country charts with an anthem of blue-collar pride:

> *Hey, Hey, the working man*
> *The working man like me*
> *I ain't never been on welfare*
> *And that's one place I won't be*

Welfare. Did the American political dictionary contain a more loaded word?

As the smoke cleared, the program that remained combined the worst of both worlds: it offered the needy too little to live on and despised them for taking it. Even as benefits peaked in 1972, the average package of cash and food stamps left a mother with two children in poverty, and over the next two decades, the value of the typical check fell more than 40 percent. Despite some offsetting growth in food stamps, by 1992 the average package of cash and stamps came to just $7,600 a year, nearly $4,000 below the poverty threshold—hence the need for boyfriends and off-the-books work. As the program's benefits were fading, so was its original rationale: to let mothers stay home with their kids. When AFDC started, fewer than one married woman in ten worked outside the home. By the mid-1970s, half of American mothers worked; why, they asked, should they pay taxes to let poor mothers stay home? That a majority of recipients were minorities further eroded political support. While the program once conjured a West Virginia widow, it now brought to mind a black teen mother in a big-city ghetto; demographically, that was a death sentence.

Its costs posed problems, too. It's true that even when its federal costs peaked at $16 billion a year, AFDC accounted for only about 1 percent of the total federal budget. That was nothing like the $477 billion the country spent on Social Security and Medicare. But count the share of food stamps and Medicaid that went to poor mothers and children and you triple the cost. Plus AFDC and Medicaid required state matching funds, insuring constant conflict in state legislatures. In addition, there were dozens of other programs that critics could label "welfare." Half of recipients ate subsidized school lunches; a quarter lived in subsidized housing. Add Head Start, disability payments, and the like, and depending on who's doing the counting, the cost of welfare could range from negligible to more than $100 billion, or 15 percent of domestic spending. Its vague definition was one of its problems; welfare could be blamed for everything and typically was.

Among those who resented it the most were those receiving its aid. One of the country's leading welfare advocates, Mark Greenberg, got the ground-level view in 1978 when he left Harvard Law School for a legal-services job in Jacksonville, Florida. His clients couldn't live on welfare, but they couldn't live on work, either—not as maids or convenience-store clerks, where they earned little, lost jobs often, and received no benefits. The most industrious combined the two, often on the sly. "Many of the hardest-working people I met were at constant risk of being arrested for fraud," he said. "They hated welfare, but if they reported their jobs they would lose their children's Medicaid." One of Greenberg's clients was arrested in a dragnet after the Fernandina Beach police, looking for secret workers, canvassed the neighbors of *everyone* on food stamps as though they were criminal suspects. The client *had* reported her job, but one caseworker had failed to tell another. "While some people had made bad choices in their lives, the suffering they endured was vastly disproportionate," Greenberg said. "People were treated dismally by public bureaucracies."

It wasn't a sustainable situation—yet the striking thing is how long it was sustained. John Kennedy had promised sweeping reform and gotten an ineffective program of "rehabilitative services." Lyndon Johnson had signed the first work requirements in 1967, but they had little funding and no teeth. Richard Nixon had tried to marry a guaranteed income to modest work rules and fell in a hail of Left-Right recrimination. In Congress, the ruling Democrats were divided among themselves; liberals wanted to raise benefits, especially in the South, while conservatives wanted to cut costs. Substantively, the challenge involved preserving welfare's safety net functions while promoting work. But the outlook for low-skilled workers was increasingly precarious. From 1973 to 1989 unemployment averaged 7 percent, about 50 percent higher than the previous three decades; among black women it was *14 percent*. Wages were stagnant among women and eroding among men. At the end of the 1970s, *half* the black women in the labor force earned a wage that left a family of four in poverty, even if they worked full-time. With the American safety net already much smaller than its European counterparts, cuts seemed especially risky.

Where jobs did exist, it wasn't clear recipients could hold them. LaDonna Pavetti is perhaps the leading authority on recipients' personal attributes; she estimated that about half of the women on AFDC had problems that could interfere with the simplest jobs. A third had severely limited cognitive abilities. Thirteen percent reported near-daily bouts of depression. Ten percent had medical disabilities. Nine percent acknowledged heavy cocaine use. Some had multiple problems—depression *and* drug abuse. The good news is that even those with the worst problems worked. The bad news is that they didn't work steadily. They bounced around like the clients Mark Greenberg saw, making beds, cleaning offices, and drawing public aid.

Women who did leave welfare for work could count on little support. The system was filled with perverse incentives ("notches" and "cliffs"), meaning that recipients who increased their earnings often lost so much aid they wound up no better off. Sometimes they were worse off. Briefing Jimmy Carter on the problem, his welfare secretary, Joseph Califano, explained that if a Wisconsin woman doubled her earnings to $5,000, her net income would fall by $1,250 and she would lose Medicaid. Carter was appalled. "When people really understand this, I'm sure they will do something about it," he said. But any smoothing of the take-away rate would simply bring more people on the rolls, at a cost of billions. The other plausible solutions—creating government jobs, offering child care, expanding health insurance—likewise seemed prohibitively expensive. One reason the despised program endured so long is that it appeared to cost less than the alternatives. While Carter had promised a "complete overhaul," his plan never even came to a vote in a congressional committee. It did, however, produce a famous quote: welfare reform, Califano warned, was "the Middle East of domestic politics."

While welfare policy was immobilized as Angie came of age, ghetto life was entering a troubling new state. Poverty rates had plunged in the sixties and plateaued in the seventies, but they surged in the first half of the eighties—especially among children. One in five kids—and nearly half of black kids—lived below the poverty line. The post-industrial economy was one part of the story, but family structure was the other. The share of children born outside marriage, 5 percent in the fifties, reached 10 percent at the end of the sixties, 20 percent in the early eighties, and more than 25 percent at the decade's close. By 1990, two-thirds of African American children were born to single mothers. Half the nation's poor lived in single-mother households. The poor were growing not just in numbers but in social isolation. The number of slum and ghetto census tracts—those where at least two-fifths of the residents are poor—doubled in two decades. Then crack arrived, and with it shockwaves of violence. This wasn't just poverty but poverty of a new and disturbing sort: brutal, stigmatizing, self-destructive.

The disaster of the ghettos brought one thing disasters typically attract, journalists. In 1982, Ken Auletta published *The Underclass*, a book influential less for what it said than for popularizing the phrase. The *Chicago Tribune* followed a few years later with a book-length series on the city's ghetto poor. *The Washington Post* sent reporter Leon Dash to spend a year living in a poor District neighborhood; he returned with a startlingly candid look at teen pregnancy. Almost all the work on ghetto life was launched with sympathetic intent, but it inevitably covered some unflattering ground: school failure, nonmarital births, drugs, crime. The focus, that is, wasn't merely on poverty but also on behavior. One startling depiction of inner-city life came from Bill Moyers's 1986 documentary on the black family. Though the two-hour CBS special broadcast was titled *Crisis in Black America*, part of its power came from seeing how rarely those caught in the tragedy viewed their lives as a crisis. The most infamous of Moyers's characters was a man with six kids he didn't support, by four women, who crowed about his "strong sperm." "Well, the majority of the mothers are on welfare," he explained. "So what I'm not doing, the government does." His name was too fitting: Timothy McSeed.

While the state of the ghettos demanded redress, the problem of self-destructive behavior wasn't one that liberalism was programmed to confront: it smelled too much of blaming the victim. The phrase "blaming the victim" itself stems from what might be considered the protobattle over welfare reform: the outcry over Daniel Patrick Moynihan's 1965 report on the black family. In sounding an alarm about the percentage of black children born to single mothers, Moynihan didn't blame welfare. He blamed "three centuries of exploitation," from slavery to industrial unemployment. But with phrases like "tangle of pathology," the report drew famously bitter condemnations and left most liberals reluctant to discuss the social problems of the ghetto— welfare included. If anything, they romanticized the lives of poor single mothers, turning Angie Jobes into Tom Joads. With economists in control, most poverty academics had gotten out of the business of talking to poor people altogether; tenure passed through data sets, not inner-city streets. The experts spoke a desiccated, technical language, mostly to themselves.

Liberals further constrained their influence when they began to argue that mothers were right to stay on the rolls until they could land "good jobs"—no maid work and no Burger King. The quest for better jobs was generally a good thing, and for southern black women it had a special resonance, since they had been exploited for generations as field hands and domestics. But as it played out in the welfare debate, the good-jobs philosophy proved problematic. Substantively, it required long stays in training programs that typically proved ineffective. Politically, it made liberals look as though they had an inherently prowelfare bias. Even at the end of the Reagan era, prominent congressional Democrats were still denouncing modest work proposals as "slavefare." The silence about self-defeating behavior, combined with the rejection of entry-level jobs, left the liberals with an increasingly cramped message: Don't expect too much from people in the ghettos. In particular, don't expect them to work—at least not in the kind of jobs most could actually get. A common liberal move was not to talk about poor adults at all, but instead shift the locus to children, who were innocent. The leading advocacy group of the eighties was the Children's Defense Fund, whose logo featured a child's crayon drawing.

In 1984 an obscure social scientist named Charles Murray published a book called *Losing Ground*, which purported to explain what had gone wrong: welfare had ruined the poor. AFDC was one program that Murray had in mind, but also food stamps, Medicaid, subsidized housing, even workers' compensation, all of them skewing the normal incentives to work, marry, and form stable lives. Such suspicions were ancient ones, but Murray gave them fresh legs with a calm marshaling of statistics and a tone of abundant good intentions. He also pushed the logic to a radical new conclusion. Don't reform welfare; *abolish* it. The "lives of large numbers of poor people would be radically changed for the better." Elegant, accessible, in sync with its times, the book created a sensation. Within a few years when Hollywood wanted to cast a hip, tough-minded undergraduate, it showed him crossing Harvard Yard with a copy of *Losing Ground*. Pre-Murray, welfare's main critics had attacked on equity grounds: it was costly, wasteful, unfair to taxpayers. Post-Murray, the criticisms became much more profound: welfare was the evil from which all other evils flowed, from crime to family breakdown. To cut was to care.

Murray ignited a liberal revival. While some critics attacked on empirical grounds—if welfare drove poverty and nonmarital births, why had both conditions continued to rise as benefits declined?— others began working toward underclass theories of their own. Nicholas Lemann started his research on the ties to sharecropper life, bringing in a racial link that Murray had ignored. William Julius Wilson published a book of masterful sweep called *The Truly Disadvantaged,* which established the reigning explanation for the rise of the underclass. Where Murray pointed to welfare, Wilson described a complex interplay between industrial decline (which deprived inner-city men of decent jobs), desegregation (which allowed middle-class blacks to escape), and self-defeating cultural forces (which took on a life of their own in communities stripped of middle-class ballast). He put little emphasis on welfare, but he left no doubt that ghetto life had entered a tragic new state, defending the word *underclass* from those who found it too harsh and chiding fellow intellectuals on the Left to speak more bluntly about disturbing ghetto behaviors.

Another important writer to emerge post-Murray was the journalist Mickey Kaus, who called for saving the underclass with guaranteed government jobs. In a long essay in *The New Republic* in 1986, Kaus, a self-styled "neoliberal," attacked standard liberal positions that had emphasized voluntary training and education and produced modest results. "Our goal, in contrast, is to break the culture of poverty" through work requirements, he wrote. Kaus took an essentially Marxist version of work's centrality to life; his subsequent book, *The End of Equality,* quoted everyone from Eugene Debs to George Orwell on the dignity of menial labor. If welfare was replaced with government jobs, Kaus wrote,

> the ghetto-poor culture would be transformed. . . . Once work is the norm, and the subsidy of AFDC is removed, the natural incentives toward the formation of two-parent families will reassert themselves . . . if a mother has to set her alarm clock, she's likely to teach her children to set their alarm clocks as well. . . . It won't happen in one generation, necessarily, or even two. But it will happen. Underclass culture can't survive the end of welfare any more than feudal culture could survive the advent of capitalism.

Murray and Kaus hailed from opposite poles—one called for a radical constriction of government, the other, for several million government jobs. But they proceeded from a common assumption, that welfare was destroying American life.

Still, not much happened. Murray's plan was too radical even for Murray—he couched it as a "thought experiment," and even a politician as antiwelfare as Ronald Reagan wouldn't get close to it. Reagan praised workfare programs, but given the costs and complexity involved he didn't push for one. Instead, his first budget, in 1981, simply cut the existing program (trimming the rolls 7 percent) by making it harder for recipients to collect aid once they got jobs. The 1981 law also gave states greater latitude to experiment with mandatory work and training programs. More than half the states opted to do so, including Arkansas.

By 1983, as the experiments were starting, half the mothers of *preschool children* worked outside the house, further eroding the rationale for letting welfare recipients stay home. That year, a groundbreaking study by two Harvard professors raised new welfare concerns. Until then, the basic facts about program usage were subject to dispute. While conservatives warned of long-term dependency, liberals said the average recipient left within two years. Mary Jo Bane and David Ellwood proved them both right. Most people who entered the system did leave within two years. But a substantial minority stayed, and over time they came to dominate; the average woman on the rolls at any given moment would draw aid for ten years. To illustrate the concept, Bane and Ellwood used the analogy of a hospital ward, with two beds turning over daily and eight devoted to chronic care; though lots of people came and went, the typical occupant of the ward was in the middle of a long stay. While liberals continued to emphasize the turnover, it became impossible, in the light of the data, to dismiss long-term welfare receipt as a figment of conservative bias.

Not long after, the first results of the work experiments appeared, with an encouraging report. Out of eleven state programs studied, nine raised employment and earnings, albeit modestly. The studies were conducted by a prestigious nonprofit organization, the Manpower Demonstration Research Corporation, and they used control groups, which lent them the gloss of hard science. Critics had called mandatory programs ineffective and punitive, arguing that the money would be better spent on volunteers. But participants told MDRC they considered the work rules fair. Plus the programs saved money— while some up-front costs were involved, the investment more than paid for itself, usually within five years. As Jonah Edelman has written, if Ellwood and Bane showed long stays were a problem, the MDRC studies showed that "mandatory work and training programs were a viable solution." Soon blue-ribbon panels were hailing a "New Consensus." Conservatives would agree to "invest" more in welfare-to-work programs; liberals would agree to require some people to join. Spend more, demand more—it was a compelling idea.

It takes more than consensus to pass a bill. It takes politicians. After ignoring the issue for much of his presidency, Ronald Reagan was preparing his State of the Union speech in January 1986 just as Bill Moyers aired Timothy McSeed. Responding to the clamor, Reagan announced he would appoint a task force on welfare reform. The group's plan, unveiled at the end of the year, urged states to turn AFDC, food stamps, and Medicaid into a "block grant," with capped federal funding but expanded local control. It was an old Reagan idea, but deaf to the politics of the moment. It arrived DOA in a Democratic Congress, which regarded it as a stalking horse for more budget cuts—far from the spend-more, require-more "New Consensus." Congress had begun hearings, which emphasized the new theory of mutual obligation. The welfare commissioners put out a spend-more, ask-more plan, and so did the National Governors Association, led by the chairman of its welfare task force, Bill Clinton, who rejected block grants. The Clinton plan called for spending an extra $1 billion to $2 billion a year but emphasized the eventual savings. Getting the governors to endorse higher welfare spending wasn't easy, but Clinton was ambitious, intelligent, and charming, and he pressed hard. The vote was 49 to 1 (with Tommy Thompson the lone dissenter). Moynihan, by now a senator, took to calling a similar plan of his own "the governors' bill," and started his hearings by quoting a Clinton welfare speech. It would prove, in the years ahead, a rare moment of harmony for the two.

No freestanding welfare bill had passed Congress in twenty-six years, and before any plan became a law, it would have to find common ground between Ronald Reagan, who controlled the veto, and the liberal Democrats, who controlled the House. Liberals wanted to raise benefits, especially in the South. Conservatives wanted to hold down costs and ratchet up work demands. The safest bet was that nothing would happen, but the governors' involvement was an unprecedented plus and lent the effort a bipartisan air. And Clinton lobbied furiously, with calls to nervous southern Democrats, who worried about raising welfare costs. At one point, Clinton, by now chairman of the whole NGA (and visibly interested in higher office), virtually acted as a legislator himself, sitting in as House members drafted the bill. The bill still ran the risk of a veto as it sat in a House-Senate conference in the summer of 1988. But it got an unexpected boost from Vice President George Bush, who wanted to neutralize the issue for the fall elections, since his opponent, Governor Michael Dukakis of Massachusetts, had the more accomplished welfare record. Even with so many moons aligned, the bill had a near-death experience, squeezing through a crucial committee by a single vote.

The Family Support Act was signed in a Rose Garden ceremony on October 13, 1988. The next day, Jewell had her first child and went on the rolls; Angie by then had three. The law created the JOBS program—the one that sent Angie to nursing aides' school—and offered states up to $1 billion a year in matching funds. In exchange, when fully phased in, it required states to make sure that 20 percent of their eligible recipients enrolled. (About half the caseload was exempt.) Spend more, demand more—the law seemed the very embodiment of the "New Consensus," and its passage was celebrated as a historic breakthrough. Moynihan was especially ebullient, predicting it would "bring a generation of American women back into the mainstream." Instead, over the next few years, the caseloads swelled by a third. By then Clinton was back in the picture, and he had a new idea.

SIX

The Establishment Fails:
Washington, 1992–1994

— disconnect

The speechwriter whose slogan ended welfare had never met anyone on welfare. That hardly disqualified him from a leading role in the spectacle about to unfold. Over the next five years, the drive to end welfare would attract an impassioned cast of the sort not found in civics class. There were the pollsters and admen of the primary season, awed by the power of the pledge to win votes, and the professors of the Clinton Camelot, vexed by its technical challenge. There was a grandiose Republican Speaker of the House, promising to liberate the poor, and his off-message troops likening them to "alligators" and "wolves." By turns surprisingly earnest and shamelessly cynical, the process swirled around an enigmatic president whose intentions were impossible to read. When the ink had dried, many would gripe the process was driven by expediency and bias rather than by a somber reading of the welfare literature. Which isn't to say that where it wound up was all wrong.

The speechwriter, Bruce Reed, came from a prosperous family in Idaho, a sparsely populated, overwhelmingly white state, and the one with the smallest percentage of children on public aid—Milwaukee alone had six times as many welfare recipients. With bookish parents who treated their children to European vacations, Reed couldn't have spent his formative years farther from the ghetto. After leaving Coeur d'Alene, he studied English literature at Princeton and Oxford (as a Rhodes Scholar), then made his way to Washington as a speechwriter and policy entrepreneur. He was trying to jump-start a struggling campaign when he set down the resonant phrase "end welfare as we know it." Reed's real interest wasn't welfare per se but the fate of liberalism. His parents had been stalwarts of a state Democratic party sliding toward extinction, and Reed had spent his childhood as a door knocker for increasingly doomed causes—"struggling," as he put it, "to defend every tenet of liberalism at the wrong end of the gun." The defining political moment of his youth came in 1980, when Ronald Reagan won the White House and Frank Church lost his seat in the United States Senate, depriving Idaho of its liberal icon and Reed of his boyhood hero. Reed's father felt so alienated he bought a shelf of books on the Middle Ages and repaired to the twelfth century. Reed, in his junior year of college, started to question his politics. One place where liberalism had erred, he decided, was in its defense of welfare.

In 1990, Reed took a job at the Democratic Leadership Council, a group formed in the Reagan years to rethink the party's liberal commitments. A few months later, the group appointed an exciting new chairman, Bill Clinton, whose distillation of his prolific interests into the twin themes of "opportunity" and "responsibility" seemed genuinely new. Clinton's tenure at the DLC reached its high-water mark in Cleveland in May 1991, when he warned that voters no longer trusted Democrats "to put their values into social policy" and used the example of welfare checks that came from "taxpayers' hides." "We should invest more money in people on welfare to give them the skills they need," Clinton said. "But we should demand that everybody who can go to work do it, for work is the best social program this country has ever devised."

Reed was dazzled. In person, he was boyish and smiling, littering his speech with pauses and "ums." But three weeks after the Cleveland event, Reed sent Clinton a fire-breathing memo, urging him to "build a mad as hell movement" and "say and do what it takes to win." When Clinton declared his candidacy in October 1991, his vague call to move families "off the welfare rolls and onto work rolls" wouldn't win the attention a dark horse needs. With a speech at Georgetown University, Clinton had another chance. It took Reed a half-dozen drafts, but he finally put down a phrase he liked: *End welfare as we know it.*

The slogan had arrived before the policy. What did it mean?

The next morning, Sunday, October 20, a colleague gave Reed a paper by a young Harvard professor named David Ellwood. The paper elaborated on ideas that Ellwood had laid out in his book *Poor Support*, which endorsed time limits on welfare but only as part of a larger expansion of aid. Ellwood pictured universal health care, job training, child care, and child support "assurance"—in effect, a guaranteed income for single mothers, since the government would make support payments if fathers did not. With those "poor supports" in place, Ellwood argued, the government could limit welfare to between eighteen and thirty-six months; then recipients would be offered a public job. Ignoring Ellwood's preconditions, Reed zeroed in on the most provocative issue—time limits—and chose a midpoint of two years. After that, he decided, welfare mothers should work.

The move from vague calls for work requirements (which Clinton had long supported) to time limits (which no prominent politician had endorsed) was a quantum leap. How would the government come up with the jobs? What would they cost? But Reed wasn't running a seminar. He gave Clinton the Ellwood paper the day before the speech, and Clinton signed off. On October 23, 1991, Clinton set forces in motion. "In a Clinton administration," he said,

> we're going to put an end to welfare as we know it. . . .
> We'll give them all the help they need for up to two years.
> But after that, if they're able to work, they'll have to take a
> job in the private sector or start earning their way through
> community service.

The pledge worked, in part, because of Clinton's credibility. As the son of a low-income single mother, he was no stranger to struggle. His friend-of-the-poor record was strong, and so were his calls for health care, child care, and wage supplements. And since Clinton had shown a long interest in welfare, both as the governors' point man and in Arkansas, he couldn't be accused, like his opponent, George Bush, of concocting the issue in a pollster's lab. But much of the electoral power radiated from the phrase itself. "End welfare" sounded definite and bold; most voters heard it as a cost-saving pledge; and as his fears about being likened to David Duke made clear, some whites welcomed it as an attack on blacks. "As we know it" offered an all-purpose hedge. After all, Clinton wasn't really proposing to end welfare; he was proposing that people work for it, in government-created jobs. Fiscally, his plan wasn't conservative at all. "I think we ought to end welfare as we know it by spending even more," Clinton said early in the race, even as his pollster, Stan Greenberg, argued that the plan "shows Clinton's skepticism about spending." While the unknowing took "end welfare" as a vow to end welfare, nervous elites detected a wink from a man they judged one of their own. Ending Welfare proved the perfect pledge for the perfectly protean candidate.

Among those unsettled by Clinton's plan was the man whose work helped inspire it, David Ellwood. Though he was sometimes described as Clinton's welfare adviser, they had met only in passing, and they never spoke during the campaign. As the architect of a mostly liberal plan with one conservative plank, Ellwood had often worried that time limits would be taken out of context. He wasn't for time limits at all unless they came wrapped in a much larger package of benefits and services. He thought the words "end welfare" sent all the wrong signals, and, as he feared, they set off an arms race. Outflanked, George Bush launched a shrill counterattack, and ten states accepted his offer to launch experiments, mostly with new penalties. Soon Ellwood was openly fretting. "I don't think these are issues that are best discussed under the klieg lights and sound bites of a presidential campaign," he said. A few weeks after Clinton's election, Ellwood wrote a paper rejecting a national overhaul, calling instead for experiments in a handful of states. "We simply do not have all the answers about how to transform the welfare system," he wrote. "For me, the greatest fear is that desperately needy people will be cut off welfare and hurt." Introduced at a meeting as the godfather of time limits, Ellwood said, "I deny paternity."

As he was leaving his office for Christmas break, Ellwood's phone rang. Donna Shalala, the incoming secretary of Health and Human Services, said she had spoken to the president-elect. Clinton wanted him to join the administration and help draft the welfare plan. Offered a once-in-a-lifetime chance, Ellwood set aside his doubts and sped to Washington, hoping the phrase "end welfare" would be forgotten. "Vacuous and incendiary," he later called it. His partner in drafting the president's plan was the slogan's author, Bruce Reed.

It is hard to conjure, at this remove, how captivating Clinton's election was to the small army of scholars, social workers, bureaucrats, and advocates who make social policy their lives. After twelve years, the words *antipoverty policy* had come to seem oxymoronic—the policy of Presidents Reagan and Bush had been not to have one. ("We fought a war on poverty and poverty won," Reagan had famously said.) Clinton raced into office like a grad student in overdrive. Universal health care! Empowerment Zones! Replicate the South Shore Bank! Out of exile to government they flowed—Harvard professors, Rhodes scholars, authors of the definitive books. It was, for its shining moment, a poverty nerd's Shangri-la.

Though it left much of the liberal establishment uneasy, the welfare plan (or what seemed like the plan) had many potential virtues. One has only to look at, say, Jewell's first years in Milwaukee to see how the themes of "opportunity" and "responsibility" might apply. The decrepit office at Twelfth and Vliet offered little of the former and demanded none of the latter. While politicians always pay lip service to work, part of what set Clinton apart was his apparent willingness to include community service jobs in the mix of welfare solutions. A term with no fixed definition, community service (or "workfare") jobs could involve scenarios with widely varying duties and pay, and it wasn't clear what Clinton had in mind. The Left feared punitive, make-work schemes, and the Right feared expensive boondoggles. But the subsidized posts had several possible sources of appeal (and might help different people in different ways): they might prompt the poor to find regular employment, polish their acculturation skills, or, if nothing else, create a safety net into which the principle of reciprocity is woven. The innovation in Clinton's formula was the conjunction: work rules *and* last-resort jobs. He didn't just talk of making work mandatory. He talked of making it possible.

Still, it seemed virtually certain that Clinton was raising expectations he couldn't fulfill. *End welfare?* No sooner had Congress passed the JOBS program than the rolls had surged to new highs. Of the 5 million families on AFDC, nearly 3 million had been on for more than two years. Putting them all in workfare posts would require an effort on a par with the WPA. While new services might move more people into private jobs before they hit the two-year wall, the first major study of a JOBS-like program had just appeared, and it had cut the rolls just 2 percent. Even if Clinton doubled or tripled that rate, enforcing a universal work requirement might still take several million community service jobs, at tremendous cost. By just mailing checks, the government spent an average of about $5,000 per family each year; a work slot (with child care for just one child) would cost about $11,700. The bill for 2 million of them would raise welfare's annual costs by more than $13 billion, nearly 50 percent. Nothing like that seemed remotely possible. Anyone armed with a pencil and napkin could see that Clinton had three likely options: start small, spend big, or riddle the rules with loopholes. There was a sense among the experts that a train wreck was coming.

The politics were as hard as the substance. Voters loved the abstract thought of "ending welfare." But Republicans wouldn't want to spend the money, and Democrats would rather spend it on other things. The public employees unions, an important part of Clinton's base, were adamantly opposed, rightly seeing an army of workfare warriors as a threat to their jobs. (Why pay someone to sweep the street if a welfare recipient will do it for free?) Shortly after his arrival in Washington, Ellwood visited some Democrats on the House Ways and Means Committee, where any bill's journey would begin. Representative Jim McDermott of Washington said, "It's stupid for the president to keep talking about ending welfare after two years." Robert Matsui of California warned, "You'll open a Pandora's box." Harold Ford, a machine boss from Memphis, summoned reporters to say that any workfare plan that failed to pay at least $9 an hour would be dead on arrival. Ford was known on the Hill as a flake, but not just any flake. He was chairman of the welfare subcommittee.

Outsiders weren't the only ones with doubts. Ellwood had come into office openly fretting. Donna Shalala, Ellwood's boss, had served as the chairwoman of the Children's Defense Fund, which had opposed even the weak work rules of the JOBS program. Shalala's predecessor at the advocacy group held an even loftier administration post. Her name was Hillary Rodham Clinton. Shalala barely mentioned welfare at her confirmation hearing, which left Moynihan ranting about the "clatter of campaign promises being tossed out the window." The biggest questions surrounded Clinton himself: did he really mean to "end welfare"? At times, he sounded surprisingly tough, like after the 1992 Los Angeles riots when he pledged to "break the culture of poverty." But when I talked to him during the campaign, he was citing the kinds of escape clauses that could render work rules meaningless. He talked of exempting people from the two-year limit if they were in "a meaningful training program," an exception of potentially vast proportions. And he said he wouldn't take away the checks of recipients who declined to work, merely reduce them—the same weak penalty that had hampered earlier welfare-to-work programs. "I don't think that you should punish the kids," he said. One likely outcome was that Clinton would send a few more people to the JOBS program, with a few workfare jobs at the end—JOBS Plus. It might be a small step in the right direction, but it wouldn't bring welfare's end.

Among the wild cards was the senior senator from New York, Daniel Patrick Moynihan, a dyspeptic skeptic and one whose support Clinton would sorely need. It would take a psychoanalytic society to fully explore the senator's feelings toward the end-welfare president. Personally he seemed to resent being upstaged as the Democrats' welfare thinker; politically he, perhaps alone, remained invested in the JOBS program, one of the few legislative triumphs of a career long on insight but short on laws; practically, he didn't see how time limits could work without an unaffordable work program (and even then he had doubts). Above all, he judged Clinton insincere, a man plying voters with promises he knew he couldn't fulfill. Moynihan spent half his time worrying that nothing would happen and half worrying that it would. As the new chairman of the Senate Finance Committee, he would have more power over Clinton's plans than any member of Congress. Upon arriving in Washington, Ellwood paid him a visit and found a gangly, snow-haired man in a bow tie, issuing a prophecy of doom. "So, you've come to do welfare reform," he said. "I'll look forward to reading your book about why it failed this time."

David Ellwood wasn't accustomed to failure. When he arrived in Washington at age thirty-nine he had already accomplished more than most scholars do in a lifetime. A tall, doughy math whiz who masked his young face with a scruffy beard, he was teaching at Harvard in his midtwenties and had tenure by the time he was thirty-five. His research on welfare caseloads was pathbreaking, and his 1988 book, *Poor Support,* became an instant antipoverty classic. As a Minnesotan who wore "Save the Children" neckties, Ellwood had the air of a do-gooder from Lake Wobegon. But he also had a habit of lapsing into lecture mode that often struck colleagues as arrogance. Professors are paid to think of themselves as the smartest people in the room. Ellwood had spent his life as a prodigy professor.

Like Bruce Reed, his bureaucratic rival, Ellwood came to welfare policy from an affluent childhood steeped in liberal politics. But while Reed heard the hoofbeats of Idaho's militant Right, Ellwood's sensibilities took hold in a pocket of splendid, benevolent isolation. The Ellwoods had their own wooded acre on Christmas Lake, a half hour away from downtown Minneapolis but a world away from its concerns. Even when he ventured overseas in high school, Ellwood wound up in Sweden. Thinking big ran in the family; just as Ellwood's embrace of time limits altered the welfare debate, his father upended the even larger world of health policy. As a pediatric neurologist, Paul Ellwood grew disenchanted with fee-for-service medicine and in the early 1970s he suggested an alternative model. He called it the "health maintenance organization," or HMO, only to grow anguished as it became a vehicle more for cutting costs than improving care. Vexed reformers, father and son, each would launch a revolutionary idea and despair as it gained a life of its own.

When Ellwood got to Washington shortly after the inauguration, welfare had already been relegated to the back burner, as Clinton turned to deficit reduction, a free-trade bill, and especially his promise of universal health care. The decision to elevate a health-care bill over his welfare plan has been endlessly second-guessed, not least by Clinton himself, who has called it one of the major errors of his presidency; some analysts think that in defining him as a big-government liberal, the decision may have cost him the Congress. Yet at the time Clinton had reasons to proceed as he did. There were 14 million people on welfare, but three times as many without health insurance.

Medical inflation was out of control, and if recipients were going to live decently as workers, they would need health care. One thing the second-guessers forget is that, given the hostility on Capitol Hill, a bill that passed in 1993 would have been a weak bill, "ending welfare" cosmetically. While the delay may have been necessary, Clinton did compound the damage by failing to provide any welfare timetable and letting the issue slip far from his view. To placate Moynihan, he promised in February 1993 to appoint a task force. But he didn't name its members for months, and the group was still doing its lost, lonely work a full year later.

Sometimes the action hides in plain sight. While he was stalling, Clinton made two moves that came to matter much more than his task force and his plan. In a speech to the National Governors Association a few weeks after taking office, he repeated a pledge to approve even those state experiments with which he disagreed. During the campaign, the stance had been attacked as a Clintonian fudge, but to the governors he defended it as federalism—letting various flowers bloom—especially if the experiments were evaluated. With everyone looking for a national bill, waivers seemed a small matter. But by the end of his first term, more than forty states were running experiments, one of which would sweep up Angie, Opal, and Jewell. While the waivers mattered substantively (long before the new law passed, the old one was coming apart a comma at a time), politically they mattered even more, since the governors' taste of state control whetted their appetite for new power. "I'm a big waiver guy," Clinton told his aides. "Let 'em rip."

In his talk to the governors, Clinton repeated another campaign pledge, to expand wage subsidies for low-income workers with kids. The "earned income tax credit" is an obscure name for an antipoverty program, and obscurity is part of its strength. While its bipartisan pedigree dates back to the Ford administration, most voters have scarcely heard of it. Because its benefits are reserved for workers, it doesn't get labeled welfare. But what the program does is send out checks—big checks, millions of them on a sliding scale to low-wage workers. In part to lure people off welfare, Clinton had promised to increase the payments so that anyone working full-time could lift a family of four out of poverty. "If you work, you shouldn't be poor," Clinton had said, in a phrase he cribbed from Ellwood. Unlike the phrase "end welfare," which was powerful because it was vague, this one was powerful because it was precise. There was an exact minimum wage and an exact poverty line, and Clinton had pledged to bridge them. When a draft plan came up short, Ellwood joined the effort to rewrite it, and a few weeks after landing in town he was summoned to the Oval Office, where the leader of the free world quizzed him on the phase-out rate. (The phase-out rate!) Clinton signed off on an expansion that nearly doubled the program's size, and with his first budget made the EITC the most important antipoverty program since the Great Society. The next year alone an additional four million families got checks of up to $2,500. Because it made it easier for women like Angie to survive on low-wage jobs, Clinton later cited the tax credit expansion as "one of the things that made welfare reform work." But because the details were technical and uncontroversial, and because it happened in an early rush of events, it attracted passing notice. The poverty reporter for *The New York Times* didn't even write about it. He—um, I—was busy looking for that national plan.

But there was no national plan. Four months after Clinton announced he was forming a task force, only its cochairs were clear: Reed, the keeper of the campaign flame; Ellwood, the academic; and Mary Jo Bane, another Harvard professor who had joined the administration. In June 1993, they were called to a meeting with Clinton, who was at his seductive best. Like Ellwood, he stressed that a welfare plan should appeal to "fundamental values." Like Ellwood, he acknowledged the complexity involved: "A certain humility dictates we should try different things." Like Ellwood, he knew the literature. Judith Gueron, the president of MDRC, briefed the group on a Learnfare experiment. While she cited its penalties, Clinton knew on his own that the program also paid bonuses to teen mothers who stayed in school; what most impressed him, he said, was the combination of carrots and sticks. The command of the data! The talk of values! The mix of urgency and restraint! Ellwood left the meeting enthralled. He wouldn't see Clinton again for nearly a year.

"Oh, that goddam task force!" Moynihan would say as, left to mark time, it grew beyond all manageable bounds, with thirty-six members splayed across seven "issue groups." For all the seeming specificity of Clinton's pledge—two years, then work—the central issues were unresolved. What would recipients do for the first two years? Would *everyone* then work? Doing what? For what kind of pay? Would their wages be matched by the EITC? Would those who broke the rules lose their whole check or only a part? The Hards were led by Reed, mindful of the campaign promise still taped to his wall. The Softs were led by Wendell Primus, Ellwood's deputy, who viewed ending welfare as a formula for increasing poverty. Ellwood was trapped in between, essentially a Soft trying to be Hard but torn and wanting consensus. They held hearings. They circulated drafts. They quarreled and leaked and quarreled about leaks. They became the butt of jokes. A series of field trips didn't resolve things, but they did prove eye-opening, even while underscoring that open eyes can see what they're trained to see. Some members had never set foot in a welfare office before. In New Jersey, Reed was struck by the bitterness between mothers and their children's absent dads, a problem he chalked up to AFDC. "It was so apparent what a destructive element the welfare check had become," he said. Primus focused on a Tennessee woman in an appalling shack, with holes in the roof and sewage in the yard. "What kind of program was really going to make her an independent, self-sufficient, taxpaying American?" he asked. Ellwood's epiphany came in a Chicago welfare office, where he watched a deaf applicant struggle with a caseworker who cared more about copying her utility bill than the details of her life. "The only reasonable reaction is to be very angry that this is not a system about helping these people," he said. Soon after, a new phrase cropped up in his talks. He started criticizing welfare as a giant, dysfunctional "check-writing machine."

In the spring of 1993, as the group was just getting started, MDRC published the most influential study of the end-welfare age. The study, of a welfare-to-work program called GAIN, compared six California counties, five of which had favored education and training, hoping to prepare recipients for higher-paying jobs. The sixth, Riverside County, had stressed basic job-search classes and encouraged most people to take the first job they could find. "Get a job, any job," was the Riverside mantra. After two years, Riverside had raised its participants' earnings by more than 50 percent, making the program about three times as effective as its rivals. Most states were still pushing education and training in their JOBS programs, so the study had the effect of turning the conventional wisdom—train first, then work—on its head. The idea of forsaking education in favor of "dead-end" jobs may sound cruel, and the thought can be taken too far (Riverside did have some education and training). But it's often what recipients want, at least initially. By the time they reached the welfare office, Angie and Jewell had already failed repeatedly in classroom settings; they wanted paychecks (or, at most, very brief training), not more open-ended classes. The Riverside philosophy quickly became the philosophy nationwide: work first.

Like many people in the welfare world, I made a pilgrimage to Riverside, where the county director, Lawrence Townsend, mixed indelicate asides ("every time I see a bag lady on the street, I wonder, 'was that an AFDC mother who hit the menopause wall?'") with odes to work's spiritual rewards. "Work is education in itself," he said, citing his own experiences unloading boxcars and shoveling manure. "It is inherently good. It is developmental. It brings hope." The notion that work is good for the soul runs deep in American life, and the talk of ending welfare revived it. Clinton, though no closer to a bill, was soon sounding similar themes. *Putting People First,* his campaign book, had mostly framed the needs of the poor in economic terms, but at a black Memphis church in November 1993, he recast the issue as one of a spiritual uplift. "Work organizes life," he said. "It gives structure and discipline to life. . . . It gives a role model to children." Elsewhere he told the story of an Arkansas woman named Lillie Harden, whom he had asked what she liked best about leaving the welfare rolls. "She looked me straight in the eye and said, 'When my boy goes to school and they say, "What does your mama do for a living?" he can give an answer.'" *That,* Clinton was saying, was success.

Years later, I had the chance to ask Clinton what got him thinking that way. "My *life,*" he began, with a force that seemed more than perfunctory:

Because I used to get up in the morning and watch my mother get ready to go to work. And we had a lot of trouble in my home when I was a kid, and she still got up every day, no matter what the hell was going on, and she got herself ready and went to work. . . . It kept food on the table, but it gave us a sense of pride and meaning and direction. . . . I couldn't imagine what life would be like for a child to grow up in a home where the child never saw anybody go to work. . . . I know that it's sometimes hazardous to extrapolate your own experiences . . . but on *this* I don't think it is.

At some level, of course, Clinton was right: even drudge work can bring spiritual rewards. And a parent's work can set an example for kids (which is really a separate topic). The issue here involves the larger context: how much will low-wage work alone change the trajectory of underclass life? What if the mothers' jobs leave them poor? What if they're still stuck in the ghetto? What if their kids still lack fathers? For a gifted young boy in Hot Springs, a working mother was a source of inspiration. For Angie's kids (and for Angie as a kid), it was often a source of more unsupervised hours in a dangerous neighborhood. But "work first" was rising beyond program design to the realm of secular religion. *childcare*

In December 1993, a month after his powerful Memphis speech, Clinton's task force sent him a confidential "draft discussion paper" that managed to be both complex and vague. It outlined nine "key features" with "five fundamental steps" plus an added "three features" to make sure the five steps are "only the beginning." Everyone got a line in. "We must guard against unrealistic expectations" (Softs). "But we must not be deterred" (Hards). The document said nothing of how many people would be involved, what the penalties would be, or how much the program would cost. "The whole question of how exactly the jobs will work is still very much under discussion," Ellwood said in an interview that day. That wasn't really his fault. No one was empowered to make a decision, and no one did. "We would like a signal from you," the cover memo asked of Clinton. The group never got a response.

"You let loose a lot of forces when you say 'End welfare as we know it,'" Moynihan complained one day. What Clinton let loose was a bidding war, with conservatives pushing ever-broader definitions of "welfare" and more literal plans to "end it." Clinton's stance on welfare had maddened the Republicans from the start, largely because he had stolen their issue but also because they judged him insincere. His incendiary verb of choice gave them the weapon they needed. Tommy Thompson made the first showy move, four months into Clinton's term. Looking to upstage the president, he proposed what sounded like a similar plan but was really the opposite. Clinton had called for two years of education and training followed by a "meaningful community service job." Thompson proposed two years followed by . . . nothing. Not "two years and work," but two years and have a nice life. The cold-turkey time limits were restricted to two counties, and Thompson needed federal permission to begin, which was part of the plan's appeal: it put Clinton on the spot. Clinton could accede and set a dangerous precedent or risk looking at odds with his own promises. After a protracted bureaucratic struggle, Clinton himself gave the green light.

The next move belonged to the House Republicans, who served up their own cold-turkey plan. Again, their idea sounded like Clinton's: two years followed by work. But once recipients spent three years in the work program, states could totally cut them off, not just in two counties but nationwide. A year earlier, some of the same GOP legislators had released a paper opposing a national time limit plan as an "untested" idea whose "feasibility . . . approaches zero." So what changed? "Clinton promised 'to end welfare as we know it,'" explained Representative Newt Gingrich, damp with mock sincerity. "Our bill gives him an opportunity to get the reform process moving." While Ellwood had come back from the field trips saluting "the great courage" of welfare families, the GOP press conference was thick with talk of drug addicts and cheats. As Representative Rick Santorum put it, "You can cut them off from AFDC permanently—end of story."

Then suddenly an attack emerged from a direction not found on most maps: Gingrich's right. Having rallied around a plan that could cut off more than half the nation's welfare recipients, the Republicans soon found it called . . . *soft*. "A cream puff." "Clinton Lite!" The unlikely force behind this assault was a dour analyst, with an undertaker's demeanor, who was about to push the debate into uncharted territory. In the welfare world, Robert Rector might be thought of as the anti-Ellwood, his polar opposite in ideology, credentials, and temperament. Ellwood came from a family of liberal intellectuals and hadn't left Harvard for twenty-one years. Rector was raised in Lynchburg, Virginia, the birthplace of the Moral Majority, and his résumé included a stint as a worker in a G.E. factory. Ellwood was famously fastidious with data. Rector once published a study saying tens of thousands of poor people had Jacuzzis and swimming pools, after extrapolating from a government survey that had found four. To the poverty establishment, Rector was a joke. But over the next two years, he would exercise far more influence than anyone in the more credentialed world. And remarkably, he proved to be the person who came closest to forecasting the law's signal result: the stunning caseload declines. Querulous, rigid, provincial, outrageous, Rector was weirdly prescient.

From his desk at the Heritage Foundation, Rector had something the academics didn't: troops. His standing with the Christian Coalition and other conservative grassroots groups made him the only welfare lobbyist who could light up the Capitol switchboard. The Gingrich plan spent too much money, he said, and didn't address the "real" welfare problem, the rise in nonmarital births. Finding two first-term Republicans to sponsor a bill, Rector produced something they called "the Real Welfare Reform Act." It would end all cash, food, and housing aid to any woman under age twenty-six who had a child outside of marriage. As one of the cosponsors, Representative James Talent of Missouri, put it, "The only way to 'end welfare as we know it' is to end welfare as we know it."

The idea of simply abolishing welfare had surfaced a decade earlier in Charles Murray's *Losing Ground*. But then no mainstream politician would touch it. Now two marquee names signed on, the former cabinet secretaries Jack Kemp and William Bennett, urging other conservatives to seize "an opportunity in the realm of politics" and "discredit the moderate pretensions of the president." Since conservatives had spent decades calling for workfare, there was a moving-the-goalposts quality to their claim that work wasn't the "real" issue. Gingrich, no stranger to cynical tactics, complained of "this stampede" to the right, but Democrats stampeded, too. The Republicans allowed states to drop people from the work rolls after three years. A group of conservative House Democrats wrote a bill that *required* it. Welfare was dead, said Nathan Deal of Georgia, and "the stench from its decaying carcass has filled the nostrils of every American."

To Ellwood's dismay, support for cold-turkey time limits was growing inside the task force, too. Clinton the campaigner had never contemplated any such thing. His template was two years of aid, followed by a community service job—not a limit on the job itself. The distinction may sound legalistic but philosophically it's profound: once you establish that even willing workers can be dropped from the rolls, you've stripped much of the safety from the safety net. But substantively, Reed argued that without a fixed time limit, people wouldn't have enough motivation to leave the work program for real jobs. And politically, he argued that "ending welfare" required a fixed end, not what he called a guaranteed job for life. About this time, Ellwood shared a draft of the plan with a dean of the poverty establishment, Henry Aaron of the Brookings Institution, who was so alarmed by the swing of events that he breached bureaucratic decorum. "I am impelled to write you," Aaron began in a letter to Ellwood, because conditions

> threaten disastrously bad welfare legislation with which you will forever be ashamed to have been associated. . . . A feral mood is loose on the Hill. . . . A Republican-conservative Democratic coalition is likely to send back legislation whose ferocity will confront the administration with a ghastly dilemma. Veto the bill and be labeled as defenders of the welfare status quo or sign a bill that betrays what you . . . stand for.

Aaron closed with an apology for being "presumptuous," but presumed a bit further. He suggested that Ellwood resign.

Rome wasn't quite burning, but Clinton was still fiddling around; after a full year in office, he was no closer to producing a plan. At the first cabinet meeting of 1994, he aired the political problem. Congressional leaders didn't want a welfare bill during the troubled heath care debate, but the longer he waited, the more he looked insincere. The group talked of how to seem committed while continuing the stall. I got an account of the discussion, and the *Times* ran the story under a provocative headline: "White House Seeks a Sleight-of-Hand Strategy on Welfare Reform." Moynihan erupted. All along he had complained that Clinton was merely playing a game—pledging to end welfare while "appointing people who have no intention of doing it." After reading of the latest delay, Moynihan walked into the *New York Post* and delivered the season's best line: Clinton, he told the tabloid, was using welfare as "boob bait for the Bubbas." As chairman of the Senate Finance Committee, Moynihan also warned that he "might just hold health care hostage" until the president sent up a welfare bill. Even by the erratic standards of Daniel Patrick Moynihan, this was a curious display of pique. After all, he *opposed* time limits, the idea behind the bill he was demanding. "Sometimes I do talk too much," Moynihan told me a few days later. But Clinton was stuck. In his 1994 State of the Union address, he agreed to produce a bill "this spring."

Friends' warnings notwithstanding, Ellwood felt a bloom of optimism. Though he had come into office alarmed at the talk of ending welfare, the field trips had quickened his criticisms of the status quo. Politically, he saw the outlines of a deal: Republicans would spend more to create the jobs, Democrats would demand that recipients take them, and voters would rally around a system that finally reflected their values—Minnesota style. It was a selective reading of the evidence, to be sure, but the Republicans *were* talking of creating workfare jobs. "I had a sense we were getting incredibly close," he said. Then he set off to find the money. As a professor, Ellwood hadn't had to confront such problems. "Many are willing to spend over $1 trillion to protect us from Soviet missiles," he had written. "Can we not spend a little for social policies?" As a candidate, Clinton hadn't fully confronted them either. "If you don't put money in there . . . you cannot crack the welfare problem," he had said. Gingrich had tackled the financing and addressed it in two ways. He would raise $20 billion by barring legal immigrants from most government programs, a non-starter for most Democrats. Even then, he had exempted about half the caseload, which sparked the wrath of the Right. Congress had just emptied its pockets twice, for the health-care and deficit-reduction bills, and none of the Democratic leaders wanted to dig in again, especially for a welfare plan. "There are things so much closer to members' hearts," warned Dan Rostenkowski, the Ways and Means chairman.

This was a bind, but a bind of Clinton's own making, obvious from the start. "There simply is no money. None!" Moynihan had warned Ellwood at their first meeting. Budget rules required that new spending come with offsetting cuts. The biggest programs—Social Security, Medicare, and Medicaid—were politically sacrosanct. That left Ellwood to forage among programs like food stamps and subsidized housing that mostly serve the poor. Substantively, this risked hurting the people he was trying to help. Politically, it gave the plan's liberal opponents something to attack: work rules were popular but budget cuts were not. In January 1994, Ellwood gave the White House a set of options, one of which would have raised billions by counting food stamps, welfare, and housing assistance as taxable income. After someone leaked it to me for a story in the *Times*, even Jay Leno got into the act: "If Clinton is going to raise taxes on the poor and cut benefits, what do we need the Republicans for?"

Politicians tend to be allergic to bad news, and Clinton was more allergic than most. It was March of his second year in office when he finally confronted the budget dilemma, summoning the three task force leaders to a meeting of the cabinet. The group offered him three options, costing from $10 billion to $18 billion over five years. "What's the least amount of money we could get away with?" Clinton asked. While the previous year he had urged them to be "bold," he now warned them about the "Tim Valentine problem." The North Carolina congressman, caught in an increasingly conservative district, had told the president he couldn't understand why ending welfare would cost money. "You have to meet the burdens of the Tim Valentines," he said. Ellwood reminded him that the welfare plan had never been designed to save money. But others in the room noticed Clinton getting that glassy-eyed look he gets when his mind has moved on.

The luxury version was out, but even paying for a Pinto was tough. There's a dissertation waiting to be written about the attempt to finance the Clinton plan, a process that pitted welfare recipients against half the gold-plated lobbies in town. Since proposed cuts in antipoverty programs had drawn flack, someone suggested "ending welfare for the wealthy" by capping the mortgage-interest deduction on multi-million-dollar homes. The Treasury secretary, Lloyd Bentsen, wasn't amused. How about financing virtue with vice, a new tax on gambling receipts? Standing on the White House lawn, Senator Harry Reid (Democrat of, hmmm, Nevada), pledged, "I will become the most negative, the most irresponsible, the most obnoxious person of anyone in the Senate." Cap the tax-free interest on annuities? The American Council of Life Insurance buried the White House in mailgrams. The embarrassing spectacle, which dragged on for months, didn't just delay the plan. It sealed its doom. It antagonized Congress. It created a blizzard of negative press. Above all, it forced Clinton into a glacial phase-in schedule. To keep down costs, he agreed to exclude from the whole program anyone then over twenty-two—about 85 percent of the caseload. Even by the end of the decade, only 8 percent of the women on welfare would be working for their checks.

At the time, the moral of the story seemed clear: presidents always forget how much welfare reform costs. So said many commentators (including me). It was only after witnessing what was yet to unfold that the deeper lesson appeared. Tough welfare-to-work programs didn't cost much, after all. They may even cost *less*, since they cut the rolls. In analyzing the Clinton plan, the Congressional Budget Office said it wouldn't cut caseloads at all, merely slow their rate of growth by 1.3 percentage points. In real life, the rolls fell more than 60 percent, and in Wisconsin the declines were about 90 percent. That's partly because the economy surged and because Congress passed a tougher law. But it's also because women like Angie responded in an unexpected way, shunning the new hassle-filled system to fend for themselves.

No one in Washington really saw it coming, but one person had a glimmer: Robert Rector, the anti-Ellwood, the uncredentialed provin-

cial. Rector argued that the experiments predicting tiny caseload declines were flawed precisely because they were experimental. Small
programs in which a few people did something modest couldn't predict large programs in which everyone did something substantial.
Work requirements would have to reach a critical mass before people
took them seriously, but then Rector predicted two things would happen. Fewer people would apply for aid. And those who did would
leave more quickly. Rector made his case as early as 1993, in something called the *Journal of Labor Research,* where he cited three obscure studies in Washington State, Ohio, and Utah. The Utah work
program had cut the caseload an astonishing 90 percent, but it only
involved two-parent families, a tiny and less disadvantaged segment of
the rolls. (Plus Utah is, well, *Utah.*) Even Rector had no idea how vast
the caseload reductions would be. "I was off by a factor of three or
four," he said.

The Clinton team paid Rector no mind, but it wouldn't have mattered if it did. The Congressional Budget Office made the binding estimates, and CBO's hands were tied, too. The analyst, John Tapogna,
couldn't just guess; he had to have data, and a raft of more rigorous
studies suggested that work programs did little to cut the rolls. It's
tempting to see the failed forecasts as an indictment of the welfare establishment—Tapogna was Ellwood's former graduate student—but
it's really a comment about establishments in general: sometimes the
experts just don't know. "We were all captive of a self-limiting exper-
tise," Tapogna said, looking back. Rector put it like this: "You've got
somebody who's spent his whole life explaining why men can't fly . . .
and there go the Wright brothers, taking off."

Short on money, long on delay, Clinton finally released his plan on
June 14, 1994, late enough in the legislative session that there was little chance it would pass. He never did find the money; CBO later
ruled that the $12 billion plan was still $5 billion short. Nor did he resolve the core issue of whether to time-limit the jobs. With Reed and
Ellwood unable to agree, they took the issue to Clinton in a May Oval
Office meeting. He sent them back to fashion a vague compromise,
involving periodic reviews to make sure people in the work program

were really looking for private jobs. Even as he released his plan, Clinton remained on both sides. "There has to be something at the end of the road for people who work hard and play by the rules," he said. But in a little-noticed exchange the next day, he defended his program by saying it had "absolute cutoffs. . . . You can just say, 'You're not eligible for benefits.'" As revealing as his nondecision was the way in which Clinton had made it—on the fly at a ten-minute meeting. Despite his fame as a policy wonk, the real surprise about Clinton and his plan was how little time he spent on it. He simply wasn't engaged. A year later, he would disown it himself, telling a columnist, "I wasn't pleased with it, either." That seemed like a typical dodge, but it may have expressed a deeper truth: he spent so little time working on it, it must not have seemed like his own.

So did it end welfare? At the time, for all the spectacle involved, there was a case to be made that it did. Yes, it had its share of loopholes and a glacial phase-in schedule. Still, if the law took effect as drafted, most recipients would eventually have to take a community service job or lose all cash aid. That was the crux of Clinton's end-welfare pledge, and in following through he'd proposed something tougher than any other president had. In retrospect, so much of the action was deferred, it was impossible to say what actually might have happened. Whatever the bill might have done later, there was something it couldn't do now—satisfy the outsized expectations the promise to end welfare had raised. "Tinkering," Tommy Thompson called it. At the rollout event, Clinton seemed subdued. The North Koreans were threatening to make nuclear arms; a showdown with Haiti's dictators was brewing; his health care plan was on life support; and the Whitewater prosecutor had just quizzed him under oath about the suicide of his friend and aide, Vincent Foster. In turning to welfare, Clinton spoke at the Kansas City bank that gave Harry S. Truman his first job—it now hired welfare recipients—and returned to his theme that work saves souls. "It gives hope and structure and meaning to our lives," he said. He repeated the story of Lillie Harden's son: when "they ask him 'what does your mama do for a living?' he can give an answer." But he also said, "Let us be honest—none of this will be easy to accomplish."

As Clinton's ebullience waned, Ellwood's grew. "I'm really proud of what we got," he said. "I really, really am." He began to imagine the plan might even catch fire before the fall elections. A few weeks later, the House held its first hearing, with Ellwood as the star witness. One of the interrogators was Bob Matsui, the California Democrat who had been skeptical of time limits all along and felt irritated by Ellwood's professorial air. Matsui thought it would be folly to debate welfare in a campaign season, when he feared the harshest measures would prevail. To make sure the administration got the message, he turned Ellwood into a piñata. *A giant check-writing machine?* Matsui declared himself offended: no one called Social Security a "check-writing machine"! *A two-year limit?* He demanded the evidence it would work. *Pass a bill this year?* Some people might say Ellwood was trying to "enhance his own résumé" before going back to Harvard. But "we would never suggest *that!*" The public flogging went on for two days, and the way congressional hearings are staged, there was little that Ellwood could do. Ellwood staggered away, knowing the bill was dead for the year. Matsui flew home to wait out the elections, figuring the climate the following year would be more conducive to temperate change.

SEVEN

Redefining Compassion: Washington, 1994–1995

On November 9, 1994, the country awoke to two words Democrats never dreamed they would hear: "Speaker Gingrich." Part emperor, part rock star, part talk-show host, he swept into town trailing spectacle and a dozen outlandish identities. He was the scorched-earth conservative who denounced his critics as "viciously hateful" and "totally sick." He was the wacky futurist who lunched with Alvin Toffler and mused about space aliens. He was a modern Moses, who delivered his flock from forty years in the minority wilderness. As he completed his rise from backbench bomb thrower to self-styled world leader, his triumph seemed absolute. Suddenly Gingrich, more than anyone else, had the power to define "ending welfare." It took Clinton seventeen months just to draft a plan; Gingrich, as leader of the Republican House, would write one and pass it in seventy-nine days.

It was a chance that Gingrich had chased throughout his congressional career. The very name of his original caucus, Conservative Opportunity Society, served as a semantic counterpoise to his favorite target: the liberal welfare state. Gingrich had looked on in disbelief in 1992, when Clinton had stolen the welfare issue from the napping Poppy Bush. Relishing the chance to steal it back, he declined to take Clinton's first call and vowed no compromise with the "left-wing elitists" in the White House. As long as the Democrats had controlled Congress, "ending welfare" had mostly seemed a rhetorical game. Now, wrote the GOP's leading welfare aide, Ron Haskins, "the time for the real Reagan revolution is at hand. . . . we can now do to the welfare state what we could not do in the early 1980s."

But beyond railing at the word *welfare*, it wasn't clear what Gingrich wanted to do. He had spent his career making trouble, not laws. He knew little about AFDC as a program, and he had never sat on the presiding committee, Ways and Means. Uncensored as ever, Gingrich ignited a furor after the election by rhapsodizing about orphanages, which his campaign document, the Contract with America, had mentioned as a welfare alternative. Yet he also showed more backroom savvy than is generally understood. In his new life as a legislative strategist, he soon hit upon the solution to virtually all his welfare woes. In policy terms, it was the equivalent of the girl next door, a vision of understated elegance that had been beckoning all along. The object of his newfound passion was something called a "block grant."

Every so often, an idea leaps from a list of perennial options and acquires the mystique of sacred doctrine. Republicans had favored block grants, like red ties and respectable cloth coats, since at least the Nixon days. One day, no one took them seriously as a welfare solution. The next day, doubts equaled heresy. In fact, someone *had* pushed block grants the previous year, an obscure Kansas congresswoman named Jan Meyers, who had badgered her GOP colleagues on the subject. But among those who had brushed her aside was Newt Gingrich. ("We thought it was too radical," he later said.) The Contract with America included a block-grant option, but as a throwaway line that commanded no attention.

Block grants differ from entitlement programs in two major ways. The first is financial. Entitlements guarantee aid to anyone who qualifies; spending automatically rises with need, and (in the case of AFDC) the states share the cost with the feds. They can't tell Angie, "Sorry, the program's broke—come back next year." Block grants offer fixed annual payments, regardless of need, and states manage as they see fit. Many housing and child-care programs are block grants, which is one reason they have long waiting lists. The second distinction is philosophical: since entitlements come with financial guarantees, they typically have more federal rules, whereas block grants set broad goals—"house the homeless"—and let states decide how to meet them. For Gingrich, the twin features of a block grant—limited federal funding and new state autonomy—combined to solve most of his problems. For one, it got him out of the financial bind that had always vexed welfare plans. As long as welfare remained an entitlement, the Congressional Budget Office would estimate work programs to cost billions and require Congress to find the money through tax hikes or budget cuts. But as soon as the program becomes a block grant, the cost-estimate game is over: Federal costs stay fixed by definition, no matter what states have to spend. Block grants also promised to bridge the ideological divide. Should the Republicans run work programs? Or just drop unmarried mothers from the rolls? With a new slogan, Gingrich could strike a posture at once radical and evasive: Let the states decide!

A state power agenda would also win Gingrich an important set of allies: the Republican governors. With their sweep of the 1994 elections, they controlled thirty statehouses, including those in eight of the nine largest states. Some, like Tommy Thompson in Wisconsin and John Engler in Michigan, were running experimental programs and could pose, with varying degrees of legitimacy, as veteran reformers. By contrast, the Gingrich "revolution" was powered by seventy-four freshmen legislators, all nationally unknown. ("We had a million freshmen who couldn't spell AFDC," Haskins, the welfare aide, said.) With Gingrich showing no signs of tempering his bombast, the governors could provide a reassuring front for an untested plan filled with risks for millions of poor women and children. "You could say to people, 'We're not talking theory here,'" Gingrich said. "Go visit Wisconsin."

One question remained: why would the governors sign on? Politically, Congress was taking the nation's toughest social problem and saying, "All yours!" Fiscally, the pact was just as perilous. The block grants wouldn't even rise with inflation, while historically caseloads had shown nothing but growth. Had the governors bought in five years earlier, they already would have lost $11 billion. Chris Henick, the director of the Republican Governors Association, wrote the chairman of the national party to warn that the governors might "resist publicly any transfers of programs, assuming these programs may be a burden to their own budgets." He added: "I wouldn't blame them." Governor George Voinovich of Ohio did resist, calling capped federal spending a "burdensome unfunded mandate." Block grants also raised doubts from a message point of view. As Ari Fleischer, a spokesman for the House Republicans, later said: "I couldn't under-stand how swapping one government entity for another was going to solve a very fundamental problem."

Yet just as Gingrich had hoped, most Republican governors couldn't wait for the chance to get their hands on the welfare program. Run-ning small experiments with big press releases, Thompson and Engler had won national fame, an example not lost on ambitious rivals. Ego was also involved. While Clinton had approved virtually every experi-ment the states had requested, the governors bridled at having to ask—seeing no reason, as Thompson liked to say, "to come in on bended knee and kiss the ring" of a Washington bureaucrat. And while they never surrendered their financial fears (or demands), with caseloads at a record high, all they had to do to break even was to keep them from growing still higher. Even with modest programs, Wiscon-sin and Michigan had already begun reducing the rolls; others bet they could follow.

With Gingrich needing the governors, and the governors wanting power, the elements of a blockbuster deal were in place. It was sealed two weeks after the 1994 election at a meeting of the Republican Gov-ernors Association, which the GOP landslide transformed into a mar-quee event. Conveniently, the meeting in Williamsburg, Virginia, had already been designed, as an organizer wrote, for "a bit of guberna-torial spleen venting" at federal power. As a place to vent at central authority, colonial Williamsburg is hard to beat; tour guides in tricornered hats still walk the streets railing at George III. The host governor, George Allen, circulated an anti-Washington mani-festo, which called for constitutional amendments to shift power back to the states. Everyone was quoting Patrick Henry. It was give-me-liberty-or-give-me-death time. Into this hyperbolic moment strode the hyperbolic Speaker-to-Be, peddling a vision of American greatness and the outline of a pact. Less federal money! More state control! Viva Patrick Henry! Welfare would only be the starting point for the block-grant revolution, with a hundred other programs to fol-low from health care to housing. As self-interest merged with true be-lief, the love fest went on for hours. The precepts were codified shortly after in a letter from Thompson, Engler, and Massachusetts governor William Weld: "We are willing to accept a reduction in funding if we are given the freedom to run these programs with few, if any, strings attached."

Would states' rights really rescue the poor? There was ample room for doubt. It was the states' failure to care for the needy that caused welfare to be federalized in the first place—their failure, in the 1920s and 1930s, to finance the Mothers' Pensions. As a creed, states' rights hadn't fully recovered from its Eastland-era service of segregation. And even as they enjoyed a renaissance as "laboratories of democracy," state bureaucracies could prove every bit as inept as federal ones. The child welfare systems of twenty-two states were in such disarray they had been placed under court supervision. While posing as reformist tigers, most governors hadn't done anything with the welfare authority they already had; they were barely meeting the minimal requirements of the JOBS program. The average state had just 13 percent of its caseload in welfare-to-work activities, which, as Jewell had discovered, often amounted to nothing more than a few weeks of motivation class. Although most conservatives celebrated the Federalist pact, the thought of governors as brave crusaders had Robert Rector of the Heritage Foundation feeling bilious again. He denounced the governors as "panhandlers," "sluggards," and "obstacles to reform rather than engines of reform." ("Rector has always been irritating," Gingrich said. "That's his major function in life.")

Leery of block grants, the Democrats prevented a bipartisan endorsement from the National Governors Association, at a meeting that turned into a showcase of frayed tempers and bad blood. Howard Dean of Vermont, the group's chairman, accused the GOP of trying "to starve children." Many critics feared a "race to the bottom," with states competing to keep services and tax burdens low. One way to think of AFDC was as a program of matching grants, since each dollar of state spending brought at least a dollar from the feds. Even in a program as unpopular as welfare, that helped sustain benefits: states could buy poor people a dollar of support for no more than fifty cents. Under block grants, the incentives are reversed; every dollar the state cuts is a dollar the state saves. And to those who said "Trust the states," critics had a retort—"What about Mississippi?"—where despite the feds paying most of the tab, the state offered a family of three just $120 a month.

But it was the Republicans whose votes counted, and among them the deal held. By the time Gingrich slammed down the Speaker's gavel in January 1995, he had united the party around a new vocabulary. "Ending welfare" meant packing it up and shipping it back to the states.

The bill shot through the House. Its secondary features would face revision in the long months ahead, but the core was set. There would be fixed federal funding. There would be vast state discretion. And there would be "hard" time limits (of no more than five years)—an idea that had sped from Ellwood's head through Clinton's mouth and into Gingrich's hands. There would also be an obscure bit of mischief around the concept of "work requirements"; the bill retained the rhetoric of work, while avoiding the substance of work programs. Work, after all, seemed expensive. While Gingrich solved the technical budgeting problem by moving to a block grant, the sums didn't seem large enough to run much of a work program on the ground. Wary of being left to foot the bill, the GOP governors wanted no federal work rules at all. As first proposed, the bill required the states to enroll just 2 percent of their recipients in "work activities," rising to 20 percent over time. And virtually anything could count as work, down to writing a résumé. That gave the Democrats a fresh line of attack—"Weak on work, tough on kids"—and earned Rector's scorn, too. "A major embarrassment," he said.

The Republicans found a solution: creative accounting. They greatly raised the percentage of families required to work. But they allowed states to count people as "working" whenever they left the rolls, whether they really were working or not. The obscure device at play is called the "caseload reduction credit." Think of it as giving states frequent-flier points every time they cut someone off welfare. Say a state is required to have 20 percent of its caseload in a welfare-to-work program and it cuts the rolls 15 percent; the new requirement becomes 5 percent. When fully phased in, the law required states to meet a work rate of 50 percent, a standard no state had ever met. But if they cut their rolls in half (as twenty states subsequently did), they wouldn't have to run a work program at all.

Oddly, it was Rector, a workfare zealot, who hatched the idea. He had visited a work program in Sheboygan, Wisconsin, where he ex-pected to see a crowd of recipients sweeping floors and answering phones. But most people had responded to work assignments by sur-rendering their welfare checks. "And I started saying the real effect of a work program is to reduce the caseload—that's what you want to measure," he said. Rector had half a point: if work programs pushed women like Angie to leave welfare and find real jobs, that's the best result. But the credit doesn't distinguish between those leaving for jobs and those leaving for homeless shelters; states get "credit" either way. They could invest in troubled women and prepare them for work. (Some, like Oregon, would do just that.) Or they could cut them off for minor infractions. (Some, like Mississippi, would do that, too.) Indeed, nothing in the bill required states to provide services to anyone—not training, not child care, not transportation—none of the benefits typically cited by the bill's defenders. Putting people to work was a discretionary activity. The core curriculum was getting them off the rolls.

The Gingrich version of ending welfare bore another watermark: more and more programs risked being labeled "welfare" and sub-jected to deep cuts. A month after becoming Speaker, Gingrich star-tled his troops by announcing he would produce a balanced budget, which no Congress had done in decades. Since he had also promised large tax cuts (skewed to the wealthy), he would need spending re-ductions far beyond AFDC. That was part of his goal. Gingrich saw social spending as the spoils system that sustained the Democratic Party (through a network of advocates, beneficiaries, and bureau-crats). A balanced budget was the stake that he could drive through its heart. His targets included food stamps, school lunches, disability payments, foster care and adoption programs, and aid to immigrants. "You cannot sustain a welfare state inside a balanced budget," he said. The $12 billion increase that Clinton had proposed became a $65 bil-lion cut.

To say the bill sped through the House makes its passage sound like a given. But Gingrich policed his precarious majority with a skill-ful mix of inspiration and fear; thirteen defectors could cost him the vote. One divisive issue involved how much freedom to give the states: should the money come with "strings" attached, or "no strings"?

Even more contentious were the fights over the so-called "illegitimacy provisions." Led by Rector, some conservatives favored a ban on aid to unwed teenage mothers that would last throughout their lives. Others with equally conservative credentials (like the National Right to Life Committee) worried an outright ban would prompt more teen abortions. With a scaled-down restriction still in place, it took an all-out effort by Gingrich himself to survive a crucial rules test by a margin of three votes. Having escaped a near-death experience, the bill passed in March 1995 on a vote of 234 to 199. Nine Democrats added their support, with just five Republicans opposed.

Democrats reacted with disbelief. An unthinkable leader ("Speaker Gingrich!") was doing unspeakable things. One Democrat suggested naming the law the "Make Americans Hungry Act." The Republican bill was *worse* than slavery, said Major Owens of Brooklyn, since at least on the plantation "everybody had a job." John Lewis, the civil rights hero, likened the Republicans to Nazis. The rancor was real, but the most notable sight wasn't the Democrats' resistance. It was the depths of their accommodation, as they found themselves surrendering ground they had defended tooth and nail. Having spent decades fending off work requirements ("slavefare"), liberals now attacked conservatives as insufficiently tough—"weak on work!" The world had changed so much so fast that even the Democratic leader, Dick Gephardt, would no longer say whether he supported something as basic as the federal entitlement. "You can't get hung up on that word," Gephardt said. "We're not trying to get people entitled. We're trying to get people to work." Worried that mutineers would give Gingrich a veto-proof majority, Gephardt managed to unite the Democrats around a substitute bill. But he kept conservatives on board only by embracing much of Gingrich's agenda: drop-dead time limits of four years and cuts totaling $9 billion. Liberals like Bob Matsui, who had thought the Clinton tonic too strong, were swallowing something incomparably stronger. The Democrats' main sponsor was Nathan Deal, the Georgian who had been railing about the "stench" from welfare's "carcass." A month after the caucus rallied around his plan, Deal joined the GOP. Now there were literally no Democratic alternatives. There were only competing Republican visions of what ending welfare would mean.

One night with the revolution in full raucous swing, I holed up in one of its marketing labs, the disheveled office of the pollster Frank Luntz. Fluorescent lights painted the air green, and all was silent except for Gingrich railing against the welfare state: "By creating a culture of poverty, we have destroyed the very people we are claiming to help." Colored lines crawled across his videotaped face—blue for Democrats, yellow for Republicans, and red for Independents. Hands on electronic dials, members of a focus group had weighed the Gingrich speech a syllable at a time. Luntz leaned forward and warned: "Here it comes—bang!" And bang it was. All three squiggles leapt in appreciation of a signature Gingrich line: "*Caring* for people is not synonymous with *caretaking* for people."

The squiggles, as much as the legislative fine print, measured the depths of what Gingrich achieved. He redefined compassion. Until roughly this point in the poverty debate, the arguments followed familiar lines. Claiming the mantle of social concern, liberals called for more programs and spending; calling for personal responsibility and fiscal restraint, conservatives resisted. Now and then conservatives managed to roll programs back, but by labeling reductions "punitive" or "mean," liberals could usually prevail. Gingrich set the old arguments on their head. While Reagan attacked poor people for abusing the programs, Gingrich attacked programs for abusing the poor. He didn't complain, as Reagan did, of high-living welfare queens; he reminded the public that poor children were suffering and said welfare was to blame. While Reagan talked of welfare recipients whose "tax-free cash income alone is over a hundred fifty thousand dollars," Gingrich talked of "twelve-year-olds having babies" and "seventeen-year-olds dying of AIDS." When I noted the change in tactics, Gingrich responded with the smile of a man well-pleased with his cleverness. "Congratulations!" he said. "You cracked the code!" The rhetoric did more than soften the message. It created a logic for deeper cuts: *The less we spend, the more we care!* As leader of the opposition, Moynihan decried the strategy as an "Orwellian perversion." But he acknowledged its reach. "You'll hear it in our Democratic caucus," he said. "'We are liberating you, breaking your chains!'" Even

Gingrich was surprised at his success. "I thought we'd be in more trouble on hurting the poor," he said.

The idea that ending welfare would liberate the poor was not wholly a Gingrich invention. Intellectually, Charles Murray had made the case a decade earlier in *Losing Ground*. Ending welfare won't mean that stingy people have won, Murray wrote, but that "generous people have stopped kidding themselves." Politically, caring conservatism found its first champion in Jack Kemp, the manic housing secretary who ran around promising to free the poor from "the government, liberal plantation." But where Kemp brought a seeming earnestness to the cause, Gingrich brought cunning and the pollsters' mad science. A management consultant named Morris Shechtman lent Gingrich the "caring-caretaking" line; in a daylong seminar for Gingrich and his staff, he called on recipients like Angie and Jewell to "grieve the unbundling of caretaking" and develop better "change-management skills." Another useful Gingrich ally was Richard Wirthlin, the former Reagan pollster, who distributed a memo about thirteen "power phrases" to "redefine compassion." "When Rep. Dunn"— Jennifer Dunn of Washington—"uses the word 'hope,'" he wrote, "her score moves up (+20)" points.

If hope was one part of the GOP message, fear was the other. Welfare may have been harming the poor, but most voters worried about the poor harming them: mugging them or bringing mayhem into their schools. Murray, the original welfare abolitionist, had moved on in *The Bell Curve* to warn of a dystopian future in which an underclass marked by low intelligence laid siege to a barricaded, cognitive elite. One reason the word *welfare* inspired so much loathing was the breadth of its reach: it conjured everything from crime to infectious disease. "You can't maintain civilization with twelve-year-olds having babies and fifteen-year-olds killing each other and seventeen-year-olds dying of AIDS," was the full text of the Gingrich refrain. Of all the allies that Gingrich summoned, the most important was the status quo, a circumstance that no one could defend. When the welfare bill moved to the floor, the leadership armed every Republican with a list of horrifying stories, including that of a four-month-old boy who "bled to death when bitten more than one hundred times by the family's pet rat." Let the Democrats defend that! What pet rats had to do with welfare, no one explained. Gingrich's point was simpler: anything's better than this.

Gingrich could operate as a breathtaking cynic, and for some of his followers the new compassion was just the old politics of race and class. In writing about welfare for *The New York Times,* I kept some of the mail I received. Some letters came in cramped grandmotherly script, with checks to pass along. Then there were notes like this: "Excuse me, but I think these little low-life scum on welfare should get exactly what life gave me, nothing. . . . They're human garbage." Or, "Dear Sir: What does it take before the liberal social reformers realize that 2000 years of civilziation [*sic*] has passed black people by." Or, "I as a middle class white person is paying for their children because the bloods can't keep it in their pants." One way to look at the billions in cuts is as what happens when a party controlled by southern white men gains power over a program that disproportionately aids black and Hispanic women. For all of Gingrich's efforts to prep his troops, some wound up with their wingtips in their mouths. Floridian John Mica made his case for ending welfare while holding a "Do Not Feed the Alligators" sign. Democrats jeered the reptilian reference, but the zoologists of the GOP pressed on. Barbara Cubin of Wyoming likened recipients to domesticated wolves.

Still, the House crusade wasn't particularly cynical or crude. Or at least it wasn't merely cynical or crude. The longer it went on, the more some members bought their lines. They didn't see themselves as people who cut school lunches to finance tax breaks for the rich. They were emancipators. Freedom riders! Liberators of the liberal plantation! After decades of predictable scripts, the debate turned downright avant-garde. Democrat Harold Ford was a black legislator from Memphis whose district abutted cotton fields and abounded with sharecroppers' children. "The bill . . . is mean-spirited, Mr. Chairman," he began. Mr. Chairman was Clay Shaw, a genial Fort Lauderdale accountant with no sharecroppers in his district—just sugar-white beaches and rich retirees. But he wasn't taking any guff. It is *your* party that defends the "last plantation in this country," Shaw erupted. "And for you to sit there and say that we are punishing kids—*we* are the ones that are going forward to try to break the cycle of poverty . . . ! No I do not believe it is the Republicans who are cruel. I think it's the Democrats!'"

Long after the dust had settled, I had the chance to ask Clinton what he thought of all this. Had his nemesis, Gingrich, used the talk of liberating the poor as a fig leaf for budget cuts? "No," Clinton began, surprising me. "Well, I think the answer is yes and no. . . . I think it was a political strategy. But I believe Newt Gingrich believed in it. I think a lot of them did." Clinton warmed to the theme: "Some of the Republicans just thought, 'I'm going to make my conservative white folks happy.' . . . I think a lot of them thought most poor people were lazy. I think a lot of them thought poor people were undeserving. I think a lot of them had a different kind of conservative insight, which is the government can't help anybody, anyway, so why are we wasting money?" Nonetheless, Clinton continued, "there were a lot of conservative evangelicals, for example, who were for this who did it out of love . . . [who believed] that work could be liberating and responsibility was ennobling and empowering. . . . So I think you had a lot of things going on at once there."

Among the oddest converts to the Gingrich cause was Christopher Shays of Connecticut, a former Peace Corps volunteer and one of the most liberal members of the GOP. With a district that included the Bridgeport slums, he was also the rare Republican with ghetto constituents. After hearing Gingrich's speech about the horror of "twelve-year-olds having babies," Shays drove home and told his wife, "Oh my gosh, I agree with this guy." In corners of his own district he'd seen equally disturbing things. While he had some doubts about whether the GOP plan was "as well thought out as I'd like it to be," Shays said, "I'll take almost any alternative over what we have now." And on the day it passed the House, Shays was at Gingrich's side. "My Speaker came up to Connecticut and started talking about some issues I had been thinking about in my heart," he said. "About . . . how we could have twelve-year-olds having babies, and thirteen-year-olds selling drugs, and fifteen-year-olds killing each other. . . . In my heart I thought I was a caring person. But I realized I was a caretaking person." Then the unlikely convert concluded with some unlikely words: "My hero is Newt Gingrich."

The rise of Gingrich left Clinton in a funk. He needed to pass a welfare bill, but what kind of bill could he get? What cleared the House in March 1995 was the opposite of what he had proposed. Funding had been cut, not increased. The work program came with no jobs. Time limits were no longer a preface to a jobs program but an arbitrary ban on aid. Clinton's idea of a social contract had been: "We'll do more for you, and you'll do more for yourself." Gingrich had amputated it: "Do more for yourself."

Clinton's name hadn't been on the fall ballot, but from coast to coast his presidency had been the issue: his wife, his health plan, his tax increase. Republican ads had shown their Democratic opponents morphing into the president. He lost fifty-two House seats, eight in the Senate, and ten governorships. Operating furtively, Clinton's new strategist, Dick Morris, urged him to "fast forward the Gingrich agenda" and sign a welfare bill. The sooner he did, the sooner he would disarm the opposition. One of Clinton's new pollsters, Doug Schoen, told him voters had him pegged as a social liberal; he needed to "get welfare off the table," Schoen said. A widely read article by Mickey Kaus in *The New Republic* called Clinton's failure to end welfare "the fundamental strategic mistake of the Clinton presidency." That was an argument that Clinton later echoed. "I should have done welfare reform before we tried health care," he said. "The Democrats might have had something to run on."

As hard as the question of what Clinton could get was the question of what Clinton wanted. In the formative hours, no one knew, including he himself. "It wasn't really until the summer that he developed a clear position on what he would accept or not accept," Dick Morris said. "On anything, really." Echoing Gingrich, Clinton made three references in a six-day stretch to the need "to liberate" the poor. Speaking to county officials in March 1995, Clinton brought up Lillie Harden again: "She said, 'When my boy goes to school and they ask him, "What does your mama do for a living?" he can give an answer.'" But when conversation turned to what to do, Clinton got maddeningly dodgy. He praised his own bill. ("I still hope it will be the basis of what ultimately does pass.") Then he renounced his own bill. ("I wasn't pleased with it, either.") He praised block grants. ("I loved block grants . . . and I haven't changed just because I have become president.") Then he criticized block grants. ("It is not fair for the federal government to adopt a block-grant system, which flat funds big things that are very important.") He emphasized the importance of last-resort jobs. (If "these people can't find jobs in the private sector, how can we require them to work?") But he also praised bills without them. He criticized the House bill. He didn't say he would veto it. The evasions hit a peak in the fall, after the chief of staff, Leon Panetta, issued a veto threat. Was he speaking for the president? The White House talking points guided spokesmen: answer "yes and no."

Clinton's defenders say the hedging was strategic, and no doubt some of it was. "We called it the 'Modified Madman Theory,'" said Bruce Reed. "If they didn't know what it would take, we could get more." Others called it a rope-a-dope, conserving the powers of the presidency while Gingrich discredited himself with his most outlandish proposals. Some ambivalence, even expedience, is forgivable on Clinton's part. He'd suffered a blow, the politics were shifting, and many of the substantive orthodoxies would later be proved wrong. As a former governor, Clinton generally trusted the states (more so than most of his aides), and he didn't think the entitlement really mattered, given the disparity in state benefits. How crucial was it, he asked Morris, when Alaska paid a mother with two kids $923 a month and Mississippi gave her $120?

But Clinton wasn't evasive on some of the issues; he was evasive on all of them. And the more he hedged, the more Gingrich set the terms of debate. As the bill headed to the House floor in March 1995, what Clinton talked about most wasn't time limits or funding or community service jobs but an obscure tool of child-support enforcement—the Republicans' failure to take the "crucial" step of suspending the driver's licenses of deadbeat dads. With the entire safety net up for grabs, *that's* where he made his stand? Nearly half the states already had license-suspension laws, and most of the men that Angie knew didn't have licenses. But the issue had scored well in White House polls. "In no time in recent memory has there been a greater need for presidential leadership on this issue," wrote Donna Shalala, the secretary of Health and Human Services, betraying an impatience subordinates don't usually display toward presidents. "[U]ntil you make it clear what we believe in and stand for, Republicans will control the debate, and we may get a bad plan that the public does not understand."

With Clinton's fidelities unclear, the administration dissolved in palace intrigue. Operating in secret through the middle of the spring, Morris urged Clinton to "attack the bill only from the right," like calling for tougher work rules. Leon Panetta, the chief of staff, attacked from the left, on issues like the entitlement and budget cuts. Shorn of influence, David Ellwood lost heart for the fight. Just as his critics had warned, the Republicans had weaponized his concept of time limits and launched a counterstrike. He resigned in the summer of 1995 and returned to Harvard, where he spent the next few years in disillusioned exile, wondering where Clinton's core convictions lay. To be sure, the fog was thick. But a moment of subtle revelation arrived in May 1995, as the debate moved on to the Senate. Reuters called the White House one night, seeking comment on the latest GOP plan. Ginny Terzano, the spokeswoman on duty, checked with Panetta, then gave a response: if the Republicans "went to a block grant" and "did not provide a safety net for children, then the president would veto the bill." A few days later, she ran into Clinton. Who told you to say that? he asked. Terzano was taken aback. The chief of staff, she answered. "That's okay," she quotes Clinton as saying. "But I really want to sign a welfare reform bill."

EIGHT

The Elusive President:
Washington, 1995–1996

In the end, Clinton got not just one but three chances to sign a bill. As welfare politics moved on to the Senate in the spring of 1995, no one knew that fifteen months of battle still lay ahead, with ambushes awaiting both sides. The Republican majority, so triumphant as the bill cleared the House, turned fractured and doubting, and Clinton, hard to read as ever, worked his way back into view. In retrospect, he called the bill a highlight of his presidency. But the only reason the final version made it to his desk was that his chief antagonist, Newt Gingrich, thought that signing it would politically destroy him.

Gingrich could push a bill through the House, but its prospects in the Senate were initially in doubt. The Senate is a graveyard for impetuous plans. The Republican majority was slimmer, and the rules gave obstructionists more sway. Bob Dole, the Republican leader, was no radical—Gingrich had once disparaged him as the "tax collector for the welfare state"—and neither was the chairman of the Finance Committee, Bob Packwood. Moynihan assured his staff that a body as august as the Finance Committee would never abolish AFDC. Then it did, just like that. Whatever affection Dole felt for the governors was quickened by his launch of a presidential campaign that needed their endorsements and mailing lists. Packwood had his own reasons to toe the party line. He was under investigation for sexual harassment and trying, in vain, to save his seat. The Left had looked for a Senate firewall. By the spring of 1995, the firewall was on fire, too.

Among Democrats, all eyes turned in one perplexing direction, toward that of Daniel Patrick Moynihan. He was the committee's ranking Democrat, and he had groomed an image as the very soul of social policy. Outside the Senate he was renowned for his mix of charm and erudition. Inside the Capitol, he was equally known for his thin record in the low art of passing bills. Aghast at the move to abolish AFDC, Moynihan had neither the instinct nor talent for a backroom fight to save it. It probably wouldn't have mattered, anyway, but it would take a dramatist to fully capture the ironies. He had spent decades demanding a national debate about fatherless families, only to despair when it finally occurred. He had spent decades feuding with the welfare Left, only to be left as its most prominent ally. Moynihan passed the spring in sputtering disbelief, then emerged in the fall of 1995 as the voice of national conscience. In speeches from the Senate floor, he was eloquent, learned, entertaining, and wholly ineffective. He may not have changed a single vote. But he did give the only speech published in *The New York Review of Books.* "Nothing I did connected," he later wrote, not without a trace of pride.

As a capstone to one of the great careers in public life, Moynihan's role in the welfare debate will be scrutinized for decades. Substantively, his worldview proceeded like this: "illegitimacy" (a normative term he preferred over "nonmarital births") was a profound new problem that the country had ignored at its peril. It was profound because it drove other problems, like crime, drugs, and indiscriminate rebellion against authority, especially among males. It was new in that it had exploded over the past four decades. But since it afflicted most industrialized countries, it couldn't have been driven by AFDC, one small American program. As a vast, disturbing condition, the rise of "dependency" deserved above all to be studied and discussed. "To ask questions. There it is," he had written, in praise of the thinker's life. As for what to do, Moynihan had never been sure. He had started his career pushing government jobs; embraced a guaranteed income; then turned to a more cautious services strategy, hoping that education and training would nudge poor mothers to work. Still, he had never been entirely convinced that single mothers ought to work, especially when their children were young; the jobs he had sought were for men. "I have spent much of my lifetime on this subject and have only grown more perplexed," he said.

One topic for future Moynihan studies concerns his gloom about the welfare poor. Not for him the polite talk that people on aid are "just like me and you." He referred to welfare recipients as "paupers—not a pretty word, but not a pretty condition"—or even "failed persons." Who knows what darkness from his ragged childhood shaded his views; his father deserted when Moynihan was ten, and the family fell from middle-class respectability to a series of cold-water flats. Moynihan would raise his hard-knocks past when it proved politically useful. But one knock he almost never mentioned was the Moynihans' own stay on welfare. What he really seemed to believe was that most welfare families would never be able to cope, and a mix of duty and self-interest demanded they be minimally maintained. "I just do what the Catholic bishops tell me," he snapped to a reporter one day. There was something refreshing about Moynihan's refusal to romanticize ghetto life. And something disturbing, too: the trio drawing checks on First Street weren't nearly as helpless as he believed. "To be dependent is to hang," he liked to say. Angie didn't think she was hanging by her check. Just cashing it.

After three decades of prescient forecasts, Moynihan was essentially left to argue that the country faced an earthshaking new problem, about which it should do nothing. With a bill speeding through Congress, that was an impossible stance to sustain. "Dear Senator," began a letter from an aide, Paul Offner. "I write to plead, even at this late date, for the introduction of a Moynihan welfare bill. . . . Democrats in the Senate are floundering. . . . you are the only one who can pull this together. . . . [W]ithout a proposal of our own—so members can say that they voted *for* welfare reform—we won't be able to hold our members. . . . the stakes are so high that we can't afford not to fight." Two weeks later, Moynihan unveiled the status-quo proposal Offner feared: more money for the JOBS program. There were no cosponsors.

That left the Senate Democrats like a lost school of fish—ready to bolt, but to where? With neither Clinton nor Moynihan to point the way, Tom Daschle, the Democratic leader, united the caucus, but he did so only with another move right (accepting "hard" time limits of five years). Clinton hailed the plan at a White House event, where Moynihan showed up, declared himself "on board," and warned it could prove "ruinous."

As the Democrats shambled toward their unity show, Republican unity suddenly collapsed, giving Clinton and the Democrats time to regroup. The bill seemed headed for quick passage when it cleared the Finance Committee in May. Within a few weeks, Dole was prepared to start debating it on the Senate floor. Then he lunched with the full caucus of Republican senators, and the next day he announced the floor debate was off: the conservatives were up in arms. "I absolutely intend to filibuster it," said Lauch Faircloth of North Carolina, with enough support for a credible threat. Chief among the conservatives' complaints was that the measure failed to combat the "real" welfare problem of "illegitimacy," since as a pure block grant, it let states decide what, if anything, to do. They wanted provisions like a mandatory "family cap," which would prohibit states from increasing grants when recipients had additional children. The uncivil war, which bogged the bill down for the rest of the summer, even featured as one of its unlikely sideshows a melee over the bill's preamble. Moderates wanted it to call marriage a foundation of society; conservatives wanted to call it *the* foundation. The "the" camp won, but only after Dole's centrist chief of staff, Sheila Burke, the "a" foundation leader, found herself pummeled in the conservative press as "Hillary Lite" and a font of "militant feminism." "Bring Me the Head of Sheila Burke" ran the *Time* account.

Once more in the thick of the fray was Robert Rector, who, operating from his office at the Heritage Foundation, staffed the illegitimacy debate as a one-man think tank and tactician. (He drafted the Faircloth alternative and his angry showdown with Sheila Burke helped spill the story into the press.) In seeking a debate over family structure, Rector had well-founded concerns; the problems of the inner city couldn't be solved by single mothers alone, even if they were working. The trouble was that no one had a clue of how to legislate a dad. The challenge of moving 5 million recipients to work was huge, but it proceeded from a template. Past programs. Evaluations. Offices and staff. In looking to deter nonmarital births, Congress had no place to start—not even any certainty that welfare played a causal role. Scholarly efforts to link welfare payments to birth rates had shown a faint influence at best; though welfare benefits had fallen for decades, nonmarital births had continued to rise. Maybe work itself would curb nonmarital births, by prompting women like Angie to demand more from their men. But even Rector made few claims for the additional measures he sought: a ban on aid to unmarried teens; an "illegitimacy bonus" (for states that cut nonmarital births); and the "family cap." "These moves were more to call attention to the issue than to provide a silver bullet," he said. "Because I don't think we know how to solve it."

The issue was politically perilous, too. Given the black-white disparities, a politician attacking nonmarital births still risked being called a racist. (Seventy percent of black children were born outside marriage in 1995, compared to 21 percent for whites.) Plus, the issue involved sexual responsibility—and how many politicians wanted to invite scrutiny of that? In demanding work, the authors of the "Personal Responsibility Act" practiced what they preached; some legislators worked so hard, they slept on their office couches. But someone charting the main players' sex lives would have found them having an affair with a junior staffer (Gingrich); having an affair with an intern (Clinton); fending off eighteen accusations of unwanted sexual advances (Packwood); or fondling a prostitute's toe (Dick Morris). That was part of Rector's gripe: without an effort by social conservatives, the issue would go ignored. He was looking for a "polemical beachhead"—a way to keep the subject in view—and with a handful of Senate allies making speeches all summer, he succeeded beyond his dreams. Faircloth: "The problem that is destroying this whole country is illegitimacy." John Ashcroft: "Illegitimacy is a threat to our nation and our culture." Phil Gramm: "We're going to end up losing America as we know it." There were other issues dividing the GOP, including child-care money and block-grant funding for high-growth Sunbelt states. But after a summer of marathon talks, Dole settled most of them. On the fractious subject of what to do about unmarried women having kids, all he could muster was a plan to take rival amendments to the floor. "We're just going to have a jump ball," he said. "But you still stay in the game if you lose."

When the Senate reconvened in September 1995, two things were clear: a bill would pass, and it would amount to a conservative revolution. After six decades of federal control, Congress would vote to hand welfare to the states, with capped funding, vast discretion, and lifetime limits of five years. The remaining disputes were secondary or symbolic. The only question was whether they would be settled in a way that mollified Democrats, giving the bill a bipartisan label and increasing the chances that Clinton would sign it. (On the "jump ball" over the illegitimacy issues, the conservatives mostly lost.) Roused from his torpor, Moynihan took to the Senate floor to remind colleagues that he owned a pen that President Kennedy had used to sign a bill deinstitutionalizing the mentally ill. That law, too, had bet on a local safety net, and it had left homeless schizophrenics wandering the streets. "In ten years' time we will wonder where these ragged children came from," he warned. "Why are they sleeping on grates?"

But the summer brought increasing signs that Clinton wanted a deal. In early August, his press secretary praised the emerging Senate plan. A few days later Clinton praised it, too, saying, "I cannot believe we can't reach an agreement here." That same day he met with his strategist, Dick Morris, who had written to advise him to "[b]rag about cuts in AFDC levels" and "never, never veto." At the White House, Bruce Reed gained control of the issue and embarked on a strategy one ally called "building a better block grant," accepting the states' rights approach with a few alterations. They entered the Senate debate with four priorities and quickly made progress on three: a "performance bonus" (to states that placed recipients in jobs); a "contingency fund" (that increased spending in a recession); and a "maintenance-of-effort" rule (that required states to keep up spending). As the debate spilled into its sixth day, September 14, the Democrats' fourth priority remained in doubt: more money for child care.

In any extended negotiation, minor matters can take on make-or-break weight. The disputed sums were small, in financial and policy terms. But the bigger issues had been resolved, and child care was something that voters could grasp. The Democrats demanded an extra $3 billion over five years: not a penny less. Republicans offered less: $3 billion over seven years. The Democrats' negotiator, Christopher Dodd, stood on the Senate floor and warned that within a few hours an agreement could be dead. With chances for a bill fading by the moment, Dole sprang a surprise: $3 billion, five years.

"That is the first time this Senator heard that offer," sputtered Dodd.

"My view is that this is what the Senator wanted," Dole said.

"We can put in a quorum call," Dodd replied.

Hardly a sound bite to ring in the new age. But next to "end welfare," those may have been the saga's most important words: a bill that Senate Democrats would support was a bill that Clinton would sign. Watching on C-Span from his White House office, a startled Bruce Reed called every Democratic office he could reach: *Take the deal!* When the Senate reconvened the following morning, Friday, September 15, the two sides had a pact. And twenty-four hours later, Clinton added his blessing in his weekly radio address. "We are now within striking distance," he said. "The Senate showed wisdom and courage." When the vote was tallied the following week—87 to 12—it brought high fives in the West Wing.

The Left came alive with panic: a Democratic president was about to achieve Ronald Reagan's welfare dream. Bishops wrote letters. Academics signed petitions. Marian Wright Edelman of the Children's Defense Fund published an "open letter," asking Clinton, "Do you think the Old Testament prophets . . . or Jesus Christ—would support such policies?" I shared the alarm, writing a piece in the form of a future encyclopedia entry that charted the suffering of the postwelfare poor. But the more telling sign is what didn't occur—no mass demonstrations, no Capitol sit-ins, no recipients with ardent demands. Nothing to suggest much political pain in signing the bill. A call from Robert Rector could get the Christian Coalition mobilized. A call from Marian Edelman was a call from Marian Edelman. It would be taken at the pinnacle of power and respectfully ignored.

The most notable challenge came from inside the administration and consisted not of placards but computer printouts. At the Department of Health and Human Services, Wendell Primus had revived an old habit from his career on Capitol Hill, of estimating how many children the proposed budget cuts would push into poverty. As the Senate reached its deal, his model spit out a number: 1.1 million. Analysts produce numbers all the time; the extraordinary thing is what happened next. Donna Shalala, the HHS secretary, raced to the White House, found Clinton in the hall, and stuck the study in his hand. She knew he was about to tape a radio address praising the Senate bill, and she wanted to head him off. "Clinton's tendency is to cut the deal too fast," she later said. "Anything I could hand him to make him slow down and think, I wanted to do." Clinton expressed surprise at the numbers but praised the bill anyway, citing the lawmakers' "wisdom and courage" for passing the "right kind" of reform. But when the study reached Bruce Reed a few hours later, he knew he had a problem—a piece of paper in presidential hands that made Clinton seem willing to impoverish kids. He assumed it would leak, and Primus did, too. (He later called the study "a stick of dynamite" lodged in the White Hall walls.) A month later Moynihan got a tip and demanded the study's release. With reporters giving chase, Reed orchestrated an absurd line—there is no poverty study—the idea being that since it hadn't passed clearance, it wasn't really a "study." Meanwhile, the nonexistent study appeared in the *Los Angeles Times*. While the lies were clumsy and bald, Reed had a substantive point: the study, for all its sophistication, was still a stab at the unknowable. It modeled the impact the law would have if past patterns of behavior remained. But the whole argument for the bill was that recipients would change: faced with unprecedented restrictions on aid, they would work more, earn more, perhaps even marry. No one could say for certain who was right. Not even an HHS computer. Trapped in its ruse, the White House agreed to redo the study and produced similar results. Yet the day the official numbers were released Clinton's press secretary said the president "may have to accept that bill anyway." To those who thought Clinton had abandoned principle, the affair only served to offer fresh evidence.

Yet Clinton didn't "accept that bill": he vetoed it, twice. It wasn't the advocates who changed his mind and it wasn't a study; it was, of all people, Newt Gingrich. With a spectacular meltdown in the fall of 1995, Gingrich did for the Left what it couldn't do for itself: he momentarily discredited the drive to end welfare. By the time the House and Senate reconciled their competing bills, welfare was caught up in a much larger fight, over whether to balance the budget. In their running battle, Gingrich appeared to be winning: Clinton had agreed in theory, while resisting specific assumptions and cuts. By mid-November 1995, federal spending authority gave out, and Gingrich tried to force Clinton's hand. He passed a bill to keep the government running, but only if Clinton made new concessions, including cuts in Medicare.

Clinton refused, and the government shut down. The Grand Canyon closed. Medical research ceased. The Pentagon stopped paying bills. Caught up in his antigovernment fervor, Gingrich had bet that voters wouldn't care, or would blame Clinton if they did. Wrong both times, he compounded his problems with a bizarre display of pique. Having cast the shutdown as a principled stand for fiscal discipline, he offered another reason: Clinton had ignored him on a trip aboard Air Force One. "This is petty: I'm going to say up front it's petty," he said at a reporters' breakfast. But when "nobody has talked to you and they ask you to get off the plane by the back ramp . . . [y]ou just wonder: Where is their sense of manners?" The New York *Daily News* drew Gingrich in diapers.

Epic fights can turn on less-than-epic events. The day Gingrich closed the government with a whine was the day Clinton won back his presidency. (And also the day he lost it: that night he met an intern named Monica Lewinsky.) The closure continued for six days, and the public blamed the Republicans two to one; Gingrich's job-approval rating sank to the depths of Nixon's during Watergate. Overwhelmed with frustration and fatigue, Gingrich broke down in an aide's office and sobbed. A second shutdown lasted three weeks, through the Christmas holidays, and Clinton looked like a sandlot hero who had faced down the bullies again. Until then, Clinton had sought political life by embracing Republican plans. He, too, favored block grants. He, too, was a balanced-budget man. Now the advantage lay in their differences, especially his refusal to accept the cuts in Medicare, a middle-class entitlement as popular as welfare was reviled. Welfare was, by contrast, a minor battleground, but this was no time for surrender. Give in to Gingrich on welfare? After a year of retreats, Clinton had a new answer: never!

He vetoed the GOP bill in December 1995 as part of the broader balanced budget. He vetoed it again in January 1996 as a stand-alone bill. Following his lead, the rest of the party reversed course, too. Thirty-five Senate Democrats had voted for the bill in September. By December, all but one changed their vote. In part, that's because a negotiation between the House and Senate had produced a significantly tougher bill. But it's also because the welfare zeitgeist had momentarily changed. The bill and the millions of lives it would touch were hostage to larger events.

Gingrich was slow to grasp his defeat. In marathon budget talks throughout December, Clinton charmed, chatted, winked, and smiled—and never surrendered an inch. "I've got a problem," Gingrich complained. "I get in those meetings and as a person I like the president. I melt when I'm around him." His wife said the gulling reminded her of a scene from *Leave It to Beaver.* Gingrich had been humiliated, but Clinton had a problem, too; having pledged to end welfare, he was approaching the 1996 election with two vetoes to defend. Gingrich swore to block any bill that would give Clinton a third chance. Dole, running for Clinton's job, was likewise opposed to a deal, since he wanted to make the vetoes a campaign issue. With Gingrich and Dole in control of Congress, their opposition to a third bill seemed to rule one out.

But among the GOP troops, other forces were taking hold, including an unlikely one: true belief. The chairman of the welfare subcommittee in the House, Clay Shaw, was a genial country-club Republican who had joined Ways and Means for the usual reasons, to work on taxes and raise campaign funds. But after a year of wielding the welfare gavel, Shaw had declared himself on "a rescue mission" to liberate the poor. ("This bill is about *hope!*" he barked, when another Republican tried to insert a measure Shaw considered punitive.) His staff director, Ron Haskins, a former U.S. Marine with a PhD in child development, was appalled to see Republicans blocking a welfare bill just to spite Clinton. "All of us are here to improve the nation's laws," he wrote to GOP members. "At the risk of seeming a little naive . . . [w]hen we reach age seventy-five and look back over our careers, will we feel we accomplished less because we didn't get full credit?" Operating outside the inner circle of power, Shaw and Haskins launched a long-shot effort to pass a new bill modeled after the Senate plan Clinton had already praised. They weren't total naifs. If Clinton signed, they would have a law. If he didn't, they would have an issue. "The politics were quite ravishing," Shaw said. "We'd win either way."

The dealmakers got a break in February, when the National Governors Association convened. In the partisan fervor of the previous year, block grants had failed to win the group's support. But by 1996, passions had cooled and self-interest had clarified: caseloads had already dropped 10 percent, so a block grant set at previous years' levels promised an immediate profit. With White House encouragement, the governors endorsed a block-grant plan much like the Senate's. Still, Gingrich and Dole remained opposed, and they found a new way to stop it: attaching a "poison pill" that would block grant Medicaid, imposing a huge health-care cut Clinton (and his wife) wouldn't abide. Shaw and Haskins couldn't believe it: *Republicans* were propping up the welfare status quo. A strategy memo from Representative Jennifer Dunn showcased a cynicism stark even by election-year standards. Emphasize "the tragedy of welfare and its crushing cruelty for the children," she wrote. But "draw opposition and, probably, a veto." Emphasize the suffering of children, and make sure they suffer some more.

By June, Republicans on the Ways and Means Committee were starting to rebel. If some worried about saving the poor, more were worried about saving their seats. They hadn't accomplished much, and Clinton was set to run against a "do-nothing Congress." The prospects for a bill improved when Dole resigned from the Senate to campaign full-time; now he could no longer block it. But Gingrich remained firmly opposed. "We're not going to give the president a bill he can sign," he told House Republicans. With that, the rebellion grew. "He doesn't care about us!" screamed Jim Bunning of Kentucky. "This is nuts!" said Dave Camp of Michigan, who collected one hundred Republican signatures urging a separate welfare bill. Perhaps Gingrich really believed what he said—that a welfare bill would save American civilization. That it would keep twelve-year-olds from having babies and seventeen-year-olds from dying of AIDS. He still wasn't willing to let one pass. Not if it might let Clinton out of a jam.

What finally swayed him wasn't a vision of liberating the needy but of something even more appealing: dividing the Democratic Party. The newest House Republican, a Louisiana party-switcher named Jimmy Hayes, clinched the case. Clinton was too skilled to be hurt by poison pills, Hayes told Gingrich. But sending him a clean welfare bill

would leave him an impossible choice: damned (by his liberal party) if
he signed, damned (by the public) if he didn't. The Democratic Party
loves welfare, the ex-Democrat said. Imagine what would happen at
the nominating convention if Clinton abolished AFDC. Picture the
pickets; imagine the protests! Hayes thought Clinton wouldn't do it:
he'd hand Dole a third veto. Gingrich thought Clinton *would* sign: he
was too wired to public opinion to resist. But he was persuaded the
price would be high. "We thought we would cause a split in their
party," Gingrich later said. And on that, "We were just wrong." With
Dole gone, momentum for a stand-alone bill had grown in the Senate,
too. Party leaders made their decision in a July 9 conference call and
announced it two days later: both houses would pass an unencum-
bered welfare bill. It was up to Clinton now.

What would he do? Even the most astute Clinton watchers could only
guess. In January, he dismissed the Senate plan he once had lavishly
praised. ("Moot.") Then he turned around and praised it again. ("A
good bill.") In February, he hailed the governors' plan as "all any
American could ever ask." The next day his spokesman criticized it. In
June, Clinton praised a protest against time limits. Then he resumed
his call for "tough time limits." A good negotiator uses ambiguity, and
Clinton was a brilliant negotiator. But after nearly five years of pledging to end welfare, he owed the country a statement of first principles.
There was lots of talk about the importance of training ("Government's going to have to train everybody"), but virtually no training in
any of the bills. There was lots of talk about community service jobs
("what the Government's going to have to do is build a jobs program"),
but nothing that made states provide them. There was, from start to
finish, great confusion over time limits. Were they a precursor to a
work program or an arbitrary ban on aid? As late as the spring of 1996,
Clinton acted as if he opposed the latter: "I don't think it's a good idea
to say, 'You can stay on welfare two years and then we're going to cut
you off, no matter how young your children are or whether you have
a job.'" But that is what hard time limits do. They cut people off *no
matter* how young their children are. *Even* if they don't have a job.

To the end, Clinton clung to the pretense that it was possible to separate the economics of mother and child: "I say, 'tough on work, yes—tough on kids, no way!'" But you can't be "tough on work"— punish women who violate work rules—without the risk of being tough on their kids. Clay Shaw, less intellectual but more intellectually honest, acknowledged from the start that some families would be hurt, including some children. "We regret that there will be a certain negative side to what we're doing," he said. "Some people are going to fall through the cracks." His argument was that their numbers would be small and the long-term gains worth it—a risky stance but a coherent one. Clinton's position was no position at all: "I don't think it's a good thing to hurt children." Did anyone? Did Gingrich?

With his dodging and dashing, Clinton did himself a disservice. He left the impression he was merely playing a cynical game to win an election—an impression that still chafed him years later. "I was really steamed when everybody said, 'Oh, Bill Clinton just did this for the ninety-six election'!" he told me. "Hell, I didn't have to do this to win the election. . . . I was going to win the election in ninety-six on the economy. I did it 'cause I thought it was right." Indeed, for all his technocratic renown, a surprising thing about Clinton's approach to welfare was that his policy preferences weren't all that strong. Block grants or entitlements, hard time limits or soft ones—he could argue it either way. ("Frankly, I thought I knew more about it than people on both sides," he said.) The pledge to "end welfare" had let loose a storm, and Clinton was borne along like everyone else, albeit on waves of his own making.

Yet beneath the maddening evasions and elisions, he did have a more consistent vision and a less self-serving one—a vision of how welfare had poisoned the politics of poverty and race. Welfare cast poor people as shirkers. It discredited government. It aggravated the worst racial stereotypes. It left Democrats looking like the party of giveaways. In the speech in which Clinton first pledged to "end welfare," he also called for a rebirth of broader progressive traditions: "We've got to rebuild our political life before the demagogues and the racists, and those who pander to the worst in us, bring this country down." He clearly saw the two causes—ending welfare and reviving liberalism—as efforts that were linked.

More than most liberals, Clinton also showed an intuitive confidence in the welfare poor. "Part of it was being a governor for twelve years and going to the welfare office and meeting people on welfare," he told me. Plus, "I'd always known poor folks. I just never thought they were helpless." While Moynihan warned that without welfare, "the children are blown to the winds," Clinton, in my later talk with him, described recipients in the same way that Angie described herself. He called them "scrappy survivors." He had never adopted the apologetic tones of mainstream liberalism. Perhaps the best speech of his presidency was his 1993 homily in Memphis, urging the black underclass to stop destroying itself. Speaking from the pulpit where Martin Luther King Jr. had preached his last sermon, Clinton chided the congregation to imagine what King would say to them now. "I fought for freedom, he would say, but not for the freedom of people to kill each other," Clinton said. "Not for the freedom of children to have children and the fathers of those children to walk away from them as if they don't amount to anything. . . . I did not fight for the right of black people to murder other black people with reckless abandon." A black audience in a poor black city interrupted with applause eleven times.

While the Left saw the bill heading to his desk as an unthinkable surrender, Dick Morris plied him with the opposite argument, which was closer to what Clinton really believed. By signing a bill, even one with some problems, he wouldn't be abandoning the poor. He'd be setting the stage for a broader liberal resurgence. Once taxpayers saw the poor as workers, a more generous era would ensue. Stereotypes would fade. New benefits would flow. Eager for Clinton to sign, Morris bolstered the case with his ubiquitous polls. One survey split respondents into separate groups. The first was asked about spending on a set of antipoverty programs—Head Start, food stamps, housing, and the like. The second was asked about the same programs but told to assume that "the president has signed a bill requiring welfare recipients to work and setting time limits." Under that assumption, support for new spending rose ten to fifteen points. To Morris, that clinched the case: the country would do more for the poor once the poor did more for themselves.

He gave Clinton the results at a campaign meeting on July 18, 1996, the day the House passed the bill. The Morris critics in the room, of whom there were many, wondered if the numbers had been cooked. If so, they were cooked by someone who knew his clients' tastes. "I just instinctively knew it was true," Clinton told me, recalling the survey years later. "I really believed that if we passed welfare reform . . . we could diminish at least a lot of the overt racial stereotypes that I thought were paralyzing American politics." He would make the same case publicly at the signing ceremony: "After I sign my name to this bill, welfare will no longer be a political issue. . . . Every single person . . . who has ever said a disparaging word about the welfare system should now say, 'Okay, that's gone. What is my responsibility to make it better?'"

Morris didn't rely on an appeal to idealism alone. In the same meeting, he emphasized another poll: it showed that a veto would turn Clinton's fifteen-point lead into a three-point deficit. Morris's accompanying memo warned, "Welfare veto would be a disaster."

On July 31, 1996, Clinton ran out of time. The House was about to vote on the conference bill, and the Democrats demanded to know where he stood. Opponents had looked to Hillary Clinton to save the day, but the signals weren't reassuring. In July, her old friend Donna Shalala went to the White House to argue against the bill. Mrs. Clinton heard her out but warned that the president was in a political bind; Shalala came away certain that she wanted him to sign. About the same time, Mrs. Clinton reached out in an unlikely direction, arranging a visit with Doug Besharov, an analyst from the conservative American Enterprise Institute; with a sanguine view of the bill, Besharov was the kind of person likely to assuage any lingering doubts. Dick Morris quotes her saying at the time: "We have to do what we have to do, and I hope our friends understand it." That's not much different from how she put it in her memoir: "If he vetoed welfare a third time, Bill would be handing the Republicans a potential political windfall."

Still publicly unresolved, the president summoned the cabinet to a sudden meeting. Everyone filed in looking for clues. Mrs. Clinton was out of town. She must be distancing herself: a hint he would sign. Elaine Kamarck, a welfare hard-liner, had been invited to attend. Clinton must have wanted her support: another signal he would sign.

At one point, Clinton turned red with indignation, denouncing the unrelated cuts in programs for immigrants. He's overdoing it, one cabinet member thought; an additional clue. Conscious, no doubt, of being studied, Clinton told the group to focus on the merits, saying that with the Democratic convention coming he could argue the politics either way. Ken Apfel, a White House aide, walked the group through the specifics. AFDC would end, replaced by a block grant with fixed funding and vast new local control. The new program, T Temporary Assistance for Needy Families, would limit recipients to A no more than five years of federal aid, and states could set limits as N short as they pleased. They would be required to enroll half their re- F cipients in "work activities." But they could reduce that target point for point simply by cutting the rolls. Those were the bill's core features, and the Republicans had dictated them. At some point, Clinton had criticized them all.

Clinton did win two debates. The bills he vetoed would have made large cuts in food stamps and Medicaid. The one before him made lesser, though still considerable, food-stamp cuts, but (except for immigrants) left Medicaid in place. ("That's why I vetoed those first two bills," Clinton told me. "I thought there ought to be a national guarantee of health care and nutrition.") He also won some of the lesser debates over the welfare provisions themselves. He got assurances of continued state spending; exemptions from the time limits (for up to 20 percent of the caseload); and more money for child care. Because of the child-care money, the new program was actually projected to spend a bit more than the status quo, a remarkable concession from a Republican Congress. But the bill came with huge unrelated cuts—totaling $54 billion—in programs gratuitously labeled "welfare." About 40 percent of them were aimed at legal tax-paying immigrants, who in most cases were barred from food stamps and in some cases from Medicaid, too. Incensed at the budget cuts, Clinton told the group he had gotten "a good welfare bill, wrapped in a sack of shit."

Buying the second premise, though not the first, most cabinet members opposed both parts of the bill. The secretary of Health and Human Services said veto. The Labor secretary said veto. The Treasury secretary said veto. The Housing secretary said veto. The chief of staff said veto. David Ellwood, "the godfather of time limits," had left the administration a year earlier. But he dashed off a distressed op-ed, urging a veto, too. Clinton then turned to someone he knew would tell him to sign: the author of the end-welfare pledge, Bruce Reed. Reed had waited five years to make the case that followed. He argued that the central provisions would work as intended, moving recipients into jobs. He said the immigrant cuts could be restored later (about half of them were). He said that if Clinton vetoed a third bill, he might never get another chance. He even argued that President Roosevelt had faced a similar decision; before creating the WPA, his celebrated work program, Roosevelt had abolished a program of cash aid, throwing millions of people off the rolls. But above all, Reed said, you promised. Clinton had pledged to "end welfare," and the only way to do it was to sign.

Clinton ended the meeting without announcing a decision and returned to the Oval Office. With the cabinet milling in the cramped West Wing halls, he summoned a few people to run through it again. Leon Panetta, the chief of staff, was an immigrant's son who said the immigrant cuts were too deep: veto. Vice President Al Gore said the current system was just too damaged: sign. Then Clinton asked Reed once more: what had FDR done?

Given what was known at the time, there were plenty of reasons to veto. Time limits had morphed into arbitrary restrictions at odds with a safety net. "Work" had evolved into a game that could be played with accounting gimmicks. No one knew whether women like Angie would be able to find jobs, much less whether the jobs would bring "meaing" or "dignity" or "hope." The package came wrapped in extraneous budget cuts, and Clinton's lapses of leadership had let the process go astray. This wasn't at all what he had promised when he promised to end welfare. "I understand why they were scared of this," Clinton later said of his liberal critics. "I was scared of it, too." But there was also one good reason to sign, and it was the reason he would cite on television a few hours later: "I will sign this bill—first and foremost, because the current system is broken." Clinton's pledge to end welfare had been turned against him by a curious mix of idealists and rogues. But in at least one sense, the rogues were right. It was time to do something different. "All right, let's do it," Clinton said. "I want to sign this bill."

NINE

The Radical Cuts the Rolls: Milwaukee, 1995–1996

Imagine for a moment that you are Angela Jobe. You are twenty-nine years old with four kids to raise. You have just quit your job. Your landlord has tired of your crowd's wild parties and is throwing you out. If you need help, you know you won't get it from the men who fathered your kids. You'll be ninety when Greg gets out of jail, and Vernon (fortunately) isn't around. You've got a new man, but the kids resent him—they always do—and so far his main contribution to your finances has been to wreck your car. You know you're not on top of the kids the way you need to be, but it's hard to raise them all alone, even harder with no money, and at least you manage to keep everyone fed. One of the reasons is welfare. You've had it for nearly a dozen years. You've never raised children without it. While you don't like to admit it, welfare is one of the few sources of stability in your life: whether you're sick or healthy, depressed or inspired, you know that at the start of each month you'll get a $708 check. And now in the summer of 1995, the country's in a fever to take it away. You don't follow the details, of course, but you can't miss the talk in the air. Black leaders warn of slavery's return. The priests say your kids will starve.

What crosses your mind?   _ uninvolvement in politics_

"I don't pay no attention to that crap!" Angie said, looking back. "I ain't thinking 'bout welfare!" Opal, the newshound of the group, wasn't thinking about it, either—she was busy in drug treatment. Jewell claimed to have noticed even less: "Didn't know, didn't care."

Even accounting for some false bravado, it is hard to square such studied indifference with the tenets of the national debate. From a distance, the threesome seemed the very definition of dependency. Together they had been on welfare for twenty-seven years; they had moved to Milwaukee just to get the benefits they now stood to lose. They appeared to embody the one assumption that the partisans on both sides shared—that the program was central to recipients' lives—which made conservatives so keen to restrict it and liberals so afraid of its loss. But as Angie and Jewell saw the world, if the money was there, they were happy to take it; if not, they would make other plans. With welfare or without it, Angie said, "you just learn how to survive."

The bill was still stalled in Congress in June 1995 when the trio left the First Street compound behind. They spent welfare's dying days apart, accumulating more of the misadventures that gave the system its bad name. If Angie felt anxious, it wasn't about welfare but the prospect of living alone. In Chicago, she had relied on Greg, and in Milwaukee she had forged a family out of Opal and Jewell. Now she was setting off on her own, with four kids between the ages of eleven and two and a loneliness she tried to ignore. A variety of men had come and gone in the four years since Greg's arrest. Angie had cared for some and tolerated others, but she sustained a relationship with none, and when she got to feeling empty inside she filled the hole with beer. Love, order, a father for her kids—there were lots of things missing from Angie's life. But, she figured, "I could always find me a job."

Just as Angie moved to her new place, another "old-ass" rental house on the near north side, the welfare office summoned her to a job-search class. Since Darrell had just turned two, she was no longer exempt, and the JOBS program was growing marginally more vigilant. Angie knew the routine: you sit through a week of pep talks, then make up a phony contact sheet listing all the employers you've called. "You think these people out here doing fifty million contacts and don't nobody hire 'em?" she said. "Come on!" She played along for two weeks, then decided it was time to go back to work. She had been off for five months.

While her dream of a postal career had faded away, the local branch was hiring, and Angie gave it a final try. This postal job, her third, was the worst. It only offered her five hours a day, and the shift began before dawn. "Who the hell want to be looking at mail that early in the morning?" she said. Since she was no longer living with Opal and Jewell, she left eleven-year-old Kesha in charge at home (with brothers ages nine, six, and two) and hoped for the best. Angie lasted six weeks until Kesha went back to school, and with that her hopes of postal glory—"a job for life"—sputtered to a close. Two months later, with the older kids in class, Angie took a job at a Budgetel. The 10:00 a.m. shift was more civilized (and Lucky's grandmother babysat Darrell). But motel maid work was nasty. Tampons, condoms, underwear—"You never know what you're going to find" in someone's sheets. With another five-hour shift, "I wasn't making crapola," Angie said. She hung on for nearly four months, but when she collected her tax money early the next year, she quit and took one of her breaks. As usual, she hadn't reported the jobs, so she still had her full welfare check.

For a year or so, Angie had thought of digging out her nursing smocks. She had lasted only three weeks in her first job at a nursing home. And lots of people made fun of a job that requires you to handle bedpans. But Angie was pushing thirty, and she had always told herself she would do something "professional" when she was grown. She practiced by taking Kesha's pulse and registered for the certification exam. In a nursing home, unlike a motel, "at least you know who peed in the bed."

While the end of group living left Angie lonely, Jewell welcomed the new privacy zone; as a homebody, she liked controlling her home. For her, the main drawback was the need to pay rent, something she never had done before. Greg's drug money had paid the rent in Chicago, and thanks to Mrs. Allen's deteriorating condition, no one had paid it in Milwaukee. At her new place, a duplex bungalow with a crack addict upstairs, Jewell discovered that she and Lucky had to pay "*all* our bills—had to pay rent and *every*-thing!" This struck her as somewhat unjust. Though welfare and food stamps totaled about $10,000 a year, rent and utilities consumed more than half, and Lucky drank too much to keep steady work. Jewell had dabbled in jobs before. Now she needed one.

Unlike Angie, who prided herself on her work history, Jewell had never given work much thought. She pictured herself doing something classy, like working in an office. But she couldn't type well enough. She did know a lot about hair and nails, and her skills as a kitchen-table beautician kept her in demand. But absurdly, the state required a high school degree to work in a beauty shop. The phone company was filling customer-service jobs; Lucky's cousin got one at $9 an hour. Jewell failed the reading test. Phone work didn't suit her, anyway, as she discovered a few months later in a telemarketing job. Talking on the phone was something Jewell excelled at. Talking to white people was not, and it proved to be the primary work of a Milwaukee telemarketer. White people made Jewell uneasy, and she avoided them when she could. Now she had a supervisor standing at her shoulder, coaching her to mimic their nasally Midwestern vowels. Jewell had a terrific telephone voice—a smooth, empathetic tone that lots of men found seductive. But she said "like-ded" for *liked* and "send-ded" for *sent,* and she had no luck getting strangers in Wauwautosa to give to the state police. Much of her shift was spent listening to them scream, "Don't call my damn house anymore!" She gave up after a couple weeks, wondering why the police needed money anyway: "Don't they make enough?"

As she scraped by on welfare over the summer, Jewell had other problems in mind. Tremmell, her four-year-old, was talking oddly, and an exam revealed he was deaf in one ear; he was going to need special help. Jewell had also taken in Opal's three girls, while Opal tried to get clean. That left her responsible for five young kids, and on some days Lucky made six. She returned to the job search in the fall of 1995 and discovered the post office was hiring temps for the holiday season. While Angie was eager to put postal work behind her, before she went postal herself, Jewell saw the vast downtown processing center as a temple of opportunity, even on a shift from midnight to six. It paid twice the minimum wage, and she could listen to headphones while she worked. Since she never even considered telling her caseworker about the job ("For *what?*"), she still had her full welfare and food stamps along with a paycheck. "Money was just coming in from everywhere," she said.

About the time she started the job, welfare resumed its lackluster efforts to push her into one. Jewell had been classified as a mandatory participant in the JOBS program for two years. But she had thrown the first nine appointment letters in the trash. When her tenth no-show finally triggered a penalty, it amounted to 6 percent of her combined welfare and food stamps, and she was flush with under-the-table earnings. Even so, she wandered in to set things straight. Lots of recipients had covert work, but Jewell now faced the special challenge of pretending to look for a job she already had. Soon, the awkwardness grew. Jewell was in the office one day when the computer spit out a list of her previous employers—all of them news to her caseworker. *Office cleaning . . . telemarketing . . . airplane seat factory.* Jewell tried to sound perplexed as her worker read off the list. "*Unh*-uhh," she said. "Somebody probably was using my Social Security card!" Technically, she could have been charged with fraud. But her current job was too recent to appear on the list, and like most caseworkers, Jewell's considered the old stuff more trouble than it was worth. Jewell was left to submit a fake job-search log, and when asked how she managed to find the only Milwaukee employers *not* hiring, she just shrugged. "Well, I went! They just didn't hire me." After two months of the obvious ruse, her caseworker put a note in the file: "Client not real motivated." "I wasn't," Jewell later laughed. "'Cause I was already working!"

Soon Opal was working, too, though as usual work occupied a place on the edge of her mental horizon. While Angie left First Street reluctantly and Jewell with a sense of relief, Opal left while coming unglued, racing to a rehab center. Medicaid financed a three-week stay, but after five years of smoking cocaine, even Opal knew she needed more than that; when her three weeks ran out, she left for a halfway house run by a storefront preacher. Pastor L. R. LeGrant required her residents to work, and Opal got hired at the Budgetel. She also started attending nightly meetings at Narcotics Anonymous, where a fellow twelve-stepper caught her eye. Within a few months, they were living together, and years later she talked of Kenny with a word she rarely applied to men. "I still love Kenny—I do," she said.

Opal was now twenty-eight—old enough to be getting herself together but young enough to rebuild a life. Kenny was a decade older and adamant about keeping them both off drugs, a welcome contrast to some of the men in her past. The kids came home from Jewell's, and as the makeshift family of five settled in, someone meeting Opal never would have surmised her problems. About then, the welfare office picked up the trail. Like Jewell, Opal was already working when she was summoned to her job-search class. Like Jewell, she ignored the notices until her caseworker reduced her check. Then, like Jewell, Opal had to master the art of the fake job search while already holding a job. Conning her caseworker was a skill Opal had; keeping a job was not. She missed too many days, and the Budgetel fired her.

Finding another job proved easy, even for a recovering addict with a trail of pink slips. Opal threw in an application at Target and charmed her way into a job as a cashier. Cash registers weren't good places for Opal; too much temptation lurked in the till. As a cashier at a Chicago Wendy's, she had taught herself to skim $100 from a single shift. The trick was keeping the math in her head—pocketing only the sales she didn't key in—and Opal, with a semester of community college, prided herself on her math. In the Target locker room, she caught wind of an easier scheme: cashiers would steer their friends through their lines, neglect to ring up most of the sale, and take a cut of the shoplifted goods. Opal sent Kenny through with a list: bathroom rug, garbage can, shower curtain, and clock—all in matching green and gold. "My bathroom was the prettiest room in the house," she said. Then Jewell and a friend gave it a try, and by the time the cart reached Opal's line it had the makings of a dumb-criminal joke. They grabbed twelve jackets, ten pairs of pants, eight shirts, six sets of pajamas, and a pile of underwear and gloves, along with a bottle of Batman soap and a jumbo pack of Charmin. The mountain of merchandise was worth more than $800. Watching on camera, the store detective noticed it heading toward Opal while bypassing shorter lines. When he saw her ring up a $90 sale, he called the cops. Jewell had nothing to say as the police took her away. But Opal went out in style. "If O. J. Simpson's innocent," she yelled, "so am I!"

The episode cost Jewell a morning in court and a $200 fine. No big deal. The real cost became clear a few months later, after her temp job at the post office ended. The postal service was hiring again, this time for *permanent* jobs. Jewell hurried to apply and with two successful stints as a temp worker she surprised herself by getting hired.

The starting pay was $11 an hour! Plus health insurance and paid vacations. She had already finished the orientation when a supervisor said they needed to talk—something about a court case had appeared on her background check. With that, the break of a lifetime vanished, done in by a cartful of shoplifted clothes. If part of the underclass dilemma wasn't just the lack of opportunity but the inability to answer when opportunity knocked, Jewell was now a walking example—and a particularly heartbroken one. She wasn't one to waste energy on regrets, but for years she talked of the post office in tones reserved for true love lost: "I would a *never* quit them. I would a *never* got fired. If they call me *now,* I'm going back."

As Opal and Jewell rode off in handcuffs in the fall of 1995, they were part of the tableau that made big-city welfare programs seem ungovernable. Tommy Thompson had been in office for nearly a decade and called himself the country's leading reformer. Outside Milwaukee, he had cut the rolls 45 percent. Inside city limits, the rolls had dropped just 7 percent, and even that was large by urban standards. Streetwise clients, incompetent staff, the undertow of crime and drugs—the sheer mass of the poverty and social disorder made the cities seem a world apart. At least by urban standards, Milwaukee's economy was strong; unemployment in Detroit and Cleveland ran nearly twice as high.

Onto this stage rambled a curious sight: an affable, paunchy, middle-aged bureaucrat in a leaky old Mercedes-Benz, convinced that he could make work programs work even in the heart of the ghetto. Nothing about Jason Turner suggested a figure about to make welfare history. He tangled his syntax and chewed cheap cigars. His shirttails were so chronically untucked that Thompson privately nicknamed him "Scruffy." But a few months before Congress passed the new law, Turner seized control of the Milwaukee program and set off the first urban exodus. In doing so, he turned an obscure patch of Midwestern blight into a policy lab that would draw visitors from around the globe. And he pioneered many of the methods that other states would use to cut the rolls.

Turner belongs to a welfare subgroup that confounds most stereotypes: the right-wing idealist. After decades of toil in conservative causes, he arrived in Milwaukee with two convictions. The first, in which he would be wholly vindicated, was that welfare recipients were much more capable of working than most experts had guessed. Even he didn't understand how many already had jobs. But he sensed that the number was high and trusted it could grow a lot higher. When Jewell said of welfare, "A lot of people was just getting it because they can get it—they know how to go out there and work," she was giving voice to the animating life-thought of Jason A. Turner.

Turner's second belief was that work—even tedious, low-wage work—had the power to save the soul. The idea that work would serve as a spiritual balm was one theme among many in the Washington debate; for Turner, it was a matter of lifelong faith. "Work is one's own gift to others," he said. "Work fulfills a basic human need." Without it, people suffer "spiritual harm." Once they became steady workers, Turner predicted, women like Angie would become happier, more self-fulfilled people, with more orderly homes, inspired children, healthier romantic relationships, and fewer problems with depression or drugs. Fumbling to make his point on television, Turner once exclaimed, "It's work that sets you free!" not realizing that he was quoting the motto on the gate to Auschwitz. He worked so late, he kept a bedroll in his office and often spent the night on the floor. The notion that, for some people, a job is just a job would not have occurred to him.

Turner's fascination with welfare began in a place where it didn't exist—the leafy precincts of Darien, Connecticut, where he grew up as the son of an advertising executive. Twelve years old in 1965, Turner was thumbing through *U.S. News & World Report* when he spotted an article on the welfare explosion. The news left him unsettled. "It hadn't occurred to me that there were whole classes of people who didn't work and who basically existed on government charity," he said. What if everyone tried that? Part of what fueled Turner's shock was his reverence for his grandfather, John Tufel, an orphan who had worked his way out of poverty and into a job as a Wall Street bond salesman; when he lost it in the Depression, he put on his suit and sold brushes door-to-door. In the moral universe of Turner's youth, nonwork was just a nonoption. While prep-school friends sat in class doodling football plays, Turner sketched workfare plans, blueprints of factories where welfare recipients would run the assembly lines. By his undergraduate years at Columbia University, he was sending them off to President Ford, hoping an over-the-transom plan to rescue the underclass might galvanize interest at the top. "One of the things that sustained me was I believed I had a solution: 'Hey guys, this is it!'"

Despite his fervor, it took Turner years to land his first welfare job. That may have been a blessing in disguise, for he used the delay in part to gain some exposure to the streets. In college, he drove a cab, mostly in the South Bronx, where he whisked around a captivating mix of drug dealers, hookers, grandmas, and kids. He also got robbed at gunpoint, twice—barely escaping the second time with his life. Having a gun stuck in his face reinforced his sense that social order was a fragile thing, not to be left untended. But it also quickened his curiosity: why run the risk of robbing someone, when a few hours of driving could earn just as much?

A second encounter with street life proved punishing in a different way. As a volunteer in the 1980 Reagan campaign, Turner had hoped to parlay his contacts into a welfare job but languished for years in the backwaters of the federal housing department. Deciding that if he couldn't save the poor, he would try to get rich, Turner cashed out his retirement plan, bought eleven cheap apartment buildings in the District of Columbia, and lost everything but his untucked shirt. The turning point came when he rented to a man who prepaid in cash and drove off in a new Bronco. Someone with a keener sense of property management might have spotted a drug dealer setting up shop. A few months later, half his tenants were smoking crack. Turner couldn't collect his rents, and District law made evictions nearly impossible. After three years of daily combat, Turner lost the buildings to foreclosure. "I got beaten," he said.

Life as a slumlord reinforced Turner's instinctive hostility toward welfare. But oddly enough, it also fortified his faith in the very people who had done him in. For all their problems, Turner regarded his tenants as a resilient lot. In a pinch, money would simply appear, from relatives, boyfriends, or God knows where. "There was nothing inherent in the people themselves that suggested they couldn't cope," he said. "They were able to support their families in a dysfunctional system. They'd do what they had to do to take care of their needs." Doing what they had to do is a phrase the Trio often use. That is, the man who was about to become their antagonist saw them much as they saw themselves; he saw them as "survivors," too.

Returning to Republican politics, Turner finally landed a welfare job, as a senior official under the first President Bush. But the Bush administration was no place for radical welfare schemes, and Turner departed four years later with his plans still on the shelf. Wisconsin offered him a second-tier post that most top feds would have found an affront. Even the title was opaque: director of capacity building. But his duties would include an overhaul of the Milwaukee program, meaning that at age forty, Turner would finally get his hands on a big-city welfare machine. He ignored the injury to bureaucratic pride and drove seventeen hours to the western shore of Lake Michigan. "I wanted to run an urban welfare-to-work program in the worst sort of way," he said.

Turner's timing was perfect. He got to Wisconsin in the spring of 1993, shortly before Tommy Thompson's showdown with the legislature's Democrats. First the governor accepted their dare to abolish AFDC. Then he had Turner lead a group to design its replacement— to do for real what he had been doing in his head since junior high school. The plan Turner proposed—Wisconsin Works, or "W-2"—was so radical that when Gerry Whitburn, the state welfare secretary, read it in his deer stand, he nearly fell out of the tree. *Everyone* would be forced to work in order to get a check: no exemptions, no exceptions, no delays. And work, not just join a job-search program. For those who couldn't find private employment, the state would create thousands of community service jobs. And it would offer subsidized child care and health care, not just to people on welfare but to a much broader class of needy workers. With its expansion of "opportunity" (child care, health care, and subsidized jobs) and "responsibility" (strict work rules), W-2 was a big, bold, serious plan, and in its broadest sense similar to what Clinton originally had in mind. Thompson, evolving from grandstander to innovator, signed off with surprisingly few changes, and Turner was as amazed as anyone in early 1996 when the proposal made it through the legislature intact. The obstacle of federal approval loomed, but when Clinton signed the welfare bill a few months later, handing authority to the states, Wisconsin was free to proceed. What started as a game of legislative chicken turned into what was, on paper at least, the boldest alternative to cash assistance since the WPA.

W-2 brought Wisconsin renown. But it is not really how the state ended welfare. By the time the program started in September 1997, the statewide caseload had already fallen nearly 60 percent, with Angie and Jewell among the first to tumble off the rolls. Indeed, Turner's success in cutting caseloads under AFDC is what made its expensive replacement affordable. In effect, he took a voluntary program that emphasized education and made it a mandatory program that emphasized work. Had someone done that to AFDC earlier, there wouldn't have been such fervor to end it.

Turner's first target wasn't the poor but the job-search bureaucracy. While the state set overall policy, and county caseworkers processed the checks, the motivation classes were mostly run by private contractors, like Goodwill Industries or the YWCA. And they got paid whether anyone got motivated or not. With a rudimentary form of performance-based contracting, Turner tied a small part of each group's pay to the number of people placed in jobs. The notion that they were *supposed* to be putting clients to work struck some of the groups as news. "I thought they wanted us to get people GEDs," the head of one agency said. As Turner put it: "Even though the program was called J-O-B-S, the message hadn't been absorbed, even by the chief executive." In each year from 1994 to 1996, the number of recipients placed in jobs rose by more than 30 percent. Since the baseline was low, and job loss high, the effect on the caseload was small. But Turner drew a lesson: "You can mobilize the bureaucracy a lot more than I had thought."

Focusing next on applicants, Turner swiped an idea from a hamlet two time zones away. He was making small talk at a conference one day when an Oregon official mentioned the news from an out-of-the-way place called LaGrande. Before opening a case, LaGrande made applicants meet with a "financial planner" to discuss alternatives: Could they move in with Mom? Had they looked for a job? New cases had plunged. "It turns out that people who apply for welfare have a lot more options than we think," the Oregon official said. The story was relayed as a curious backwoods development, not the makings of major new policy. But a light went on in Turner's head: the idea that the poor have other options was both an article of faith and the lesson of his days as a rent collector. Back in Wisconsin, Turner dialed up the "financial planner" herself, a former restaurant hostess named Sandy Steele, who was chosen for her welcoming persona; LaGrande wasn't at all trying to drive people away. Still, nearly a third of the applicants withdrew their forms rather than sit through the session. Never mind an hour of counseling, Turner thought: why not require every applicant to spend a few weeks looking for a job?

The idea clashed with the reigning administrative premise—that eligible families ought to get aid—and legislators wouldn't go along. But Turner found a loophole that allowed a pilot project. And to persuade local officials, he drove around Wisconsin with a giant speakerphone, piping in upbeat Sandy Steele to explain how she had done it. By the time he won permission to go statewide in March 1996, Turner required every applicant to spend a few weeks sitting in motivation class and filling out employer logs. Someone could always fake it, of course, but the more the hassle factor rose, the more the rolls went down; as soon as "Self-Sufficiency First" began, case openings fell by a third. Over time, the concept gained a new name—"diversion"—and variations were launched, amid significant controversy, in thirty states. In some cases, diversion *did* become a tool for driving the needy away; some of the most serious problems arose under a program later run by Turner himself as welfare commissioner in New York City.

Despite the ebbing applications, Turner still needed a program for those already on the rolls. For them came Turner's third initiative and his most potent: for the first time in the history of AFDC, he established a real work program in the heart of a major city. While the idea was one he had mulled all his life, he once again grabbed the details from an eccentric westerner, a Utah liberal named Bill Biggs, whose work had won a curious following on the Right. The Biggs story began in 1981, when Utah abolished the small, optional part of AFDC that served married couples. When the next year's recession left families sleeping in their cars, the legislature created a state relief program, but imposed a work requirement. Biggs took charge. The Emergency

Work Program, as he designed it, had two distinctive features. One, it really involved work; Biggs had recipients cleaning the highways, not sitting in motivation class. Even more unusual, it only paid people for the hours they logged on the job. This feature, known as "Pay for Performance," sounds exceedingly routine: you work, then you get paid. But most welfare-to-work programs took the opposite tack, sending recipients their monthly grants and threatening to reduce them later if they broke the rules. *Reduce*, not eliminate: on the rare occasions when penalties were imposed, they didn't amount to much. In practice, as Jewell had discovered, you got paid whether you showed up or not.

Biggs wasn't trying to cut the rolls. He was trying to help people get jobs, so he wanted to imitate a real workweek. Nonetheless, the caseload fell nearly 90 percent from the levels of the previous program; rather than work for welfare, most people quickly found regular jobs, even in Utah's down economy. Turner *was* trying to cut the rolls, and he proceeded in Milwaukee along similar lines. Through the county government and nonprofit groups, he lined up thousands of community service positions, where recipients could be sent to sweep floors, answer phones, or sort the mail. And he reduced their checks for every hour they missed. Wisconsin's version of Pay for Performance was even stricter than Utah's. The beleaguered Clinton administration, eager to look tough in the welfare wars of 1995, let Wisconsin punish those who didn't comply by taking away their food stamps, too. Under the old system, Jewell could ignore her work notices and still collect a cash and food stamp package worth more than $800 a month. Now if she failed to appear, $10 of food stamps was all she would have left. With the welfare world focused on the national bill, the experiment initially got little attention. But flying in below the radar in welfare's final hour, Turner put the whole safety net in play.

Turner launched Pay for Performance in March 1996, five months before Clinton signed the new federal law. With that, the city's caseloads collapsed. They fell 24 percent in the program's first year. They fell 66 percent in the two years until the transition to W-2 was complete. During that time, about twenty-two thousand Milwaukee families stopped getting welfare, meaning that about one city resident in ten was someone Turner had removed from the rolls. Nothing like it had ever been seen in a big-city welfare program. Outside Milwaukee, the rolls fell even faster, 93 percent over the two-year run-up to W-2. It didn't take a time limit to cut the rolls. It didn't take a surge in the economy. It simply took a work requirement, strictly enforced. "The numbers just blew me away," Turner said.

Why would so many ostensibly destitute people decline to work for welfare? One reason is that, as with Angie and Jewell, many were already working. Covert work is by definition hard to measure, but a Milwaukee researcher named John Pawasarat got a glimpse by comparing two state databases. One identified every city resident on welfare. The other showed everyone with earnings. Although only 12 percent of the recipients had said they were working, 31 percent appeared on the quarterly wage earners list—nearly a third had jobs. Over the course of a year, more than *half* of the people on welfare worked. And even that understates the amount of hidden work since the wage file omitted jobs in other states and informal jobs like babysitting or doing friends' hair. Many people didn't show up at the work program because they couldn't be in two places at once. For those who didn't already have a job, the work rules were a goad to get one. Working off her cash and food stamps, a woman on welfare would be earning the equivalent of the minimum wage—$5.15 an hour. Most entry-level jobs paid at least $6, and state and federal tax credits effectively raised that to about $9—offering at least the surface hopes of getting ahead. Plus, some of the jobs that Turner set up were transparently dull or dumb. In the most notorious case, women were sent to sort coin-sized toys called "pogs" into piles of different colors. When they finished, a supervisor dumped them, and the next crew started again. Faced with tedious or demeaning tasks, thousands of Milwaukee women had the same thought as Jewell: "I ain't gonna be doing that! I'll work and get my *own* money!"

Even those who piled the pogs weren't sure to get their checks. In his zeal to ferret out the guilty, Turner created a system that often punished the innocent, too, through an obscure change in the state's check-writing software. Let's say Jewell was assigned to work at a food bank but overslept. In the past, no penalties were imposed unless proof of her absence made a cumbersome trek—from the food bank to a work-program case manager (typically at a nonprofit agency like Goodwill) and then to a county eligibility worker, who had to go into the computer system and request a payment reduction. As long as the paperwork was missing, Jewell got her full check. Turner reversed the default mechanism. Now it was proof of Jewell's attendance that had to navigate the traffic jam. Until her eligibility worker got a time sheet and entered the hours she had actually worked, the computer wouldn't issue her payment. With that, the number of families penalized each month rose a dozenfold, to more than four thousand. This solved the problem that Turner had in mind: women who ignored the work rules no longer got paid. But thousands of women who did comply didn't get paid, either, simply because their paperwork was missing. Congressional investigators later found that 44 percent of the penalties were imposed in error. While the lost income was typically restored, it could take weeks just to get a caseworker on the line—and presumably the people who had agreed to work especially needed the cash. Unrepentant, Turner eventually retreated on tactical grounds, reverting to the old software. ("It just wasn't worth the advocates running around with a case of someone not getting their check," he said.) But in the collective mind of the city's poor, one thought seemed to be forming: *Why mess with these people?*

Not everyone who left, left for a job. Some turned to relatives, some to boyfriends. Some were too sick, depressed, or addicted to navigate the bureaucratic chaos. Even seeking a medical exemption demands an ability to function that some people didn't possess. One of the saddest sights I encountered in Milwaukee was that of Amber Peck, a fiftyish woman who lost her check, her apartment, and after a drug binge, her spot in a homeless shelter. We met on a snowy February night, and I gave her a ride to a cross-town church that had opened its floors to the dispossessed. She said that while she had understood the work rules, she couldn't bring herself to comply. "I stay depressed all the time." Then gripping two shopping bags filled with old clothes, she picked her way across an icy church lawn to lie on the hard, lonely floor.

In prosecuting his war, Turner was fully prepared to see such abject destitution rise. One of the failures of welfare, he argued, was that it papered over recipients' problems. By paying the rent, it let drug addicts ignore their addictions and the mentally ill postpone seeking help. "You want to get people into a situation where they have to resolve their issues," he said, a process he called "thrusting them into the public square." Whether much issue-resolution occurred is a matter of some doubt. A few years later, I went looking for Amber Peck, wondering whatever had become of her impossibly sad silhouette. The trail led to a low-income Samaritan named Eula Edwards, who answered the door in a torn housecoat and talked of having raised three dozen foster kids. She had taken in Amber after meeting her at a place called Power House Delivery Church. By the time I arrived, Amber was locked up on a drug charge, and Edwards was relieved. Before her arrest, Amber had been beaten on the streets and all but left for dead. "I used to be worried 'bout her all night," Edwards said. "At least now we know where she's at."

Still, Milwaukee saw nothing like the waves of dispossession that some people had feared—no children "sleeping on grates." (Amber Peck's teenage children had moved in with friends.) During the program's first winter, about forty-one additional families a night slept in the city's shelters. In the course of a year that translated into hundreds of additional homeless families, and in a shelter system as small as Milwaukee's they often exceeded the number of beds (hence the church floors). Nonetheless, by any reckoning, the homeless accounted for a tiny percentage of the ten thousand families who left welfare the first year. Food bank usage also rose that year, by 14 percent. Child welfare cases remained *lower* than they had been at welfare's peak. A smattering of critics still warned of "genocide." But Ramon Wagner of Community Advocates, a leading social services group, expressed surprise at the lack of more obvious distress. "We thought there'd be a more dramatic impact," he said.

Turner was amazed. He had never imagined that so many people would simply walk away. What he discovered in Milwaukee would soon become evident nationwide: welfare families depended on welfare less than anyone knew. "They must have had a lot more options than even I had realized," he said.

Angie received one of Jason Turner's first work notices. Two weeks later, she found her own job. She had already started to renew her nursing license when the Pay for Performance letter arrived, and a big nursing home was hiring. She timed her start to get a paycheck for Redd's tenth birthday. It was as easy as that.

Angie had landed plenty of jobs, and she resisted the notion that welfare hassled her into this one. "I ain't call that hassle—just 'cause they make you get up off your ass and look for a job," she said. "I was looking for a job, anyway." But this time several things were different. One is that she had to tell her caseworker right away; otherwise she would have been sent to sort pogs. Another is that when she got discouraged, she couldn't take one of her breaks; welfare would have made her work, too. In the long run, the aim was to mold her into the steady worker she imagined herself to be, with rising income and inspiration for the kids. But in the short run the rules just left her poorer, since she could no longer double-dip. Angie kept a partial welfare check during a brief transition. But after four months the payment dwindled to $11, and then it disappeared. With that, twelve years and about $60,000 worth of welfare payments ended, and she never received another. The state happened to process her final check on August 22, 1996, the day Clinton signed the new law.

In welfare theory, this would seem like a baccalaureate moment: she was off the welfare "plantation." After a lifetime of "dependency," she was fully, genuinely, that American hero, a working-class stiff— star of country music, socialist art, and beer ads everywhere. So how did it feel? Angie's smooth face puckered. "I never think about shit like that!" she said. "I always work, anyway." What did it mean? "It means I be a broke motherfucker for the rest of my life!"

Jewell, who had just lost her post office job, got the same letter as Angie. At first, she tried to beat the system. She was doing a little volunteer work at her son's school and passed it off as full-time community service. "I had got real cool with the teachers, so I just told them to say I was volunteering up there," she said. When that didn't work, she signed up for a course to become a nursing aide. Her mother was doing it; Angie was doing it; "Let me go ahead and have something under my belt," she decided. Six weeks later, she was on the job at a nursing home. As usual, Jewell didn't tell the welfare office she was working. But Sheriff Turner's new software tracked her down. Before issuing her next check, the computer tried to tabulate her hours on a workfare assignment. Finding none, it closed her case. The old system had sent Jewell a check every month for eight years. In five months, Turner pushed her off the rolls and into a full-time job. Like Angie, Jewell says the timing was pure coincidence. But on the bus to the nursing home each morning, she was astonished to find women heading to community service jobs—working for *welfare.* "Ain't no way I would wanna be working for free when I could be working somewhere and getting paid!" she said. Her contempt for the program happens to explain what made it so effective: "I didn't feel like going through all that; I just started working."

In Angie and Jewell, Turner's first theory found corroboration: lots of welfare recipients could work. Whether emptying bedpans would "set them free" was another matter. And Opal would pose the kind of challenge that Turner hadn't fully imagined. Within a few years, it would be hard to say whose failures were more disturbing—Opal's, with her self-destructive ways, or those of the celebrated system that squandered millions and did nothing to break her fall.

PART III

After Welfare

TEN

Angie and Jewell Go to Work: Milwaukee, 1996–1998

Nursing aides do difficult, dangerous work. They get hurt twice as often as coal miners and earn less than half the pay. They traffic in infectious fluids, in blood, urine, vomit, and poop. They handle corpses. They get attacked by patients. Above all, they lift. They lift people from beds and wheelchairs; they lift them from toilets and showers. They lift at awkward angles and times, and the people they lift can slip and resist. Nearly one in six nursing aides gets injured each year, and nearly half the incidents involve back injuries, where the risk of recurring problems is great. Coal mines and steel mills have grown safer with the years. Nursing homes have grown more dangerous. Science has prolonged patients' lives, while insurers have shortened hospital stays, sending ever-sicker patients into nursing-home care. In the decade before Angie started her job, the injury rate among nursing-home workers rose nearly 60 percent. Turnover is epidemic: a typical home often replaces nine of ten aides each year. Nationally, the job pays about $7.50 an hour, and one in five nursing aides lives in poverty. Although they are the foot soldiers of the health-care system, about a quarter have no health insurance.

Angie liked the job. She liked it more than lugging mail and a lot more than cleaning motels. She liked the bright, clean building. She liked break-room gossip and the teamwork of patient care. She liked the residents and the stories they told, especially the nursing-home rebels, who reminded her of herself. "Ain't no telling what might come outta they mouth!" she said. She liked her medical smocks. While others might call the job "wiping butts," Angie liked to look in the mirror and think of herself as a "nurse." Clinton and others had argued that work would bring new purpose and meaning. As a pioneer of postwelfare life, Angie offered an early test case and a promising one.

It didn't seem so at first. After renewing her license, she applied at a nursing home close to her house but was sent to a sister home eight miles south in the overwhelmingly white suburb of Greenfield. (The Greenfield population is 1 percent black.) "Wilderness," she fussed, making the trek in a $300 Oldsmobile as uncertain as her sense of direction. She found it strange that everyone at Clement Manor knew her name, then discovered that in a building with two hundred people, she was the only black worker on duty. Angie had never spent an entire day surrounded by white people and was surprised when "they didn't make you feel out of place." Soon, she made her first white friend, a coworker named April. Angie showed her how to put cornrows in her daughter's hair, and on Angie's thirtieth birthday April came along to a club. "She talked, she hung out—she just like she was black!" Angie said. Walking in to Clement Manor, Angie had wondered if she would last the day. But by the end of her first shift, "I knew when I woke up in the morning, I was going back."

With nursing aides in short supply, there's interest in what makes them tick—why suffer all that lifting and pulling when fast food pays as much? One theory is that aides are inherently drawn to the caregivers' role. "Often they have been caregivers of someone in their own family," said Robert Friedland, a nursing-home expert at Georgetown University. "They find something intrinsically valuable in doing the work itself." Angie's not one to put herself on the couch, but that's an insight she summoned on her own. "I think it was because of my Daddy," she volunteered one day. In her case, she *hadn't* taken care of him, which gnawed at her conscience. As Roosevelt Jobe drank himself to death, he hadn't looked after her, either. Angie was busy running the streets, and Roosevelt was too drunk to notice that his teenage daughter was pregnant. "I was mad at him, yeah, but that don't mean I don't love him," Angie said. "People make mistakes. He tried to mend it. He didn't have enough time." She saw her father for the last time just before she moved to Milwaukee, and after a separation of several years she was shocked by his decline. He couldn't even go to the bathroom on his own. "I had to hold his penis," Angie said. "That'll fuck up your head." They spent a tender two hours together in a park, the nicest father-daughter moment of their lives, and a month later he was dead. "I felt so guilty," Angie said. "I did not do nothing for him."

Five years later, Clement Manor gave her a second chance. The job tapped a vein of energy and imagination dormant in other parts of her life. She certainly had more patience for her patients than she did for her kids. Years later, she still laughed at the stories from the ward. "Okay, we had this man—he had dementia," Angie said. "He was always walking around with his pants down! He never kept 'em pulled up. *Never!*" Angie cackled. "He had a lady up there that liked him, *old* lady! She'd put makeup on her, dress in a little dress. If another resident sat next to him, *boooh,* she ready to fight! Even if they old and they can't remember nothing, they remember about sex. S-e-x! You'd catch him in somebody's bed in a minute!" A few weeks into the job, Angie's first patient died. "Scared-er than a motherfucker!" is how she felt when she had to clean him. She had never seen a corpse before. But after washing his body and combing his hair, she left the room thinking that dead people weren't so bad; unlike her kids, Angie would say, they can't talk back to her. In a less flippant mood, she put it this way: "It was easy, because he was suffering. And he just looked so much more at peace when he was dead." Another patient, as Angie moved to scrub her, barked, *"Get your hands off of me, you nigger!"* On the streets, that would have sent Angie's fists flying; on the ward, it made her laugh. ("Old people, sometimes they stuck in their ways. You overlook the things they say.") She smiled at the frightened old woman and, in the calmest voice she could muster, explained, "The nigger is cleaning your ass, 'cause you can't do it yourself—so you might as well let me."

The commute was harder to forgive, especially after her axle fell off. Then she had to get up at 4:00 a.m. and catch two buses to a 6:30 shift. Angie kept her enthusiasm for nursing homes but found a job closer to home, a place called the Mercy Residential & Rehabilitation Center. A 10 percent pay cut brought her down to $6.50 an hour. But it was "one bus, straight there."

By the end of 1996, the year she left welfare, Angie had worked nine months and earned $8,200, a pittance ideal in only one sense: it left her with an earned income tax credit about as large as anyone could get. As soon as her W-2s arrived, she hopped a bus to H&R Block and filed for a combined state-federal bonus of $4,700. The sum swelled her annual earnings by 57 percent. After a vast, if quiet, expansion at the start of the Clinton years, the $30 billion program became a pillar of post-welfare life. In Milwaukee, furniture stores ran annual tax-season sales, and car dealers brought bookkeepers to the lot, to help customers file. Despite the program's size (it spends more than AFDC did at its peak), not a lot is known about where the money goes. But one survey, of 650 workers in Chicago, offered some encouraging clues. While nearly a fifth spent the whole sum on what economists call consumption and Angie calls "surviving"—food, clothes, and overdue rent—more than 70 percent of the workers used at least some of the money for strategies to get ahead. They saved, moved, went back to school, or bought a reliable car. Angie had a foot in both camps. She bought the kids new beds and sank most of the rest, about $2,000, into another car. A "nice car." A car on the outer edges of what she could afford.

The salesman said he knew the previous owner and promised the car had been fastidiously maintained. It broke down five times in the first few weeks. Then it threw a rod. In the spring of 1997, Angie had the useless hulk towed back to the lot, where it sat as a smoldering monument to the salesman's empty assurances. "It was towed more than it was driven!" she said. A poor black woman with a melted engine is not one of society's more empowered figures. But what she lacked in automotive sophistication, Angie made up for with fury. She spent four hours in a waiting room standoff, listing all the people she would call—billboard lawyers, the television station, the "Bureau of Better Business." Then she drove away with a fine green Chevy and a feeling of vindication.

The car promised to change her life. Without it, she was stuck on an inner-city bus line, where wages ran the lowest. With it, she could "work the pool"; she could moonlight through a temp agency at short-staffed nursing homes. Pool work offered no job guarantees and often meant working at troubled sites. But it paid a premium, and pool work in the suburbs paid even more. After six months at Mercy,

Angie was earning $7 an hour. In South Milwaukee, fourteen miles away, she could earn more than $10. "Think I didn't find South Milwaukee?" she said. She found it in the morning, and she found it at night. She found it in manic double shifts that started before the sun rose and ended long after it set. Although the suburban cops made her nervous—"My black ass ain't supposed to be out there"—Angie's ambitions outran her fears. After a few months of juggling two jobs, she left Mercy to work the pool full-time. She made $1,600 in May; $1,300 in June; and $2,000 in July. Through six months of gyrating schedules and fatigue, she was on pace to earn nearly $20,000 a year.

Her success bolstered her confidence, much as the advocates of work had hoped. "You know how you might want to change your life around, do something different?" she said. What Angie wanted was her GED, for her pride above all else; she had been trying on and off for a dozen years. It's easy when you own a high school diploma to forget what it took to get one. Signing up for a class, Angie dragged home a workbook that ran a thousand pages. Square roots, onomatopoeia, the Pythagorean theorem, plate tectonics, cumulus clouds, the Townshend Acts, $2 \times (x^2+1)$—it was all there, a four-pound brick of stuff she should have long ago learned and forgotten. She was ten years older than most of the students and felt like the chaperone. As a onetime high school poet, she started with the literature review, huddling in the break room with "Sonnet 43": "I love thee to the depth and breadth and height / My soul can reach, when feeling out of sight." ("I always *liked* poetry," she said. "I just could never understand that shit.") In verse, as in person, Angie was more direct. Though with the move to Milwaukee her writing had waned—she wondered if she had run out of time or out of things to say—she responded with a poem about Roosevelt Jobe:

> He was here now he is gone
> Gone to a place where
> the sky is blue
> the wind is still
> the trees and
> the grass is green and bright
> He is gone to a place to be at peace with life.

In the tradition of student crammers everywhere, Angie pulled an all-nighter before her first test. In the morning her heart was racing; what if people laughed? She felt no shame in being poor, but looking dumb she couldn't abide. What she suffered next hurt worse: the computer crashed and tests were canceled for the day. Remarkably resilient in most aspects of life—she could stare down corpses or used car salesmen—Angie didn't find the courage to return for another four years. "I was really, really hurt," she said.

She did keep working, and in the summer of 1997, she treated herself and the kids to their first family vacation—four days down South for the family reunion. The trip was not to be undersold as a marker of achievement. She bought each of the kids a new outfit and had Jewell do her hair. She fried up a cooler of chicken. Then she loaded a rental car and drove fourteen hours to Monroe County, Mississippi. Darrell had just turned four, and her mother had never seen him. Carloads of kin drove in from Chicago, and praying over the backyard feast they formed a portrait of mainstream achievement. Two of Angie's cousins were cops; another cousin worked for a bus company or airline—Angie was never sure which. One uncle parked rental cars at O'Hare. Another owned a beauty salon and a house with a swimming pool. No one asked Angie what she did for a living or whether she got welfare. They just fussed over her kids, teased her about her weight, and stuffed her with ribs and pie. Her presence said all that had to be said: Angie was making it.

Nursing homes didn't have the same effect on Jewell. She started at a place known for being rough on aides, the Bel Air Health Care and Alzheimer's Center, which had three hundred beds and a dementia ward that Jewell came to dread. Her patients threw food. They played in their poop. They moaned at phantom pains. "It was just like a big old crazy house!" she said. "Had to rassle with some of them." At $8.30 an hour, Bel Air paid more than most places outside the pool. But getting there involved a long bus ride, and Jewell was chronically late—"no special reason, just late." The average Bel Air aide stayed for eight months. Jewell lasted seven. "They terminated me because of my attendance."

She got fired two weeks before Christmas, 1996—her first without welfare—but Jewell wasn't worried. Lucky had wandered into a job at a rubber factory that paid nearly $10 an hour. Plus tax season was around the corner, and Jewell had $4,100 in credits coming, about as taxes much as the average state paid out in welfare all year. She bought clothes and furniture for the kids and a Grand Am for herself. A few months later she got a job at Mercy Rehab, the nursing home where Angie was working. Mercy had a homier feel than Bel Air, but Jewell found it chronically short staffed, and she lost the Grand Am when a drunk driver hit her. (Neither of them had insurance.) One weekend, three months after she started, Jewell learned she was slated to cover a whole shift with just one other aide—the two of them would have to wash, dress, and feed sixty patients. "*Unh-uh,*'" she thought. "They're not fittin' to work me like that!" She didn't go in, and she didn't go back. After quitting in May, Jewell hardly worked the rest of the year. Her mind was on other things.

Life with Lucky wasn't happy and hadn't been for a while. She had lived with him for nearly five years, and he was the only father her two boys had known. But Lucky was always drunk. Screaming drunk. Obscene drunk. Falling-down-and-passing-out drunk. At twenty-eight, she thought she might like another baby, but Lucky had driven her to Norplant. As Jewell launched her nursing career, one of Lucky's best friends moved to town, with a story as vivid as his name: Kenyatta Q. Thigpen. The last time Jewell had seen him, a decade earlier, he was a mischievous kid in Jeffrey Manor, three years behind her and known by his graffiti *nom de guerre,* Mirf. Jewell hadn't paid much attention to Mirf. But Ken caught her eye. At twenty-five, he was a tall, muscular man with a dimpled smile, copper skin, and soft hair tied in a ponytail. They were playing Spades at her brother Robert's house when Jewell noticed the change. "Oh, he looks so nice," she thought. When Ken dropped in a few days later, Lucky got drunk and passed out; Ken and Jewell stayed up most of the night, playing video games. Soon after, she took him out for a hamburger. Then she gave him a call. "Should I *say* something?" Jewell asked herself. She decided it was too risky. Then she said it anyway: "What's up with you and me?" Ken pretended to be surprised. "What you want to be up?" he said. He left town to visit family in Mississippi, and needing a place to stay when he returned, he moved in with Lucky and Jewell. She had just started working on the Alzheimer's ward when their covert romance began.

After years with Lucky, Jewell found Ken an oasis of innocent fun. He didn't drink or do drugs; he liked kids; and while he didn't have any of his own he played the generous uncle with élan. He liked bowling, theme parks, and video games. He taught Jewell to drive a stick shift and took her to play miniature golf. He even liked to shop. He made her laugh with funny faces. Once when Jewell blew him a kiss, he leaped in the air to catch it. "He's silly!" she said. "We could talk about anything." Still, not many people leave Jeffrey Manor as innocents, and Ken certainly hadn't. His probation officer noted that he had "described his childhood as so-so, as both parents were addicted to cocaine." "So-so" was a generous view. Until he was twelve, Ken boasted of having the most popular, cookie-baking mother on the block. After she got addicted to drugs, he spent the rest of his childhood refereeing his parents' brawls and their smoke parties. Losing the house, the Thigpens split up, and his mother moved to a shelter. His father hung on to a steel-mill job, while Ken stole cars, lived here and there, and finished raising himself. As a high school linebacker with a vicious hit, he had hoped to play college ball. That didn't pan out, and a few weeks after graduation he started selling crack to his mother's friends. "I ain't qualified to do nothing else," he thought. "I ain't working in no McDonald's."

Ken soon discovered he had the qualities a good drug dealer needs. He was smart, personable, and hardworking. He was savvy about marketing; anyone who brought him five clients got a round on the house. And since he didn't consume his product, he didn't burn up his profits. Plus, he was tough. Because of his ponytailed good looks, some people called him "Pretty Boy." But his attitude toward collecting debts brought another nickname, "Batman." "I used to beat them niggers' ass down with a baseball bat," he said. He figured a reason that he didn't have kids is that one of his victims returned and blew off one of his balls. Among the talents that Ken seemed to lack was the knack of avoiding the cops. By the time he arrived in Milwaukee, he had spent half his adult life behind bars.

As their romance blossomed in the summer of 1996, Jewell and Ken were each making a new start. Jewell was leaving welfare for work. Ken was dabbling in modeling school and, despite passing thoughts of quitting the trade, building a new drug business. While traffic was slow for the first few months, he caught a break with a $10 sale to a "go-getter" of a woman named Tina. Among the things she knew how to go get were stolen checks; she had bribed someone at a currency exchange to cash them, and Ken soon had part of the take. Another thing Tina attracted were men willing to pay her for sex. "Once I got hooked up with her, I really took off," Ken said. "Not because of the drugs, but because she was a ho—and she became my ho."

In Ken's line of work, sex and drugs meet at an economic crossroads. What addicts demand are drugs. What they can supply is sex, even when their pockets are empty. Crack houses are filled with bingeing women eager to sell a $10 blow job to finance another high. "It don't make no sense to sell your body for a bag," Ken would say. "Come with me and I could make you a hundred dollars or two hundred dollars." Some people call this pimping, but that's a word Ken generally avoided. He saw himself more as a talent scout, a middleman in the great American tradition. In Tina he realized he had a star of unusual wattage. She had caramel skin, delicate braids, large breasts, and long legs. Plus, she could "conversate." Her escort service charged $225 and took a third for setting up the date. Ken provided drugs and protection—"the Be There"—and pocketed most of the rest.

As the enterprise grew, Ken found that coveted commercial force, "synergy." Selling drugs, he met women who wanted to sell sex. Selling sex helped him sell more drugs, since half the johns got high. His products went together "like Bonnie and Clyde," he said. Since the sex workers spent *their* earnings on crack, "no matter how the date goes, I'm gonna get all the money." Until he met Tina, Ken was scuffling by on about $200 a week. With her, his weekly take rose five- or sixfold, and since none of it went to the IRS, he had the take-home pay of someone making $100,000 a year. As the child of addicts, he knew the rap on dealers—parasites preying on the community, blah, blah. "That's a bunch of bullshit," he said. "If I turn my back on them, all they gonna do is go two houses down and get it from someone else." He'd sell to pregnant women as long as they had the cash. "I didn't make the rules, I just follow them."

In explaining how it worked, Ken sounded less like a ghetto badman than a middle manager. He set standards so that Tina would know "what I was going to expect out of her and what she could expect out of me." He pumped her up when her spirits were down: "I just told her if you gonna sell pussy, you gotta be the best at what you do. Ain't none of that selling pussy one day and laying up the next day." And when he had to, he made clear that poor performance brought repercussions. "You can pay me or you can pay the doctor"— so went a favorite refrain. "The first time I beat her up, she told me she wasn't going to work," he said. "*Smack!* 'What you mean, bitch, telling me you ain't going to work?'" Someone with a psychoanalytic bent might wonder if, in beating his whore, he was channeling the rage he felt toward another addict, the mother who had abandoned him. Ken didn't have such a bent. He just said he put in long hours and expected his subordinates to do the same. "It was like a job to me."

That Ken sold drugs was not something Jewell found notable. "That was every black man's job," she said. "I think if *I* could sell drugs and get away with it I would." The sex trade was something she knew less about. She was astonished, when Ken took her to a crack house, to find women ducking behind closed doors only to suddenly reappear, still working their lips and clutching their cash. "The shit these females would do!" Since she had never tried drugs, she couldn't fathom what made addicts act that way. She also thought, "I really don't care, since it ain't me." What she did care about, more than she expected, was Ken. At the start, she thought she was just having a fling, but the more it progressed, the more she saw "a match made in heaven." For months, people were talking. Then Lucky came home early from work and discovered the rumors were true. Too afraid to fight Ken, he turned his fury on Jewell. "Do what you gotta do," she said, refusing to deflect his blows. Ken left for Tina's, and Jewell stayed with Lucky. But she continued to see Ken whenever she could.

Jewell says the tumult had nothing to do with her flagging interest in a job. But she quit shortly after Lucky discovered the affair, and she hardly worked for the next seven months. She didn't have welfare. She didn't have work. She didn't even have food stamps or health insurance; like many former recipients, though she still qualified, she found the new bureaucracy so hard to deal with that she gave up. About a third of the families leaving welfare were in a similar position—

left for months without welfare or work—and their means of survival was a national mystery. Welfare-rights groups went as far as calling them "the disappeared." No one could see how they got by. Jewell's circumstance offers some clues: she had a private safety net. Lucky got fired from the rubber factory but found temp jobs here and there. Thigpen & Associates was throwing off cash. Opal gave Jewell a $65 book of food stamps each month. And after Angie returned from Mississippi, she and her kids moved in. That left nine people sharing a two-bedroom house, but Angie helped pay the rent. "If I got fired, there was always somebody else to help out," Jewell said. "So it really didn't matter."

Her mind told her that cheating on Lucky was wrong. But her heart had a mind of its own. In the summer of 1997, Lucky got locked up for driving without a license. Jewell threw a barbecue to welcome him home, and when Lucky got drunk and threw a beer bottle at Ken, Ken hit him so hard he broke his knuckle on Lucky's head. After the fight, Jewell delivered a harder blow. She told Lucky she wanted him gone.

Angie came home from Mississippi and raced back to work. The Chevy ran like a dream, and the nursing pool paid like one. "You could work seven days a week!" she said, and some weeks she did. In her first month back, she made another $1,800, two and a half times what the average person earned after leaving the Wisconsin rolls. Work made Angie feel useful. It bred empathy. At some level it really did become what Jason Turner had audaciously imagined, her "spiritual gift to others." What it didn't bring was any obvious social benefit to her kids. The most stirring case for putting mothers to work was the promise of planting new values and goals that would transform the next generation. Clinton had been so taken by Lillie Harden's story— "When my boy goes to school and they say 'what does your mama do for a living,' he can give an answer"—he flew her in from Arkansas to stand beside him as he signed the bill. Explanations of just how work would benefit kids were varied and a little vague. One theory emphasized new discipline: an alarm clock would act like a social metronome, imposing new order at home. Another stressed inspiration: watching their role-model mothers buckle down on the job, the kids would do the same in school. Their mothers' toil at indecent wages might even serve as an object lesson, warning children of the need to hone their skills and minds. In the storybook version, a bread-winning woman like Angie might meet a bread-winning man. You can almost picture the new house—small but neat, in a safe neighborhood, with better schools.

Angie's kids didn't live in that house. They squeezed in among the racy subplots at Jewell's. Angie's exit from welfare, a signal event in policy terms, barely registered on them. "Doesn't make no difference at all," said Redd a few years later. "She was working when she was on welfare." A change in family dynamics can take years, of course, and it can happen without children articulating it. But the kids' absences from school, alarming when Angie was on the rolls, grew even worse when she got off. During Angie's last five years on welfare, Kesha, Redd, and Von missed a combined 21 percent of their scheduled school days. Over the next three years, their absentee rate rose to 26 percent. In the course of an elementary school education, that's the equivalent of missing two full years. Angie valued education in an abstract way. She had even kept her notes from a high school debate about the importance of staying in school: "We as black women already has two strikes against us . . . if we don't have a good education, that may become another." But there were days when she just didn't have the energy to get the kids out the door. And days when she was already long out the door herself by the time the school bus came. While affluent parents endlessly complain of their kids' overscheduled lives, Angie's suffered from the opposite blight, long blocks of empty, unsupervised time, which grew longer the more she worked. Their childhoods passed on a sea of boredom, dotted by landfalls of chaos.

At fourteen, Kesha was an open, oddly innocent girl, who alone among the kids still poured out her thoughts in letters to her dad. She also had a severe case of asthma, which compounded her problems in school. With only one functioning lung, anything from cold weather to a whiff of cologne could bring a disabling attack; it was the rare day that passed without one. Landing in Milwaukee, Kesha had responded with courage, and not just physically. Failing second grade, barely able to read, she had struggled uphill to a fourth-grade report card that had shimmered with As. Kesha "has great potential for success," her teacher had written home. But with her transition to middle school two years later (Angie's first off the rolls), Kesha's progress slowed. She felt lost among the five hundred students. She didn't like switching classes or going to gym, and she wouldn't take her medicine in front of her classmates. (Her highest grade, a C, came in, of all things, sixth-grade Japanese.) As Angie moved in with Jewell, Kesha was starting seventh grade, and her schooling crashed: she was absent nearly half the year. Two weeks in the hospital set her back, but so did the unsteady housing, Angie's long hours, and Kesha's fights with Angie's new man. She ended the year with nearly straight Fs, and her education never really recovered.

Kesha felt especially close to her aunt Jewell, her great counselor in fashion and grooming. But Kesha soon had an unlikely new friend in Jewell's rival, Tina. Tina took Kesha shopping, paid for her to have her hair and nails done, and let her spend the night. Kesha understood she was being used as a pawn in Tina's rivalry with Jewell, but she didn't understand where Tina got the money. Or she didn't until Tina pulled out her slitted skirts and boasted that an evening's work could bring her $1,000. "If that's how she wants to make her money, that's on her," Kesha later said. "She was cool." Rather than bring Kesha a new role model, that is, Angie's first years off welfare left her passing time with a prostitute. Later I asked Angie what had gone through her mind. Was she just grateful to have someone buy Kesha things? Was she too tired to give it much thought? Did she genuinely have no qualms about Kesha's weekend visits with a call girl? Angie shot me one of her sour looks. "I'm not supposed to let my kids visit her 'cause that's her chosen profession?" she said. "I ain't got nothing against prostitutes. You don't judge people about stuff like that!" Whether her indignation reflected secret regrets or genuine belief, I never could tell.

Role-model theory took a curious bounce in Redd's life, too. If he had a role model, it wasn't Angie but Ken, the rare grown man who paid him any attention. "When I call him and wanna do something, he come gets me," Redd said. "Plus, he had that dust." Dust—money—loomed large to Redd, and even at twelve, he figured out where Ken got his. As a pudgy, picked-upon child, Redd was impressed by Ken's power over Tina and thought, "I got to find me a girl like that." For a school essay, he chose to write about Las Vegas, because "ho-ing is legal out there." Redd had always struggled in school, but by fourth grade, as Angie left welfare, his behavior grew as worrisome as his grades. His fifth-grade teacher could barely contain himself: "His disrespect toward authority is blatant . . . and demeaning to me as an adult." Redd got suspended for fighting so often that Angie told the school to stop calling her at work and asking her to come get him. "Keep him there!" she said. Equally unhappy in sixth grade and at home, Redd started smoking weed and got two pit bulls. The weed made him giggle. The animals made him feel safe.

Von was afraid of the dogs; in that, as in most things, the brothers formed a study in contrasts. Athletic where Redd was sedentary, even-keeled where Redd was explosive, Von was the only one of Angie's kids diligent about school. "School's fun," he said. "You benefit more from going to school than not going." Every inner-city school's got a kid like Von, an unmined gem waiting for someone to discover his shine. The question was whether anyone would notice before the mudslide of living swept him away. Riding the school bus one day, Von made a crack about a classmate's hair. She taunted him back, Von looked away, and Redd rushed over and punched her. Redd got suspended, but Von was the one whom Angie whipped, for walking away. Don't *ever* punk out on your brother when he's fighting your fight! Von was so mad when he got back to school he hit the girl himself. This time he got suspended. But he didn't get a whipping.

If there was a point on which the kids united, it was a resentment of Angie's boyfriends, who had wandered in and out of their lives since their father had gone to jail: Vernon, Johnny, Sherman, and then Johnny again. "I just really wanted them out," Von said. Angie often seemed to feel the same way: she once chased Sherman with a baseball bat until he jumped out the first-floor window. Kesha got so mad at Johnny, she threw a giant pickle jar from an attic window onto his head. "Every time we see a guy with Mama, we ready to fight him," Redd said. "We just real protective about Mama." About the time she left welfare, Angie finally sat down with the kids and explained what their father had done. He was helping his friends jump some guys, she said. The shooting was an accident. Though their father was serving time for murder, he hadn't even fired a shot. Kesha, at twelve, was quick to forgive. "It was an accident," she said. For Von, who was three at his father's arrest, it was a story about a virtual stranger. But Redd was disturbed. He could forgive his father's role in the shooting; what he couldn't forgive was his refusal to testify against his friends. He just couldn't understand why any child's father wouldn't do all he could to get home. "That's bogus," he said.

Soon after Angie moved in with Jewell, a friend brought her a message: the butcher at the corner store wanted to "talk." Marcus Robertson: big smile, shaved head, soft, dewy eyes like Greg's. "I don't want to talk to him!" she said. But she talked to him every time she stopped in for a loaf of bread. Her on-and-off relationship with Johnny had ended, and among the trio Angie missed congregate living the most. Opal had a boyfriend—Jewell had two—"and I was by myself, as usual." Marcus took Angie to a diner, and a few months later, when she moved to her own place, Marcus came along. Angie never said much about Marcus, then or in the years that followed. He brought home beer. He babysat. He was the rare man she knew who vacuumed and the only one the kids couldn't drive away. But he smoked too many blunts to keep up much of a conversation. And Angie's attitude spoiled early on, when she learned he was messing around. Twenty-three years old, eight years her junior, just out of jail for selling drugs, Marcus was in no settling-down way. The discovery of his infidelity didn't kill the relationship, only Angie's professed investment in it. "I like Marcus, but I don't like to be bothered like I'm his wife," she would say. She let him share her new house. But she never gave him a key.

One night soon after they met, Marcus borrowed Angie's car and headed out to party. He said he would stay at his mother's house, and he awoke there, hungover, the following morning to the blare of Angie's voice.

"Where the car at?"

"In the yard."

"Ain't no motherfucking car out there!"

Angie's green Chevy—literally and metaphorically her engine of progress—had vanished. Angie usually said it was stolen, as in a random crime. Once, she said the real story was that Marcus was selling a little crack, and his sister, seeing him asleep, drove off with his drugs and money. Opal and Jewell thought that Marcus lent it to another woman, who got it towed. Wherever the car went, she had no insurance, and its disappearance in November 1997 spelled the end of Angie's MVP season in the Welfare-to-Work League. She told it as a clear tale of cause and effect: without the car, she lost her job with the nursing pool and sank into a trough of discouragement and debt. The full story is more revealing. Angie found another job, with a pool that transported its workers in vans. The job paid the Christmas bills, but it offered fewer hours and lower pay, and she quit in January over a $10 charge for a van ride she didn't take. The driver said he honked and she didn't come out; Angie said he didn't show up. "Plus they try to talk to you smart," she said. "I got smart right back!" It was tax season. Three days later, she went to H&R Block and collected $5,200. That was twice what she needed to buy another car and return to the nursing pool. But she and Marcus had just moved into the new place on Concordia Street, and she wanted to fix it up. She bought a washer, dryer, refrigerator, and stove. She bought the boys new bedroom sets, since they had destroyed theirs again. And when the money ran out, she got on the bus and applied for a welfare check. Angela Jobe, working-class hero, was trying to get back on the dole!

One person who wouldn't be surprised is Toby Herr, who founded an employment program called Project Match in Chicago's Cabrini Green. Herr got her start as an employment expert in an unadorned way, piling some women in her car and driving off with the want ads. Her first surprise was how many found jobs. Her second was how quickly they lost them. Sick kids, drug problems, fights with the boss—the reasons ran the gamut of housing-project life. Only half her clients became steady workers, and on average it took them more than five years. Most programs stress their successes. Advertising her setbacks, Herr coined a phrase that became a maxim of the field: "Leaving welfare is a process, not an event."

While Herr's findings about job loss have been widely acknowledged, the causation is more complicated than it may seem. A large "barriers" literature has arisen, documenting impediments like depression, illiteracy, domestic violence, and especially the shortage of child care. But the focus on barriers goes only partway in explaining who works and who doesn't. The more barriers a poor mother has, the less likely she is to work; yet plenty of women work despite multiple obstacles, as Angie had. Depending on definitions, her barriers had at various times included shortages of child care and transportation, a severely asthmatic child, bouts of depression, and the lack of a high school diploma. Not to mention the Colt 45s. The barriers discussion also comes with an implicit logic: you fix the barriers and then go to work. Angie's back-and-forth moves (Jewell's, too) show the process to be more nuanced. All women leaving welfare have barriers. The challenge is learning to manage them without losing the job. Herr's training was in human development, not economics, which put her subtly at odds with others in the field. While services like child care and transportation are essential, she argued, new workers ultimately succeed by acquiring something else: a strong "work identity." Seasoned workers, when faced with personal turmoil, see the job as a pillar to cling to, rather than the thing to let go. "It's about making the psychological leap," Herr said. Cars and babysitters come and go. Work identities stay.

In her breakneck dash from the welfare rolls, Angie seemed to have the ultimate work identity. But liking a job isn't the same thing as internalizing the need for one. Angie also faced an especially immobilizing "barrier": troubled love. Conflicts with boyfriends get none of the attention reserved for child care and cars. But women leaving welfare are constantly undermined by the men in their lives, either deliberately, because the men resent their success, or simply because the lives of poor men are so infectiously troubled themselves. And a broken heart is debilitating in a way that a broken carburetor is not. To Herr, a woman with a tenuous work identity and an unfaithful man is behaving in wholly familiar ways when she turns from the job to focus on her home.

Angie didn't assemble the story like that. But the pieces are there. She applied for welfare the month that she and Marcus had their first big fight (one that landed her in the emergency room when she accidentally cut her own hand). She talked about wanting comfort at home ("I had to get my house together"). She talked about turning toward her children ("My kids really hadn't had nothing new"). She talked about being physically drained ("After a while, your body wear out—you need a break"). She said she didn't reject the notion of using her tax money to replace the lost car. She just didn't think of it. "I really wasn't thinking 'bout no car."

Angie had been losing jobs all her life. What happened next was new. She tried to get back on the welfare rolls in March 1998, just as Wisconsin completed its transition to W-2. A caseworker explained she could get a check. But first she had to sit through a self-esteem class. Then she would be assigned a community service job. The job would pay $673 a month, about half of what she could make in a nursing home even without a car. "Ain't nothing wrong with my damn self-esteem!" Angie said. The next day, she went back to Mercy Rehab and reclaimed her old job. Typically, when Angie tells the story, she supplies a negative spin, casting herself as a needy woman turned away. "They gave me a lot of yada, yada, yada. I said, 'Screw 'em,' and found me a job!" But that's mostly Angie's sardonic style. "They just did what they supposed to do," she said one day. "If they probably woulda gave me AFDC—who knows?—maybe I'd be on there, now."

Jewell became a steady worker, too—not with Angie's self-conscious pride, but simply because she had to. Her private safety net fell apart. Angie moved out, Lucky got fired, and Jewell was trying to put him out anyway. As stories of work identities go, Jewell's was disarmingly simple: when she had to work, she did. "It ain't like I had help no more," she said. "How the bills gonna get paid?" She tried a little more nursing home work, but old people continued to vex her. The want ads showed an opening at a large tool-making plant called G. B. Electric. As a "scanner," she worked the shipping line between the "pickers" and the "packers," making sure orders were properly filled. It didn't strike her as meaningful work, and it paid less than the Alzheimer's ward. But she showed up every day, and by the end of 1998 she had earned nearly $12,400. The average woman, in her second year off the Wisconsin rolls, earned about $8,100. Jewell was a sudden success.

Things grew even more complicated at home. Out of pity and

habit—and because she needed a babysitter—Jewell let Lucky back in the house. But she wouldn't let him back in her heart. Her life tumbled forward like a Nashville lyric: living with one man and loving his ex–best friend. Jewell felt so close to Ken that she sometimes pictured them as the same person: "He's the male version, I'm the female." But with Thigpen & Associates thriving, Ken's thoughts were on commerce, not love. "I wasn't in love with no woman—I was in love with the money," he said. "Jewell was like an escape for me." Ken's latest hire was a sixteen-year-old runaway. He brought her to Tina to learn the trade, then sent her to live with Jewell, explaining: "You know how to ho'. I want you to live with Jewell, so you'll know how to be a woman." Jewell took her in for a year. Around the same time, Ken gave Jewell a ring. He had it wrapped in paper and ribbons, and Jewell felt giddy as he guided it onto her hand. Opal made a big fuss and called it a "wedding ring." Jewell said it was just a "friendship ring" but hoped to be proven wrong.

Jewell had the ring, but Tina had the man—Ken lived with *her*—and neither wanted to share. As Jewell started her new job, she and Tina went to war. Jewell derided her as a hooker and an addict, but Tina was just as disdainful of Jewell for selling herself for $6.50 an hour. Over the phone, she called Jewell a "welfare recipient" and mocked her poverty. Jewell thanked her for whoring, laughing that through Ken she got a cut of the cash. When Jewell was hospitalized with bleeding ulcers, Tina woke her with a phone call at dawn to gloat about having Ken to herself. One of the rare times Jewell and Ken argued was after Jewell drove to Tina's and tried to beat her up. "Ain't nobody fittin' to jump on my whore, bruise up her face," Ken said. Through it all, Jewell continued to work. As inventories of work "barriers" go, Jewell had quite a list: a shortage of child care, chronic stomach pain, little work experience, and no high school diploma. And what category would Tina come under: "Hassles with Your Boyfriend's Hooker"? Maybe it helped that she didn't care about the substance of her job. Or maybe there wasn't much substance to care about; Jewell didn't think of her work as a "gift" to her fellow man, and with a teenage prostitute sleeping on her couch, it scarcely brought a storybook life to her kids. She wore her headphones, scanned her tools, and watched the clock. After six months as a temp worker, she got promoted to a regular job, with a raise to $7.50 an hour and a chance to buy into the health plan.

The turmoil around the house grew. Her hotheaded brother Robert shot at an undercover cop, sparking a two-week manhunt tracked on the local news. The police banged on Jewell's door with drawn guns, and helicopters circled her job. Robert got seven years, and Jewell took in his son, a happy-go-lucky three-year-old named Quinten. Jewell was barely scraping by herself, but she didn't hesitate. She said having three boys made her feel like the star of her own TV show. "*My Three Sons*—remember that?" she said. A few weeks later a new problem arose: a neighbor accused Lucky of rape. Lucky professed his innocence, and Jewell didn't know whom to believe. She also said, "I didn't really care." She had been trying to put Lucky out ever since she had let him back in, and the pending case of sexual assault (eventually dropped) was the final straw. The judge put him on house arrest, but that only caused Jewell new grief: it was her house. Now, he *couldn't* leave. It was the law.

Of the three old Jeffrey Manor friends, only Ken was free. One way he had avoided trouble was by refusing to set up a drug house; too many people come and go, and "that shit cause drama." But when a friend got arrested in the summer of 1998, Ken took over the lease. Business was lagging, and the house had a large client base. One day, Ken and Jewell made plans to hit the outlet mall. When she arrived at the crack house to meet him, Jewell's heart fell. Ken was in the back of a squad car, cuffed. The police had found a loaded rifle, a box of plastic bags, and about $400 worth of cocaine, some in the toilet and some in Ken's pocket. "Drama," just as he feared. Now Jewell's home life got *really* complicated. Awaiting trial, Ken was put on house arrest, too, but he didn't have a house. He couldn't keep staying with Tina: she had filed battery charges after one of their fights, so legally he was barred from her home. He couldn't go to Jewell's, either: even if he and Lucky weren't enemies, he figured you could only have one house arrest per house. For Jewell, that settled things: Lucky had to go. "Ooow, you making me *sick*," she told him. At ten and seven, Terrell and Tremmell cried and begged to go with him. Jewell felt awful, too; she knew that after six years he was the closest thing they had had to a father. But with Lucky finally out of the house, Ken was free to move in. And she had never wanted anything more.

Two years after leaving the welfare rolls, Jewell really did feel transformed—not by a job but by a gangster with dimples. She gave herself to Ken as she had never done before. She told him, "This is not just my house, it's *our* house: everything in here is *ours*." She pledged "to keep everything honest" and "never lie." Straggling in at dawn, Ken woke her each morning to play video games. When she turned thirty, he made the weekend a rolling set of surprises: Friday, new coffee tables; Saturday, roses; Sunday, the cake. The family mostly sided with Lucky, and Angie grew especially caustic. "You ain't no good," she said, one night after too much beer. "I hope something bad happens to you!" *You hope something bad happens to me?* Angie's words got under Jewell's skin and festered there for years. Jewell had guilty feelings of her own. But that's different from having regrets.

One problem remained: possession of cocaine with intent to distribute. Ken had placed a bet he could beat it at trial, but he had already been convicted when he moved in with Jewell. With sentencing ahead, Jewell set her sights on probation. Ken figured he might draw a few months of work release. He felt confident enough to keep a hand in the business, even on house arrest. His first sentencing hearing was postponed, but something in the judge's tone left him spooked. He put $6,000 in the bank for Jewell and returned the next week, prepared for the worst. Jewell couldn't go with him; G. B. Electric was strict about missing days. She kissed him good-bye, borrowed his pager, and awaited the good news. It was night at the county jail when Ken was finally able to put through a call. "They gave me two years," he said.

ELEVEN

Opal's Hidden Addiction:
Milwaukee, 1996–1998

One of the things I liked about Opal, the first few times we met, was her abundance of seeming candor. Stuck in a tedious job-search class in the presence of a reporter, most women on welfare would at least feign an earnest streak. They wouldn't saunter across the room, mock a practice job interview, and announce their delight in the dole. They wouldn't insist, as Opal did, "I *like* that welfare check!" She had the room roaring. We met in the summer of 1997, when Wisconsin's war on welfare was building to its peak. Jason Turner's first work program, Pay for Performance, had already cut Milwaukee's rolls by a third, with Angie and Jewell among the first to go. But it was an experiment grafted on to the old system, and in any given month it left more than half of the caseload untouched. Turner's new program—Wisconsin Works, or "W-2"—promised to extend the work rules to everyone: no work, no check, no exceptions. As the most ambitious of the new state programs, W-2 inspired lavish fears and praise, and with its rollout only weeks way, Milwaukee's welfare offices became an international media draw. Japanese television and *Le Monde* were on hand, and everyone was abuzz with sightings of "Maria!" (Shriver, that is) and the *Dateline NBC* crew.

The scene around Opal hardly conjured the words "Republican work program." Among the groups chosen to run W-2 was the Opportunities Industrialization Center, a social services agency with a black nationalist gloss and a talent for courting Tommy Thompson. Having agreed to run his first work program a decade before, when others had balked, OIC had banked his gratitude and a decade of subsequent contracts. With $57 million of W-2 money coming in, the group had renovated an abandoned theater on Martin Luther King Jr. Drive, where bow-tied Muslims glowered at the doors and recipients milled about, looking peevish and bored. I spent an hour in a room of corralled indigents, listening to a job counselor read from an almanac of occupations. It was social work as farce:

> *Mathematics:* reading graphs and stuff like that—it gets real deep when it comes to mathematics. . . . *Agriculture:* that thing with cows gets real deep—giving them those hormones? . . . *Social studies:* like socialization, only you studying it. . . . *Forestry:* why don't we see any more wolves? Somebody eating them?

As a showcase of private-sector efficiency, Opal's classroom was no more promising. One woman was eating chips for breakfast beneath the No Eating sign. Another was drunk. The instructor, Darlene Haines, was complaining to the class that she didn't feel qualified to teach. "It's kind of hard for me," she told the group. "They just kind of threw me into this." As she left the room, a chorus of operatic warnings rang out. "They're building orphanages and prisons!" the chip eater said. "It's going to be like Mississippi!" Haines returned with breaking news: Potawatomi Bingo would hire anyone who passed a drug test. Someone asked if marijuana was a drug. Things went downhill from there. "I can tell this isn't working," Haines sighed.

Needing a body for a practice interview, she called on a short, dark woman in the back wearing a look of boredom. Opal, inconspicuous until then, came forward with a mime of contempt. Head rolling, limbs flopping, she crossed the room in an arc of attitude and slouched into a chair. "I know how to *get* a job," she said. "I just don't know how to *keep* a job." Then as Haines launched into her role as the fictitious employer, Opal sprang to life. Her spine straightened. Her gaze locked in. "I am a courteous person," she began. "I am hardworking. I am dependable."

Haines looked startled. "What motivates you to work?" she asked.

"Being around smiling people," Opal said, smiling.

"What are your greatest achievements?"

"Well, I graduated from high school, and back in ninety-six, I completed a thirteen-week nurturing course."

"If I asked you, when could you start?"

"It would be next Monday, so I could arrange my babysitting situation."

"That won't be an issue?"

"No, I won't let it affect my job performance."

"*Girlfriend!*" the chip eater gasped. "And you said you wasn't motivated!"

Then Opal's limbs went limp. "I'm one of those women who don't *want* to work!" she said. Dragging herself back to her seat, she looked concerned that no one would believe her.

"The sister's gonna make it!" Haines said.

Opal, in fact, was working. Chased by the tightening rules, she had found a part-time job cleaning a hospital lab, and I joined her there the following night. Swabbing and scrubbing in a musical voice beneath posters of the digestive tract, Opal created a mood of easy intimacy. She didn't airbrush her wild adolescence ("I was out of control!"). She didn't disguise her motives for moving to town (welfare in Milwaukee "pays the most"). Her candor seemed the only aspect of her character she cared to defend. "I am an honest person!" she said. Though her formal education had stopped at a semester of community college, her account of welfare history could have been drawn from a grad-school text. AFDC was created in the 1930s for white widows, she said, "but with so many African American women on it" the politicians decided "it was just out of control." If the rolls were still predominantly white, "none of this W-2 would even be in effect."

In describing her streetwise past, Opal offered an unprompted aside. Lots of her friends had gotten high, but drugs had never tempted her. "Even though I fought and hung out with those people, I never did drugs," she said. When I visited her apartment, I noticed a sign that proclaimed it a "Drug-Free Zone." The man she introduced as her fiancé, Kenny Gross, was wearing a no-drugs pin. At that point, Opal had been smoking crack for seven years. And the drug was about to carve a destructive new path through her life.

self fulfilling prophecy

"My Mama said I was bad since I was a baby," Opal was saying a few years later. We were driving around the South Side of Chicago on a survey of her youthful haunts: the projects where she had lived as a girl, the alleys where she had started to drink, the schools from which she had gotten expelled, the apartment where she had first smoked cocaine. Like her childhood, the trip began with the grim high rises of Stateway Gardens but passed through creditable working-class zones, and the accompanying narrative was equally eclectic, able to support multiple theories of her addiction. Opal began with biology. "I never knew my daddy, but he was a hard-core drug addict," she said. "Plus my Mama drank a lot, so I probably got it from both sides." One could add child psychology, wondering how much nurturing she got as the last of a young single mother's five kids. "It was like Viella raised us," Opal said of her oldest sister. In a later conversation, Kenny, her boyfriend, traced Opal's addiction to the murky realm of self-esteem: "Opal never thought she was attractive. She thought she was so dark." Mere proximity may have also played a role: she married a drug dealer. While the return to old streets and rebellions set her in high spirits—"Them was some *fun* days"—traces of loneliness showed. Three of her siblings had regular visits with their father, but Opal was left to speculate about hers, something she still did wistfully. He was so high the one time he came to visit, her mother wouldn't let her see him. "I always think, 'Would things be different if I had known my father?'"

One subject that doesn't arise in her childhood story is welfare: her mother was hardly on it. Half the time Opal was growing up, her mother worked two jobs. Like her cousin Hattie Mae, Ruthie Mae Caples was raised on the Eastland plantation, a granddaughter of Pie Eddie Caples, and she was still picking the Eastlands' cotton when she had her first child in her teens. After a detour to southern California, she joined the extended family in Chicago and found a job at a Zenith plant assembling TVs. Working her way out of the projects by the time Opal started school, Ruthie Mae settled at Fifty-ninth and Michigan—rough but not projects rough. That leaves Opal in that great class of troubled people often assumed to have been raised on welfare, who grew up with hardworking, single moms. "My Mama was at work *all* the time," Opal said.

Her siblings settled uneventfully into blue-collar lives. A brother made a navy career and another drove a truck. One sister worked as a medical clerk and the other in a bank. Yet "badness" acquired a power for Opal early on.

"I was just bad!"

"Man, we was bad!"

"We were some bad teenagers, boy."

"Bad as hell."

"Just *bad*!"

While Angie and Jewell saved their rebellions for adolescence, Opal got kicked out of sixth grade. "Running the halls, not going to my classes, talking back to the teachers . . . What didn't I do?" she said. She got caught spray painting a field house and trying to set it on fire. Corporal punishment didn't work; trips to Aunt Vidalia's brought the kind of rough-justice whippings honed in plantation days. The Jubilee CME Temple didn't work, either, though Opal liked singing in the choir. Trying to keep Opal out of trouble, her mother sent her to a public high school for girls. Opal got expelled in her sophomore year. In junior high school, she had started to drink—gin and juice, Wild Irish Rose, whatever she could find. "We used to get drunk and throw up all in the alley," Opal said. "Man, we used to trip!" She also found a protector. With a flashy wardrobe and a chassis for a chest, Robert Lee Johnson, her first boyfriend, made a fatherless girl feel safe. They stayed together throughout high school and married at City Hall two years after Opal's graduation, on her day off from Wendy's. Her mother wasn't there—she had to work—but she sponsored a reception shortly after, on Valentine's Day. Opal, at twenty-one, wore red and planned to stay with Robert Lee forever. For all her problems, Opal, unlike Angie and Jewell, entered adulthood with a diploma, a marriage, and a job.

Opal's mother got Robert Lee hired at Zenith, but third-shift work on an assembly line didn't hold his interest. One day he came home with what looked like a bag of soap chips. Crack was new to Chicago, and Opal was stunned to hear how much selling it would bring: $200 in an afternoon. "*Oowww*, we fittin' to have a *lot* of money!" she said. The ambience of the drug scene was ready-made for Opal's sense of adventure: the guns, the men, the scales, the cash, the pagers, the commotion. She and Robert Lee lived behind the Calumet Building, a high-rise filled with prospective clients, and Opal spent her nights on the back porch, drinking, watching the alleyway fights, and lending Robert Lee a hand. She had their first child at twenty-two, a girl they named Sierra. But that didn't slow them down, and neither did Robert Lee's arrests, one while Opal was still pregnant and another before Sierra turned one. With a single conviction for selling cocaine, he drew probation.

In Opal's tellings, the one letdown of married life was the discovery of Robert Lee's affairs. She was pregnant and visiting him in jail one day when she found a mysterious Tanya on his list. Stopping by McDonald's, she judged the cashier, Rene, too eager to slip him free food. Opal wasn't one to take betrayal passively. Slipping a suspicious key off his ring, she let herself into Rene's apartment and discovered Robert Lee in the living room, ironing his clothes. Opal found Rene and beat her up, and she swapped blows with Robert Lee, too, in knockdown, lamp-busting brawls. Opal doesn't scare easily, but at five foot eight, two hundred pounds, Robert Lee could scare her. Still, a decade after splitting up, she refused to get divorced. "I was in love with him," she said.

One thing that Opal couldn't understand was why people smoked cocaine. What could make them rob their families, neglect their kids, even sell their bodies to get it? "I saw how bad they looked and I said, 'Man, how could they do that?'" Robert Lee's brother had started smoking Primos, cigarettes laced with crack, and when Sierra was about a year old, he rolled one for Opal. She smoked it and felt nothing. She tried it again. "And you know what?" she said. "It didn't take no time at all to get hooked. But you don't *know* you're hooked." A few months later, Opal was pregnant with her second child and getting high constantly. "I used to think of all kinds of lies," she said, about why Robert Lee's drugs were missing. She said that his brother smoked them. Or a friend smoked them. Or she sold them and spent the money. One way to see Opal's theft of the drugs is as revenge for Robert Lee's affairs. (Enlisting his brother as a confederate gave her betrayal an incestuous edge.) Another is as pain relief: Opal had been medicating herself since her days of alleyway gin. When Robert Lee caught her rolling a Primo, she told him it was for a friend. "And he believed me!" she said. "Or he acted like he believed me—he was codependent."

But he wasn't blind. Opal smoked crack throughout the pregnancy, and shortly after the baby arrived, she burned through the rent money. Robert Lee sent her home to her mother, hoping that might set her straight. But "I was gonna do what I wanted to do, when I wanted to do it," Opal said. While the new baby, Kierra, was born free of cocaine, Opal grew so thin her relatives feared she had AIDS. Opal and Robert Lee reconciled, and soon she was pregnant again. So was Rene. Opal was back living with her mother when her third daughter, Tierra, was born in the spring of 1993. By then she was twenty-six years old, severely depressed, and she had been smoking crack for three years. That's when Jewell came home for a visit and happened to give a call.

The drug that captured Opal had ancient appeal—some cultures thought coca leaves a gift from the gods—but crack didn't make its American debut until the first half of the 1980s, appearing in Miami, Los Angeles, and New York, and exploding, by mid-decade, across the country. Crack is cocaine mixed with an additive, then cooked, cooled, and "cracked" into smokable pellets. Compared to powder, the champagne drug of the seventies, it had two advantages. Reaching the brain through the lungs, not the nose, it was much more efficient than snorting. It was also much cheaper. A gram of coke cost $100, but a crack vial could be bought for as little as $2.50. Suddenly, everyone could afford it. To say that crack makes you feel good hardly captures its appeal. People who smoke it resort to words like *euphoric* and *invincible,* describing a sensation that unites pleasure with power. "I felt I could handle anything, do anything," ran a women's magazine account. "Crack has you up and on the go," Opal said. "You on a *mission.*"

From the outside, the behavior of addicts defies explanation. In biochemical terms, the explanation is clear: the euphoria is a rush of dopamine, a neurotransmitter that tells the brain it is experiencing intense pleasure. Food and sex cause dopamine to surge, as do all drugs of abuse, from nicotine to heroin. Crack causes it to surge to mighty levels. It's a climax. A winning lottery ticket. The dunk that secures the championship ring. The problem is that the brain adjusts: it needs these new levels of dopamine just to feel normal and still more to feel high again. But chronic drug use actually causes it to get less. The body then inflicts a double whammy by activating a chemical, CRF, that suppresses the brain's sense of pleasure. With that, Mardi Gras is over, and the cops are on Bourbon Street swinging their sticks. Crashing, the crack addict grows paranoid, desperate for more dopamine. At the start, people smoke to get high, but over time they smoke to feel normal again. They smoke to "get straight."

As powerful as crack is, not everyone who tries it gets addicted. An addict develops a kind of brain disease, albeit one of her making. The drug hijacks the circuits that govern motivation and reorganizes them around the lone task of getting more crack. In the paradigmatic cocaine experiment, once a lab rat discovers that tapping a lever will deliver the drug, the tapping takes over her life. She doesn't eat, she doesn't sleep, she doesn't feed her young. She binges until she drops dead. While some people manage to stop on their own, most need the structured help a treatment program can provide. Even then about 80 percent relapse within a year, a figure that helps explain why public support for treatment programs is hard to sustain. For treatment to succeed, it literally has to change the brain.

Leaving a program, a drug user often feels a surge of well-being, a rush of health and competence for three to six months. But old cues can still trigger old cravings. Physical prompts, like a glimpse of a crack house, can do it. So can emotional ones: happiness, sadness, a song. Cues are so powerful that lab rats get a dopamine surge just by looking at their levers. When they relapse, addicts rarely relapse a little. They pick up where they left off. They binge, as if making up for lost time.

Two years after she got to Milwaukee, Opal got clean. Fleeing First Street after a four-day spree, she spent a few weeks in residential treatment before moving to the halfway house run by Pastor LeGrant. The preacher made three demands: get a job, pay the rent, and attend her storefront church. For all her earthly transgressions, Opal took pride in her spiritual roots—"I love sanctified churches"—and the

House of Faith made her feel at home. She was off to a good start in the Twelve Step world when a man at a recovery meeting captured her attention. He would have been hard to miss. If his purple pants didn't stand out, the spray of gold jewelry would. It was a look that said to Opal "sophisticated gentleman." Sitting beside her, Kenny Gross noticed Opal, too, noticed her short white shorts. Watching him eye her, another Twelve Stepper leaned over and warned, "Those shorts are going to get you in trouble." One rule of recovery, an emotionally fragile process, is to avoid the roller-coaster of romance for a year. And there was another reason for Opal to be wary. "He used to be one of the baddest pimps in Milwaukee!" her housemate said. But the image of Kenny in fur coats and feathered hats only piqued Opal's interest. As soon as she got an overnight pass, she took him to the Budgetel. "It was magic from then on," she said.

Kenny was a decade older than Opal and had been clean for three years. Still, even at thirty-eight, he radiated his old street vibes. He had a quick temper and a face that seemed angry even when he smiled, which wasn't often. He seldom kept a job for more than a few months, and with an aggressive sideline peddling rings and chains, he drew snickers from Opal's friends. Like Opal, he was raised by a working single mother, and like Opal he was drawn to the streets—nearly killing himself on a diet of heroin, coke, and pills. He got sober at the urging of a cousin dying of AIDS, and about sobriety he was deathly earnest. He wore his clean date on his NA medallion and defined his life's purpose as mentoring younger addicts. As Kenny once (inadvertently) put it, having once been a pimp, he was determined to become a "seductive member of society." Even at the Budgetel, all he wanted to talk about was The Program. "You on a *date*, nigger!" Opal said. "I don't wanna hear about no program!"

Opal was smitten. With the First Street family scattered about, she invited everyone to meet him at a sobriety picnic. Kenny arrived with a suit and Bible, offering temperance lectures. Lucky and Robert smuggled in beer and dubbed him "Preacher Man." Opal delivered an ultimatum: if Kenny wanted to keep seeing her, they had to move in together. Their first six months passed peacefully. He got a job as a short-order cook. She had welfare and some short-lived jobs. The girls came home from a stay at Jewell's—Sierra was six, Kierra, four, and

Tierra, two—and Opal enrolled in a nurturing program to improve her parenting skills. Kenny, seasoned at spotting cons, judged her to be sincere. "Her kids are her heart," he thought. They even talked of getting married someday.

Still, there were warning signs. Opal's rush toward romance was one, itself a form of addictive behavior. Her arrest for ripping off Target was another. One of the Twelve Steps requires people to take a "fearless moral inventory" of themselves, which is hard to do during a shoplifting scheme. Opal left the courtroom as her case was called—"I wasn't fittin' to admit I was guilty, even though I was"—which left her walking around with a warrant out for her arrest. Mindful of cues, Narcotics Anonymous tells addicts to avoid the "people, places, and things" they associate with getting high. But Opal wasn't about to avoid Angie and Jewell, even though there was usually a party nearby. She skipped NA meetings. She had a beer. Then, Kenny's special gold chain disappeared, the one with the abstinence medal. It took him a week to calm down, but when he did she told him what he already knew. She sold the chain, but not the medallion; no drug dealer wanted that. Opal's relapse, in the spring of 1996, occurred somewhere around the sixth month, toward the outer edge of what the statistics predict.

Kenny's sense of betrayal came in a double dose; his previous girlfriend had relapsed, too, and the last thing he wanted was another doomed affair. But he had slid back on his own first try. Hesitantly, he stayed, and Opal appeared to get clean, though he could never be sure. Kenny pushed her to get a job, and so for the first time did welfare. Opal made just enough effort to keep them both at bay. Jason Turner had just launched Pay for Performance, but by acknowledging her addiction, Opal managed to avoid a work assignment. Instead, she was sent to a brief outpatient program and told to look for a job on her own. It wouldn't have taken much of a sleuth to suspect she was stringing things along. In the logs she turned in over the next three months, she claimed she applied for 240 jobs, or about one every three hours, including six at the same Taco Bell, all without an offer. ("They don't check—come on.") Eventually she went back to the nurturing class and found a job at McDonald's, where she got fired for eating an apple pie and calling her boss "a fag." Someone at the nurturing program then helped her find the hospital job—with a path to full-time work at $10 an hour. However circuitous her path, Opal made her way into the best-paying job of her life.

She spent her first paycheck on crack. "I had been thinking about it a long time," she said. "I had wanted to do it so bad." Every addict's relapse is painful, but Opal's carried a special mix of guilt and defiance, since living with Kenny amounted to having a drug counselor at her side. Kenny's whole world was The Program—the nightly meetings, the sobriety club, the Twelve Steps as Ten Commandments. Kenny was drawn to the program's authority; Opal was programmed to defy it. "Why can't she just *get* it?" he would wonder. "Why don't you leave me?" she would say. She would binge. He would explode. She would cry and promise to quit. Despite himself, a part of him always believed her. He cheated on her; she caught him; they fought. When peace had been made, Opal would sometimes explain her thinking. "Opal looked at it like this," Kenny said. "If there's food, the rent's paid, kids took care of—she owed herself to get high." She told him—she told herself—she could handle it.

By the summer of 1997, Opal's brinksmanship with welfare was skating toward a new brink. She had slid past the JOBS program (with its weak penalties) and survived Pay for Performance (with luck), but the program the state was about to unveil, Wisconsin Works, called itself loophole free. The first thing that was radical about W-2 was its theory of "universal engagement": *everyone* was supposed to join in. The sick, the addicted, mothers with young kids—everyone was supposed to do something if they wanted a check. The second radical notion involved what they were supposed to do: work. Not just look for work or prepare for work, but spend at least part of the week in some sort of community service job. Most states avoided community service jobs, which were expensive, difficult to administer, and in the small-scale experiments of the past had shown a poor record of leading to private employment. In betting on them, Wisconsin hoped to achieve at least three things. One was diversion: forced to work for welfare, those with other options would leave. Another was acculturation: participants would learn the so-called soft skills, like grooming and punctuality. And a third was reciprocity: rather than getting something for nothing, the poor would give something back. The state promised to create the jobs by the tens of thousands.

If W-2 seemed unusually tough, it also seemed unusually generous. While the jobs would form the core of a "simulated workweek," they were supposed to be tailored to each recipient's needs. Other services could be layered on, like drug treatment or GED classes. And Wisconsin promised child care and health insurance, not only to families in W-2 but to a wider group of the working poor. Another distinctive element of W-2 lay in its administration: much of it would be privatized, with profit-seeking corporations invited to join nonprofits in submitting bids, in what the state called an effort to improve efficiency. Certainly there was much to worry about. Could everyone really work? Would the jobs prove useful, to recipients and society? Would the most vulnerable be driven from the rolls, like the miserable Amber Peck? Had the state gone too far in eliminating training—consigning people to a dead-end future of impossibly low wages? Still, by accompanying the rhetoric of work with the girders to support it—child care, health care, and the semblance of a last-resort job—Wisconsin's plan for "ending welfare" displayed a rare seriousness. To his credit, Thompson seemingly had created a program as big as his boasts.

And Opal seemed a good window through which to observe it. Though I didn't know she was using drugs as I watched her spoof the job-search class, I found her compellingly bilingual, fluent in the language of the streets and of the working-woman's world a notch above. With her disarming mix of intelligence and self-deprecation ("I *like* that welfare check"), she seemed just the kind of woman whose fortunes could swing either way. I included her in a preview of W-2 I wrote for *The New York Times Magazine.* Opal and the girls caught a bus downtown to a photo shoot, and a few weeks later a memorable cover appeared. In the back stood the serious, dark-suited men who had launched the welfare revolution, Tommy Thompson and Jason Turner. Across the front in pink shirts skipped Opal's girls, as if to a promising future. In the middle sat Opal, wearing a janitor's uniform, a finger wave from Jewell, and an enigmatic smile. Opal, of all people, was the W-2 poster child. "Has a job, but can she keep it?" the cover line asked.

TWELVE

Half a Safety Net:
The United States, 1997–2003

As Opal swabbed hospital floors and slid back toward addiction, the new American safety net was appearing, one state at a time. Politically, the battle had been fought with glib slogans about trusting states over "arrogant federal bureaucrats." But the challenge at hand was immense. On one side stood 4.5 million poor single mothers with an unknowable mix of problems. Nine out of ten said they were jobless; nearly half had preschool kids; most got little (if any) help from their children's fathers; and about half lacked a high school diploma. Who could say how many like Opal were secretly smoking cocaine? On the other side were fifty state bureaucracies whose historical line of work had been limited to mailing them checks. They were operating in a politically charged atmosphere, with a low-paid, undertrained staff and substantial financial risks; if caseloads went up, they had billions to lose. The optimistic scenario was that states would undergo a vast "mission change," converting the old check-writing offices into job-placement machines. Federal law did allow another option: just kick people off the rolls.

Texas set some time limits as short as a year. Michigan set no time limits at all, pledging to use state funds for families who exhausted their federal aid. Oregon invested in casework, Rhode Island in child care. Mississippi placed its faith in the Lord, with Governor Kirk Fordice asking churches to pick up the charity load. "God, not government, will be the savior of welfare recipients," he said. While I started with doubts about state control, the effort brought much to admire. After decades in the check-writing trade, the average office was talking up jobs and however fumbling its ways—"that thing with cows, gets real deep"—moving people into them. Services expanded, especially child care, and for a surprising number of people, like Angie and Jewell, a small push or pull was all it took. At the same time, just as feared, many families got lost in the chaos—dropped from the rolls whether God proved their savior or not. And that's not to mention the bigger question framing the postwelfare years: how far would a low-wage job go in changing a poor family's life? Yet with caseloads plunging everywhere, the law had barely taken effect before it was crowned with claims of success. "The debate is over," Clinton said a year after signing the bill. "We know now that welfare reform works!" At that point, the average state program was about six months old. From the White House down, one trait most welfare abolishers shared was a weakness for their own PR.

For all its surface variety, the focus of the new system could be summarized in a word: work. The states pushed poor women to find it faster, keep it longer, and look for it as a condition of aid. Virtually every state regarded an entry-level job as preferable to the education and training efforts they had run in the past. And recipients who broke the rules risked big penalties, often the loss of all cash aid. Despite all the congressional talk of shoring up the two-parent family, no state made a serious attempt to reduce births to single mothers—a root cause of welfare but a socially charged one, and a problem to which there was no obvious solution. When word leaked that aides to New York City mayor Rudolph Giuliani planned "family-strengthening activities," the soon-to-be-divorced leader not only dropped the idea but publicly denounced it. Politicians like to do what they know how to do, and they more or less knew how to run job-search programs. From Harlem to Watts, waiting-room posters sounded a similar call: "Life works if you work first."

About three-quarters of the states made applicants do something before coming on the rolls, a process Jason Turner called "securing the front door." In some places, the requirement involved nothing more than sitting through a single orientation, though even that kept some people away. In New York City, where Turner became welfare commissioner, a required job search dragged on for four weeks, diverting about half of those who would have applied. With one missed

dis·heart·end

day in a four-week program, a New York City applicant could be
forced to start all over. One Harlem manager said the highlight of her
career came the day she reopened the office as a "job center" that required applicants to complete a search for work. "Half the people
said, *'Job center?* I didn't come for no job center!' This man said, 'No,
no! *Ah-plee-ca-cion! Ah-plee-ca-cion!* No job, no job!'" She laughed
so hard at the memory of her scattering clients she could barely finish
the story. "I could not believe that those two little words—*job
center*—could clear the area."

There's no doubt the hassles drove off people who had other ways
to get by. But they also drove off people who needed help. The diversion effort in New York City involved not only the mandatory job
search but aggressive attempts by front-line workers to verbally dissuade people from applying. In what a federal judge called a "culture
of improper deterrence," many refused to even distribute applications during an aid-seeker's first visit to the office. "No matter how you
phrase it," explained the newsletter of a Queens welfare office, "the
goal . . . is the same: redirect the participant to another source." One
consequence, in New York and beyond, was that eligible families
stopped applying for other programs, such as Medicaid and food
stamps, which were supposed to be part of the remaining safety net—
at a cost of skipped meals and untreated disease. Nationwide, about
two-thirds of the adults who left welfare lost Medicaid, even as the
number of uninsured grew. Among children eligible for food stamps,
the proportion of those who actually received them fell by about 20
percent. Scared, angry, or simply confused, all kinds of families
stopped thinking of the welfare office as a place to get help.

For those who made it onto the rolls, states had to place a rising
share in specified "work activities." A dozen activities qualified, from
short-term training to sweeping the streets. By far the most common
was the job-search class, which Riverside, California, among other
sites, had shown the quickest and most cost-effective way of moving
people off the rolls. Some classes left recipients to search on their
own; others armed them with résumés, leads, and donated suits.
Their quality ran from mediocre to downright awful. I once sat
through a class in Riverside, California, at the peak of its job-

placement fame. "Hopefully we can get you employed as soon as possible," the instructor began. "I shouldn't say hopefully. . . . I keep losing my train of thought." Down the hall, the recipients took upbeat, alliterative names—Kind Kathy, Willing Wanda, Dependable Dave. Then they gave themselves a round of applause and turned to a video that declared, "The employed lifestyle is better!"

There was no shortage of silliness involved. But among the early lessons was that that even silliness worked: requiring people to do *anything* was usually better than leaving them to do nothing. For Acerbic Angie or Jazzy Jewell, the hassle was a goad to make better plans. For some others, any activity offered a respite from lives stunted by terrible isolation. In Milwaukee, I spent two weeks at the YWCA's "Academy of Excellence," where one woman was so timid as it began she could barely speak her name. Another flamboyantly announced, "Ain't no such thing as bad sex, y'all!" then fled in tears when the talk turned to violent boyfriends. A certain esprit did evolve, even in such a care-worn group. The women wore mortarboards at their graduation, and some brought their kids to watch them collect the only diploma they might get.

While job-search class might not seem tough, the penalties for skipping it were. In nearly three-quarters of the states, recipients who missed an assignment could lose their whole check, a penalty known as a "full-family sanction." As a weapon of welfare reduction, time limits got much more attention, in part because the concept was easier to understand. But sanctions had a much bigger effect. By 1999, sanctions had eliminated a half-million families from the rolls—about six times the number cut off by time limits. Because of sanctions, between a quarter and a half of those enrolled in the typical program wound up losing all or part of their check.

At times, the tough penalties were all for the best. In Oregon I met a methamphetamine addict who said losing her check helped save her life. "That was part of the reason I went into treatment," Lori Furlow said. With weaker sanctions, New York found it harder to persuade troubled clients to get help. About a third of New York City's huge caseload was in the penalty process at any given time, and officials there griped about the "happily sanctioned"; able to ignore the work *factic*

rules and still collect three-quarters of their cash and food stamps, some people did just that. But if weak penalties hurt some clients, so did strong ones—that's the dilemma of sanction policy. The goal should be to lure people in, not to drive them away. There was so much confusion in the system, however, many people who lost their checks didn't even know what they were supposed to be doing. Taking an in-depth look at one hundred sanctioned families, Utah found that about half had problems their caseworkers hadn't realized: illnesses, chronically sick kids, boyfriends who beat them if they left the house. "We were sanctioning people we shouldn't have been sanctioning," said Bill Biggs, the official in charge. It's natural to think that the plunging rolls followed a rational order, starting with the easy cases and proceeding to the hard ones. In truth, the process of "ending welfare" played out like a freak storm, hitting here and missing there. The sick, the addicted, the depressed and confused—all joined the employable and the secretly employed in a mass flight from the rolls.

For those unwilling or unable to hold jobs, the rules could be unforgiving. But the new system also brought needy workers new support, with child care, tax credits, and health insurance among the main examples. Overall spending on poor families *grew* in the postwelfare years, even as its focus shifted from nonworkers to the working poor. The expansion of the earned income tax credit is the obvious case in point. By the end of the decade, it offered workers up to $3,900 a year, a sum that went far in smoothing the transition from the rolls. For a typical woman leaving welfare, that turned a job that paid $6.50 an hour into one worth $8.35. Sixteen states, including Wisconsin, layered their own credits on top of the federal one. Not coincidentally, two days before he signed the welfare bill, Clinton also signed a law that raised the minimum wage (to a still-paltry $5.15)—another nod toward the notion that "people who work, shouldn't be poor."

There were other supports for new workers. The number of children in subsidized child care doubled in just three years. By the end of the decade, thirty-three states spent more on child care than they did on welfare checks. Although there were no formal guarantees, in practice everyone leaving welfare for work qualified for at least a year. In addition, all states expanded child-care programs for the broader population of low-income workers (not just those on the welfare rolls). In some states, the programs were modest and waiting lists long. Still, in general, child-care shortages kept fewer people from working than initially feared. Nearly all states loosened the asset rules that had made it hard for recipients to own reliable cars; some helped workers buy them. Nearly every state let recipients who found jobs keep more of their welfare checks during a transition (through something called an "earnings disregard"). The states also got much better at collecting child support, more than doubling the percentage of the cases in which the absent fathers paid. Even then, only about half the women leaving the rolls collected anything, but those who did averaged about $2,000 a year.

The health insurance story was less encouraging. Despite Clinton's hopes of a medical safety net, as Angie left welfare in 1996 about *half* the women streaming off the rolls wound up uninsured, as did nearly 30 percent of their kids. Medicaid's tight eligibility rules were part of the problem, but so was the unwelcoming bureaucracy; many families didn't get enrolled even when they qualified. In 1997, Congress took a step in the right direction by creating the State Children's Health Insurance Program, which spends about $4 billion a year to insure the children of needy workers. By the end of the decade, most states covered children up to twice the poverty line, meaning a family of three stayed eligible as its income approached $28,000. But adults remained out of luck, typically losing their Medicaid eligibility before their earnings reached $10,000. Even at the end of the decade, 37 percent of the adults leaving welfare had no health insurance. It's unconscionable that by staying on welfare, Opal could see a doctor for free while Angie and Jewell each lost coverage and went without needed care.

Nonetheless, despite its holes, the rise of a "work-based safety net" did ease the transition off welfare. A study by David Ellwood makes the point: in the mid-1980s, a typical mother of two leaving welfare for a minimum-wage job would have come out just $2,000 ahead, even with only modest work expenses, and the whole family would have lost health insurance. By the late 1990s, that same woman would have gained $7,000 and her kids could get Medicaid. As welfare (greatly) increased its hassles, work (modestly) increased its rewards.

What happened next astonished everyone. The welfare rolls collapsed. They collapsed in Boston and they collapsed in Phoenix. They collapsed in New York City. They fell fastest in states like Wisconsin and Florida, which made aggressive moves. But they also gave way in Texas and Illinois, which showed little bureaucratic zeal. They plunged where the economy boomed, and they plunged in stretches of the poverty belt, from New Mexico to West Virginia. Historically, the rolls had never fallen more than 8 percent in a year. By the time they leveled off in 2001, they had fallen for seven straight years by a total of 63 percent. Seven states cut the rolls by more than three-quarters. In Wisconsin, a half-dozen counties at some point in the year had a W-2 caseload of *zero*. Three million families—more than 9 million people—left the rolls nationwide.

Explaining what caused the rolls to vanish is harder than it seems. Certainly, the economy helped. Nationally, the unemployment rate fell to 4.0 percent, its lowest level in thirty years. Shorthanded employers who would have once shunned recipients all but begged them to apply. But previous booms hadn't cut the rolls. And the correlation between caseloads and state unemployment is faint at best. One study found that states with more unemployment had *greater* caseload declines, perhaps because they passed tougher laws. The tax-credit expansion also helped reduce welfare: the more work pays, the more people work. But the District of Columbia, with one of the largest local credits, had some of the smallest caseload declines. The auspicious economics surround the story like good weather—necessary, perhaps, for cutting the rolls but not sufficient.

Two prominent economists with contrasting politics—Rebecca M. Blank and June E. O'Neill—separately estimated that policy changes did three times as much to cut the rolls as the economy did. But which policy changes? In general, the places with the toughest sanctions had the steepest declines. But sanctions were tough in Tennessee, moderate in Oregon, and weak in Arkansas, and each cut its rolls similarly. Time limits may have encouraged families to leave welfare and bank their remaining time. But the rolls fell more in Michigan, with no time limits, than in Texas, Virginia, and Connecticut, with short ones. In general, the rolls fell faster under Republicans than Democrats. But they fell nearly as much in two of the most liberal states (California and Vermont) as they did in two conservative ones (Arizona and Tennessee).

Clearly something happened that neither economics nor policy fully explains. Rebecca Blank found that *half* of the caseload declines came from something her model couldn't detect. Part of what the era brought was a sudden cultural change, what social scientists sometimes call "message effects." From the TV news to waiting-room posters came the same strident message: "Get off the rolls!" In Creek County, Oklahoma, the rolls fell 30 percent even as the legislature was still debating the law, a decline officials largely attributed to the mere rumors of what was coming. In its mysteriously powerful convergence of events, the late 1990s can be thought of as a bookend to the 1960s. One era, branding welfare a right, sent the rolls to sudden highs; the other, deeming welfare wrong, shrank them equally fast.

The unexpected declines brought unintended effects. White families left welfare faster than blacks, and blacks left faster than Hispanics, who consequently composed a growing share of the rolls. The notion that most recipients are white, long misleading, grew plainly untrue. By the end of the decade, blacks and Hispanics outnumbered whites by a ratio of two to one. (The rolls were 39 percent black, 25 percent Hispanic, and 31 percent white.) As race changed, so did place: the caseload grew even more concentrated in big cities. In Wisconsin, where the trend was extreme, 85 percent of recipients lived in Milwaukee. Welfare, that is, increasingly became what most voters already assumed—a program for urban minorities.

At the same time, falling caseloads brought one problem that states welcomed: it left them rolling in dough. States literally had more money than they knew how to spend. The irony here should not be missed. The authors of the law set out to slash welfare budgets. Instead, by freezing federal payments at historic highs while caseloads fell, ardent conservatives achieved something that even liberals hadn't dared to propose: a huge rise in per capita welfare spending. Over six years, states collected $59 billion more than they could have under the previous system, when falling caseloads brought reduced federal dollars. By 1998, Wisconsin collected $22,000 for every family left on the rolls. Having promised to do more with less, the governors wound up with more—much more—than anyone had imagined.

Antipoverty windfalls are unheard of. Since the money came with few constraints, states had nearly unlimited reach to improve poor people's lives—not just those on the rolls but the broader working poor. They could have subsidized rents for needy workers or supplemented their wages. They could have helped entry-level workers like Angie and Jewell train for better jobs. The great expansion of child care largely stemmed from the welfare windfall. But in a perfectly legal maneuver, states also used billions just to sustain programs they had previously financed themselves. That freed funds for other uses but did nothing for the poor. Roads got paved, bridges painted, and taxes cut—all on the federal welfare nickel. In the first few years alone, New York diverted $1 billion into budget swaps. Wisconsin channeled $100 million into a property-tax cut. Most states tried to mask such schemes, but Minnesota spelled it out in the budget: "Replace state spending with federal dollars." In some states, huge sums simply gathered dust as officials bickered or dithered. Two years into the new welfare age, Wyoming had failed to spend 91 percent of its federal money. In New Mexico, the nation's poorest state, a third of the federal money went unspent as a defiant Republican governor, Gary E. Johnson, refused to implement a plan passed by Democratic legislators. He relented only after the state supreme court found him in contempt. But by then, he had already cut the rolls in half, mostly through eligibility cuts. With nearly $70 million of its welfare money unspent, New Mexico still had no job-placement agencies in counties where unemployment ran as high as 33 percent.

"What about Mississippi?" the skeptics had asked, when Congress insisted it could trust the states. Early in the new welfare age, I made a trip to the Delta, where Mack Caples, on the far side of eighty, still puttered in the Eastland fields. Nearby, things were proceeding about as feared: unemployment rates hit double digits for two hundred miles around, but the state was still purging the rolls. In Washington

County, where caseloads had fallen more than 30 percent, twice as many families had been sanctioned off the rolls as placed in jobs. Most of the jobs that did exist were distant or unappealing. The de facto capital of the Delta is Greenville, where twenty-seven recipients had moved from welfare to work in the month before I arrived. Of them, ten were packed off to a catfish plant an hour away. They left town at dawn on a company bus and spent their days severing fish heads in a jungle of conveyor belts and saws. The job paid the minimum wage, and annual turnover ran 300 percent. "You work in the cold, you work in the wet—and of course you're around guts," the manager, Donald Taylor, observed pleasantly. He praised the state for barring aid to anyone who quit. "If they can go back to Uncle Sam, you can't keep them in the plant."

A few years later, a study in the *American Journal of Political Science* tried to quantify the factors that shape state policy. The most important was race: the more blacks on the rolls, the tougher a state chose to be. That would come as no surprise in Mississippi, where Governor Fordice wore a tie with a Confederate flag to a meeting on minority set-asides. The racial rub was obvious in the Delta, where with few exceptions employers were white and welfare families black. Lured by a state subsidy, Kevin Cunningham, a gregarious Greenville insurance agent, hired a receptionist off the rolls. She was a well-spoken woman who played piano at her church, but he worried her friends might decide, "She knows where the cash drawer is." He warned her, as she started work, that "business language isn't Ebonics."

Hard luck stories were everywhere. Patricia Watson quit the catfish plant after coming home from work to find her six-year-old daughter missing and her teenage babysitter not even aware that the child was gone; for quitting, Watson was barred from all state aid. Curley Barron had rescued her nephews from foster care and was raising them with the help of a welfare check. But she gave them back when the state ordered her to stop caring for her disabled mother and join a work program. "It doesn't make any sense," she said. "The kids were a ward of the state—they weren't mine." Even by Delta standards, things were rough in Glendora, which made a cameo appearance in civil rights history as the place where Emmett Till was beaten before being dumped in the Tallahatchie River. All but three of its eighty-eight households had once gotten public aid. After being dropped from the rolls, a mother of four named Carrie Ann Bridges took a night job at a poultry plant seventy miles away. Coming home after midnight, she fell asleep and drove into a ditch, killing herself and her aunt.

The Delta would challenge any welfare plan. Two time zones away, Oregon presented a contrasting view of state autonomy. Of all the states, it probably worked hardest to help women like Opal, the so-called hard to serve. In Oregon City, a blue-collar suburb of Portland, caseworkers gave them a different name—"drawer people"—since under the old system, that's where their files had resided. With the rolls already cut in half, about three-quarters of those left on welfare had mental health problems. Half acknowledged drug or alcohol abuse, and 30 percent had criminal histories. Of the sixteen recipients I met in Oregon, eleven described incidents of childhood sexual abuse, a problem that gets no attention in the welfare literature but correlates with any number of problems that make it hard to keep a job. Women who were molested as children are more likely to abuse alcohol or drugs, suffer from depression, or become victims of domestic violence. In my conversations with welfare recipients over the years, talk of childhood molestation has arisen with eerie regularity. "I don't call it anything special," one Oregon woman told me, "because it seems like it happens to everybody."

While Oregon, like most places, pushed recipients to take entry-level jobs, it also offered a long list of services for those who didn't soon get one. With the caseload 80 percent white, it was the rare state where welfare hadn't figured in politics, and state spending was unusually high. Caseworkers could send addicts to treatment or depressed women to mental health clinics. They had job-placement counselors fluent in Russian and Vietnamese. Oregon made a special commitment to drug treatment, financing a residential program with a tax on beer and wine. Oregon had its problems, too. A system that emphasizes caseworkers' discretion rises and falls on their talents, which even in Oregon were often mediocre. Some applicants were just too troubled to find their way on the rolls, especially since they had to do a month of job search first. I met an indigent mother who was turned away even though her boyfriend had just beaten her, her landlord was evicting her, and she was scheduled for major surgery. She was told she couldn't get a check until she spent a month looking for a job.

Nevertheless, up and down the I-5 corridor, it was possible to glimpse what conscientious casework could achieve. There were few better examples than that of Rita Davis, who launched an earnest, vexed search for work after her husband left her. Sexually abused by her father in her teens, she had spent her adult life struggling with anxiety. She read at the seventh-grade level. And she weighed 325 pounds, one reason she was sent away jobless by a dozen temp agencies. Unremittingly earnest, she struggled to tell her story through deep, steadying breaths. "I'd call up on the phone and they'd say, 'Oh, you sound like the perfect person,'" she said. "Then they take one look at me and they blow it off." After months of rejection, she met a caseworker who spotted her hidden talent for numbers and persuaded an accounting agency to give her a job, with the state temporarily subsidizing her wage. That's when a new problem arose. Body odor. "I don't know what it is," Davis said. "I take a shower every day." Her doctor didn't know either. Her boss called the welfare office and complained that it was driving clients away. The caseworker rushed over with two sacks of deodorant and shampoo, and Davis experimented until something worked. Soon she won a promotion, from receptionist to bookkeeper. Poor, obese, abandoned, and abused, she had been relegated to a kind of nonexistence until—of all things—a welfare program came to her rescue. "I love this job," she said. "Somebody is able to look past my size and see me."

What happened with Rita Davis wasn't unique; every program, even Mississippi's, produced some inspired casework. In the new welfare age, someone really looking for help was much more likely to find it. Yet for all the talk about work requirements, the system harbored a strange little secret: many of the people left on the rolls weren't doing very much. The thought is sufficiently counterintuitive that it bears some explanation. After all, the new system was constantly called tough, and compared to the old one it was. But it was toughest in the application stage and during the first few months, when recipients risked losing their checks if they skipped the ubiquitous job-search class. After that, they could still be kicked off for failing to complete an assignment. But many people didn't have assignments, at least not consistent ones. When job-search class didn't lead to a job, it often led nowhere at all.

Seemingly the law prohibited this, by requiring states to place half their recipients in work activities. But the "caseload-reduction credit"—those frequent flier points for bureaucrats—cut the rate, point for point, for virtually every downtick in the rolls. By 2002, the rolls had fallen so far (60 percent) that twenty states could meet the work rate without putting a single recipient to work. Only ten states had to meet a work goal of 10 percent or more. In other words, to comply with the law, most states had to do . . . nothing.

Just how much they actually did became a topic of sharp dispute. Federal reports showed that in 2002 states enrolled a third of their caseload in eligible work activities. But the majority were recipients with regular jobs who collected some transitional welfare under the loosened earnings rules. Of the remaining caseload—in a sense, the core caseload—only 15 percent were participating in eligible welfare-to-work activities. Yet because of the caseload-reduction credit, every state met its participation requirement every year. The states argue that the federal numbers are misleading because they omit activities—like drug treatment or part-time work—that don't count toward the official rates. The states did their own survey and reported that 61 percent of recipients had some sort of assignment. But if there was underreporting in the federal numbers, there was overreporting, too; not everyone on the roster of a job-search class was actually looking for a job. In an odd inversion of welfare politics, the conservatives who had pushed the states-rights revolution began accusing the states of laxness, while liberals, fearful of onerous new rules, defended the states' judgment and skill. The truth is that no one really knows how much the average recipient was doing. But if my own travels were any indication, the answer was often "not much."

Why? Certainly the states had the funds. But keeping recipients productively engaged is hard work—much harder than it sounds. It's not as if women like Opal were lining up for help. You had to motivate people who didn't want to be motivated. You had to tailor programs to daunting needs. You had to penalize those who failed to comply, promptly and fairly. And you had to do it with a staff that was typically low-paid and poorly trained. Every state did some of this hard, creative work, more than in the past. But few sustained it on a wide scale. Nor did they have to. The mixture of hassle and help they offered was enough to cut the rolls. And cutting the rolls brought the sheen of success. It's easy to make a churlish complaint about people getting something for nothing. But the real concern is for the recipients themselves: hundreds of thousands of the most troubled families were left to idle on the rolls. That's especially worrisome in an age of time limits, when after five years, or in some places less, they could just be given the boot. With a booming economy, piles of cash, and vanishing caseloads, states had an unprecedented chance to help those left behind. What they managed to construct was at best half a safety net.

THIRTEEN

W-2 Buys the Crack:
Milwaukee, 1998

Opal blew it. And in her case so did W-2. Having starred on the cover of *The New York Times Magazine*, she was fired by the time the issue hit the stands. It's not clear whether a binge caused the firing, but the firing, in the summer of 1997, gave way to more binges. "I *wanted* to go get high—I did," she said. "I was so scared to come home and face Kenny that I stayed gone for a day and a half." When she got back, Kenny said the police had taken the kids—though really he had left them with Jewell—and as Opal tried to leave for the police station, they started to fight. Kenny had his own demons raging. He demanded that Opal take him to confront the drug dealer, a stunt that could get someone shot. A few weeks later, she binged again. This time Kenny just acted hurt. "If you love me and the kids, why would you do that?" he asked. It was a question with no rational answer, only a chemical one.

Opal had lost lots of jobs, but none as promising as the one cleaning the hospital lab, with its path to a double-digit wage. In a three-page letter to her boss's boss, she pleaded for another chance. "I really, truly love my jobs," she wrote. "The choices I make now will be positive and aim at proving to myself and others that I am a strong bla"—she crossed out "black"—"woman who've had ups and downs in my life and is willing to live my Life to the fullest." The hospital manager didn't bother to read it. The timing seemed ominous. She was fired a month before the launch of W-2; in theory, cash welfare was finished. The only way anyone could get a check now was by working a community-service job, an option that Opal had ruled out. ("I don't work for free!") Opal had outlasted Angie and Jewell, but even she felt certain that her luck had come to an end. "I know I won't get no more cash from them."

Then she did. Opal's caseworker at the Opportunities Industrialization Center was Darlene Haines, the same woman Opal had dazzled in class with her spoof of the job interview. Haines was a blustery, gold-toothed woman with a hard-luck past, quick to boast of her savvy. "I don't play when it comes to gettin' people jobs," she said. Some of her clients called her a "hood rat," a ghetto woman putting on airs. But Opal liked her. Haines kept the cover of *The New York Times Magazine* on her wall—she was in the picture, too—and the sight of Opal posed with the governor made other clients gripe. "She's out there doing drugs," one said. With a few calls, Haines discovered that Opal's problems included a warrant for her arrest. Soon after, Opal showed up at OIC with an agitated look and a notice saying her benefits were slated to end. Haines took her into a private room. "They're goin' round saying you're using," she said. "They *who*?" Opal answered. Then she began to cry and admitted that she had been smoking cocaine.

This, in W-2 theory, was the perfect exchange. Among Jason Turner's complaints about the old welfare system was that it let recipients hide their real problems. He had talked of "thrusting them into the public square," where their needs could be addressed. With her tearful confession, Opal was accordingly thrust. But from there, theory and practice diverged in the hands of Darlene Haines. W-2 pictured addicts like Opal combining a community-service job with a drug-treatment program. Instead, Haines did the one thing the program expressly forbid: she simply sent Opal a check. She said she feared that if she cut Opal off, the kids would suffer. ("Women she likes, she gives them money," one of her coworkers complained.) A few months later, Haines herself was gone from OIC. She went on to jobs at rival agencies, Goodwill and Maximus, until her conviction for check forgery; she had a temp job at a bank where she altered a check and tried to cash it as though it was made out to her. Then Haines moved to the other side of the desk, as a W-2 client herself.

I saw Opal a few days after her encounter with Haines. Family life was in a fragile state. She was drinking beer and chain-smoking Newports, and she said she had been reading the Bible to ward off the urge to get high. With Opal spending her money on drugs, Kenny had pawned his jewelry to pay the rent, and the power company had shut off the lights. Despite her binges and depression, Opal had found a job in a factory that made diaper wipes—something she hadn't told Haines—and along with welfare she had an unemployment check: she was *triple*-dipping. "Drug addicts are some of the smartest people in the world," she said, more in sadness more than in pride. " 'Cause we're able—I'm not gonna say me—to manipulate, to get whatever they want."

Two months later, when I saw her in January 1998, Opal was a different person. "I'm in better spirits—can you tell?" she said. She said she had stopped getting high. Kenny had given her a special Christmas present, a green Tommy Hilfiger coat, and she wore it with schoolgirl pride. Sierra, Kierra, and Tierra seemed better, too. Unprompted by Opal, they sat down to dinner and launched into a prayer. To make it to the factory, Opal had to get up at 5:00 a.m. and catch two buses across town. But she talked about packaging diaper wipes as though she'd found her calling. By now she had reported the job, so her W-2 benefits were about to end: her next check would be her last. She had just gone to H&R Block, and with a big check for tax credits coming, she had plans to refurnish the apartment. Opal, the unlikely poster child for welfare reform, was sounding like one. "Now I *have* to work," she said. "I'm better off."

Opal quit two weeks later, on her thirty-first birthday. With $4,000 of tax money in hand, a sunrise bus to an assembly line plant no longer held its allure. She decorated the apartment just as she had planned, with a green-striped sofa, matching love seats, and a new dining room set. It all wound up in the drug dealers' hands, with everything she owned. The most remarkable thing about Opal's collapse was its sheer velocity. It took about thirty days.

The first thing Kenny noticed was the air freshener. Then Opal started to chain-smoke again. They were supposed to be living in a drug-free building—the manager could demand a urine test—but there were people getting high on every floor. A neighbor had a drug-

dealing son, so Opal no longer had to catch the bus to see Andrea, the
crack-house proprietor she had met in jail. She could buy drugs down
the hall. Kenny realized Opal had stopped wearing the Tommy Hilfiger coat. She told him she had lent it to Jewell, but he saw it on the
drug dealer's back. "I was gonna *kill* him, not just shoot him," he said.
"Not over the coat, over the fact that he was killing her and wouldn't
care." A few weeks after Opal quit her job, Kenny went to Chicago for
a sobriety convention and came home a few hours early. He found
Opal as he'd never seen her, on the bed unable to speak. She had sold
a television and a VCR and had another wrapped up to go. "She was
looking crazy—it was like the devil," he said. Opal was so high, she
later said, she felt like she was having an out-of-body experience, like
she was watching a stranger's dream. She could hear Kenny storming
around, demanding to know where she had sold their stuff. High as
she was, she knew better than to say. Someone could get killed.

Though Kenny had five sober years behind him, no one's recovery
is secure; if The Program had taught him anything, it should have
taught him that. Having once put women on the street, he now found
himself babysitting for a woman on the lam. He lost his job, which was
nothing new. But blaming Opal was a more alarming sign, since it vi-
olated the ethic of personal responsibility at The Program's core. Out
of work, out of money, and low on self-respect, Kenny walked into a
liquor store and bought a miniature Courvoisier. It was his signature
drink in his days as a pimp, and just staring at it made him stir. He
could smell it. And taste it. He could feel its glow. The liquor store was
next to a music shop, and Kenny used the rest of his money to buy a
Gospel tape. He put the bottle on his dash and sat in the lot, letting
the music play. *Should I?* he asked.

Most addicts who buy a bottle find a way to say yes. Kenny's first effort at sobriety had ended that way: six months clean, one sneaked
drink, and he was back on the streets. In subsequent years, his counselors had urged him to answer temptation with a mental image. See
the big picture beyond the small bottle, "Get something up under
your feet." In the big picture, he wasn't homeless anymore. He wasn't
stealing to get high. In the big picture, young guys trying to get sober
looked up to him. Kenny stared down the bottle and delivered his ver-

dict aloud: "I got a lot of people who depend on me, and I love myself today. So this is not the way out." When he went home shaken and told Opal what had happened, she drank the Courvoisier.

Kenny moved out a few weeks later, in the middle of March. "I looked at the Opal I met in the program, and she wasn't that Opal anymore," he said. "She chose drugs over me." With Kenny gone, Opal had no brakes at all. "Now I can just get high whenever I want," she figured. She wanted to every day. The next month passed in a blur. She got three bags of dope for the microwave and four for the end tables. She sold her jewelry, her clothes, her food stamps. With nothing to eat, she bummed milk from the neighbors for the girls. One day, she failed to pick them up from the day-care center that kept them after school. "I didn't forget—I was just high," she said. The center gave them to Kenny's mother, and Opal stayed gone two days. The girls started wetting their beds, and a social worker took them aside and asked if their mother used drugs. Sierra, at eight, knew enough to lie. But Kierra, six, felt trapped. "I don't think I want to tell you that," she said.

By the spring of 1998, as Opal hit the skids, the state's rolls had fallen about 85 percent. Whatever its shortcomings, the system had proved skilled at one thing: diverting people who were basically able into entry-level jobs. Opal, crazed with cocaine, posed a challenge of a different order. Everyone had known such cases existed, and W-2 had ambitiously promised them an individualized plan, one that combined a workfare job with services like drug treatment. Enthusiasts thought the rigor of work would itself have therapeutic value. Others feared the inordinate demands would drive the hardest cases away. What happened with Opal was a scenario neither side envisioned. First, W-2 ignored Opal's collapse. Then it abetted it.

As Opal started coming unglued, she called OIC to get back on the rolls. Darlene Haines was gone, and a new caseworker, Opal's third in a year, knew nothing of her addiction—though she would have had she looked in the computer. She told Opal not to bother coming in: just go look for a job. Instead, Opal spent the next few weeks selling off her possessions, until she grew so desperate she called back and confessed she was using drugs. On paper, what happened next went according to plan. The agency gave Opal an assignment that combined treatment with a community service job. But then it just forgot her. Special cases were supposed to be monitored by specialized workers; Opal's case wasn't monitored by anyone. It was assigned to a worker in a different department, Sonya Gordon, who waited two months just to schedule their first meeting. Opal fell into a bureaucratic black hole.

Looking to do just enough to reclaim her check, Opal showed up at the treatment program. But she mostly skipped the job, with a nonprofit agency that put people with disabilities to work at light assembly tasks. Treatment was a low-budget affair without urine tests, and she continued to get high every day. With no one at OIC handling her case, no one sent her a check. The treatment program ended. Out of food and facing eviction, Opal started calling OIC three times a day. But she couldn't even leave a message; her caseworker's voice mail was full. She couldn't reach a supervisor, either. OIC had a $57 million contract and about half the cases it had budgeted for. You'd think someone could answer the phones. (I once called an OIC worker and got a voice mail that advised, "Try to call only once a week.") Finally Opal just walked in, asking to talk to someone. Had a caseworker ever gone to her home, she could have seen all she needed to see: no food, no furniture, three frightened kids. Had the receptionist even looked in the file, she would have known that the thin, disheveled woman seeking help was a mother on drugs. Instead, she said the office didn't see walk-ins. She told her to make an appointment.

Sunday was Mother's Day. Opal and Jewell usually spent it together, but this year Opal didn't show. Jewell stopped by on Monday after work, and when Opal wouldn't answer the door, she waited outside, figuring Opal would come out soon to get the girls from day care. Opal emerged looking wild-eyed and wasted, and Jewell walked her to the day-care center. The girls looked terrible, too: hair uncombed, clothes askew. Back at the apartment, Jewell was shocked to discover that all the furniture was gone. She knew that Opal had been smoking Primos, but she had no idea things had gotten so bad. Jewell was furious: "How could you do this to the kids?"

"Fuck you, bitch!" Opal screamed.

"Fuck *you*, bitch," Jewell said.

Just then, Kenny pulled up. Though he had moved out two months earlier, he still came by every week or so to drop off cigarettes or milk. He hadn't gone back in the building, so he, too, didn't know she had sold everything. He arrived just in time to hear Opal telling Jewell that their days as cousins were through. Jewell went home, called Opal's mother, and told her to come get her grandchildren right away. Kenny gave Opal the news. "It's over," he said. "You don't have nothing left to sell but your body, if you haven't already started doing it." Opal put up a fight, but she knew she'd been beaten. She couldn't face her mother like that. She hated Kenny. She hated Jewell. "I should kill myself," she said. Kenny didn't take her seriously, but he didn't take any chances. He bought her a beer, made her drink half, and doused her with the rest. Once she smelled sufficiently drunk, he drove her to detox, one place he trusted to keep her safe. Her mother rushed up from Chicago for the kids, and Opal cried herself to sleep, a ward in a ward.

Detox was just an overnight solution; Opal had no place to go after that. The shelters were full, Medicaid wouldn't cover another residential program, and at forty, Kenny still lived with his mother; he couldn't take her there. He picked her up, cast in his conflicting roles—ex-lover, accuser, counselor, best friend—and they drove around so broke he had to stop by a friend's to bum gas money. They wound up at a sobriety meeting, Opal's first in a year, and a Program friend gave them a place to spend the night. In its bittersweet way, it felt like a date; they stayed up listening to recovery tapes and talking of better times. The next day Kenny pulled a rabbit from a hat. One of his old counselors ran a halfway house called Project HALT. Opal met none of the conditions to get in: she wasn't working, she couldn't pay the rent, and she hadn't stopped using drugs. But Kenny didn't see any other options. On top of all else, Opal was two months pregnant, with a child she claimed was his.

I caught up with her a few days after she arrived. She was fiddling with the blinds in a sad little room, trying to capture fading light through a dirty window. Opal recounted her collapse in matter-of-fact tones: the yearning for drugs, the good-bye to the girls, the thoughts of suicide. She was a woman in suspended animation, a detached observer of a shattered past and a future she felt powerless to change. The moment she sprang back to life was when she spit out her scorn for Jewell. "I ain't never gonna talk to her again!" she said. Yet Jewell may have kept her from losing the kids. A few days after she left her apartment, Opal returned to gather a few things. While she was there, an investigator arrived, saying someone had filed a child-welfare complaint. If Opal's mother hadn't gotten the girls, the state of Wisconsin might have had them.

From her dingy room in the halfway house, Opal started calling OIC again, pleading for a welfare check. Sonya Gordon, her caseworker, finally returned her call. If she was curious what Opal was doing in a place called Project HALT—"Hungry, Addicted, Lonely, and Tired"—she didn't say. She did say that nearly two months after inheriting the case she hadn't looked at it. She'd have to talk to a supervisor and call back. When she did, she compounded the errors: she agreed to send Opal $700 as back pay. There were any number of reasons Opal didn't qualify for a W-2 check. She hadn't worked for it, of course. Even more basic than that, she didn't have custody of her kids. But OIC didn't know.

Opal cashed the check and headed for Andrea's, telling herself she'd be back for dinner. She stayed for six months, making the crack house her home. Sonya Gordon transferred the case to yet another caseworker, Opal's fifth in a year, and the checks continued to flow. Pregnant addicts were a big concern in Wisconsin that year. Just as Opal moved in with Andrea, Tommy Thompson signed a "Cocaine Mom" law, authorizing courts to force pregnant women into treatment programs. "The unborn child is going to be preserved and protected and . . . healthy when born," he said. Meanwhile Opal was pregnant and living in a crack house—and Thompson's celebrated welfare program was buying the crack.

FOURTEEN

Golf Balls and Corporate Dreams: Milwaukee, 1997–1999

> *The Company's services are designed to make government operations more efficient and cost effective while improving the quality of the services provided to program beneficiaries.*
>
> —MAXIMUS, INC.

In theory, the people sending drug money to Opal had a motive to clean up their act: fear of the competition. After twenty-eight months, their contracts expired. If the Opportunities Industrialization Center wouldn't answer its phones, if it sent checks to pregnant women in crack houses, then it risked being replaced by its rivals. In practice, the agencies acted less like competitors than like members of a welfare cartel. With Milwaukee split into six exclusive regions, the contracting produced a kind of ethnic and ideological partition. One contract went to the black grassroots group (OIC). One went to its Hispanic counterpart (United Migrant Opportunities Services). Two blue chips of the public service world were dealt in (the YWCA and Goodwill Industries, which ran two regions). With a common consultant and common agenda—keeping state regulators at bay—the agencies showed more interest in sticking together than in raiding each other's turf. Think OPEC, not the Cola Wars.

The exception was the fifth agency, Maximus, Inc., which did want to take over the city. As a national, profit-seeking corporation, Maximus wasn't just the new face in town but the ultimate symbol of privatization: a welfare agency that traded on the New York Stock Exchange! The state saw a paragon of market-based virtues—efficiency, discipline, accountability—and considered letting Maximus run the whole Milwaukee program before bowing to the political imperative to include local groups. Critics saw a cold, distant corporation, looking to profit off the poor (and some just seized on any opportunity to attack W-2). When Opal moved to Andrea's, she didn't just land in a new service region. She landed in an ideological battle zone.

As a business, Maximus arrived in Milwaukee on a wave of spectacular success. In 1975, its founder, David Mastran, left a job at the Department of Health, Education, and Welfare to start a consulting firm in his basement. Two decades later he was master of an empire based in Reston, Virginia, with contracts in nearly every state. Along with consulting, Maximus ran programs itself; it collected child support in Tennessee, helped enroll Texans in Medicaid, and processed Connecticut's child-care payments. By allowing states to privatize their programs, the 1996 federal law set off a gold rush for similar contracts; one Wall Street analysis saw more than $2 billion a year coming up for grabs. Formidable rivals, like EDS and Lockheed Martin, the aerospace giant, were fighting for the business, but with its long record and tighter focus Maximus was thought to have an edge. The W-2 contract was a coup. No welfare experiment was followed more closely, and Maximus hoped to leverage the publicity and prestige into market share nationwide. The company went public on the eve of W-2's launch, and the share price rose by two-thirds over the next nine months. Mastran's stake was worth more than $100 million.

While W-2 brought special opportunity, it also posed a special challenge. The other W-2 agencies had run local programs for years; Maximus had to start from scratch, in a place where grassroots opinion ranged from suspicion to hostility. To lead the effort, the company hired a local Goodwill executive named George Leutermann, who had gained some national prominence a few years earlier with an employment program in nearby Kenosha. Leutermann brought Maximus instant connections: his family had run a Milwaukee grocery store for one hundred years, and he had spent a quarter century working in Wisconsin social services. For Leutermann, Maximus had an equal allure: one day, he was a cog in a bland bureaucracy, the next he was checking on his stock options as a corporate VP. With the chance to set up W-2, Leutermann, at fifty, wasn't just running a program but launching a new product line. "Over the next two years, we plan to replicate many of the systems we are testing in Milwaukee for use in other markets," he told the *Milwaukee Business Journal*.

Leutermann made a splash. Though his face sagged in a hangdog look, he held forth with the quick, glib rap of a man born to sell. Knowing the knock that Maximus faced—rapacious profiteers—he set out to soften the corporate image with an aggressive marketing campaign; there were billboards, bus ads, and CD-ROMS, even Maximus fanny packs. A succession of minority fetes and fairs wound up with a Maximus check. A team of "community outreach" specialists came on board, most of them local minority women, with generous salaries and vague promotional duties. Spin to the smooth jazz station, and you could hear the Maximus jingle:

> *People helping people*
> *That's us*
> *We're here at Maximus*

In theory, the thing that made W-2 different was its stress on community service jobs: everyone was expected to work. But the heart of the program that Leutermann designed was another motivation class. Grandly reincarnated as "MaxAcademy," it grew into a weeks-long festival of assessment tests, Successory posters, and inspirational speakers, distinguished above all by empty seats. Attendance, though mandatory, was wretched. Leutermann called the class a way to polish the so-called soft skills, like punctuality and grooming, while getting to know clients more deeply than the usual office visits allowed. His detractors suspected he was equally drawn to its promotional qualities. Every visiting dignitary was routed to the class, and if enough clients didn't show up, employees would pose in their place. When *Nightline* came to town, MaxAcademy supplied the lead.

NIGHTLINE: "You are watching a revolution in progress."
INSPIRATIONAL SPEAKER: "You have to be aggressive when
you're out in the workforce. . . ! You gotta want it!"
NIGHTLINE: "Twice a week, employers are here interviewing."

Cut to George Leutermann. For a VP looking to scale the ranks, it
doesn't get much better than that. But no sooner was the program up
and running than a group of disaffected managers began voicing a
common complaint: the clients weren't doing anything. W-2 was built
around the theory of "full engagement." As state officials described it,
the average client would perform forty hours of weekly activity, of
which thirty would involve real work. But the W-2 policy manual cast
things in looser terms, demanding "up to" thirty hours of work. Or, actually, up to thirty hours of "work training activities," which could include the old job-search routine. The manual writers said that they
were just trying to accommodate the occasional need for discretion,
not create a big loophole. But the real-world practice of W-2 became
much looser still. Many clients waited months for assignments. Others ignored them and got paid anyway. While Opal's ability to keep
drawing a check may seem like a strange aberration, Maximus managers were busy swapping written complaints about clients in similar
straits: "Job-seekers are essentially in limbo." "[M]any job seekers
with W2 placements are not assigned activities." "The no show rate is
high and we are losing people." "Today, Northwestern Mutual Life, a
very important employer, is on site. . . . However there is one critical
element missing, JOBSEEKERS." Six months after the program's
start, Steve Perales, the second in charge, warned that "virtually no
referrals are being made to the CSJ unit," the one that assigns community service jobs. While about 1,100 clients were supposed to have
community service jobs, just 507 had gotten assignments, and "only
about 88 are actually participating," he wrote. That is, in the country's
most famous work program, only 8 percent of the clients were working. "What they were doing, I don't know," Leutermann later told me.
"They were doing nothing."
One reason for the disarray was a shortage of caseworkers. Under
state rules, each caseworker—a Financial and Employment Planner,

or "Fep"—was supposed to manage no more than fifty-five clients. Some Maximus Feps had more than twice as many. The woman who would next handle Opal's case had 108. Four months after the program's launch, Mona Garland, a senior manager, wrote a memo warning that Maximus had thirteen caseworkers and needed twenty-eight. Leutermann argued that the state had placed too much emphasis on Feps. While W-2 had cast them as centralized problem-solvers, Leutermann pictured them as traffic cops, routing clients to more specialized services. But Garland, who became an embittered critic, suspected Leutermann had another thought in mind: caseworkers, unlike inspirational speakers, don't get you on *Nightline*.

In June 1998, ten months into W-2, the state produced its first quantitative look at the agencies' performance. The computerized audit, called a 740R report, examined what activities clients had been assigned. Of interest as a midterm report card, it also hinted at the criteria the state would use for contract renewals. A follow-up report would cover similar ground, and those who passed would gain the "right of first selection," a chance to keep running the program without another public bid. Agencies that failed could reenter the competitive fray, but they would be doing so under a cloud and could find themselves losing a lucrative contract in a particularly humiliating way. Since Maximus was using W-2 as a national exhibit, that would wreck the whole business plan. Failing wasn't an option.

Most of the Milwaukee agencies performed poorly, and Maximus looked especially bad. Sixty-seven percent of its clients had no work assignments. An internal Maximus analysis, a few months later, found that 46 percent of the clients had no assignments at all, work or otherwise. "I had no clue that we were in that kind of shape," Leutermann later said. "We were just out of whack all over the place." At the time, he exploded and blamed Garland. "[O]ur dismal performance" is "a major setback," and "our track record portends continued problems," he wrote. Garland responded with a blizzard of old memos, e-mails, and reports to say she had been warning him. The evidence of idle clients was kept from public view—neither Maximus nor the state had a motive to vet their failures—but amid the finger pointing, one issue got resolved. Maximus would hire more caseworkers.

As Opal lay around smoking Primos, Michael Steinborn sat at home, drinking vodka for breakfast. Sometimes he thought he *needed* a social worker. He had no clue he was about to become one. Some social-work careers begin in flights of youthful idealism; Michael's began at Ladies Night at a Milwaukee pickup joint. He was out with a high school friend, Jose Arteaga. They had both grown up in the inner city, sons of small-time landlords, and as classmates at the Jesuit high school, they used to have long, philosophical talks about how the ghetto had gotten so screwed up. Now at thirty, Michael was poor and screwed up himself, and Jose was a rising star at Maximus, director of case management. By the end of the night, Jose had an inspiration: Michael should come aboard as a Fep. *Yeah,* Michael thought. *Right.*

It was late and they were drinking, but they each had a reason to act like they were serious. Michael's reason was simple enough: he needed a job. In the decade since he had dropped out of Marquette, he had driven a taxi, delivered pizzas, swabbed toilets, attended fire fighters' school, rushed into a marriage, had a son, and gone through a bitter divorce. Joining a friend on the crew of a landscaping firm, Michael spent a few years mowing city lots, and then had a better idea—they should start a landscaping firm of their own. Michael's friend Alvin was black, so his 51 percent share gave them minority contractor status. It also gave Alvin the ability to cut Michael out, which he did, unsentimentally, once the business took off. Michael was devastated. It took a tackle from his sobbing girlfriend, Jai, to stop him as he tried to run after Alvin with a butcher knife. In the two years since, Michael had done some sheetrock and roofing jobs, but mostly he brooded and drank. By the summer of 1998, he owed ten months' worth of back child support and Jai was pregnant, due in a week. He needed some cash.

Jose's motives were more complex. In part, he wanted to help a friend, and as the chief of Feps he needed bodies. But he also thought that Michael would bring something to the job. Like all the agencies, Maximus had drawn most of its Feps from the old welfare program, prizing the veterans above all for their familiarity with the state computer system. Jose thought too many acted like data entry clerks, tidying their software screens but forgetting the client. "Their people skills weren't there," he said. Michael, on the other hand, had been doing protosocial work since his preteens, when his father first sent him out to collect rents. Jose saw him as a no-bullshit kind of guy, tough but empathetic. The kind the system needed. A few nights later, he showed up in Michael's kitchen with a bottle of tequila and a sheaf of paper. Taping flowcharts to the wall until 1:00 a.m., he offered a crash-course on W-2 as it existed in theory:

Point Number One: Only Work Pays. Free money was gone. Clients had to earn their checks in a simulated workweek. The bulk should be spent actually working, while the rest could be devoted to activities like training, treatment, or classes. For every hour clients missed, their checks got reduced by $5.15, the equivalent of the minimum wage. The idea was to model the workaday world.

Point Number Two: W-2 Provides the Jobs. The jobs progressed along a four-part ladder, with each a step up in difficulty and pay. At the bottom rung, W-2 Transitions, even the physically or mentally impaired might, say, perform light assembly tasks in a supervised setting. At the top was the ultimate goal, regular, unsubsidized employment. In between, most clients would be assigned to community service jobs—answering the phone at a food bank, perhaps, or sweeping a school. The bottom rung paid $628 a month, while regular community service paid $673. Grants no longer grew with family size, though for all but the largest families they paid more than the old system. In addition, the state provided child care, health care, and transportation, the support services that workers needed.

Point Number Three: Casework Is the Key. There *was* no casework in the old system, just a stream of checks. W-2 promised every client an individualized employment plan and a caseworker to help see her through. Quarreling with the boss? Drinking too much? Part sheriff, part shrink, the Fep was supposed to monitor progress and get to the bottom of things.

As the kitchen course came to its inebriated close, Michael liked the theory: he hadn't hung around the ghetto all his life without accumulating some disdain for welfare. But he wondered if the bureaucracy could pull it off. And for his own role as an agent of reform, he had no enthusiasm at all. As a high school student, he had taken a test of occupational interests and scoffed when it cast him as a future social worker. "You think I'm gonna be some underpaid, overworked *social worker*?" he had said. Office work dealt a blow to his muscular self-image. Office workers had soft hands. Still, though it pained him to admit it, the $28,000 salary was more than he had ever earned. Leaving for the first day of work, he kissed his baby, Christian, goodbye and headed off to log an office worker's day. "Your daddy's going to make some money," he said.

It started poorly and went downhill from there. His first battles weren't with clients but rather with the computer system that tracked them, a befuddling institution called CARES. The central nervous system of W-2, CARES had more than five hundred screens, each known by an opaque four-letter code. There was no doing the job without knowing the program, and despite three months of training, Michael thought he never would. Need to change someone's work assignment? Go to WPAS. Check her living arrangements? That's ANLA. Issue her check? Type "Y" in AGEC, but change the date in SFED, otherwise the check may not go out, even when AGEC said it did. For all the talk of making Feps bold new problem solvers, fluency in CARES was particularly prized, since it was the sole repository of the data that would govern contract renewal. It didn't matter when Michael used his lunch hour to drive clients to job interviews; there was no CARES screen for that. (He pictured one: SCKR, for "sucker.") What mattered was whether he had correctly coded their employability plans.

Facing a parade of addled clients, Michael found himself thinking more about keystrokes than the substance of what they said. Disabled child? Dying mother? "Shut up!" complained a voice in his head. "I'm trying to remember the transaction code!" His befuddlement reached its dark apogee with the arrival of a large, sobbing woman free-associating about her troubles. Michael entered the driver flow and dutifully posed the questions on his screen.

SOBBING WOMAN: I got into it with my sister's boyfriend. . . .
MICHAEL: What are your employment goals?

WOMAN: . . . he hit me in the head with a two-by-four . . .

MICHAEL: Foreign languages? Written or verbal?

WOMAN: . . . my brother's retarded . . .

MICHAEL: Distance from the nearest bus line?

WOMAN: . . . we're out of food . . .

MICHAEL: Volunteer work or hobbies?

Volunteer work or hobbies! "No, I don't want to hear that you've been at food pantries for the last two months," he thought. "What I want to know is whether you play volleyball!" A coworker suggested the information might help him guide clients to the right job, but Michael kept picturing a gnome in Madison darting out of the computer room: "A knitter! A knitter! We've got a knitter, folks!"

In its pitch to investors, Maximus had promised to outdo government with "a professional work environment that is more conducive to employee productivity." Michael had a different view: half the place was coming unglued. At least two of the caseworkers he came to know were addicted to crack. Another was hospitalized for job-related stress. A Fep with whom he shared an office went off on gambling jags, staying out at a casino all night, then sleeping at her desk. "Baby, I gotta take a little nap," she'd say as she locked the door. Another Fep walked off the job with a message on her screensaver: "God has something bigger and better for me than this place." Michael thought he might just be a magnet for office misfits. But the memo traffic inside the agency showed broader disarray. Leutermann warned that one caseworker was "going off the deep end lately," causing "all kinds of problems about his behavior in the bathroom." Another Maximus worker chased his supervisor from his office when she told him to clean up his files. "I am a Marine combat veteran that deals with Post Traumatic Stress Disorder," he wrote. "I lost my head." A flirtatious caseworker, rebuffed by a colleague, walked into his cubicle and bit him. As the incident report noted dryly: "He then told her to get her Monkey Ass away."

Given the power that caseworkers exert over poor, troubled women, welfare offices need to use special caution; predatory workers may pressure their clients for sex or drugs. Sometimes no pressure is needed. After Michael drove a client to a job interview, she sent him

a card with a smiley face. "If you give me the chance, I'll ride you like
a horse," she wrote. "Your voice just makes me melt!" Not everyone
summoned Michael's self-control. A MaxAcademy teacher was quietly
pushed out the door after a client complained that he was urging her
and others to join a drug-peddling scheme. An internal report explained: "She said some of these women have told her that they have
had sex with him because they are afraid he will cut off their benefits."
A different caseworker resigned when his client announced she was
carrying his baby. "Dumb ass . . . should have paid for the abortion
like I asked him too!" she announced in the Maximus office. She went
public only after another client told her MaxAcademy class that she
was sleeping with him, too. Maximus kept the story out of the press,
and the mordant office joke had it that the women were enrolled in
"W-3," a program of lifelong checks for clients who kept their mouths
shut. "Mike, you're a bright guy," one colleague said. "Get out while
you can."

Maximus encouraged the hiring of family and friends, calling it an
effective way to lure and keep talent. As head of the office, Leutermann certainly practiced what he preached. He put his wife, his son,
and his niece on the payroll, along with his mistress and his mistress's
mother. The gossip about the boss's affair reached the point that
Leutermann urged subordinates not to mention it in front of his wife.
In a memo titled "Rumors and Soap Operas," he wrote: "Our office
continues to suffer through a problem of useless, superfluous, and often insidious rumormongering. . . . MAXIMUS does not have time to
fixate on this type of drivel." Leutermann's girlfriend, a senior Maximus manager, was pregnant with his child when he hired her; at the
time he circulated the memo, they had an eight-month-old son. The
woman who rose to the number-two job in the Maximus office, Paula
Lampley, had her son on the payroll, too, until he drew thirty years for
reckless homicide; Romell Lampley, an employment counselor, got
angry at his girlfriend's stepfather and ran him over with a car. "This
project has had more than its share of complaints," wrote David Mastran, the CEO, ordering an investigation. "If we are doing nothing
wrong, why are we receiving complaints?" The incident at hand involved an employee's complaint of racial discrimination, but Beverly
Swann, the Maximus executive sent to the scene, warned that the

problems went deeper. "I asked the question what message would you like to send the CEO and the response was clearly 'things are not what they appear to be,'" she wrote. "There is a perception that management are [sic] hiring friends, relatives, and former displaced associates." Years later, Mastran told me, "In all of our projects, we never had personnel problems like we had up there. It got out of control."

Perhaps he was thinking of Corey Daniels, the caseworker originally assigned to train Michael. Everything about him set off Michael's bullshit detector. He wore a platinum Dennis Rodman do and watched soap operas at his desk. He flashed wads of cash and boasted of his Cadillacs. Playing his voice mail on the speakerphone, he deleted clients' messages as soon as he heard their names. *Bo-rring! Heard that!* "The guy's a flipping goof," Michael said, demanding a new trainer. A background check would have shown that Daniels was also a convicted forger, with an arrest record that included kidnapping, battery, and impersonating a police officer. "You appear to be living a double life," a judge had warned, while giving him four years for passing forged checks. Maximus hired him while he was out on parole. A few months after his tutelage of Michael, Daniels was back in court, charged with extorting nearly $4,000 from his clients. Four of them brought similar complaints: that Daniels had threatened to reduce their checks if they didn't give him a share of the money. Michael, still new to office work, wondered what he had gotten into: "Drug abuse, check kiting, knocking up people—what is it about this place?"

He did find a Fep to admire. His new trainer, Elizabeth Matus, was a soft-spoken Nicaraguan immigrant who could do what Michael could not: talk and work CARES at the same time. For two months, he scarcely left her side. He wouldn't eat. He couldn't sleep. He stayed at the office until 9:00 at night, studying the CARES manual. "This isn't like putting up drywall," he told himself. "You're messing with people's lives." Then, ready or not, his password arrived: he was XMI28W, a full-fledged Fep. As if from a B movie, a clerk wheeled in seventy case files, some of them literally covered with dust. Most of the clients had been idle for months, while collecting checks. They needed appointment notices, work assignments, employability plans. With the state review approaching—and the corporate showcase at stake—Michael had two months to turn a pile of lost lives into CARES codes that could pass official muster.

One of those files was Opal's.

The crack house where Opal took refuge was a mustardy complex cast in an otherworldly light by the all-night gas station next door. The inside was otherworldly, too, a dark space of torn couches and acrid odors that slumbered until noon and buzzed until dawn. The building divided into four apartments, and discreet dealers operated from three. The fourth, where Opal lived with Andrea, was a rollicking bazaar, notorious enough to attract motorists off the nearby Interstate. Opal paid $250 a month to sleep there, pregnant, on the couch. No one knew where she was. Like a foreign trek, life at Andrea's combined adventure, escape, and a kind of liberating anonymity. It let her indulge her secret self, away from disapproving eyes.

W-2 kept paying the way. With her new address across district lines, OIC transferred the case, and Opal's introduction to Maximus had the makings of a dark spoof. Dragging herself in from the crack house, Opal discovered her case being reviewed by someone she knew from the recovery world as a fellow addict. The Maximus worker couldn't have been any happier to see Opal than Opal was to see her, especially if Opal was right in surmising that she was still snorting heroin. ("She had them blisters up her nose! You can tell!") "How you been doing?" the caseworker asked. Opal avoided an answer. She handed over an old drug-referral note and concocted a story about being in treatment. That bought her another month's check. Someone handed her a form asking about volunteer work and hobbies. "Reading, skating," Opal wrote.

More faux social work followed. When Opal missed her next appointment, Maximus arranged for a home visit, just what you'd want in the case of a pregnant woman on drugs. Except the home visitor never went in the home. He knocked on the crack house door and handed Opal an appointment notice. A look inside would have revealed a drug nest. A call to the police would have disclosed a warrant for Opal's arrest. A check with the Milwaukee public schools would have revealed that she didn't have her kids. Instead, Maximus sent

Opal to MaxAcademy. "That's wasteless," she said. "I been to so many motivation classes." She went one day and got another month's check.

As usual, welfare wasn't Opal's only way to get by. One of the dealers who hung around Andrea's was a small-timer in his late twenties, a rail-thin man with a pocked face and oversized nose, whom everyone called Bo. He wasn't much to look at, Opal thought, and he didn't have much to say. But she had a $300-a-day habit, and he had a pocketful of crack. Soon, Opal was calling him her "friend" and laughing behind his back about her ability to wheedle or steal his drugs.

Restless after four months in hiding, Opal finally walked to a pay phone and told Kenny where she was. A week later, I picked them up and the three of us headed off to a Red Lobster. Kenny looked dapper in a red turtleneck, with cubic zirconia sparkling in his ears and a No Drugs button on his chest. Six months pregnant, Opal was disconcertingly thin, with matted hair and bags beneath her eyes. But she sallied forth in gold lamé shoes, regal even in exile. Drugs were destroying her family and her health, but not her love of the fantastic tale. "I live in a crack house!" she began. It was a difficult sentence to parse—part apology, partly a boast. "That house is *booming*. I ain't never seen so many white people do drugs in my life! Doctors, bus drivers, men that own their own construction companies!" Andrea and her sister smoked cocaine, Opal said, and their daughters sold it. "It's like a family thing," she said. She griped about the rent Andrea charged her, but the dealers had to provide drugs to the house—and "now, I'm the house."

Kenny poured a dozen sugars in his tea and took it all in. "Daughter sells drugs to the mother, so you know she's going to hell," he said.

"So are you!" Opal said, raising the sore subject of his affairs. "You just fornicating."

"Thank you, Pope," he said.

Opal described her daily routine: sleep past noon and stay up till dawn, especially "if it's my day to watch the door." Kenny tried to sound more incredulous than he was. "Your day to open the door! What: they got your name on a refrigerator? 'Opal's day to open the door?' *I* used to work the door. The guy that works the door is the first to get hit upside the head when the robbers come through." Opal was thinking less of robbers than cops. The police had raided an adjacent apartment, and she couldn't understand why they hadn't burst into Andrea's yet. "The police don't want no white people doing drugs," she said. "They fittin' to raid it." Given the pending theft charges from Target, she seemed resigned to going to jail. "It seems like it's going to happen."

She said she had talked to her daughters several times "since I been AWOL." Kierra and Tierra had taken her absence in stride, but Sierra, the oldest at nine, had cried and asked when Opal would return. "I'm sick right now," Opal had told her. "When Mama gets better, I'm a come home and get y'all." She said she felt sad. She said she felt "self-pity." She said she felt "ashamed of what I'm doing." She didn't say she felt ready to stop. After dinner, she packed the leftovers in a box and stole a bottle of steak sauce. Then she rode back to Andrea's, where she was still living a couple months later when her case reached Michael's desk.

Whatever Maximus could blame for its failures with Opal, it couldn't blame a shortage of cash. As she spent her welfare money on Primos, Maximus went on a grander binge, showering the town with more than $1 million of billboards, TV ads, and corporate tchotchkes and financing the spree out of welfare funds. Like a Mafia wiretap or the Watergate tapes, the bookkeeping has the lurid appeal of shabby sin exposed to daylight. The company spent $100,000 of program funds on backpacks, coffee mugs, and other promotional fluff. It spent tens of thousands on employee entertainment, including meals, flowers, parties, and retreats. It spent $3,000 to take clients roller-skating at the zoo. In one of the more inventive uses of welfare funds, it doled out $2,600 for professional clowns to liven up Maximus events. Though Maximus later agreed to repay $500,000 to the state and donate another $500,000 to community groups, the true extent of the waste will never be known because the records were in such disarray. In nearly three-quarters of the transactions later examined by legislative auditors, Maximus either couldn't show what it had purchased or explain its relevance to W-2. Entries in the auditors' report literally read like this: Vendor: "Unknown." Item purchased: "Unknown." Welfare funds expended: "$5,302." For any welfare program to spend money like this defies comprehension. Why would a profit-seeking enterprise indulge such chaos and waste?

The answer starts with the financial incentives of W-2. It was designed as a risk-management system, much like an HMO. Each agency got a fixed payment to serve its region; in return, the agency financed everything from clients' benefits to caseworkers' telephone bills. Just as HMOs were supposed to profit by keeping people healthy (and out of hospitals), W-2 agencies were supposed to keep them employed (and off the welfare rolls). The more an agency cut its caseload, the more its profits would grow. Given those incentives, the most obvious fear was that the agencies would find ways to cut needy people off—*not* that they would pay women like Opal to sit around crack houses. But the rolls immediately fell so much that the financial pressures vanished. In offering the contracts, the state had budgeted for fifty thousand cases; when W-2 began, only twenty-three thousand people enrolled. Rather than rolling the dice, the agencies were rolling in dough.

The catch is that unrestricted profits were capped at 7 percent of the contract, or $4.2 million in Maximus's case. After that, the agencies kept only 10 percent of any leftover funds. Maximus knew its $4.2 million was in the bank. So it had little incentive to cut costs, since it would keep just a dime of each dollar it saved. In other words, it found itself with a big pot of someone else's money to spend. And spend it did, lavishly and foolishly, in a drive to burnish its corporate image. "I have permission to make seven percent on this contract, period," Leutermann said. "We're using it as a national exhibit."

Hoping to win over local skeptics, Leutermann hired a $60,000 PR chief with a half dozen $40,000 and $50,000 assistants for the "community outreach" team. Inside the agency, they were resented as deadwood, and Leutermann let most of them go as soon as the contract was renewed. He also tried to buy goodwill more directly. Lots of companies make charitable donations; Maximus made them with tens of thousands of program dollars that were supposed to be helping welfare recipients. Leutermann covered the ethnic bases, from the African American State Fair and the Black Holocaust Museum to the La Causa Celebrity Waiter Festival and Granny Shalom House. The Women in Public Policy Luncheon, the Hispanic Chamber of

Commerce, the Charlie Lagrew Fiddle and Jig Contest—likewise, all dealt in.

In the big scheme of things, Granny Shalom didn't cost taxpayers much. The advertising blitzkrieg did. State auditors estimated that Maximus spent $1.1 million on its marketing campaign. Bridgette Ridgeway, who spent two years overseeing the effort as a Maximus consultant and staff member, estimated the cost to be about twice as high, at $2.3 million. There were Maximus water bottles and Maximus visors. There were Maximus golf balls, towels, and tees, for all those golfers on the Maximus rolls. ("The golf balls were a bad idea," Leutermann later acknowledged.) There was a Maximus jingle. Make that *two* Maximus jingles; the first, rendered in a minor key, was recommissioned after a consultant warned that in "keeping with the Maximus image, the music should not reflect sad or dark tones." In one of Leutermann's wilder schemes, Maximus spent more than $23,000 to bring in Melba Moore, the once-upon-a-time Broadway star (and former welfare recipient), for what flyers called an "exclusive inspirational concert for Maximus families." She drew about two hundred people, putting the per-ticket cost at about $125.

Leutermann argued that as the new name in town, Maximus needed a PR campaign to counter the negative rumors spread by its critics and reassure wary clients. "Had we been given a fair shake from the start, that would never have been necessary," Leutermann later said. "But we were being painted from Day One as the for-profit, nasty assholes of the world." Advertising can be appropriate; the question is whom does it aid? It's one thing to leaflet poor neighborhoods, another to make sure that local pols tee off with Maximus balls. Among the expenses the state subsequently deemed *proper* was a share of the costs of hiring two of Tommy Thompson's cronies, for advice on how to target political donations and win new contracts. Much of the advertising occurred around the 1998 summer meeting of the National Governors Association, which was held in Milwaukee. Collectively, its members controlled a multi-billion-dollar welfare market, and Leutermann hit them with everything from TV ads to CD-ROMs; his goal, he wrote his boss, was "to put MAXIMUS on the lops [*sic*]"—lips? laps?—"of every one of the fifty-five governors who will attend" from Maine to Guam. Ridgeway, the former PR chief, became a Maximus critic after Leutermann let her go. "My department bought media on specific radio stations because we knew that politicians would listen," she said. "It wasn't what's best for the clients."

Maximus wasn't the only agency taking a joy ride on welfare funds. OIC spent $67,000 to sponsor the *Ray Rhodes Show*, the weekly football rundown hosted by the coach of the Green Bay Packers (a show more likely to be seen by legislators than welfare mothers). United Migrant Opportunity Services spent $23,000 from a different welfare contract to advertise at Milwaukee Brewers' games. A more disturbing report emerged when auditors looked at the Goodwill subsidiary, Employment Solutions, Inc., which ran two Milwaukee regions and therefore was the state's largest W-2 agency. Auditors found it spent more than $270,000 of program funds outside the state, mostly in an unsuccessful attempt to win a contract in Arizona; the contract went to Maximus. The audits didn't appear until 2000 and 2001, long after the money was spent. And the salient point is that they were done by the auditing branch of the legislature, not by Thompson or the subordinates he put in charge of his showcase program. On the day the legislative auditors released their findings, the state's top W-2 official, Linda Stewart, issued a competing press release. It complained the auditors had failed to credit her own "vigilant efforts at monitoring and oversight."

The waste, though concealed for years, finally came to light. Not so with the deeper problem of W-2, its neglect of so many clients. What George Leutermann called "our dismal performance" on the state's first client activity report, in June 1998, didn't tell Maximus anything its managers hadn't known: casework was weak to nonexistent, and most recipents were idle. If anything, the report understated the casework problems, since it only measured one aspect of the agency's performance, the assignment of work activities. In August, Maximus examined several hundred cases against a fuller list of state rules, such as proper caseworker ratios and employability plans; 78 percent failed. In truth, none of these measures got to the bottom of things. They focused on process, not results. They asked whether clients were told what to do, not whether they did it and certainly not whether doing it made sense. Keith Garland, the Maximus manager of quality control, studied attendance at MaxAcademy, the agency's signature effort. More than three-quarters of the people assigned to the class never showed up for a single day. Out of a caseload of nearly fifteen hundred, Garland said, "We had maybe one hundred people doing something." As for the rest: "We didn't know what people were doing. We didn't have a clue."

With so many people (like Opal) doing nothing, why did they still get checks? In a given month, Maximus reduced its payments to only about one client in four, and hardly anyone had her whole check taken away. That pattern was typical statewide. The bureaucratic chaos offers one explanation: people couldn't be punished for skipping assignments they hadn't received. Finances offer another: having maximized their profits, agencies had little self-interest in withholding benefits. Caseworkers disliked the sanctioning process, which was time-consuming and brought complaints from angry clients. But a subtle shift in welfare politics also played a role. By the end of 1998, Tommy Thompson was finishing his third term, and he had cut the rolls by 90 percent. Politically, he had nothing to gain by pushing more families off welfare. On the contrary, the new national concern was reaching "the hard to serve," and savvy officials were trying to show they had preserved a safety net. The entire history of W-2 reflects a move away from Jason Turner's Work or Else theory toward a more erratic and diffuse set of practices. In part that's because the original vision was too rigid (not every client was best served by a community service job) and in part because the bureaucracy never really tried to pull it off. For all those reasons, an unspoken assumption often prevailed: when in doubt, give 'em a check.

A few months after Maximus learned of its "dismal" results on the client activity report, the state announced the criteria it would use for contract renewal. There were, among other standards, three major measures of casework. The Feps could each handle no more than fifty-five clients at a time. They had to keep 95 percent of their employability plans up-to-date. And they had to make sure 80 percent of their clients had a full slate of assignments. This was more bureaucratic bunk. The state didn't ask whether Opal got a job—it asked whether she had an employability plan. Plus, it was easy to manipulate the data. In grading the agencies for contract renewal, the state's sole source of information was the computer system, CARES. The state had no way to know whether the assignments in the computer were real, much less whether clients were doing them. For months, Maximus tried to round up its clients and give them something to do. But if all else failed, the policy manual did permit another option: just type something in the system and send the client a copy. "It became a CARES game," says Mona Garland, the former operations manager. "You just go in there and code them this, this, and this to make CARES look right and ultimately meet the right of first selection. . . . They may not really be assigned to thirty hours, but you go into CARES and make it sound like they're assigned to thirty hours. The job-seeker may not even know." When I asked George Leutermann about this, he said: "I would imagine some of that did happen."

It happened to Opal. Finding her file in his dusty stack in November 1998, Michael Steinborn quickly sent her an appointment letter. As usual, she didn't show. One reason he needed to see her was to update her employability plan, since without one her case would fail to meet state standards. When she didn't appear, he simply went into CARES, wrote a plan, and stuck it in the mail. It showed her aspiring to become a teacher's assistant. And to get her started, he gave her the assignment he gave everyone. "Opal Caples?" he said to himself. "It's MaxAcademy for you!" He didn't know she was addicted to crack. He didn't know she was pregnant. He didn't know she was living in a drug house while her mother raised her kids. He had never met her. But with that, his casework was up to standards: Opal's case was now passing. "CARES is a fantasyland," he said.

The state took its computerized snapshot of the caseload on January 29, 1999. A few weeks later, Maximus, like all the Milwaukee agencies, learned that it had passed. Its "national exhibit" was safe. State officials were just as relieved. In scoring the agencies' performance, they were also scoring their own, and the last thing they wanted was any hint of failure. Thompson was mulling a run for president and pushing W-2 for a prestigious Innovations in American Government Award, which is cosponsored by the Ford Foundation and Harvard's John F. Kennedy School of Government. He won. In bestowing the $100,000 prize, award administrators called W-2 "one of the nation's best examples of government performance." One of the qualities they singled out was its financial efficiency. The other was the quality of its casework.

For Maximus, there was more good news. By the end of the year, with George Leutermann leading the charge, the company won a prized $100 million contract in New York City, where Jason Turner had gone on to serve as welfare commissioner; just as planned, W-2 proved a springboard to greater things. Six months later, the legislative auditors' report would appear, and the talk would shift to Melba Moore and clowns. But for a fleeting moment, more fleeting than he knew, Leutermann was on top of the world. "The company hired me because of the quality issue," he told a local business paper. "There is nothing worse than a pitch man not having substance to back him up."

Opal never read her employability plan. She had been missing for six months when Kenny ran into Angie and Jewell and told them where she was. A week later, the two of them knocked on her door. Opal came out, and they sat in the car, where the three women fell into the irreverent banter that marked them as family. Opal didn't say a word to Jewell about turning her in to her mother. Jewell didn't say anything to Opal about smoking cocaine. She just listened to Opal's spirited drug-house stories. "Girl," Opal said, "you see some tripped-out shit over there." More visits followed. Then Angie urged Opal to move in, and a few weeks before the baby was due, she finally did. With that, Angie achieved what W-2 had not; she got Opal out of the crack house.

Opal was miserable. She missed Andrea's, not just the drugs, but the rush of late-night excitement. There was nothing to do at Angie's but lie around, and lying around left her depressed. Angie and Marcus argued all the time, and Opal had never much liked Angie's kids, who didn't want her around. ("Opal's a *drug addict*," whispered Darrell, Angie's five-year-old. "I don't talk to Opal.") The house smelled like the pit bulls that Marcus was raising, and the dogs had chewed up the top floor, forcing everyone into uncomfortably close quarters. Opal shared a bed with Kesha, who at fourteen felt an excitement about the baby that Opal didn't share. Kenny resisted Opal's claims that the baby was his, and he soon stopped coming by. Back in touch with her mother, Opal called one day and said she wanted to give the baby away. Her mother told her she was talking crazy; babies aren't something you give away. It was another thing to fight about.

As Angie came in one morning, Opal told her it was time. "Stop playin'," Angie said. Then Opal dropped her pants to show that her water had burst. "We fittin' to have a baby!" Angie screamed, jumping up and down. Angie went with Opal to the hospital, and Jewell joined them after work. Bo, Opal's new man, did not, seeing no reason, he said, to come out and "hear you holler." It was nearly midnight by the time Brierra Caples arrived, surrounded by her exhausted mother and two crying aunts. "What y'all crying for?" Opal fussed, pretending to be annoyed. But once the swaddled infant was laid on her chest, all that she could think about was what a beautiful daughter she had. The talk of adoption ceased. She told herself what she was soon telling others, it was time to start doing things right. "You ain't going nowhere, girl," Opal said in the delivery room. "You stayin' right here with me."

drug testing after birth of baby?

FIFTEEN

Caseworker XMI28W: Milwaukee, 1998–2000

Opal's return from the streets didn't register on Michael Steinborn, who had mailed off her employability plan a few weeks earlier but still hadn't met her. With his roster of "job seekers" fifty-something names long, Michael had other problems. One was now standing before him on the coldest day of the year, a candidate for hypothermia.

"*Mi-ike!*" she rasped. She stood so close it was all he could do to keep from backing away. She talked with such a loud lisp he thought she might be retarded. She had lost half her teeth, and her skin looked almost plastic. If she weren't so big in the butt, he would have guessed she was smoking crack. That's the thing he had noticed about addicts: their butts were the first thing to go. As her sandpaper voice silenced the room, the receptionists stopped to stare. "I need a coat, *Mi-ike!* You're my caseworker now, *Mi-ike!*" Michael felt his loathing for his job surge to new highs. "She's a mile a minute with the 'Mikes,'" he thought. "My new best friend."

Since inheriting her case months earlier, he had known her only as a computer code. She hadn't answered his appointment letters. (Typical.) She hadn't complained when he docked her check. (Not typical.) Now here she was in shirtsleeves with the wind-chill factor 24 below. Coats weren't part of Michael's job. That's what all those high-priced "community outreach" specialists were for. But given days to produce, the outreach team produced only excuses. Bunch of nail-filing bitches, he thought. The waste around this place. "They haven't gotten you a coat?" he said. "Look at me *Mi-ike*—does it look like I have a coat?" There was a thrift shop down the street. Michael promised her a coat.

Sometimes when Michael hatched a plan, his body moved faster than his brain. He was halfway out the door when he remembered he only had $4. He climbed back up the stairs, bummed a loan from a coworker, and ran four blocks through the snow. The drifts swallowed his office-worker shoes and buried his toes in ice. The thrift store was out of coats. There was another thrift store two blocks away, and after another frigid sprint Michael was surrounded by coats. There were blue coats and black coats, long coats and short coats; there were so many coats that he was losing his way when a voice came into his head. It was the familiar voice of self-reproach, his *You Idiot!* voice, and it reminded him that he wasn't there to make a fashion statement: just pick one, you idiot! He chose a blue ski jacket with a pink collar, nicer than anything he had expected to find. It cost $11. He had $9. His You Idiot! voice returned: Maximus has a $58 million contract, and you—idiot—can't afford a used coat. He humbled himself before the store clerk, who indulged herself in a show of disdain but let the difference slide.

It wasn't exactly a landmark in the annals of social work. But climbing the Maximus stairs, Michael allowed himself a frisson of satisfaction. The nail filers had sat around all week; Michael Steinborn, can-do guy, had gotten something done. She lifted her arms over her head and made a sour face. "Mi-ike! It's a little snug when I do this, Mi-ike!" The slapstick line came to mind: "Then don't do this!" But the coat had another problem. The zipper didn't work.

Back he went, six blocks through the snow. Back to the sign that warned: "No Exchanges. All Sales Final." What was he supposed to say? Special exceptions for guys like him, dumb-ass social workers with ice in their shoes? The clerk found him too pathetic to bother with; Michael walked out with a lined denim jacket and a zipper that zipped.

"Mi-ike!" she said. "The other one was better looking than this!"

Mi-ike wasn't going back in the cold. *Mi-ike* wasn't wearing a coat himself. He left his at home because his clients' kids kept wiping their Cheeto hands on it. *Mi-ike* said he was done talking about coats. "Okay, Mi-ike!" she said. How about a bus pass? Four days later, in shirtsleeves again, she told Michael's supervisor that no one had been willing to find her a coat.

A social worker! He couldn't believe he was a social worker! Six months earlier he was an unemployed jack of the building trades, drunk by noon and wondering how he and his pregnant girlfriend were going to get by. Now he was a "Financial and Employment Planner," dispensing career advice. He hated the grip of starched collars on his throat. He hated the new-carpet office smell. He hated the officious, self-satisfied talk of some of the senior staff. Above all, he hated feeling responsible for any part of ghetto life, just as he had as a kid collecting his father's rents. "Son, take it from me," his father had warned, after another tenant had trashed an apartment and skipped out owing a big debt. "They'll take and take, and then they'll spit you out." (When he wasn't griping about his tenants, Ted Steinborn was running them on errands and bringing them bags of used clothes.) Growing up in the family business, Michael took pride in never backing down from a fight and had his nose broken three times. The last thing he brought to his profession was a sentimental view of the poor. "I never wanted to be a sucker for a sob story," he said.

Yet as a caseworker Michael was surrounded by sob stories, and just like his father he believed some of them. He could carry on, and did, about his clients' bad-faith betrayals: their games, their evasions, their weak alibis. "You're lied to on a constant basis," he said. But sometimes he felt he was lying, too, talking up the promise in all these dead-end jobs. "People will call and say, 'I got a job!' I feel like saying, 'You're going to have a really fucked-up time living on $6.41 an hour.' But my job is to bullshit them, to say, 'Hey, that's great, it's a first step.'" Clients liked Michael. ("My guardian angel," one said.) Clients trusted Michael. ("Like a brother," said another.) Clients had crushes on Michael. To an extent rare among the city's 150 caseworkers, Michael's career served as a tutorial on what conscientious casework can (and can't) achieve.

Shortly after the coat debacle, Michael's supervisor caught him with an application for a job cutting plate glass. "Are you leaving us?" she asked. He was, sooner than he knew. The next day, when he got to work he just kept driving—nowhere, somewhere, anywhere but here. Resigning with his gas pedal, he spent thirty minutes feeling freed, and then he felt like a loser. He didn't get the plate glass job, and a no-call, no-show was a firing offense, the kind of stunt his clients would pull. Michael assumed he had burned his bridges until his buddy Jose, the manager, called and promised to smooth things over. Give it a second chance, he said. You owe yourself. What he didn't say was that, being shorthanded, Maximus couldn't afford to lose a caseworker, even one as disenchanted as XMI28W. "You fucker," Michael said. "You just want my XMI on the caseload." The next morning, he was back. "I had a new son," he said. "I had to feed him."

The promise of individualized casework—made lavishly in W-2, and echoed in many other programs—is more extraordinary than it sounds. Personalized attention, if it ever existed, was chased from the system two generations ago. Welfare-rights groups called it paternalistic and discriminatory: aid was a right, not a privilege. And budget offices deemed it frightfully expensive, especially as the rolls surged. By the late 1960s, the average caseworker was the equivalent of a postal clerk, a low-paid, rules-oriented cog. In his original proposal for W-2, Jason Turner wrote: "More of the success of Wisconsin Works will ride on the talents . . . [of the] 'financial planners,' than any other collective feature of the new design." He listed some of their ideal attributes: "Creative, intuitive, optimistic, a people person . . . a paradigm shifter, and a problem solver rather than an enabler." But having recruited heavily from the old system, W-2, like most programs, still mostly had postal clerks.

It wasn't as if most clients were eager for a stranger's help, especially when the stranger controlled her check. To Opal (or for that matter, Angie and Jewell), "personalized casework" was a euphemism for someone dipping in her business. Hoping to strengthen ties to their clients, officials in Oswego County, New York, tried an especially client-friendly program called Pathways. The *only* thing clients had to do to keep their checks was appear at a single monthly group meeting. Still more than a third either couldn't or wouldn't attend. "I was shocked," said Toby Herr, the Chicago social worker who designed the program. "They would give up their whole check rather than come. They wanted no part of it." In Milwaukee, the challenge was compounded by the balkanized private system, which ignored the fact that poor people constantly move. One in five clients changed regions

work the system

each year, starting over with a new caseworker who knew nothing about them. Add the turnover *within* agencies, and you get what Opal got in her first year on W-2: six caseworkers at two agencies, of whom one was a fellow addict and another would be convicted of check forgery. And Wisconsin's bureaucracy was typically celebrated as among the country's best.

Yet shortly after Michael went AWOL, something strange occurred. He decided he might be good at the job and that the job might do some good. Casework requires a balance between inspiration and caution, hope and reality; balance wasn't Michael's forte. He skipped lunch to drive clients to job interviews. He brought them his son's used clothes. He stayed up past midnight to rewrite one woman's résumé. (She didn't show up the next day.) He offered to babysit while another enrolled in a training program. (She still didn't go.) When a client showed up desperate for diapers, he blew off his plan for an end-of-the-week beer and gave her his last $10; he knew he'd never get a voucher out of the bureaucracy on a Friday afternoon. Michael had a calculator routine. Follow along, he would say. W-2 pays $673 a month. There are 4.3 weeks in a month and forty hours in a week. Pivoting the calculator, he would show what welfare paid: $3.91 an hour. "Do you think you can do better?" He was waiting, as he put it, to see "the lightbulb go on inside someone's head."

Michael thought he had seen it all, but some things hit him afresh. One seemingly demure twenty-one-year-old always had new hairstyles and clothes. He wondered how she was getting by, especially since he'd been reducing her check. One day, she burst into tears and told him; an old man was paying to kiss her between the legs. He wasn't surprised at what she was doing, only at how much it upset him. Michael was stunned to discover that another client had a terminal liver disease. He had pegged her as a malingerer until the doctor warned she had five months to live. What's more, the county was threatening to drop her from Medicaid. The sick woman wanted to fax in her forms; the county worker told her to "fax your ass over here." Michael stood over the county supervisor's desk, ranting so wildly she started to call the security guard. "They just screw people left and right!" he said, sounding more like a welfare advocate than an agent of welfare repeal. In retrospect, Michael began to think of this period as a crazy jaunt, his SuperFep stage. "I came into this job because I needed money," he said. "Then, I started thinking, 'Maybe I could make a difference.'"

One afternoon, a nervous client named Kimberly Hansen told him she was ready to get out of the house. At twenty-five, she had been home for six years, caring for a daughter with cerebral palsy. But child care was going to be a problem: the girl needed a day-care center with transportation, wheelchair access, and someone who could feed her through a gastrointestinal tube. Previous caseworkers, following the book, had fobbed her off on an ineffective child-care referral service. Michael spent three hours calling around town and got her appointments to inspect two places. The next thing he knew, she filed a complaint with Legal Aid. The group dragged him to a refereed appeal. Absurdly, there was nothing to appeal. He hadn't reduced Hansen's check; he had pledged to keep sending it in full until she found child care. But the Legal Aid lawyer bore in. *You don't understand what you're dealing with here! This child has special needs!* Even Hansen was taken aback. "Michael really did try to help me," she protested. She had called the lawyers with a panic attack, not with a concrete complaint.

A few weeks later, she returned to his office, this time with her daughter, Mercedes. Any grudge Michael felt disappeared. Mercedes was in a wheelchair, paralyzed from the neck down. She had difficulty lifting her head or controlling her saliva flow. Still, she was immaculate, and Hansen hovered over her to keep her that way. Michael turned his head, fighting the impulse to cry. She was obviously a mother of unusual devotion; the last thing she needed was him giving her grief. "I didn't pity her as much as I respected her," he said. He went back to working the phone and helped her find the child care.

She got a job. She lost the job. She fell into a pit of depression. A doctor warned the depression stemmed from her fears of leaving Mercedes, but she wouldn't go to counseling. There are "perverts out there" in day-care centers, she told Michael. Since Mercedes can't talk, if someone tried to hurt her, Hansen wouldn't even know. Months passed until she felt ready to work again. When she did, the day-care center wouldn't let Mercedes return. Hansen owed $40 in late fees and "Ebenezer Day Care," as Michael dubbed it, wouldn't budge. Neither would W-2, which paid child-care bills but not late fees. Michael brokered a repayment plan: Hansen would pay $10 every other week. She missed the first payment. She was stuck at home, as paralyzed as Mercedes, when SuperFep leaped into the breach; he skipped lunch and drove across town to make the payment himself.

The effort went about as smoothly as his trips to the thrift store. Again, he had to borrow the money. Then the center wouldn't take cash. A money order alone wasn't good enough, either; the center demanded a signed agreement, pledging the balance. "She's really in a bad way," Michael pleaded. Rules are rules; blah-diddy-blah; your lack of planning isn't our emergency. He forged her signature and faxed the agreement. His supervisor warned him he was in too deep. Someone discovering that he gave Hansen money might imply he was expecting something in return. But Michael trusted her, and his trust was repaid. When I met her six months later, she described Michael as a "brother." Sometimes Michael felt good about that. Sometimes he reminded himself that she still didn't have a job.

Michael had just donned his SuperFep cape when Opal finally walked in, a few weeks after having Brierra. W-2 hadn't yet caught her attention. But with his gym-rat build and Marlon Brando eyes, Michael did. "He was fine!" she said. "Fine, fine, fine, *fine*-looking white man! I was flirting with him the whole time." Michael didn't notice. As a mother of a newborn, Opal was, for a rare moment, a caseworker's dream: he put her on maternity leave, and they were done for three months. When the leave expired and Michael insisted she do something for her check, he no longer looked so fine. "Michael Stein-some-shit," she would call him.

For now, he had another challenge: the Woman Without a Coat. She reappeared just after his meeting with Opal—loud, raspy, and coatless still. He tried to act indignant about her claim that he hadn't helped her. But his resolve melted in a hail of denials and her loud, sing-songy *Mi-ikes*. "I never said that, Mi-ike! I never told a lie about you!" She popped up in his office, talking gibberish: God is money, the Devil is deaf, beware the millennium bug. But in between her story trickled out. She was thirty-nine, with a grown daughter and a ten-year-old son. She was raised in the ghetto, but not on the streets; her mother was a church woman and her father kept a job. She played high school basketball, got her diploma, and landed a clerical job. Then a decade ago she went to a party where people were smoking a new drug. She figured it couldn't hurt to try it once. She stole, she whored, she slept in the gutter. Treatment programs couldn't keep her off of crack. Only her mother's death, two years ago, gave her the resolve to get clean. Her mother had been "about taking care of business," she would say, and now she was taking care of business, too. "I lost my soul on crack, Mi-ike. I'm about business now, Mi-ike, I'm about business."

At first Michael wasn't sure if he cared. But her stories had a morbid pull, and there was something obligating about her trust. Michael was particularly impressed with the impeccable manners of her son. Sit up straight, she would fuss. Look at the man when you speak. Oddly, he started feeling half pleased when the receptionist announced, with a sarcastic aside, that his train wreck of a client had arrived. While Michael didn't say so, she wasn't the only member of the tandem who often felt desperate about getting through the day. At one point, she brought him a crinkled sheet of greeting-card verse: "Obstacles are only what you see when you take your eye off the goal." He tacked it to his wall.

Bonding was one thing. Binding her to the scaffold of W-2 was another. In January, Michael assigned her a community service job, sorting clothes at the St. Vincent dePaul Society. She never showed up. In February, she called from a pay phone and announced she was going to be a nursing assistant. "Mi-ike, I'm in a training now!" Michael snapped at her: That's not how it works! You can't assign your own activities! "Why not, Mi-ike, if it'll help me get a job?" She didn't get her certificate, but Michael let her keep half her check. "I just didn't have the heart to cut her off," he said. In March, she got an eviction notice after falling four months behind on the rent. Michael grew newly concerned. Most landlords wouldn't carry her that long, and hers was no philanthropist. Michael asked if she had been having "rent dates," swapping sex for shelter, and her denials left him unconvinced. Maximus had a unit to deal with evictions; unfortunately, it was the same one that dealt with coats. She was still looking for a new place when the landlord removed her front door.

It took him weeks, but Michael found a solution. A nonprofit group, Community Advocates, would pay her security deposit. In exchange, it would become her "protective payee," cashing her W-2 check, paying the landlord, and giving her whatever remained. Most recipients balked at losing control of their money, but Michael's client quickly followed through, even putting down $10 for a key. All she had to do was to pick an apartment. SuperFep had gotten it done! But she didn't pick an apartment. She moved to a shelter. And the next thing Michael knew, she was sitting in his boss's office, complaining that no one would help her. He got her to a private room and lost his considerable temper. What was she doing in a homeless shelter? How could she do that to her son?

Her answers didn't make sense. All the vacant houses were on the south side, she said. She grew up on the north side. "I can't live on the south side, Mi-ike." Jesus, she was acting goofy; it was almost enough to make him think she was back on drugs. He was so pissed he started to taunt her: what, are your *connections* on the north side? She flared up and taunted him back: I walk by my connections all day! It took Michael a moment to grasp what she was saying. He hadn't been serious. She wasn't still using. She wasn't still smoking crack? "Yeah, I'm smoking crack!" When was the last time she smoked? Three days ago. She told him she had been clean two years. "I told you what you wanted to hear."

Michael felt the room spin. He felt like a total chump. He had poured some subconscious drive for redemption into a crackhead who had scammed him. "A small part of me knew it the whole time," he said. "I felt really stupid and really useless as somebody who was supposed to be helping her. And I felt very sad for her son." More shouting followed when Michael urged her to return to treatment. No way, she said; treatment programs tell you it's your fault. To some extent, Michael said, it *is* your fault. Don't you think I know that? Don't you think I hate myself every day? It more or less ended there, the conversation and the latest disillusioning chapter in the life of Super-

Fep. No hard feelings, he said with a parting embrace. But he needed to refer her to a more specialized caseworker. "Do what you got to do, Mi-ike. I always do."

A few weeks later, Michael was sitting at his desk, staring at the Excuse Woman. She never did *anything*, this one. The bus was late. The dog was sick. She lost the address. She forgot to call. Doing his best not to look like a man having a breakdown, he excused himself and crossed the hall to his supervisor's office. Question: who could he see about the company's counseling program? He was having a little problem with—how to put this?—managing his anger. He was having a problem with the idea that "financial and employment planners" were going to help "job seekers" scale the "work ladder" to achieve "self-sufficiency." In fact, he found the whole notion ridiculous, and he didn't want to be held responsible for the next calamity. He returned with a pamphlet for Employee Assistance and flashed the Excuse Woman a look of contempt. "What kind of fantasy world are you living in?" he asked.

He went home that night and told his girlfriend, Jai, he was looking for another job. They lie and cheat and lie some more. They bear out the cynic's adage: no good deed among Feps ever goes unpunished. He got no argument from Jai. Her own mother had spent years on welfare and left her for relatives to raise. "I'd tell them their sorry ass was always gonna be in the gutter," she said. "He calls them 'job seekers,' I call them 'money seekers.' I'd cuss 'em out and lose that job!" Michael was going back to hanging drywall. You nail it and it stays in place.

Who was he kidding with his calculator routine? Even his successes were emptying bedpans and swabbing hotel rooms. There's no such thing as a bad first job! Your kids are going to be proud! He'd been to a conference where Tommy Thompson had given that speech, and it had made him cringe. "I'm the guy the politicians hire to tell themselves they're doing something about the underbelly of society: 'Oh, we've got W-2! Isn't it a great program!' It's a farce. It's sickly comic. There's some delusion that we're going to take these people to the next level—that's not going to happen." Michael's midnight resolve faded with morning light. He couldn't quit; he had to pay the rent.

To boost his spirits, he hung up a MaxAcademy "Certificate of Completion" that belonged to a woman he hardly knew. Angiwetta Hills had walked in at closing hour, looking as ragged as her tale. She had lost her job, moved to a shelter, and gotten dropped from the rolls when Employment Solutions, the Goodwill subsidary, failed to properly transfer the case. Here we go again, Michael thought, bracing for a tirade. Instead, she apologized for the way she looked; she had left her clean clothes at a relative's house and hadn't been able to change. Michael spent hours restoring her benefits. Then she surprised him with perfect attendance in Motivation Class. It wasn't exactly a new life. Or even a new job. But the surprise ran in both directions: she hadn't expected a caseworker to work so hard to straighten out her case or offer such reassurance. "He said, 'Everything's going to be all right, Angiwetta. You put in your half and I'll put in mine,'" she said.

His expectations of Dinah Doty ran just as low. At twenty-three, she was a high school dropout, pregnant with her fourth child, and about to be evicted. He rushed to get her a special grant, but she got evicted, anyway. She was pleasant enough, but very street, and Michael had her pegged as a lifer. Once her maternity leave expired, he gave her the calculator spiel: $3.91 an hour, can you beat it? The next week, she announced she had a job as a clerk at a homeless shelter for nearly $8 an hour. And she seemed so—Michael felt embarrassed to say it—*proud*. "Michael gave me that motivation to get up and basically open my eyes," she told me. "I have children to take care of. We conversate about it all the time. Michael understands where I'm coming from."

On that, she may have been more right than she knew. He had lost his business, wrecked his marriage, and wasted his shot at a college degree. There were days when he felt so disgusted with himself he couldn't look in a mirror. And he told that to some of his clients. "I say, 'I *know* what it's like to be down and out. I *know* what it's like to not even be able to get out of bed because you're drunk from the day before and you're too depressed.'" While Michael thought he had nothing to learn about the tragedy of ghetto life, he learned something, anyway. "They don't want to be perceived as vulnerable," he said of his clients. "But when you cut away the exterior, they're sad—sad for themselves, sad for their children, sad that they haven't done more with their lives. And they're just aching for you to listen. Not necessarily to solve their problem, just to listen. I'm not sure if I knew that before and chose to forget it or if I'm learning it for the first time."

The case he saw as his biggest success can be seen as a tribute to either his ample gifts or his slender expectations. In his first stack of dusty cases sat the file of Shelley Block, who had collected $6,000 the previous year without doing a thing. Michael sent letters. Michael made calls. Michael took away her check. That made his telephone ring. "What—you don't give out checks?" she said. He told her to come see him in the morning. "I don't *do* mornings," she said. Finally, she darkened his door. Literally. She weighed more than three hundred pounds. She had a pierced tongue and a tattooed neck, and she was as cynical in person as she was on the phone. Michael found her enchanting. "Everything she said made me laugh," he said. When she talked, vaguely, about becoming a nursing aide, Michael told her the truth: she was too fat to stand up all day. "I respected him for that," she told me. He lured her to MaxAcademy just to get her out of the house. Then he arranged a work assignment at Maximus, to keep her in sight. They talked—about her boyfriend, her boyfriend's crack problem, her days in a street gang. "He made me feel like he actually cared," she said.

One day, she arrived in his office especially depressed. She had dumped the crackhead boyfriend, who then broke in the house and beat her up. Michael responded with the best you-are-somebody lecture she had heard. "I see you as an authority figure," he said. "I can see you sitting behind a desk, making sound money. Don't ever let anybody put you down." When she got back to the car, her mother asked why she was crying. "Michael just makes me feel real good about myself," she said. Not long after, when Michael fell captive to one of his depressions and told her he wanted to leave, she turned the lecture around. "I told him, 'Don't quit! You're too good at what you do.'"

After a year on Michael's caseload, Shelley Block got a job. It was nothing that either one of them would mistake for a social triumph: a part-time job at an after-school program, driving a bus. It paid $7.25

an hour. It might lead to something better. But probably not. "Fep of the year," he said to himself. "A part-time bus driver. Big deal." Not long after, one of Michael's coworkers was down in the dumps, griping about the caseworker's lot. The clients don't listen. The system's a mess. The whole thing's a big con. Michael stunned himself with his response. "We do God's work here," he said. For a moment, he believed it.

SIXTEEN

Boyfriends:
Milwaukee, Spring 1999

Angie did her share of God's work, too. She had been doing it now for three years: lifting, washing, dressing, and feeding the infirm. She did it before sunrise and after midnight. She did it when her feet were sore and her back had shooting pains. She did it in an old Polish neighborhood that once rioted to keep black people away. She did it without complaint. Stepping off a bus eight years earlier, looking for a welfare check, Angie was someone society carried. Now she carried those who couldn't carry themselves. "Angie has a sparkle," said her supervisor, Wendy Woolcott-Steele. "I think she's ace."

Angie's story had a special luster, but it conveyed a common theme: whatever the frustrations of SuperFeps or the failures of the bureaucracy, poor single mothers, defying predictions, went to work at unprecedented rates. Although they didn't all sparkle, about three-quarters of the women leaving the rolls in the late 1990s worked in the subsequent year. Six in ten worked at any given time, and those with jobs worked nearly full time, about thirty-five hours a week. No doubt the surging economy offered ideal conditions. Yet previous booms had largely left welfare families behind, and the gains were greatest among the most disadvantaged, which discounts the notion that a rising tide simply lifted all boats. The employment rates of never-married women rose nearly 50 percent, while those least affected by welfare policy (married, college educated, or childless) scarcely changed. In its curious mix of hassles ("They gave me a lot of yada, yada, yada. I said, 'Screw 'em' and found me a job") and help (child care and tax credits), the drive to end welfare created a singular employment machine. "It succeeded beyond, I think, what any-body could have rationally predicted," Clinton told me. And on one level he was right.

But the advocates of the law had talked on other levels, too—not just of putting poor people to work but of the rewards that work would bring. "Work organizes life," Clinton had said. "It gives mean-ing and self-esteem to people who are parents. It gives a role model to children." The celebrations of the law were celebrations of its social bequests—of *meaning* and *role models* and transformed kids. Of parables like that of Lillie Harden and her son. About the time Angie let Opal move in, Tommy Thompson invited another welfare-to-work success to tell her story during his State of the State Address. Michelle Crawford had gone from two decades of depression and drugs on wel-fare to a job at a plastics factory. Facing the legislature beside the man she nervously called "Government Thompson," she stole the show. "Today, I'm working as a machine operator, providing for my family," she said. Then, with flawless timing, she pointed toward the gallery where three of her children were watching. "Now, I tell my kids that this is what you get when you do your homework!"

The author Mickey Kaus went so far as to argue that the rising work rates presaged "The Ending of the Black Underclass."

> [B]y definition and in practice, working-poor mothers aren't in the "underclass." A maid changing sheets in a Marriott is no longer cut off from the world of work. . . . She can't afford to develop an attitude that sets itself in op-position to the mainstream culture. Her children will grow up knowing the discipline of a working home, and they will have at least one working "role model. . . ." If women know they . . . are going to have to work, they are apt to ask that men contribute by going to work. Young women will be less likely to have children out of wedlock.

Ordered lives, elevated hopes, inspired kids: it was a lot to hope for from a low-wage job. Three years into her postwelfare life, Angie Jobe—indefatigable worker, hard liver—offered one ground-level view.

Taking in Opal was God's work reprised, but there was a price to Angie's charity. With the pit bulls having destroyed the attic, Angie was out of space. The boys shared a foldout sofa in the living room, while Opal, Kesha, and Brierra squeezed into one bed and Angie and Marcus shared the other. The Concordia Street house was a shambles. The second-floor balcony dropped rails like rotted teeth, and so many roaches swarmed about that Opal lay awake worried that one would crawl in Brierra's ear. Angie blamed the landlord for not fixing things. The landlord blamed Angie for not paying the rent and tried to evict her twice. Before Marcus had gotten the pit bulls, someone had tried to break into Kesha's room. Two days after Opal moved in, there was a shooting in the abandoned apartment below. Opal's arrival settled things. Angie decided to move.

With tax time near, Angie had another windfall coming: $5,300, the equivalent of five months' pay. In truth, it was enough to subsidize a move to a better part of town. But Angie didn't know anyone in a better part of town. And she had neither a car nor the instincts of a housing pioneer. She found four bedrooms in a duplex on the near north side, at 2400 West Brown. The street took its name from Samuel Brown, the nineteenth-century settler who had turned his farm there into a stop on the Underground Railroad. By the time Angie arrived, the street cut through so many vacant lots it looked like it was being reclaimed by Farmer Brown's fields. Jewell had been living on Brown Street when gunfire had forced her to sleep on the floor and when Lucky had been shot in the hand. And a few years later, Brown Street would make the national news when a gang of boys, some as young as ten, armed themselves with shovels and bats and beat a neighborhood man to his death. Opal knew the area, too; Andrea's crack house was a short walk away. But at $450 a month, the price of Angie's new house was right. And Angie figured it wasn't much different from other places she had lived.

Just before the move, she and Opal stopped in for a look. The friendly new landlord was there, gluing down new living room carpet and throwing up a fresh coat of paint. "I want everything to be just right for you, Miss Jobe," he said. Opal thought that he might be a little too friendly. She noticed that without Marcus around Angie was friendly, too. "Oh, I want everything to be just right for you, Miss Jobe," she sang, as they got out of earshot. "Shut up, creep," Angie laughed. Angie worked the day of the move, so she missed most of the adventure. The kids packed their clothes in Hefty bags. The apartment had no appliances, so Marcus had to rent a trailer to tote the refrigerator and stove. His $500 Chevy broke down twice, bringing out Jewell in the snow to give him a jump. They finished at 1:30 in the morning. "We had a ghetto move," Kesha said.

The practical thing for Angie to do with the money that remained would have been to buy a car. Until she got one, Angie would be stuck with the lower wages along the bus line. Instead, she bought furniture again. Darrell got a new bedroom set, having destroyed his with more bed-jumping games. The living room got a new black-and-green couch, and the windows got window blinds. Angie didn't have a dining room, but she bought place settings for her dining room table and put it in the living room. Then she banned the kids from eating there. Sometimes when there's turmoil inside, you yearn to set appearances right.

Maybe it was her years in Catholic school, but Angie still believed in salvation, her own and that of others. Opal was pledging to kick the cocaine and get the girls back from her mother. Angie thought she could do it. The birth of Brierra had brought a surge of maternal diligence, to the point where Opal asked a hospital social worker about treatment programs. She didn't realize the social worker was attached to the county child welfare agency. When the conversation triggered a visit to Concordia Street, the caseworker grew so alarmed at the pit bulls and roaches that she threatened to take Brierra away. Opal beat a quick retreat to Jewell's and the incipient investigation fizzled. But so did Opal's talk of programs. "If I go to one of them, I got to cut the drinking out, too," she said.

Her short stay at Jewell's brought problems. Soon after Opal moved in, Jewell's car broke down. Jewell left Opal $100 to have it towed, and when she got home from work, Opal was gone. So was Jewell's money, along with a bunch of her video games and her pearl-handled .22. Jewell wasn't surprised that Opal would steal. But she was stunned that Opal would steal from her. From *family*. While Angie was trying to play Good Shepherd to Opal, Jewell's ethos was an eye for an eye: when Opal returned the following day, Jewell barred her from the house, kept her clothes, and temporarily took her food stamps. Jewell eventually let go of her anger but not her residential ban; Opal wasn't allowed in the house unless Jewell herself was there. Angie made a minor show of taking Opal back. "Let her come over here," she said. "I ain't got nothing to steal." It was a line that would make Jewell laugh.

Angie got a package deal. In taking in Opal, she not only got an infant, Brierra, she also got Opal's "friend" from the crack house, Bo. "I ain't fittin' to be Cuckoo for Cocoa Puffs," Opal said—not crazy for some man. But as her talk of sobriety faded, her talk of Bo increased. She said he made her feel "giddy-ish." Giddy was hard to understand— he was pitted, scraggy, dull, and dumb—but one could guess a source of his appeal. "Drugs!" Angie said. "'Cause he ain't no good-looking motherfucker!" What Bo saw in Opal was harder to say; most dealers didn't want a girlfriend consuming their goods. Her ability to win him over was both a tribute to her survival skills and his lack of alternatives. Mostly, they argued. On maternity leave from the work rules she had previously ignored, Opal had too much time on her hands, and she spent it in a jealous dudgeon. In a typical incident, she would accuse Bo of sleeping with his ex-girlfriend and threaten to leave; Bo would feign indifference but compensate with Pampers or a used VCR that someone had traded in for drugs. If Angie had misgivings about the soap opera in her living room, she kept them to herself. She figured it was Opal's business and nothing the kids hadn't seen.

Shortly after the move, Opal got $400 in tax credits from a month's work the previous year. The next morning, Jewell was standing in Angie's kitchen, bouncing a yo-yo. It was Saturday, and she had promised to take Opal shopping for baby clothes. Opal wasn't there. "Gone all night?" Jewell said.

"You shoulda gone yesterday!" Angie fussed.

"Oh, Opal," Jewell said.

Von arrived home from a fifth-grade basketball game, aiming a Sprite like a machine gun. "Y'all win?" Angie asked.

"We lost by five."

"Y'all always lose," she said. "Y'all the Bad News Bears."

"Opal, Opal, Opal!" Jewell said.

Darrell, who was five, chimed in. "She probably got lost over there," he said. Everyone knew where "over there" was. Andrea's house.

Bo walked in at midday, not knowing Opal was missing. "Where Brierra at?" he asked. Brierra was with Kesha (as usual), and Bo left on a scouting mission.

"Bring her back!" Jewell said.

"I mean put her on your back and carry her!" Angie said.

No one was going to find Opal until Opal was ready to be found. She had stayed at Andrea's until 4:00 in the morning, smoking up her tax money, when one of the night's big spenders told her he was tired of overpaying for dime bags. He wanted a quarter, a quantity the size of a Ping-Pong ball. It sells for $250, but not to an unknown white guy on Brown Street in the middle of the night. Opal knew a place to get one, and they got back to his house at sunrise on Saturday to celebrate their luck. By Sunday morning, when Opal came home, she had been partying for two nights and a day. Angie held her tongue. She had problems of her own.

case worker perception

One of them was Marcus. Like many poor black men, Marcus looked worse on paper than he did in person. On paper, he was a sporadically employed eleventh-grade dropout with a history of drug dealing and carrying illegal weapons—technically a habitual criminal. In person, he was an aimless but mostly placid soul who, lacking a father, had spent his youth seeking brotherhood in a gang. His twenty-five-year-old body was all hard edges—shaved head, tattooed biceps—but any air of menace was offset by a pair of basset hound eyes; he showed more interest in smoking blunts than in doing anyone harm. When they came to blows, Angie usually counted herself the aggressor. "I have a worse temper," she said. "He have to psyche hisself up to be mean."

The story of Angie and Marcus is, among other things, the story of the limits of a social reform that almost exclusively targets one gender.

In the end-welfare years, poor women went to work in record numbers. But poor men did not. And young, low-skilled black men—the sea in which women like Angie swim—continued to leave the job market at disconcerting rates. Despite the booming economy, the employment rates of young black men fell faster in the 1990s than they did the decade before. By the end of the nineties, only about half of young black men had jobs, compared with nearly 80 percent of Hispanics and whites. Theories abound: disheartening wages, high prison rates, the flight of urban jobs, employer discrimination even toward those with no record. (Does anyone draw more suspicion than a young black man?) Flooding the labor market with competition from women may even have made things marginally worse. It may be an exaggeration to say that behind every successful worker like Angie lurked a jealous, potentially disruptive man. But it's not a huge exaggeration.

David J. Pate Jr., a doctoral candidate at the University of Wisconsin, spent two years tracking black men in Milwaukee with children on welfare. On average they earned $8,800 a year and owed $6,500 in back support. Three-quarters had a high school diploma or less. Two-thirds had criminal convictions. Though their average age was thirty-four, many couldn't secure a badge of adulthood as basic as a driver's license or an apartment—a quarter still lived with their mothers. Where others have seen cavalier dereliction, Pate (who also runs a fatherhood program) viewed the men through sympathetic eyes. He saw wounded castaways—rejected by employers, chased by the courts, and exiled by the mothers of their kids. With the mothers in new relationships, some of the men couldn't see their children no matter how hard they tried. In the men's minds, the mothers' failures loomed large, especially when the mothers were on drugs: why should my money go to *her*? Pate may be right in arguing that "most of these men aspired to be good fathers." But the modesty of their gestures was revealing. "I buy diapers all that," boasted Deion, a jobless twenty-one-year-old. I once spent a day in a Milwaukee class that forced absent fathers like these to write their own obituaries through the eyes of the children they scarcely knew. "He really wasn't involved in our lives," stammered one man, imagining what his two-year-old twins might someday say over his coffin. He added a hopeful "but we respect him." By the time that Pate finished his study, two of the thirty-six men had been murdered.

If working mothers will save the underclass, having one hadn't saved Marcus. After stepping off a bus from Memphis, Mary Williams made a career slinging greens at Perkins, a Milwaukee soul-food palace. But Marcus's older brother was locked up for selling drugs, and his sister was strung out on drugs. "His mama real nice—I don't know how she got all them crazy-assed kids," Angie said. The same could be said about most people Angie knew. Like Opal, Marcus met his father just once, and his father was drunk at the time. "My mama was my daddy," he said. At fifteen, he joined the "Brothers of Struggle," neighborhood guys with bankrolls and loud cars. He tattooed a six-point star on one arm and put "Love Mom" on the other. Marcus thought the gang "stood for something," though he couldn't say just what. "You had all these guys behind you," he said. "Like a family." After dropping out of school, he cut meat in corner grocery stores and helped his guys sell weed and cocaine.

His twenty-third year was rough. He got caught in a drug house, selling crack. He got robbed at shotgun of two pounds of marijuana. Then his gang brothers accused him of stealing the weed and broke his arms with two-by-fours. Being hospitalized and sent to jail tempered his enthusiasm for the gang life, without quite extinguishing it: he would still earnestly recite the catechism of the six-point star: love, knowledge, wisdom, life, loyalty, understanding. He had been out of jail and working for two months, when Angie walked in the grocery store and Marcus saw more stars. "I just wanted to know her real bad," he said. She was eight years older, a woman of the world. She radiated class. On their first date, he took her to an all-night diner. "You can't just take Angie to McDonald's or Burger King," he said.

At the start, Angie may have cared for Marcus more than she liked to admit. She was lonely, he was handsome, and he introduced himself with a smile. He cooked and cleaned and watched the kids; occasionally he bought them clothes. On Mother's Day, he surprised Angie with flowers and balloons. There was one problem, Angie said: "Motherfucker just not faithful." As they got together, another woman spotted Marcus with Angie and dumped a pile of his clothes in the street. Angie knew there were others. "My day is coming," she would say. By the time she moved to Brown Street, it had come. Angie was staying out half the night, "talking" to a coworker named Tony. There were nights when Angie didn't come home; she'd say she stayed at Jewell's. One night Marcus confronted Tony, who assured him there was nothing going on. Opal thought Marcus had to know but was pretending that he didn't.

The kids viewed Marcus with a mixture of indifference and contempt. If Angie didn't respect him, why should they? But they also spent a lot of time alone with him—and a lot of time just alone. Angie worked the second shift, 2:00 to 10:00 p.m., which left her gone during most of their free hours. Just shy of fifteen, Kesha arrived on Brown Street with a wide smile, crooked canines, and the burdens and privileges of the oldest child. She was still enough of a little girl to dote on her kittens and keep a kitchen play set in her room. And enough of a teenager to always have a boy on her mind. "Dear Mom, I have a lot of questions about sex," she wrote after Marcus spotted her kissing one of her neighborhood suitors. "It's not like going to do anything elec because I'm not really. . . . You going to have to understand that I'm start to be a young lady." Hospitalized with asthma for weeks at a time the previous year, Kesha had missed half of seventh grade and failed nearly every course. Virtually raising Brierra, she was absent a good bit of eighth.

While Kesha had babies and boys on her mind, Redd seemed to have nothing in mind at all. Still, he would talk the paint off the wall in an effort to make himself heard. At thirteen, he spent his free time in the cramped living room, filibustering the walls, a portrait of growing, inchoate rage. "Apply yourself," Greg had written from prison. "Start going to the library at least twice a week." Instead Redd bought a CD and rapped to "I Don't Give a Fuck." His father was just another stranger. If Redd had troubles that were going unheeded, Von had potential that was going unshaped. At eleven, he was still a boy focused on boyhood stuff—cars, sports, and video games—and alone among Angie's kids, he felt invested in school. But Von "is always catching up, rather than being up," his fifth grade teacher warned. "Being up" was part of the problem. As Angie and Marcus had started to quarrel, Von had stopped going to bed; he waited until his mother was safely home, "'cause I knew they was gonna come in fighting when the bars closed." The semester that Marcus moved in, Von's school absences rose 50 percent. Darrell, at six, crawled in my lap whenever I walked in the door. He was all but walking through life with a sign that read Someone Hug Me.

I dropped in one night around the dinner hour. No one was talking about dinner. Angie was at the nursing home, feeding her patients. Marcus was gone. Opal was emitting operatic groans. Her three months of maternity leave had expired, and Michael Steinborn had promptly scheduled her for MaxAcademy. She was due there the next morning at 8:00. "I'm not going to be able to do it," she said. Von was practicing his pickup lines. "I'm a player, not a hater," he said.

But the real player was Kesha, who was mulling the problem with her latest boyfriend, Larry. They had met on a four-way telephone call and talked every day for a month before meeting face-to-face. Then one day, Kesha was at Jewell's, and Jewell said Larry could come by, and—

Darrell broke in. After a long absence, his father had started to visit again. "My daddy got a job, Kesha!"

"Mama told you that," Kesha said.

Darrell said he told his father, "I didn't know you had a job!"

Kesha wasn't interested in Darrell's daddy; Kesha was interested in Larry. So . . . Larry came over, and he was six-foot-one; and they played video games and put on some music; and Larry clapped and yelled, "Hit that note!" as Kesha sang along. Then they went to get some Tater Tots for Jewell, and Larry had to go. "And he was like, 'You ain't gonna give me no kiss?' And I said, 'Boy, what's your problem?'" This part of the story made her smile. "Then I gave him a hug and kiss!"

"*Ooow,* you *kissed* him!" Her brothers were listening in.

"Stop dippin'!" Kesha said, delighted with the audience.

The boys started to sing: "In the bedroom . . . In the hallway . . . We can do it anywhere."

Though nearly two months had passed, Kesha hadn't seen Larry again. He lived too far away, and she was wondering if they should break up. "I don't want no kids," she said. Then: "I want a daughter." Then: "I want to get married before I have a baby. My mama didn't

ever get married. I want a big wedding. I never been to a wedding."
Angie had never been to a wedding, either. "If it's in the summer I
want to have it in a big old church," Kesha said. "I think it'd be a lot of
fun if you be together a long time. My mama been with my dad for
seven years before he went to jail—"

Kesha's vision of domestic bliss vanished as Marcus stormed in. "It
smells like must through the whole house!" he said. It was 8:15 p.m.
The breakfast dishes were still in the sink, and the boys' room was
buried in clothing drifts three feet tall. Darrell added more bad news:
Redd had skipped school. "Your ass is mine!" Marcus said. "My mama
said it ain't!" Redd said, and ran to his room.

Kesha called Darrell a "tattletale punk" and slapped him on the
head. Marcus was so angry—*this mess! these kids!*—he looked ready
to charge the wall. "You were told to do the dishes last night!" he
screamed.

"Last *night*?" The sarcasm dripped from Kesha's voice and pooled
on the unswept floor. "This is a whole new day, Marcus."

Darrell bawled from Kesha's slap. Redd ran to the pay phone
across the street and tried to reach Angie. But she was too busy with
patients to come to the phone. "Go call your motherfucking mama,"
Marcus said, disappearing into his room. "And when you're done
come deal with me!" Kesha rolled her eyes. It was almost 9:00 and no
one had eaten. No wonder tempers flared. "We're all hungry," she said.

"Goal-setting is very important! . . . If you fail to plan, you plan to
fail! . . . Getting a job is a full-time job!" The motivation lady was
preaching the next morning, but Opal wasn't in the mood. She was
slumped in a chair, eyes barely open, as the waves of aphorism
crashed overhead. Angie had come home and fought with Marcus all
night, then roused Opal and ordered her to class. "Last name, first
name, Social Security number! This calendar is what you will follow
each and every day while you're here at MaxAcademy. . . . Problem
resolution, dressing for success—we'll have workshops! . . . We've
had people from all over the world watching us, from Germany, Sweden! . . . It's all about children—that's why we're here!"

Two other people had shown up, neither with greater interest. Opal would give it one day. She had sat through so many motivation classes, she complained the curriculum was out of order: assessment tests belonged on the second day. "We changed it," the instructor said. As Opal played along with her number-two pencil (yes, she would like to "study ruins"; no, she wouldn't like to "grow grain"), Michael stopped by. "How's the baby doing?" he said. It was only their second meeting, and—now that he had stuck her in MaxAcademy—less pleasant than her first. Taking her aside, he noted she had missed her last appointment and said he didn't buy the excuse about babysitting problems. If she didn't attend the classes, he said, she couldn't get a check.

Opal glared. "I don't want to be here," she said.

"You really don't have any option," he said. "I take that back. You do have an option—you don't have to participate in the W-2 program." Caseworkers can sound nasty when they want but there was nothing nasty in Michael's voice. "I pulled your case history," he said. "You don't call, you don't show. I pulled your employment history. It's sketchy at best. . . . Do you have your GED?"

Opal clucked her tongue. "I have a high school diploma!" she said. "And some college!"

Michael looked skeptical. He told her to spend a few weeks in the class, to establish a morning routine. "Sometimes you need to be pushed in certain directions," he said.

"I don't."

"We'll see."

He gave her a week to find child care. After that, he warned, every hour's absence would be deducted from her check. Opal dragged herself back to class, leaving a trail of artificial braids on the rug. Even bodily she was coming unglued. "'Well you *say* you got a high school diploma,'" she fumed. "Like I was lying!"

Two days later, Mercy called in too many aides, and Angie got sent home. She figured it was just as well. Her feet were tired and she had errands to run, but she was waiting for Kesha to come home from school. In the morning's confusion, Redd hadn't been able to find the coat that Jewell had bought for his birthday. Angie was hoping that Kesha had worn it. Opal, who had been acting irritable all morning, came out of her room just before Kesha was due to arrive. Kesha didn't have the coat, she said. The crack house did.

Angie gasped. "You took Redd's birthday coat?" And the Play Station. And the CDs. And Kesha's radio and Von's new video game, Crash Bandicoot. Opal had been slipping in and out since dawn, auctioning off the kids' stuff. Angie was no stranger to fury, but Opal's betrayal propelled her to new heights: stealing's one thing, even stealing from me—but how could you steal from my *kids*? Opal started to pack and leave, but Angie demanded something more painful, a humiliating public confession as each of the kids walked in. Everyone yelled at Opal that day. Angie yelled, Bo yelled, Kesha, who was all but raising Opal's baby, yelled most of all: "You're a thief! You hurt people! You should leave that shit alone!" Marcus grabbed his gun and started toward the crack house until Angie reeled him in. "You don't go to no dope spot and tell 'em you want your stuff back," she said. "Marcus ain't wrapped too tight." Opal agreed to replace the items with her next welfare check and spent the afternoon looking contrite. Despite her anger, Angie, unlike Jewell, refused to put her out. "I wouldn't do that to Brierra," she said. Opal "would be in a shelter, just doing it again." At dinner, Opal asked Angie to go with her to a sobriety meeting, Opal's first in a year. When they got there, they found the meeting had moved. Looking back, Angie saw the trip as part of the con. "She knew they didn't have meetings no more," she said.

One good thing about the rhythm of the house was that it left no time to brood about old trouble; new trouble was always on the way. The next day, Opal's mother drove up from Chicago and left the girls for spring break. Eight kids, one bathroom, and a limited supply of food didn't make for a happy week. Opal's four daughters slept with her, piled in the bed with Bo. Redd tried to keep them from eating the cookies. Von put gum in Sierra's hair; Sierra put gum on Von. Opal locked Von out of the house, and when Von shook his finger in her face, Opal put him in a headlock and threw him to the floor. "When I got through with him, he was *real* hurt," she said.

The cocaine was playing tricks with Opal's eyes, highlighting the transgressions of everyone else, while blinding her to her own. She didn't approve of Angie's nagging: "She think she can be my mother!" She resented Angie's request for rent: "And spend all my food stamps? She is ripping me off." She didn't approve of Angie's parenting: "Them kids ain't never in school." She criticized Angie's consumption of beer: "I said, 'You ain't nothing but an alcoholic.'" Angie knew that Opal was busy cataloging her sins. But her refusal to put Opal out had grown to a point of pride. "You can't get angry any more," she said. "All you can do is pray now—just hope she find her way."

Jewell kept her distance from Angie and Opal, clucking her tongue at the antics. "Ain't neither one of them doing what they really supposed to," she said. By contrast, Jewell's house formed an oasis of tranquility. Jewell kept more regular hours than Angie; she didn't drink; and she kept her kids on a tighter leash. Like Angie, she had taken in a needy relative, but her nephew Quinten had just turned five, so she didn't have to worry about him pawning her stuff for drugs. The aura of or-der—or maybe just the big TV—made Jewell's place a favorite desti-nation for Angie's kids. She had a white tiger-skin sofa and rug and a stack of G movies from *A Bug's Life* to *Babe*. Jewell's house felt like Jewell, racy yet domestic.

In some ways, Jewell's success on the job was even more impres-sive than Angie's, since she started with so little experience. After eight years on welfare, she was a 9-to-5 scanner of nameless objects on an industrial shipping line. But work was simply something she did. What she cared about was Ken, whose prominence in Jewell's post-welfare story was unlikely to get featured in a State of the State Address. Jewell's wages paid some of the bills. The remnants of Ken's drug and prostitution money paid others. While most of Jewell's friends might wait six months for an imprisoned man, they wouldn't wait two years, especially for one deftly promising nothing in return. Jewell decided the separation was a test—"to see if our love is strong enough"—and wrote him every other day. "That's all she talk about," giggled her seven-year-old, Tremmell. "Oh, I miss my boo-boo!"

Tina, Ken's hooker, missed Ken, too, and in his absence Jewell's conflicts with her grew. Jewell said Tina wrote Ken letters peddling the lie that Jewell was smoking crack. She said Tina called G. B. Electric and tried to get her fired by claiming that Jewell had threatened to beat her up. (After that, Jewell said, she *did* threaten to beat Tina up.) One day, Jewell emerged from work to find that the car that Ken had left her was gone. Jewell remembered that Tina had a key, and since

Jewell didn't have the title, the police said there was nothing they could do. Soon Jewell found a hospital bill collector at her door, seeking payment for treating her venereal disease. "I ain't got no gonorrhea!" she said. Then she realized she left some papers in the car. Tina had her Social Security number. *fraud*

Ken and Jewell were together when he left, but not *together.* He didn't fully think of Jewell as his girlfriend, and he had Tina turning tricks. In person Jewell had stopped short of making demands, but in his absence her boldness grew. She told him to stop "waiting on some Miss America or Miss Hollywood to come to your life." She told him she wanted him to herself. Mail is everything to a man locked up, and Ken had nothing but time to ponder Jewell's devotion. She wrote him twenty times in the first month alone and sent him money and clothes. As Jewell grew more open, Ken did, too. "I really don't know what my problem is," he wrote. "[I]ts a man thing," he tried to explain. One letter said, "I'm willing to give it a try." Another called her a "soulmate."

> [Y]ou may not be that Miss hollywood or Miss America as you say but you are everything in a women that a man could want sense of humor, best friend, a sister I never had and a great Lover . . . you are like a dream. . . . I can't make any promises but I am willing to put effort into it. . . . I want to keep our relationship sacred.

"I couldn't stop reading it," Jewell said. At first, he signed off, "Okay, Ken" or "I'll holler at you." Then came a letter that said, "I love you" and one to "my gorgeous wife." How much was love, how much was loneliness, even he couldn't say. There were tensions, too; needing someone to watch Quinten, Jewell had let Lucky back in the house, and he intercepted Ken's mail. "I know he's your rent-a-dad," Ken fumed, routing his letters through a friend, but "make his Ass stand outside." Still, the sheer force of Jewell's devotion was one that Tina couldn't match. When Tina promised a package that she never sent, Ken wrote her to say they were through.

He had been gone for two months when Jewell got a letter that made her spirits soar. "Hello there my sexy wife," it began.

I almost feel as you do. . . . I feel that we're so close in our
love that when I'm not with you I'm just not where I want
to be, everyday we spend apart is starting to feel like
twenty-four more hours of lost, lonely time slowly ticking
away. . . . So until you're in my arms please remember you
are always, always on my mind; you are never, never out of
my heart and you are needed more than ever in my life.

"Finally!" Jewell said. She strolled through the aisles of Sam's
Club, pointing out the brand of diapers they'd wrap their baby in. She
told him that her friends hadn't believed her when she said they were
going to get married. *Married?* Whatever he felt toward his "sexy
wife," a wedding was the last thing on Ken's mind. He was up for parole after six months and eager to get back to business, with Jewell or
without her. "I said, 'Till death do us part,'" he wrote back. "So do that
math."

Till death do we part—do the math. Ken started to say it all the
time. Now and then, when her spirits sagged, Jewell wondered what
it meant.

As Jewell chased her vision of the happy home, Angie's home life con-
tinued to fray. A week in April marked a calendar of chaos at 2400
West Brown. *Sunday:* Opal's tooth had been aching for weeks. Bo's
Mama told her to spray it with perfume, and she vomited all over her
room. *Monday:* Angie left for work after lunch and never came home.
She called Marcus the next day to say that she had stayed at Jewell's.
She didn't care if he believed her. *Tuesday:* Kesha was ready to fight
Marcus, this time over a kitten. When her cat, Oreo, had gone into la-
bor, Kesha had donned surgical gloves and stayed up all night, deliv-
ering the litter herself. Now the kittens were ready to be weaned, and
Marcus had promised one to a friend. "Bet you ain't taking my kitten!"
Kesha screamed, standing on the bed with her fists balled up. With
Angie at work, it took Opal and Jewell to pull her away.

Wednesday: When morning arrived, Angie was home, and the
fight was still in swing. "Jewell! Jewell!" Opal reported. "I tell you, if

you woulda seen your niece, it woulda knocked you out! Angie told her fifteen times to get up and go to school. Kesha said, 'Mama, you make me sick—I ain't goin' nowhere!'"

Mama, you make me sick? "I woulda grabbed her by the collar!" Jewell said.

"Grab her by the collar?" Opal said. "I woulda grabbed her by the hair and dragged her out the house!"

"Wouldna been a crochet left in her hair!" Jewell said. "Redd, Kesha, and Von—they gonna whup her."

"If I was a man," Opal said, "I would not be living with Angie and putting up with her disrespectful-ass kids."

Thursday: Marcus was thinking along similar lines. Angie was gone—he wasn't sure where—and he and I were sitting in a bar. Angie gave him little time, he said. The kids gave him nothing but lip. He cooked and cleaned and ignored the snubs, but they stung more than he showed. "The kids don't listen to nothing I say—they don't respect me," he said. "But whenever they need a pair of shoes, who do they ask? Sometimes I'm like, 'Man, I should pack up and leave.'" Saying so only left him more melancholy; where would he go? "Deep down, each of them got they own way to love me, I guess."

Marcus got home at 1:00 a.m., full of Courvoisier. Angie rode up ninety minutes later, with Tony at the wheel. Marcus swore he saw her kissing him! He knew she had been messing with that man! Suddenly Marcus was banging on the car window and running for his shotgun. As Angie climbed the steps, Marcus was shooting at Tony's taillights. Angie brushed past him with a laugh. Hadn't she warned him that her day was coming? She taunted him with an R. Kelly song about feminine revenge—"When a Woman's Fed Up"—and locked herself in the bathroom. The next thing she knew, Marcus had blasted a hole in the ceiling outside the door.

"I was thinking, 'Damn! This motherfucker's trying to *kill* me!'" Angie said.

Kesha grabbed a skillet. Von used his fists. Marcus dropped the gun, and as Angie came out he grabbed her by the throat. "When a woman's fed up!" she sang again. Marcus sobbed with rage. Redd ran to the pay phone and called the police, who found Angie on the porch in the rain, swinging at Marcus with a broom. They wrote it off as a drunken lovers' squabble and sent Marcus on his way. Up all night, the kids stayed home from school the next day. Other than that, the only thing hurt was Marcus's pride and the friendly landlord's ceiling.

"Freedom!" Angie announced the next afternoon. "He can't come back no more. . . . That's *my* house. *I* pay the bills!" A few days later, Marcus was back, sweeping the kitchen as though nothing had happened.

SEVENTEEN

Money:
Milwaukee, Summer 1999

"Who the hell is FICA?" Angie fumed. "They be eatin' my ass *up*." If Opal and Marcus were one source of frustration, her pay stub was another and closer to her heart. Leaving welfare, juggling multiple jobs, Angie had done all a welfare reformer could ask. And she had done it with a kind of willed faith that work would eventually pay. "I want my own house," she said, after some Brown Street kids tossed a rock through her window. "With a fence!"

On the surface, she was making good progress. Had she stayed on welfare, her cash and food stamps would have come to about $14,400 a year. In her first three years off welfare, her annual income (in constant dollars) averaged more than $24,900. On paper, she was up more than $10,000—a gain of nearly 75 percent.

Yet it didn't feel that way. Usually she said she has "a little more money, but it ain't that much." On a bleak day, she said, "No, I'm not better off economically—not yet."

While that may just sound like Angie grousing, it's a pretty fair read of the evidence. Like almost all recipients, Angie never lived on welfare alone; she had boyfriends of varying means and a series of (mostly) covert jobs. Quantifying the help from her boyfriends is hard. But through the tax returns lying in the bottom of her closet and her old welfare records, it's possible to see how Angie's part of the finances really worked. A comparison of her last four years on welfare with her first three years off produces a box score that looks like this:

	On Welfare	Off Welfare
Earnings:	$ 6,500	$16,100
Tax Credits:	$ 2,300	$ 5,600
Payroll Taxes:	$ -500	$-1,200
Cash Welfare:	$ 8,400	$ 0
Food Stamps:	$ 4,800	$ 4,400
Total Income:	$21,500	$24,900

As a strategy for promoting work, the law did its job: Angie's annual earnings more than doubled. Adding in tax credits (and subtracting FICA), the amount she brought home from the workplace rose by $12,200 a year. Yet the drop in welfare and food stamps cost her $8,800. On balance, she was up $3,400, a gain of 16 percent.

Or was she, really? The more she worked, the more her work expenses increased. There was bus fare, babysitting, work uniforms, and snacks from the vending machine. In Angie's case, the child-care costs were minimal, since the kids mostly minded themselves. But figure just $30 week for bus rides and the stolen car, a conservative estimate, and you wipe out nearly half the gain. In leaving welfare, Angie also lost her health insurance. The kids remained on Medicaid, which was crucial with Kesha's asthma attacks. But for twenty of her first thirty-six months off the rolls, Angie earned just enough to get disqualified. On welfare, she could call a cab and get driven to a doctor for free. But, with pains shooting down her back from lifting patients, Angie walked around uninsured.

Other than her back, Angie was healthy. Jewell was not. After she left welfare, her earnings rose *sixfold,* to nearly $13,000 a year. But her public aid fell 93 percent—she lost all of her welfare and most of her food stamps after she failed to file the monthly earnings reports required of people who work. While her overall income rose from about $14,700 to $16,600 (a gain of 13 percent), she also lost her health insurance for two years, and Jewell had bleeding ulcers. "I just dealt with that pain," she said. "I just got a lot of Tums, Rolaids, stuff like that." In the end, she was hospitalized and her wages were garnished to pay the bill, a circumstance that struck her as nothing unusual.

health care

"Anybody that works is gonna get their check garnished," she said. "Everybody in Milwaukee owes a hospital bill."

In going to work, Angie and Jewell didn't just face new expenses. They also faced new uncertainty. Angie's income soared for a year, when she bought a car and worked two jobs. Then it crashed for three months after the car was stolen. So the experience registered less like a stable advance than a roller coaster ride. In Jewell's case, the ride was particularly steep. Her income leaped to $25,000 when she worked in the Alzheimer's ward, then fell to $8,000 the next year when she lost her job and focused on Ken. On welfare, they had a senile land-lady who forgot to collect the rent. Off welfare, Jewell had rent to pay and her nephew Quinten to feed. Angie had Opal and Brierra.

So *did* they come out ahead in economic terms? Probably, a bit. And their earnings may grow with time, which wouldn't happen on welfare. Still, three years after they left the rolls, their material lives didn't *feel* much different. Their economic progress, such as it was, vanished in the noise of living.

To understand the economics of the postwelfare years, you have to juggle two competing ideas. The first is that most poor single mothers fared better than expected. The second is that they continued to lead terribly straitened lives. Earnings surged, welfare fell, and net in-comes inched up—but not necessarily enough to keep the lights on. By national standards, Angie was a great success: she earned 50 per-cent to 75 percent more than the average woman leaving the rolls. Sifting through the piles of economic data, it's hard to know what to emphasize most—the amazing ability of poor mothers to work or the questions about what their work will achieve?

The case for encouragement starts with earnings trends: from 1994 to 2001, the poorest half of single mothers saw their annual earnings *double*. That universe includes most of the women who left welfare as well as many who might have gone on it absent the new law. (Among the poorest quarter of single mothers, the rise in earnings was proportionally even greater: 150 percent.) Mostly that's because the women worked more. But the wages of entry-level workers also rose. While it was common to talk of recipients being shoved into minimum-wage jobs, most earned in the range of $7.50 to $8.25 an hour (in today's terms)—well above the legal minimum.

Poverty rates brought more good news. Most of the conservatives who backed the law would have been happy to replace welfare with work, even if poverty levels didn't change. But poverty rates fell sharply—for some groups to record lows. Poverty rates are arbitrary and odd, and they generally undercount need. Crudely devised four decades ago as a multiple of food costs, the formula hasn't changed other than to grow with inflation. The numbers undercount poverty by ignoring work expenses and the increased costs of housing and health care (which have far outpaced inflation). But they also ignore billions distributed through certain programs like food stamps and tax credits. Their all-or-nothing quality is oblivious to nuance: the year she left welfare, Angie would have been poor with $18,437 and not poor with a dollar more. Nonetheless, the numbers retain an important symbolism, and since the methodology behind them hasn't changed, they can be useful in tracking trends.

Poverty rates didn't just fall; they plunged. And they plunged most among those groups targeted by the bill. America's child poverty rates, the highest in the industrial world, hadn't changed in fifteen years. Suddenly they dropped more than 20 percent. Poverty among blacks, Hispanics, and single mothers fell to all-time lows. Nearly *half* the country's black children were poor when Clinton first pledged to end welfare. By the time he left office the figure had fallen by more than a third, to 30 percent. The last president to preside over an economic expansion, Ronald Reagan, removed 290,000 Americans from poverty. The Clinton years multiplied that figure 22 times, moving 6.4 million people across the poverty line. More than half lived in families headed by single mothers. "This is the first recovery in three decades where everybody got better at the same time," Clinton said, just before leaving office. "I just think that's so important."

The bad news is that while incomes rose, they rose from distressingly low levels. Extrapolating from an hourly wage of $7.50, one would expect to see annual earnings of about $15,600. But most women leaving welfare earned much less. A few found only part-time work. Many more went months between jobs. In her first year and a half off the rolls, Jewell quit one nursing home (too much work), got fired at another (chronic tardiness), and ran through four temp jobs. Even Angie, a much more experienced worker, went jobless for two and a half months after her car was stolen and she fell into a funk. Only about a third of those leaving welfare nationwide held jobs in every quarter of the following year.

So what did former recipients really earn? In ballpark terms, if you count everyone leaving welfare (including those without jobs), the average woman earned less than $9,000 in her first year off the rolls. Count workers alone, and the figure grows to about $12,000. Count steady workers (excluding those who go back on welfare), and you can get to $14,500. Their paychecks did grow with time; in Wisconsin, the earnings of the average "leaver" rose 26 percent over three years. Still, their annual earnings over the three-year stretch averaged just $10,400 (even when you exclude those who didn't work at all). With earnings of $12,700, Jewell was well ahead of the pack. With $16,100 Angie was a star.

Nationally, most people leaving welfare did come out ahead, at least on paper. But that wasn't the case in Wisconsin. Maria Cancian and three colleagues at the University of Wisconsin examined the records of eight thousand of the state's former welfare families. Although their earnings and tax credits surged, their public aid dropped even faster, cutting their total income by about $2,600 in the first year, a loss of 20 percent. Even after three years, a minority of those leaving the rolls—40 percent—had incomes higher than when they were on welfare. Wisconsin had unusually high benefits, so families leaving welfare had more to lose, and in cutting the rolls so deeply the state pushed more marginal cases out the door. The before-after comparison might look different in, say, Chicago. Nonetheless, the Cancian study recorded something of note: the most celebrated welfare program in the world on average left poor people even poorer.

A focus on averages can leave things out. Even as poverty levels fell, the ranks of single mothers in "extreme poverty"—living below half the poverty line—rose by nearly 20 percent. Nationally, about one welfare mother in five earned nothing after leaving the rolls. How they survived remains unclear. There was no parallel rise in public destitution, no sidewalk encampments of homeless families, as Daniel Patrick Moynihan had feared. Spending among the very poor rose, even as their incomes fell, suggesting they had more resources—boyfriends or relatives to take them in—than the Census Bureau could measure. While reliable data on the very poor are scarce, the best guess is that about 7 percent of single mothers grew poorer in the second half of the 1990s. The worst of them, like Amber Peck in Milwaukee, parceled out their kids, then trudged through the snow to sleep on church floors.

Opponents of the bill sometimes cite such families as evidence of its failure. But a policy that fails the most marginalized few isn't necessarily a failure overall, especially if it brings significant improvement to the lives of most others. What's more surprising is how much hardship persisted among the seeming winners, among workers like Angie and Jewell. By warning, as Senator Moynihan did, of "cholera epidemics," critics set the bar for suffering awfully high. Large numbers of welfare-to-work *successes* report problems in obtaining basic necessities—fewer problems, perhaps, than when they were on welfare, but not dramatically fewer. Depending how the question is asked, a quarter to a half of former recipients report shortages of food. Similar percentages cite an inability to pay rent and utilities. Half said they lacked health insurance at a given moment, meaning that many more experienced a period without insurance sometime in their first few years off the rolls. Sheldon Danziger and four academic colleagues tracked seven hundred Michigan families for four years. Those who moved from welfare to work had nearly twice the annual income of those who stayed on welfare but "similar levels of material hardship." They were less likely to go without food or shelter but much more likely to go without needed medical care.

In my own travels through postwelfare life, I was struck by how many working families complained about facing depleted cupboards—or about just plain going hungry. I spent some time with Michelle Crawford, the Milwaukee woman Tommy Thompson featured in his legislative address. ("I want to run for president," she remembered him telling her, "and I want you on my team.") While her pride in landing a job was real, so were her struggles to buy a commodity as basic as milk. To fool the kids, she sweetened a powdered mix and hid it in store-bought jugs. "Then we ran out of sugar," she said. Food wasn't on my mind when I stopped by Pulaski High School to talk to some students with welfare-to-work moms. But it was on the minds of the kids, who commandeered the conversation with macabre jokes about Ramen noodles and generic cereal. When I asked how many had recently gone to bed hungry, four out of five raised their hands. "Go to my house, look in the refrigerator—you'll be lucky if there's a gallon of milk," said a senior named Tiffany Fiegel. Then she burst into tears.

The persistence of so much hardship poses a paradox. If incomes were rising, and poverty falling, why did so many people skip meals and fall behind on the rent? The answer is that the near poor live only slightly better than the poor. The Economic Policy Institute, a Washington research and advocacy group, examined two databases that measure hardships like shortages of food or medical care. Material deprivation did fall once families crossed the poverty line. But it only fell a bit. Real freedom from grinding need didn't occur until families reached twice the poverty line—until a woman like Angie, with four kids, had an income of nearly $40,000. In Wisconsin, fewer than one former recipient in ten had an income of twice the poverty line the year after leaving the rolls. If past trends hold true, most never will: a decade after leaving AFDC, two-thirds of former welfare families still hadn't gotten that far.

One can quibble about the math, but the basic point is clear: there's a threshold that families have to cross to feel their lives have changed. And most haven't crossed it. Angie went from 103 percent of the poverty line during her last four years on welfare to 114 percent during her first three years as a worker. With an extra mouth to feed in Quinten, Jewell went the other way, from 98 percent of the poverty line on welfare to 93 percent off it. "How well am I doing?" Angie said one day. "I ain't gonna call me poor—but I *am* poor." The Census Bureau couldn't have put it any better.

To say that Angie lived on $25,000 makes her life sound more forgiving than it was. The tax money came just once a year and went mostly to big-ticket items—cars, refrigerators, bedroom sets. Food stamps went to food. Marcus pitched in, but his help was erratic and typically in-kind—a package of pork chops, a new coat—as opposed to something Angie could count on for the bills. (Help from Opal was similarly sporadic.) What Angie really lived on was her take-home pay, about $1,120 a month. The result was come-and-go economics: what comes, goes.

Nearly 60 percent went to shelter costs: $450 to rent and $200 to utilities.

Seventy-five dollars went to Walgreen's for items, like toothpaste and toilet paper, that food stamps wouldn't buy.

Seventy-five dollars went to Jewel-Osco, for groceries when the food stamps ran out.

Fifty dollars went to the Lorillard Tobacco Company, since Angie's body wouldn't function without a pack of Newports every other day.

What was left was about $270 a month, or $9 a day. With that, Angie had to buy the remaining stuff of her life: bus fare, haircuts, gerbil food, video games, winter coats, check-cashing fees, doctors' bills, Colt 45s, Halloween candy, Christmas presents, Kesha's color-guard uniform, Redd's rap discs, Von's basketball shoes, Darrell's birthday party at Chuck E. Cheese, and the occasional pizza supreme. It was a budget with no room for error. And a life with lots of error. "Cash money in my hands?" Angie said. "It's like the wind blows and it's gone."

The biweekly pay cycle had a rhythm all its own: two weeks of anticipation followed by the realization that the money had been spoken for twice. As a rule, food came before rent, and rent before utilities, which Angie relegated to the lower-order status of optional necessity. "If you ain't got no place to stay, all the gas and the lights in the world wouldn't make no difference," she said. In her first six months on Brown Street, she paid on the light bill once. "Paid on" is how she put it, since the bill was never fully paid. She owed more than $1,400, but with Kesha using a nebulizer the power company was slow to disconnect. The week after the fight with Marcus, Angie picked up a $490 paycheck, hoping to treat herself to an outfit and a plastic plant. Once she paid the rent and bought a bus pass, she had $23 and 12 days to go. Among Angie's coping skills was a healthy dose of denial: she refused to open the bills. "If I ain't got the money, I ain't got the money," she said. "No need to be worrying myself to death."

By the spring, the tax money was gone; Michael was cutting Opal's check; and Marcus lost his job when the corner grocery closed. To cap it off, a bureaucratic screwup cost Angie her food stamps. Angie was too proud to say that anyone in the house went hungry—"We survive! Ain't nobody starving in there!"—but it wasn't unusual at the end of the month to find the refrigerator reduced to a box of fish sticks and a bottle of ketchup. Half the household fights, it seemed, revolved around a shortage of food. Opal was supposed to help stock the fridge, but she sold some of her stamps for spending money and kept a cache of snacks locked in her room. One morning, after she beat Darrell to the last drop of milk for the cereal, the five-year-old flung himself to the floor.

"What you crying for, boy?" she said.

"I ain't got nothing to eat! I'm hungry!" he said.

"You need a good butt-whipping, Darrell!" Opal said.

Darrell wasn't the only one missing a meal. Called in to work on her thirty-third birthday, Angie was broke and didn't eat all day. The loss of her food stamps left her incensed. The program required an eligibility review every three months. Arriving for her most recent appointment, she discovered her caseworker had gone on a leave of absence. In welfare jargon, that had left Angie in a "vacant zone"; she no longer had a designated worker but could see whomever was free. No one was. A few weeks later, Angie got a notice saying she had been cut off for failing to complete the review.

"QUESTIONS: Ask your Worker," it said.

"Worker Name: VACANT."

It took two months of calling to get another appointment. When she did, the bus broke down, she got there late, and no one would see her again. Having worked until midnight the previous night, Angie was out of patience; she responded with an off-color tirade that nearly got her thrown out of the office. A supervisor calmed her down, but she still had to come back the following day, when ten minutes of paper pushing restored her stamps. The foul-ups had cost her $500, but she arrived home trying to pretend she didn't care. "Hell no, because I *work*!" she said. "I done got over all that, waiting on food stamps! I *hate* to be bothered with them. I wish I had a job that paid $10, $11 an hour—I wouldn't *have* to be bothered with them."

"That still ain't enough," Opal said.   *frustration*

"You could make it," Angie said. "You just have to budget."

But Angie didn't earn $11 an hour. She earned $7.82, and while her income placed her in the postwelfare elite, it still didn't pay the bills. She needed a pool job to make more money, and she needed a car to work the pool. With some of her friends moonlighting as home health aides, Angie put in an application. "I need two jobs to get me what I need!" she said. "One job ain't gonna make it."

A job was the last thing on Opal's mind. She hadn't slept in two days. She feared toothaches more than childbirth. Her head was exploding in pain. Pull 'em, she said. The dentist said her gums were infected. The infection could travel to her heart. The worst-case scenario, however remote, included the risk of death. Take an antibiotic; come back in a week. "Let's do it right," he said. Opal pleaded: *"Pull 'em!"*

The pain must have been extraordinary to lure her to a dentist's chair, a place she avoided even more than Motivation Class. She had been leaving her teeth in food for years, the latest in an Easter egg. She had tried aspirin, Chloroseptic, perfume, and Tanqueray; she had been sent home by the emergency room. There are thirty-two teeth in the human mouth. With a practice focused on indigent care, Dr. Celestino Perez had once pulled twenty-eight. Opal needed only ten teeth pulled. "You can take it awhile longer," he said. Blinking away silent tears, Opal disagreed. She was starting to sign a waiver, absolving him of liability if the procedure went awry, when I threw my thin influence behind the antibiotics, promising to rush her back if the pain didn't ebb. She climbed down from the chair and dragged herself home, a perfect portrait of wretchedness. If years of tooth rot couldn't get her attention, I wondered how W-2 stood a chance.

A week later, she was back in the chair, looking terrified. "I gotta shot with a needle?" she said. By the fourth shot, her chest was heaving. The sixth made her legs buck. By the tenth, she merely looked confused. Novocain was one drug she wasn't used to. "My nose numb," she said. Numbers twenty-eight and thirty popped right out, but thirteen, an upper-left bicuspid, put up a fight. It had broken off below the surface, so Dr. Perez had to peel back the gum. The root was so rotten it snapped in his pliers, startling everyone with its crack.

He grunted. She gurgled. Her head jerked around. "My hand's getting tired," he said. *"Unnhhhhh!"* As the bloody stump succumbed, the dentist smiled. Three down, seven to go; come back in a week. "God, I just love this stuff!" he said. Opal made her way to the door still searching for her nose.

Welfare was inflicting blows of its own. When she didn't return to MaxAcademy, Michael pulled the attendance sheets and docked her check. He hadn't figured out she was using drugs (though he should have, since it was noted in her case history). Still, she finally had a caseworker she couldn't completely con. She suddenly seemed like a textbook example of a tough case meeting a tough law. In theory, the possible outcomes appeared to be these: (a) Opal could surrender her resistance and work for a welfare check; (b) Opal could leave W-2 and find a job on her own; (c) Opal could get kicked off the rolls and sink into deeper destitution. The answer turned to be (d): the bureaucracy screwed up again.

As it happened, Maximus didn't have jurisdiction over Opal's case. In moving to Brown Street, she had moved to a region run by Employment Solutions, the Goodwill subsidiary. Once the error came to light, Michael transferred the case, and his dealings with Opal were done. In the name of private-sector efficiency, Opal was packed off to her third agency and seventh caseworker in less than two years. "I don't feel I did a damn thing for Opal," Michael said soon after. At Goodwill, Opal told her new caseworker, Darcy Cooper, that she had her high-school diploma and wanted to work as a teacher's assistant. Cooper was impressed. "Very intelligent—very highly intelligent," she told me afterward. "Very goal oriented." Cooper gave Opal some time to find child care. In the meantime, she sent her a full check.

"Thigpen, Kenyatta Q., # 362246. . . ." Jewell worked the eraserless pencil, looking too nervous to breathe. The Fox Lake Correctional Institution didn't tolerate mistakes. No hairpins, no wallets, no Spandex, no tube tops, no paper money. No more than one rosary per visitor. No exceptions. The reception area was clean, cold, quiet, and hard, like an autopsy room. While the prison was just eighty miles from Milwaukee, it lay across a landscape of one-stoplight towns that looked as though they had fallen off a feed-store calendar. Jewell didn't trust her car or her map-reading skills; she didn't trust the small-town police. The trip made her feel her blackness intensely. The only time she got to see Ken was when I could give her a ride. A few weeks earlier, I had picked her up when she got off work, and we drove two hours to arrive at 7:23 p.m.—thirty-seven minutes before visiting hours ended. A fat guard with a walrus mustache had barely looked up. No new visits after 7:15. No exceptions. This time, Jewell took the day off and spent $150 to have her hair done. Ken had just had his parole hearing, and she was coming for the news.

[handwritten margin note: let down / expensive to be poor]

Jewell finished her form, removed her rings, and eyed another adversary. The Fox Lake metal detector was a tin-pot dictator, a court with no appeals. The wire in a bra, the button on a jean—anything could set it off. There was no follow-up scan; what the arch said, goes. Another visit nearly ended in defeat when her pants zipper made it buzz. Jewell was accustomed to feeling powerless when dealing with Authority; she had mutely turned to leave when I spotted an old woman with a friendly face coming from the visiting room. The woman went home in Jewell's Fubu jeans and Jewell cleared security in a rare out-of-style moment, in stranger's baggy yellow shorts. "Hands to the side. Walk slow. You've got three tries." The Walrus was working again. The arch buzzed. Jewell checked her hair for pins. The arch buzzed again. With the reception area empty, there were no shorts to be cadged. Jewell took one step back and two hopeful steps forward toward the visiting room. The arch acquiesced. "You've got three hours," the Walrus said. She looked like she had won the lottery.

Whether she was winning Ken was less clear. The drive to end welfare was, among other things, a drive to raise marriage rates; as a thirty-year-old mother of two, Jewell suddenly had her prospects, if not the kind the bill writers had in mind. While it had been eight years since her old boyfriend Tony had gone to prison for murder, he had just sent her a drawing of a wedding band. "Marry Me," he wrote. Ken's rival, Lucky, had moved out again, but he had sent Jewell a picture of clenched fists breaking free of their chains: "To my wife, I'm coming home." Ken, in his letters, sounded marriage-minded, too, referring to Jewell as "my wife," "my sexy wife," "my gorgeous wife," and "wifee." But the separated lovers had hit a low point the previous

[handwritten margin note at bottom: inmates are vulnerable and have time to think about past relations on outside]

month, after Jewell promised to send money and clothes and failed to follow through. Having given her something he usually withholds—his trust—Ken got so angry he cursed out a guard, and his next letter came from the hole. "I blame you because if you wouldn't pissed me off I wouldn't have a fucking attitude," he wrote. "[T]hat came from trying to show you the soft side of me. . . . I will never look stupid again for no female. . . . I will be girl less." They weren't used to fights, and that one quickly passed. Yet now and then a trace of doubt crept into Jewell's voice. "If we stay together, it's just something to show us that we're meant to be together," she said one night. *If?* Does she ever have—"No—no doubts, no nothing!" she said.

Trends in family structure nationwide were similarly hard to assess. The welfare bill proved spectacularly successful in putting poor women to work, but that was only half of its stated purpose. Shoring up the two-parent family was the other. "Marriage is the foundation of a successful family," reads the first line of the Personal Responsibility Act, which goes on for three pages to chart the statistical correlations between single motherhood and social risk. Launching his attack on welfare in 1994, Newt Gingrich had warned that the growth of non-marital births threatened American "civilization." That year, 32.6 percent of children were born outside of marriage. As Jewell was visiting Ken in prison, hoping to have his baby, the figure was up to 33.0 percent, and a few years later it hit 34.0 percent. There may be no statistic that said more about the prospects of the next generation. By 2002, 23.0 percent of whites, 43.5 percent of Hispanics, and 68.2 percent of African Americans were born outside of marriage—a total of 1.4 million kids. That doesn't mean that the welfare bill had *no* effect on childbearing. The increase in nonmarital births slowed to a crawl and did so just as the attacks on "illegitimacy" hit fever pitch. It would be remarkable if that were pure coincidence.

Looking beyond births, some researchers have found potentially good news in subsequent living arrangements: fewer children living with lone single mothers and more living with two adults. Examining the National Survey of America's Families, a database of 40,000 households, Gregory Acs and Sandi Nelson of the Urban Institute found a notable shift in family composition in the postwelfare years. In 1997, about 48 percent of low-income children lived with a lone single mother; five years later, the number had fallen to 42 percent. But just half of that reduction in single parenthood came from increased marriage between mothers and their children's biological fathers, which statistically produces the best outcomes for kids. Most of the rest came from cohabitation, which was less encouraging. On average, children raised in cohabiting homes fare no better than those raised by single mothers alone. (Kesha grabbing a skillet to defend Angie from Marcus is an example of a cohabiting home.) Examining a database from the Census Bureau, Wendell Primus found the decline in lone single motherhood especially pronounced among blacks and Hispanics. The share of low-income black children living with married parents rose from about 20 percent to 23 percent over five years. But the share with cohabiting mothers also rose. And the Census data don't specify whether the marriages brought biological fathers or stepfathers to the home. To the extent it was the latter, past studies predict a high risk of conflict with the kids. Both Angie and Jewell spent a good part of their adolescence warring with stepfathers.

If changes in family structure were unclear, the impact of welfare policy was even more so. Policies specifically aimed at reducing nonmarital births (like "family caps" that eliminate extra payments for additional kids) generally showed weak results. And there was no other obvious policy pattern. The District of Columbia had some of the most permissive welfare rules, and also the largest reduction in the share of children born to single moms. Even as Wisconsin was eradicating its welfare rolls, the share of children born to single mothers *rose*—at a pace more than twice the national average. For all the praise heaped on the two-parent families, the end-welfare years brought little new information about how to promote them.

Jewell was a marriage-promotion movement all her own, with a target audience of one. She reached the visiting room to find Ken in the clothes she had finally sent: tank top, jeans, new gym shoes. Elated just to see him, she waited awhile before asking what the parole board had done. "They played me," he said. "What?!" Jewell was crushed. At the hearing, he had stuck to his story: the drugs weren't his; he wanted to go home and take up a trade, maybe computers. The hearing officer had called his story "bullshit" and warned him to learn from his mistakes. Even with good behavior, he had nearly a year left to serve. He asked Jewell: can you wait? He said he knew it was hard. It *was* hard, harder than he knew. Jewell had never been alone before. But she'd never had a cause, either. "I'll be there for you now *and* when you get out," she said. The visit sped past. Ken joked that they should prick their fingers and seal a pact in blood. When Jewell said she already had a pact—her "friendship" ring—Ken said that whoever had given it to her must love her very much. "They do," Jewell said.

Despite the disappointing news, Jewell left the prison in an upbeat mood. In the distance from Ken she had found a new closeness, but at home an opposite dynamic was in play. For all her closeness to Opal and Angie, a new distance was creeping in. Opal's problems were obvious enough. But for reasons Jewell couldn't understand, Angie acted as though she didn't like Ken. Or maybe, Jewell thought, Angie didn't like the sight of her in love. She spent most of the ride back to Milwaukee airing her frustrations. "She's always saying little stuff. She told me once, 'You changed!' She said she never let a man come between me and her friendship. How did he come between our friendship?" With Opal, Jewell's conflicts had been out in the open; with Angie, they smoldered.

Even so, once we hit the city line, she made Brown Street her first stop. Family was family, and Jewell had news. "He got to do the remaining time," she said, sitting on Opal's bed.

"Girrl!" Opal oozed empathy. "Even if one person on your parole board say you can't be released?"

"It was only one," Jewell said.

"I thought it was four or five, like you see on TV!"

Angie had little to say about Ken or his parole. ("Whatever make her happy," she harrumphed later.) But standing beside Opal's dresser, she saw a flyer from the welfare office with a list of jobs and starting wages: "$8.25 an hour!" Angie said. That was more than she made after three years. They were all in places she couldn't get to without a car.

A second job was her way to get one. But six weeks after signing up with a home-health agency, Angie still didn't have a client. May brought birthdays, Kesha's and her own, and she came up empty on both. June brought graduation bills. With Von finishing fifth grade and Kesha eighth, Angie gave them each $100 for outfits and put off the rent. Two months after he shot up the ceiling, Marcus was adding to her woes. He was out of work and obsessively jealous, threatening to follow her wherever she went. Angie tried to send him home to his mother's, but he wouldn't go. Food was tight again; having fought to get her food stamps back, Angie still hadn't received them. When she called the office, she learned they had been sent by certified mail and signed for two weeks earlier, on Friday, June 4. Angie remembered the date. Mercy had been overstaffed and sent her home, and when she got there Opal was gone. Angie's heart sank: Opal and the food stamps had disappeared the same day. With Opal in Chicago, seeing the girls, Angie left for work, stopped by a friend's, and came home at midnight full of frustration and beer. Just then, her "friend" Tony drove up. Marcus spied him and climbed in the car. As they drove off to settle their differences, Tony had his gun; Marcus left his behind, afraid of what he might do.

Angie ignored them. Though it wasn't clear whether a felony or a peace talk was under way, Angie was brooding about the stamps. It could have been Marcus, she told herself. But Marcus doesn't steal. "The only thing he might a stole was my heart and broke it," she said. Maybe it was the upstairs neighbor; yeah, that was it. It *couldn't* have been Opal. It *wasn't* Opal. But what to do if it was? Angie mulled the question in a drunken soliloquy that was, by turns, angry, funny, wounded, and wise. "I love her, but drugs mess you up," she said. "It's not like she's a bad person—she's sweet as pie. . . . But she's tripped her kids to nothing and herself, mainly, to nothing. So what the hell would she care about coming over and tripping me to nothing? . . . All that shit I said, 'I'll never kick you out'—that don't mean shit. . . . I'll be unforgivable hurt."

She was still parsing moral codes an hour later, when she heard the front door rattle. After a half dozen Hennesseys on his rival's tab, Marcus was back. Angie laughed. "You're drunk!" she said. "You're fucked up!"

Marcus smiled and looked my way. "Did you tell him who Tony is?"

"Tony's my guy!"

Whatever had happened at the bar, Marcus wasn't ready to say. "Am I heartbroken?" he asked himself. "No, I'm not heartbroken."

"You all right?" Angie asked. "'Cause I want you to be all right."

"I'm not talking to you," Marcus said.

"I don't care. You think I care?"

It was 1:00 in the morning. She was out of food. Her men were facing off with cognac and pistols, and she was trying to decide whether to put Opal out. This struck Angie as just the time . . .

. . . to pick a portfolio of stocks. Eight years after arriving in Milwaukee, three years after she had left the rolls, Angie had climbed to a rarified height in postwelfare life. She had qualified for a 401(k). The enrollment deadline was the following day, and she wanted a hand in assessing her tolerance for risk. She foraged in her bedroom and returned with a booklet called *Help! Which Investment Options Are Right for Me?* "What would make you more upset?" it asked.

(a) Not owning stocks when the market goes up.
(b) Holding a stock when it drops.
(c) I have no experience and can't respond.

"I'm number two!" Angie said. "Hold the stock and it drops, I'll be *pissed!*"

"Angela, Miss Angela!" Marcus broke in. "How you doing?"

"Fine. Love ya!"

"Do you?"

Angie laughed. "I love *me,*" she said. "Tired of you!" Tickled, she broke into song. "Love me, tired of you! Love me, tired of you!"

Marcus grinned and talked about getting a four-pack. "Get yourself a *job,* nigger!" Angie said.

"If you were invested in a stock and it suddenly declined 20 percent in value, what would you do?"

(a) I would never own a stock.
(b) Sell a portion to cut my losses.
(c) Sit tight, ride it out, maybe even buy some more.

"I ain't gonna buy no more!" Angie said. "But if my money already there, what the hell else can I do? I ain't got time to be calling them!"

Tallying her risk tolerance, the pamphlet judged Angie a "moderate" investor. "Yes, I *am*!" she said, giving it a toss. "I already know where I'm putting my money at—IBM computers and shit, cause that's the future, *computers*!" She would put in $6 out of every $100 she earned, and Mercy would add $1.50, to vest if she stayed seven years. "Marcus get outta my bed," she called. He'd gone off to sleep, but Angie removed him to the couch. It was 2:00 a.m., and Von warned her she was due to work the first shift, just a few hours away. "Won't be the first time," she said. She got to work at dawn and started buying computer stocks, shortly before the tech bubble burst.

Opal stayed in Chicago a week, warring with her mother. Opal wanted the girls for the summer. Granny wouldn't let them go. Little girls want to be with their mother no matter their mother's condition. When Granny finally took a poll, the vote was Milwaukee 3, Chicago 0. They were back at Angie's for all of two hours when the fights began. "This is my worst nightmare!" said Redd. "A house full of girls!" said Von. By day two, Opal and Angie were at odds. "Ain't no motherfucking food in the house," Opal fumed. While she denied any knowledge of the missing stamps, she had given Angie $200 out of her allotment to restock the cabinets. Now Angie was at work, and Opal was complaining that she hadn't bought enough groceries. "Ain't no meats in there!" she complained to Jewell. If Angie's charity toward Opal was admirable, it was also increasingly costly, for herself and her kids. But putting Opal out required a greater willingness to enforce boundaries than Angie yet possessed. Of the three, Angie had found the greatest comfort in the First Street family. Perhaps if she evicted Opal she would be telling herself that ultimately she was on her own, too.

On day three, Kesha had a fit. Her condom had disappeared. The romance with Larry had reignited, and everyone but Angie was worried. One of Angie's friends had tried to get Kesha on birth control pills. But Kesha, who had just turned fifteen, said she didn't need them. Then she spied a condom in Larry's wallet; wrote "Kesha-N-

Larry" on her bedroom mirror; and kept the condom on her dresser. "It's mine," she said. "He's going to use it on me!" After Opal's girls spent the night in her room, the prized packet vanished. They found it, beneath the bed, just in time to keep Kesha from meting out blows. "I ain't sexually active now," she said. "But I'm gonna be in the future. Maybe two months."

Perhaps Angie wasn't alarmed because she wasn't around very much. She had finally gotten an assignment as a home health aide. Angie had worried about working in a stranger's house, and her client, Karen, had worried, too; she was confined to a wheelchair with multiple sclerosis, and her last aide had stolen from her. But the two of them hit it off. After two hours with Karen in the morning, Angie headed to Mercy after lunch, stretching her workday from breakfast to 10:30 at night. But two weeks into the new routine, she got her first paycheck: $178.42. To celebrate, she bought the kids a pizza. No one was in the mood. "You found my mama?" Tierra, the six-year-old, asked everyone. Opal had gotten her welfare check on Wednesday, disappeared on Thursday, and left a message on Bo's pager Friday afternoon: "I know y'all mad at me, but I still got two hundred dollars, and I ain't coming back tonight." Angie raged. "I could think of a million and one things I coulda done with that money—paid on the light bill!" she said. Plaster fell from the gun blast to the ceiling. Newspaper still covered the broken window pane. And there on the table lay the pizza box, perched like a cardboard crown. Angie, God bless her, tried.

The job with Karen, months in the making, ended within a few weeks. Solving one problem (too little money) aggravated another (too much time away). Angie quit working for Karen and switched to the first shift at Mercy. Angie *hated* first-shift work. First shift made her alarm clock bleat at 4:30 a.m., it made her whole body rebel. But if she started at 6:00, she could leave at 2:00 p.m. and try to be home more. "I don't want Opal to be in the mood to take nothing, and I don't want Marcus in the house," she said. "I can kill two birds with one stone." Karen was facing a spinal operation and pleaded with Angie to stay. But Karen mostly needed help in the mornings. While she tried to create some dinner-hour work, Angie felt bad about sitting around and laid herself off. "Don't you let nobody take your money away like that," she warned Karen. "You might need that."

blood suckers of poor

Shortly after, a friend told Angie there was an easier way to get a car. W-2 would loan her the money. This struck Angie as unlikely news, but it turned out to be true. To help people stay off welfare, the program offered "job access loans" (of up to $1,600) for cars, uniforms, or even rents. This was another example of what states could have done with their welfare windfalls, rather than siphoning them into suburban road projects, and Angie was a perfect candidate. She was also a mark for a used-car salesman, and she nearly got talked into a $7,000 Dodge that would have been destined for repossession. It was bright red. He offered financing. All she had to do was sign. Angie tried to believe the car man when he said she could afford it, then came to her senses just in time. "I'd be signing myself over to the Devil," she told him, pulling herself away. A few days later, she put a deposit on a rusty old Cutlass that wasn't half as pretty. But it cost only a quarter as much, and she figured it would run long enough to get her started at the pool.

Under the logic that ruled Angie's life, when something went right, something was about to go wrong. Marcus was losing his mind. While Angie and Marcus had always fought, she felt he had crossed a new line. She put him out every night and woke up to find him back: waiting on the porch, lying on the couch, using the shower. She rose before dawn to find him staring in her bedroom window. In the middle of car shopping, she had gotten a restraining order. But it wouldn't take effect until the police could put it in his hands. Following her to the bus stop a few days later, Marcus warned if she tried to evict him he would burn down the house. Angie had the worse temper of the two. "I think I'm gonna buy me a gun and blow his fucking head off," she said.

Angie came home from buying her car and went to bed early. The kids woke her up at 1:00 a.m. Marcus had been drinking; he was standing on the porch and somehow he had gotten a key. "Your door's open," he yelled. Angie had had enough. Enough double shifts and enough unpaid bills. Enough wounded male pride. "I'm a very violent person," she once said. "Not violent toward everybody—I'm violent toward people trying to hurt me." She picked up a screwdriver and told him to come in. He taunted her from the porch. She locked the door, and he opened it. Then she heard him drop the key. As he bent to grab it, she flew out the door in her nightgown and knocked him down the stairs. "You trying to hurt me?" Marcus laughed. "Trying to *kill* you," she said. Then she stabbed him in the back. Opal was in the middle, trying to pry them apart, and the screwdriver passed through her hand.

It took three calls to summon the police, but they arrived at 4:00 a.m., served the order, and drove Marcus away. Had he kept his wits about him, it would have ended there. Maybe he didn't realize how angry Angie was. Maybe he didn't understand that he was legally barred from the house. Maybe, as he said, he just wanted his clothes. But he was back at dawn, daring Angie to call the cops, and this time they kept him. He wasn't disturbing the peace anymore; he was violating a court order. And with his record as a chronic offender, he faced up to three years. "Marcus felt I wasn't going to go to this extreme," Angie said. "Wrong brother!" She spent the morning in bed, reading a romance novel. In a few days, she could pick up the car. And with the car, she tried to tell herself, there was no telling where she might get.

EIGHTEEN

A Shot at the American Dream:
Milwaukee, Fall 1999

"I need a whole new life," Angie said, and for a moment she thought she had one. She lost a man, found a car, and glimpsed a vision of hourly wages climbing to double digits. She stopped drinking beer. She did her hair. She did jumping jacks in the living room. She got up early and cleaned the basement. With no one rattling her window at night, she let Opal's daughter Sierra sleep beside her. "I been sleeping heavenly," Angie said. She sensed a return to an earlier, idealized self: younger, stronger, lighter, free. With a week of vacation coming, she talked about driving to Mississippi. "If I don't go to Mississippi, I'm a get me a hotel room." She knew of one with a spa. "I deserve to romance myself."

Then the old life rushed back in: Angie was the only one working in a house with eight kids. Von and Kierra fought all day. Kesha's cats had fleas. Redd's summer-school teacher said he had an attitude. Kesha dumped Larry, the boy with the condom, and started dating the upstairs neighbor, Jermaine. One day, Opal's seven-year-old, Kierra, said, "I'm gonna get paid today!" She couldn't say why—or she wouldn't get paid—but the secret spilled: she had caught Jermaine in Kesha's bedroom, and they had tried to buy her silence. "She gonna be pregnant, Angie," Opal warned.

The week Angie picked up her car, she got her annual raise: 20 cents. "Cheap bastards!" she said. "I'm a damn good worker. I'm worth more than twenty cents!" A few weeks later, she came home from work to find her lights shut off. Opal had given her some money for the bill, but Angie had bought school clothes instead. The cutoff was her third in as many years. How the power got reconnected is a bit of a mystery. Angie said she got a note from the asthma doctor, re-iterating Kesha's need for a breathing machine; Opal said Angie's cousin broke the lock and turned it on. When her vacation arrived, Angie got no farther than the neighborhood bar. She spent the night dancing alone.

One evening after the lights returned, Angie dragged in from a double shift. It was nearly midnight. She had worked sixteen hours. She was due back at dawn. Out of toilet paper, Angie had tried to swipe some from work, but even there she met defeat: the place had been picked clean. Angie usually treats her setbacks with mordant humor; this night she wasn't laughing. "Ain't got a pot to piss in or a window to throw it out of!" she spat.

"Why you working so hard?" her friend Barbara asked.

Angie shot her a withering look. "I got bills to pay!"

Kesha's face had swollen from the fleas, and Von worried that his would, too. "Mama, you sure there's no bugs in that blanket?" he said.

Angie didn't answer. "Gotta be back at 6:00 a.m.," she groaned. "I gotta get my ass in bed."

Two months after she got her car, Angie finally did it: she drove five miles west to the edge of town and applied for a nursing-pool job. At Mercy, she had just cleared $8 an hour. Top Techs Temporaries, Inc., paid up to $14 for some weekend shifts. Wendy, her Mercy supervisor, argued she was making a mistake. Lot of aides left for pool work only to return after months of canceled shifts. "They think they're going to be millionaires, but then they can't get the hours," she told me. But Angie wasn't quitting Mercy; she was just looking for extra pay. She filled out the Top Techs forms, got back in her car, and found it wouldn't start. She ate lunch and tried again; all that was driving was the autumn rain. Speeding past on an ugly afternoon, the commuters heading home for dinner had no way to know that the drenched woman trudging down the road was a welfare-to-work marvel trying to work two jobs. Angie had the car towed and caught a bus to a bar. "Three hundred and fifty-nine dollars and eighty-two cents!" she moaned when the bill came in. Still, her good humor was back. *Fourteen dollars an hour.*

Angie kept her thoughts about Marcus closer to her chest. Shortly after his arrest, she got a call from a prosecutor, asking if she wanted to press charges. "Look, I don't want the man to go to jail," she said. "I just want him to stay away from me." The prosecutor agreed to drop the case, and then reconsidered; this was a violation of a restraining order, and Marcus had a record. Marcus spent a week trying to make the $500 bail, and as soon as he did he headed to Angie's, this time with a police escort. Ostensibly there to collect his stuff, he was trying to collect his wits. He was no stalker—he was her man!—and now he could be facing three years. While the police gave them a few private minutes, Angie wouldn't engage. You chose your own way, she said. The next week, Angie went to a block party near Jewell's house. She disappeared into the crowd and when she emerged a few hours later Marcus was at her side. Opal and Jewell were stunned, and more surprised still when Angie let him come back to Brown Street for the night. The next weekend, he took her to a bar. When she ran out of hair gel not long after, Angie drove to the grocery store where Marcus had found a job, knowing he would get her a jar. "Oh, is the love coming back?" asked Marcus's boss. The kids were still applauding his absence when Marcus was back in the house.

Angie had little to say on the subject, but Opal and Jewell chewed it over good. Jewell stressed economics. "Us women that just got off W-2 can't make it out here by ourselves," she said. While Marcus didn't directly pay the bills, she noted that Angie had lost her lights just after she kicked him out. "Every little bit helps," she said. The difference between Marcus and no Marcus might be the difference between gel and no gel, beer and no beer, lights and a night in the dark. Opal, a student of both money and men, didn't slight fiscal concerns. She'd once heard Angie scream at Marcus, "I don't love you—if you ain't got no money, I don't want you around!" But Opal argued that Angie had feelings at the start. "It only got financial when they started having hard times." All Angie would say was that the restraining order, which remained in force, gave her a legal leash. "He have to go when I say go," since a call to the cops at any time would send him back to jail. One day, Marcus tried to bring her a microwave. Angie would have none of it. She didn't want anything to imply he had squatting rights.

Angie had no such leverage over Opal. No one did. Not her mother. Not her man. Not her lovely pigtailed daughters. And certainly not W-2, which had accomplished no more in Opal's life than the programs it had replaced. At the beginning of the year, Angie and Jewell had thought she could turn things around. She had gone to rehab once before and gotten clean. She was too smart, too strong, too much a *survivor* to squander her life on cocaine. "She's trying to get herself together," Jewell had said. No one would say that now. Opal, the woman who could light up a room, had vanished in a fog of listlessness and gloom. Most days, she didn't get up until dusk. On her feet, she exploded in fury. "I'll hit you so hard in the motherfucking mouth I'll knock your ass on the floor!" she screamed at Redd. They were fighting over a pancake. Opal wasn't Opal anymore but an imposter in her own skin.

As summer stretched into fall, the only one blind to Opal's problems was the woman being paid to address them: her new caseworker, Darcy Cooper. Months after she inherited Opal's case, I stopped in to see her, only to leave wondering which Opal Caples she claimed to have met. "She was out there looking for a job," Cooper said. "She did everything she was supposed to do." Opal had left ten teeth in the dentist's pliers just before they met. "Opal looked good, appearance-wise," Cooper said. "It seemed like her home life was intact." How she felt confident in Opal's home life wasn't clear, since Cooper had never visited her home. Opal did report that she had been stabbed, one hint that her home life wasn't "intact." In six months, Cooper had met with Opal twice, both times in her cubicle at Employment Solutions, the Goodwill subsidary. Yet even at that, her cheerful credulousness must have been hard to sustain. Opal had given up. In the past, she had faked or flirted her way to a monthly check; when she had to, she pleaded. Now she had her own safety net—Angie and Bo—and W-2 could do what it pleased. A letter arrived, warning that she was halfway through the five-year federal limit—in welfare theory, a wake-up call. "I don't be reading that shit," she said. "I ain't trippin' about that check, long as I have my food stamps and medical card."

Still the checks kept coming. First, Cooper gave her a month to look for child care. Then, the stab wound bought more time. After that, Cooper had Opal fill out Employer Contact Sheets, the same forms she had been forging for years by thumbing through the Yellow Pages. Opal didn't even finish making up a list. She was literally too tired to fake it. "I told her 'Miss Cooper, I don't just be home sleeping'—which I do," Opal said. While some caseworkers acted callous or cavalier, Cooper just seemed myopically nice. She told me she had heard that clients sometimes fake the job search, but "to me, it seemed like she was actively doing it." She sent Opal another check. "We all have days when things don't go our own way," she said.

Others showed less understanding. To qualify for W-2, Opal had to identify Brierra's father, so the state could try to collect child support. Opal repeatedly missed her appointments, and the child-support office told Cooper to close the case. Cooper entered the case-closure codes. But even that didn't end Opal's aid. Across the country, hundreds of thousands of families were dropped from the rolls for minor infractions, or no infractions at all. In Opal's case, the computer seemed to have a gremlin inside: whenever it saw the words "Opal Caples" it churned out a welfare check. She got $673 for October; $673 for November; and $673 for December. By the end of the year, the tally of cash and food stamps topped $11,000. Even Opal was amazed. "I didn't do nothing," she said. "They just sent it."

Goodwill's incompetence was hardly unique, but it merits a moment of special attention, given the marker laid down by the program's aggressive young CEO. William Martin was barely thirty when he took charge of the $112 million contract, with one of his assets being his political ties to the administration that had awarded it; he had helped run Tommy Thompson's Milwaukee office. At the program's launch, Martin sounded like a business student on Nō-Dōz. W-2 was about "getting to yes" and finding "win-win opportunities." It was about "cutting-edge, private-sector, customer-centered growth." While welfare had left people "wards of the state," Martin, the descendant of a line of southern black preachers, said he had never met someone he couldn't put to work. "We start from a moral premise that it's simply unconscionable to leave somebody on welfare." Two years later, Opal looked like—well, a ward of the state—and Martin was articulating a

many mothers choose not to

new moral premise. "We try to give people the benefit of the doubt, rather than hold to the mechanics of everything," he said, when I asked about Opal's case. "If they had the wherewithal to make it on their own, they wouldn't be in the program."

Someone did "get to yes": William Martin. As Goodwill ignored Opal's downward slide, Martin collected $62,000 in performance bonuses, bringing his year's pay to more than $172,000. He also gave bonuses averaging nearly $10,000 to more than half his staff. In time, the project attracted the legislative auditors, who found some of what they had seen at Maximus: tens of thousands of welfare dollars spent on staff parties, embossed briefcases, and the like. They also found something that disturbed them more: Martin was using the W-2 contract as a marketing fund, spending money earmarked for client services to seek contracts in other states. This was not a "win-win" situation. State auditors deemed it a violation of the law. While Martin called it a bookkeeping error, among the expenses the auditors disallowed were nineteen first-class plane trips to Arizona, where Goodwill was battling Maximus for the next privatization prize. The day after they requested the agency's credit card records, Martin came forward to say he had discovered another $160,000 in unallowable costs. At Maximus, the auditors had found reckless extravagance; at Goodwill, they suspected a cover-up, and the headline in the Milwaukee paper soon read, "W-2 agency under FBI investigation." Martin was forced out of Goodwill, and after repaying a half million dollars, Goodwill was forced out of W-2, with its chief executive, John Miller, pleading "bumbling rather than trickiness." With that, Goodwill and Maximus, the two leading players in privatization, became the two leading emblems of waste and abuse. And they can scarcely be dismissed as an unrepresentative slice of the W-2 bureaucracy: together, they handled *half* the state's cases.

In the end, the real scandal was of the sort that financial auditors don't track: the scandalous absence of casework. With the rolls down 90 percent, the state was collecting more than $40,000 in federal payments for every family left on the rolls. Yet Opal had bounced between seven caseworkers at three agencies, at least two of whom had been on drugs themselves. And none of them had made the slightest difference in her life. There was another thing that Darcy Cooper didn't know about Opal: she was pregnant again. While Opal had urged Angie to take precautions with Kesha, she was too lost to heed her own advice, and another unwanted pregnancy, her second in two years, only added to the violence of her moods. "I'm gonna kick your motherfucking ass!" she screamed at Sierra one day. The girls had stayed in Milwaukee for the fall, still wanting to be with their mother, and the nine-year-old had taken a schoolbook from her room to read somewhere else in the house. While Opal kept saying she wanted an abortion, either she lacked the energy to pursue one or decided a baby would help her keep Bo. By October, her body started to swell. "Girl, just get ready," Jewell said, rubbing Opal's stomach.

At the end of the month, Angie lost her lights again, for the second time in three months. Opal ran an extension cord to the neighbor's outlet. Then she plugged in her boom box, and sat in the dark, listening to Al Green.

> *I'm so* tiii-red *of being alone,*
> *I'm so* tiii-red *of on-my-own.*

When Angie walked in at dinnertime, the only thing lit in the house was the tip of Opal's cigarette. Opal finished her smoke and left for Andrea's. "You know where to find me," she said.

expensive to be poor

Once Ken's drug money ran out, Jewell lost her lights, too. She owed only $500, a third of Angie's debt. But without an asthmatic child, she had to pay in full. That left her with no money for heating oil, and as the fall temperatures dipped to the 30s, she warmed the house with an oven. With her wages being garnished to satisfy her ulcer bills, Jewell was surrendering $99 out of each biweekly paycheck. At least Angie thought if she wrung enough shifts from her tired body, the system would reward her. Jewell bought no such notion. A supervisor called her off the floor at G. B. Electric one day to praise her work and add a quarter to her hourly pay. "He musta liked my eyes," Jewell laughed. The competing explanation—that work brings rewards—was one she didn't consider. "They don't care about no black person there!" she said. When a white coworker hurt her leg, the company

unfair treatment

gave the woman a desk job; when Jewell hurt her back, she had to miss four days without pay. "I wouldn't even want to go no further there," Jewell said one day. "They'll use you until they can't use you no more. That's what I think: they'll use you until they can't use you no more." Jewell had few convictions about the world. But she was adamant about that.

Her vision of the future boiled down to a vision of Ken. Jewell wanted him for herself, of course: for adventure, romance, and sunrise video games. But she also increasingly wanted him as a father for the boys. Although Terrell's father hadn't seen him since he was a baby, he had recently called to propose a visit. "He's not gonna come," Terrell said, and after encouraging him to give it a try, it pained Jewell when the eleven-year-old proved right. Tremmell's father, Tony, had sent a card calling him "the smartes, smoothes, handsomes the most educated son in the world." But the return address had an inmate number and would for another seventy-seven years. When she first had children, Jewell had thought fathers superfluous: "If they around, they around, if they not, they not—I'll do it by myself." Now she thought that boys got something special from a man. "It's financial and discipline," she said. "I think a male have a lotta effect on the kids when it comes to doing right and wrong. A mother could tell a child do something, and she'll have to holler or scream or spank 'em. I seen a lotta cases where the man can only say it one time and the child will do it." Though her sense of herself as a "strong black woman" was undiminished, a decade of raising her boys alone made her think "they need both of their parents."

Jewell was speaking off the cuff one day as we made another drive to the prison. But she was getting at the ultimate question about the postwelfare world: how much does having a working mother—a single, low-income working mother—enhance the life chances of the kids? Will it bring them a new shot at the American Dream? Bill Clinton, among others, saw working mothers as a source of inspiration; critics saw kids left in substandard care while the only parent they had was away. Either scenario—rising achievement or rising neglect—had a plausible logic. Now there is some data. Studies of a dozen programs have followed poor children as their mothers went to work, and collectively they have examined everything from changes in meal times and reading habits to criminal arrests. So it's possible to make some educated guesses about what difference a working mother makes. So far, the answer seems to be "not much." In one sense, that's reassuring: poor kids have suffered no obvious damage as their mothers left home to work. But they haven't inherited a new life trajectory, either. From the standpoint of child development, it hasn't much seemed to matter.

The small differences that have emerged are mostly counterintuitive. A few work programs have shown benefits to *younger* children. That's contrary to the conventional theory that young kids most need their moms. To the extent the programs helped, they appeared to do so not by turning mothers into role models but by getting more kids into formal day care. Reforming welfare, that is, didn't reform the house; it got the kids out. At the same time, there's a hint that adolescents did worse as their mothers left welfare for work. This, too, challenges the role model theory: presumably adolescents, contemplating their own passage to adult life, would be at just the right age to extract a positive lesson from the example of a working parent. Yet when Minnesota mothers joined a work program, their teenagers performed worse in school. In Canada, adolescents grew more likely to smoke, drink, and use drugs. In Florida, they grew more prone to school suspensions and criminal arrests. One theory is that the teens of working mothers get less supervision just when they need more: think Kesha and Jermaine. Another is that they inherit more burdens at home: think Kesha and Brierra.

But what's most striking aren't these small differences. It's the long list of things that don't seem to change when mothers leave welfare for work. As a leading review of the literature put it: "the list of 'dogs that didn't bark' is impressive and includes parental control, cognitive stimulation in the home, family routines, and harsh parenting." Another set of authors found "the children of current and former welfare recipients generally look similar" and identified "the role of poverty, more than welfare status per se, as a marker of risk in children's lives." A third researcher found that "[h]ome environments changed little." In wondering how far work will go to reorder poor women's lives, it's worth remembering the New Hope Project, a nationally renowned jobs program just down the street from Angie. New Hope was uniquely generous, offering guaranteed jobs, subsidized wages, health care, child care, and attentive casework. And it did achieve its main goal—putting more poor people to work. But it had little impact on the rest of family life. Psychologists found virtually no improvement in parents' mental health even under such ideal conditions. They found no rise in self-esteem. No improvement in feelings of "mastery." Even after two years in the program, the average participant still registered levels of depression considered cause for a clinical referral. The researchers came up with measures of parental "warmth," "control," "monitoring," "aspirations," and "cognitive stimulation." They asked whether New Hope families had dictionaries, magazines, or library cards; if they took trips to museums; if they went to church. Same result: families in the work program looked no different than families down the block. The program did have one outstanding finding; it significantly raised the school performance of six- to twelve-year-old boys. While researchers weren't positive why, the leading explanation stresses the program's success in getting children into after-school programs. Here, too, it seems, success came not from changing the home but from getting children out.

The studies are early and no doubt imperfect. Maybe working mothers convey something to their kids that social science can't measure. Or maybe they will with time. Women leaving welfare for work often *say* they feel better, even if their scores on mental-health tests don't rise. But it's one thing for a mother to feel some pride and another for her to alter the trajectory of her children's lives. Especially when the children are still growing up fatherless and poor. Angie, Opal, Jewell, Greg, Kenny Gross, Marcus—they all had mothers who worked. What none of them had was a functioning dad and the emotional and financial support that a second parent can bring.

Jewell was still talking of stand-in fathers when we reached the Fox Lake gate and hoping that the man inside would provide her boys with one. The denial of parole had left Ken shaken up; he was approaching his twenty-eighth birthday, and jail was getting old. With another nine months to serve, he enrolled in a masonry class. He hated it at first. He was used to making money by looking pretty, not by mixing mud. But he heard that masons make big bucks, and soon Jewell found puzzling words like mortar and trowel cluttering their conversations. Ken got straight As and became a teaching assistant. ("He does have the skills to go to work for a bricklaying company," Ken's instructor told me. "I wouldn't say he's a lost cause.") One morning Ken woke Jewell with a call. "He told me that when he get out, I ain't gonna have to work no more," she said. She got busy making plans. Maybe they'd move back to Chicago. Or maybe she'd go to school. She had always wanted to be a nurse—not an aide, but the real thing. If not a nurse a beautician, then. One with a real salon. They'd have a girl named Shavell. Or a boy named Travell. One thing certain was that her career as a scanner of industrial tools would end.

I waited while Jewell went inside.

"Till death do we part."

"Do that math."

"We ain't gonna rush things."

Jewell returned two hours later with a report of their conversation. "He said he want to spend the rest of his life with me. He said he wanna grow old with me. And if he was married, I'd be the woman he'd want to marry.

"But he never asked me," she said. "He never asked me to marry him."

It's a test, Jewell kept telling herself; the waiting is a test. Inside the prison, she fiddled with the ring that Ken had given her and told him that she would never take it off. His smile made his dimples stand out when he told her that a ring even more special might be hers someday.

Angie's nursing-pool plan was jinxed. The day she filed her Top Techs application, her car went dead; the day she finished her orientation, her lights got cut off. Her life had turned into allegory: literally, figuratively, she was a woman without power. At least there wasn't much food to spoil. Then again, there wasn't much food. The car bill had set her back on the rent, and she rolled into November still owing for October. The landlord winked and reduced the debt. So far Angie had only winked back. But "if I was by myself—whatever he wanted," she said.

Finally Top Techs called. She made it to the office by 5:00 a.m. and caught a van to Oconomowoc, thirty miles away, where the affluence of the nursing home seemed as exotic as the town's name. "Man, they closet is so big!" she said. At $11.50 an hour, Angie's wage was looking big, too. The next day was Saturday; she returned to the pool. She worked Sunday, as well. After just a few shifts, she got a raise of $1 an hour. She may have been running ragged to reach the next county by dawn, but she talked like a woman who had just glimpsed a future of boundless shimmering wealth. "I made $98—just for that one day!" she said. "Should I leave Mercy? Forget about my 401(k)?" She cut back to a seven-tenths' schedule at Mercy to make more time for the pool.

The next week, as Angie was walking out the door, Top Techs called to cancel. It was 4:30 a.m., pitch black, and bone-achingly cold. The scheduler offered her the second shift. But that wouldn't get her home until midnight, and she was due back the next day at dawn. Angie got back in bed. On Wednesday, Top Techs canceled again. Thursday made it three days in a row. This was just what Wendy, her supervisor at Mercy, had warned her about: big dollars, few hours. Everyone was looking for Christmas money, Angie figured. Things would look up soon. Not long after, Top Techs called three times in a day: we need you, we don't, we do. "I wish they'd make up their mind," Angie grumbled. One night she worked till 10:30 in the outer suburb of Waukesha. But the van didn't come for more than an hour, and she didn't get home until 1:00 a.m. "They leave you trapped out there!" she said. She could have driven herself, but she didn't know the way, she didn't trust her car, and she didn't trust the Waukesha police, especially at midnight. "My black ass ain't supposed to be out there." racial profiling

As Angie started the Top Techs job, her old friend Lisa moved back to town, and Angie took her in. Lisa had been a core member of the First Street crew, and they instantly clicked again. But her arrival left seventeen people in the house, with enough kids to field a football team: Kesha, Redd, Von, Darrell, Sierra, Kierra, Tierra, Brierra—and now, for a month, Chaquita, Pierre, Chakiera, and Charlesha. Even Angie found it a bit much. The more time Angie spent at work, the more time the kids spent alone. At fifteen, Kesha had none of the rebel's instincts that Angie had shown at that age. She didn't drink, smoke weed, or hang in the streets. She even chose a crosstown high school for its prelaw program. "I always told my daddy that I was gonna be his lawyer and help get him out of jail," she said. But she was absent half her freshman year, and finished the second semester with Fs in every class but band. Kesha spent much of her time taking care of Brierra and the rest upstairs with her beau, Jermaine. At the other end of the age range, Darrell, at six, was so starved for attention that sometimes he called Angie a half dozen times in an eight-hour shift. Even Angie's boss, Wendy, noticed. "He just wants to talk to his mama," she said. One day Angie's cousin appeared at the house with a computer marked M.P.S., for Milwaukee Public Schools, to whom it seemingly belonged. Kesha used the graphics package to sketch pictures of a baby. Von used the machine to record his raps. Earlier in the year, his faux pickup lines had cited Fred Flintstone and Elmo. Now he went for the sixth-grade gangsta sound. "Fuck that, nigger!" he chanted to the hard drive. "Let's go get some weed. We fixing to bust somebody tonight. I ain't playin' no game."

Von *was* just playing, or so Angie thought. Her real worries centered on Redd. Though he was only thirteen, Angie could feel him slipping away. He never had taken an interest in school, and now in seventh grade he scarcely tried. When everyone in his class wrote Brett Favre, inviting the Packers star quarterback to visit, Redd alone refused; a summer-school teacher had called him a "dummy," and he was afraid of misspelling his words. His temper was worse than his spelling. Small setbacks, like a classmate's taunts, would leave him banging his head on the wall. He had a stack of suspension notices six inches deep. A single day's report had him "threatening a student, disruptive, hit another on the head, disrespectful, hiding in bathroom—a little bit out of control." Redd had been five when Greg went to jail, old enough to remember the loss, and scarcely a day went by when he and Marcus didn't fight. "He say [Marcus] ain't his daddy, he don't have to listen to him," Angie said. "He better listen to some damn body. That the only daddy he got. Gonna wind up in the same place his daddy at."

As the year progressed, so did Redd's problems. He cut school. He smoked a lot of weed. Like Kesha, he found someone three years older to "date." Though Angie didn't know it, Redd, not Kesha, was the first of her kids to become sexually active, at age thirteen. Angie worried that with his streetwise airs he was trying to emulate Greg. She also worried he didn't have the mettle to pull it off. "Redd is as sweet as pie, but *wanna* be bad," she said. "Redd is a kitten. Redd is a baby. . . . He's a ticking time bomb." Most of his teachers shared Angie's fears, and some just gave up on him. But at least one saw some promise, calling him "artistic," "thorough when you want to be," and praising his "sense of humor." Among the papers that survived in the bottom of his closet is a middle-school essay called "A Grimmer Mouse."

> He has small pointed ears and a big round body. . . . I found him in the woods crying in a box. I took him home and tried to feed him. . . . He was running around the house tring to find a place to sleep. So I built him a place to sleep in a bigger box with hay in the bottom of the box. He kicked the hay around + started to use it as a bath room. Then I notice he like to be under things, away from the light and people. I took another box and put a blanket in it and put it under my bed. There he sleeps and he is happy living under my bed. His predator is bright light and loud kids. The light because it hurts his eyes . . . The kids are because . . . loud nose inerfer with his hearing.

He came across it one day as he was showing me some school things. I asked him why the mouse had been crying.

"Cause he was just left out there by himself," Redd said. "Somebody who was supposed to be bathing him, feeding him, washing him, and stuff wasn't doing it."

Why not?

"Probably 'cause they didn't have no money to feed him and stuff."

How did that make him feel?

"He was crying, 'cause he was sad."

Was he angry, too?

"He had to be mad, 'cause he was chewing on a tree."

Redd suddenly stopped and looked up. Until then, he said, he hadn't realized that he had been writing about himself. "That's about my daddy," he said. "He wasn't here."

The more time I spent at Angie's, the more it felt like *everything* was about Greg. He had been gone for eight years, but his absence had left a hole that nothing had been able to fill—not welfare, not work, and certainly not the parade of men filing through Angie's life. Since moving to Milwaukee, Angie and the kids had seen him just three or four times. But he hung over the house like a private gravity field. Kesha wrote most often and treasured his typed responses. ("I miss you and love you babygirl.") She was now the same age as Kathryn Miles, the girl killed by Tony's wild shot as Greg watched his buddies' backs. Her father didn't mean to hurt the girl, Kesha said. "Can't hold it against him forever." But Von could hold it against him and did. "What's a grown man doing out shooting a little girl?" he said. "I don't care if it's an accident. You shouldn't a been there in the first place." That Greg had turned down a plea bargain only deepened Von's disdain: "Dude chose his friends over his family." Flipping through the family photo album, Von and I found a picture of a smiling Greg crouched behind one of his toddler sons; it could pass as a warm father-son moment—or it could have if they weren't holding a rifle. I asked what that was about. "Ask that crazy dude," he said, the crazy dude being his dad. Redd said if his father were around, Angie would benefit. "It wouldn't just be this guy, that guy—there'd be somebody to help Mama." But as for himself, Redd said, "I don't miss him. I don't think about him. I don't care that he's gone."

At the start of the school year, Greg had contacted the boys after a long silence and apologized "if I in any way made you feel unloved." He also offered his advice: stay out of the streets, listen to your mother, apply yourselves. When that didn't work, Angie asked me to arrange a visit. We needed the warden's permission for Greg to see Angie and three kids together, and once it came through, we piled in my car for the hundred-mile drive to Joliet, Illinois. The kids hadn't seen him in two years, but no one was talking about Greg. Redd slept, while Kesha and Von kept up an astonished commentary on the high cost of highway tolls. When the Stateville Correctional Center rolled into view, it looked like something that had wandered off the set of *Scared Straight*. It's a gloomy old fortress with thirty-foot walls and, until a few months earlier, a death chamber inside, obviously a much rougher place than where Ken was doing his time. The guards didn't thumb old magazines. They sat behind bulletproof glass.

While I had planned to wait outside, Greg had put me on his visiting list, and Angie invited me to meet him. He'd formed a dozen incongruous identities in my mind. He was a four-year-old boy, leaving Missouri on a bus, never to see his father again. He was a ten-year-old escaping the Chicago projects after someone dropped a brick on his head. He was Hattie Mae's "little gentleman" and Angie's soul mate. He was the charismatic street entrepreneur who'd commanded a crew of men. He was a letter writer of obvious intelligence and an affectionate, worried Dad. He was a drug dealer, a convicted murderer, a man whose crazy scheme had killed a teenage girl. We spent an hour in waiting-room limbo, then climbed the hill to the main cell block, passed through two sets of menacing doors, and entered a nicotine-dim room of hard chairs and vending machines. A handsome man in a denim shirt was standing there, slightly stooped from stomach surgery. He had a soft, polite voice and big, beautiful eyes. "Thanks for bringing the kids," he said. It was easy to see how Angie had fallen in love with him. And nearly impossible to picture him doing what he had done.

I left them to a private visit. When they emerged an hour later, Kesha and Von looked as though they'd come from a funeral, and Angie had her arm around Redd, who cried all the way to the car. A heavy silence fell over the drive home, and no one discussed what was said. "He really miss Greg—what can I say?" Angie later said about Redd. She didn't add—she didn't have to—how much she missed him, too.

Angie's day in prison was Marcus's day in court for violating the restraining order. I picked him up when we got back to town and encountered a portrait of defeat. While a guilty plea had limited his sentence to sixty days of work release, he worried less about going away than about what he would come back to. Ever since his arrest, Marcus had tried to make amends. He had cooked and cleaned and taken Angie out. He had left when she told him to go. But he realized he amounted to nothing more than an afterthought in the house. Angie "was like a gift—a gift I wasn't able to receive," he said. "I don't know how many times you could tell a person you're sorry. I mean, I'm *sorry*." That Angie and the kids had just returned from seeing

Greg completed his emotional rout; he knew he would never compare. We pulled up to the house, where he sat in the car pining so long the kids came out and stared. With the restraining order still in place, just walking through the door was a crime. Marcus finally mustered a weak smile and got out to break the law. "I'm a sucker for love," he said.

Marcus, Opal, the kids, the bills—Angie's problems never got solved. They orbited her like planets. They stuck to her like gum. A few weeks later, trying to gas up her car, she found that someone had stolen her last $20. Opal professed her innocence, and Angie had another suspect, her cousin's girlfriend. Still, she did something she had thought about for months: she told Opal it was time to go. What if, as usual, the shelters were full: would Angie really put her out? "Yes, yes, yes, yes, yes—I'm really tired!" she said. Opal called the shelters; the shelters were full; and Angie stopped bringing it up. As November turned to December, Opal had been there a year.

Angie's work plans turned circular, too. The money at Top Techs was great when she could get it, but she couldn't get it enough. She could get all the hours she wanted at Mercy, "but I don't make jack." Although Angie resented the Mercy pay, she did feel comfortable there. One day with her car in the shop, she woke Wendy at 4:00 a.m. to say she didn't have bus fare. Wendy got up and gave her a ride. ("Stuff happens to people," Wendy said.) On Thanksgiving, Angie cooked all night and slept through the morning shift. Wendy was less forgiving ("that little toad!"), but they had a history. While Angie had spent most of the year plotting her exit from Mercy, the pool felt too risky to count on full-time. She would hope for more pool hours later. For now she needed two jobs to earn one inadequate living.

Christmas was coming. Kesha wanted a VCR. Redd and Von wanted a weight-lifting set and Darrell, a Nintendo 64. Angie bought Marcus a coat, and she planned to treat herself at a male strip club on Christmas Eve. In all, she was facing bills of $500, or more, in a budget already in the red. She stormed through December like a one-woman nursing brigade, pulling doubles at Mercy and trekking to Oconomowoc whenever she could. "I wish you would tell Santa about me," she laughed one day. "I'm a good, hardworking woman who can't seem to get up off the ground."

financial pressure

In the middle of December, Angie and Opal had a new fight. Opal's food stamps arrived one morning, and by the time Angie dragged her out of the crack house she had burned through nearly $300 in a single afternoon. The house was out of groceries—again!— but Angie didn't have time to lecture; she was rushing to get Kesha to a color-guard show. The next day, Angie's friend Barbara called. She mentioned that she had lent Opal some money. But Opal said she couldn't pay her back because her food stamps hadn't come.

This, in the world of 2400 West Brown, was a minuscule lie, a transgression so slight that on another day Angie might not have noticed. It was a satellite sin, an outer-orbit derivative of the real dilemma: another month short on food. But it left Angie in a rage. She walked into Opal's room and said something she hadn't planned to say. *Get out.* Go. Leave within forty-eight hours. "I said, 'Why you keep *lyin'*?" Angie said. "Why you keep trying to *use* motherfuckers? Don't make no sense!" Opal wasn't surprised, just angry—angry at Angie, and though she couldn't admit it, angrier at herself. She threw back every accusation she could muster—calling Angie a drinker, a hyp-ocrite, a bad mother. Angie was still simmering the following day. "She told me because I work all the time, that don't mean you're a better parent: 'Kids need their parents around them.' Yeah, they might do. But I buy my kids stuff when they need it. . . . You don't take care of nobody but yourself. . . . That girl crazy! But you know, it ain't nothing but the drugs—drugs make you say anything." Angie urged her to go back to rehab and offered to go with her. "Maybe I shouldn't drink as much beer." Opal had closed her ears.

Angie knew it was Christmas. She knew it was cold and the shelters were full. She knew that Opal's departure—to a room in Bo's cousin's house—would be freighted with sad symbolism: Opal would be haul-ing away her stuff on Brierra's first birthday. But "I ain't doing her no good here," she said. "She told me that a long time ago: I'm 'enabling' her—she learned that in rehab." Angie laughed. "Shoot! Why don't you take your ass back there and learn something else?" Yet under-neath she was as earnest as could be. "If I don't put her out, she ain't never gonna get herself together," she said. "I love you," she told Opal. "When you get yourself together, I'll be there for you."

I stopped by on the eve of Opal's departure. Opal was packed and locked in her room, and Angie was propped up in bed at midnight with a Colt 45. Great heaps of stuff spilled everywhere: report cards, pay stubs, unopened bills, CDs, an iron, mounds of dirty clothes. A milk crate held a battered TV, and Marcus sprawled on the bedcovers. Having failed to report to the work-release program, he was a small-time fugitive. Despite the showdown with Opal, or perhaps because of it, Angie was in an expansive mood. All in all, she figured, it hadn't been a bad year. She had worked three jobs and bought a car. She had earned about $18,500, a personal record. She had started a retirement plan. She had been shot at by Marcus and ripped off by Opal. She had lost her lights twice and run low on food more times than she could count. Someone had just egged her car. Too bad the shelters were full, she laughed. She needed one.

So how had the new law changed her life? Had ending welfare worked? While I had posed versions of the question before, they never seemed to grab her, and I was starting to understand why. On welfare, Angie was a low-income single mother, raising her children in a dangerous neighborhood in a household roiled by chaos. She couldn't pay the bills. She drank lots of beer. And her kids needed a father. Off welfare, she was a low-income single mother, raising her children in a dangerous neighborhood in a household roiled by chaos. She couldn't pay the bills. She drank lots of beer. And her kids needed a father. "We're surviving!" is all Angie said. "'Cause that's what we have to do."

Were the kids proud that she works? It was a question that often arose when I talked about Angie with middle-class friends, most of whom took it as an article of faith that the answer had to be yes. Angie paused. "I don't think the kids think about that," she said. "They'd like it if I'd just sit around with them all day." She raised her voice to a mimicking squeal: "'Why you always at work?' Shoot! Why you think I gotta work? Ain't none a you got a job!" It was possible, of course, that the kids felt prouder than she knew and that the power of the example she set would become clearer with time. I asked if she thought her struggles to grind out a low-wage living would encourage the kids to stay in school. "Do I think they're going to finish high school? Hell, no!" Angie said. Watching her own mother struggle hadn't inspired her. "I just hope they understand what I'm doing, trying to make they life a little better. I ain't expecting nobody to be no rocket scientist. Just get up and make a life for yourself. And don't be selling no drugs."

Did she worry that Kesha would follow her path and become a teenage mom? "Sex ain't what's on Kesha's mind now," Angie said. "When she's ready, she'll let me know."

Marcus wasn't so sure. Kesha did spend a lot of time with that eighteen-year-old boy upstairs. . . .

Angie shot him a censuring look.

"No—I know she ain't having sex," he said. After a pause, he whispered, "She might as well move up there."

Angie yawned and talked on. In the hours between midnight and dawn, she found her sacred space, turning the jumble of junk and a flickering TV into her makeshift sanctuary. Finally, the beer cans were empty. The GED workbook was covered with dust. The kitchen clock flashed its usual time: 88:88. In the real world, it was almost 3:00 a.m., and in two hours Angie's alarm clock would drag her cussing from her sleep. She wasn't betting that an $8 or $9 an hour job would prove anyone's salvation, the kids' or her own. Still, by the time the sun rose over Milwaukee, she would be at the nursing home, complaining that she was broke and tired and desperate for a little sleep. Then she would get someone dressed and fed and ready for the day. Angie wasn't one to boast, but that did make her proud. "I work," she said.

Epilogue:
Washington and Milwaukee, 1999–2004

I started to write about ghetto poverty in the early 1980s, when the field felt as filled with defeat as Angie with her lights cut off. *Homelessness, the underclass, AIDS, crack*—the decade challenged dictionaries to keep pace as it redefined urban suffering. Whether I was writing about welfare or the broader fabric of inner-city life, I soon had the same formula reflexively in mind: things were bad and getting worse. Every reporter's early encounters leave indelible impressions. In St. Louis, poverty registered as a sound, the wails of teenagers mourning a gang murder. In Detroit, it arose as a scent: Lysol, body odor, and spaghetti sauce wafting through a homeless shelter. In Chicago, poverty was the menacing sight of high-rise projects stretching to the horizon; "American apartheid" it was sometimes called, and so it seemed. As dispiriting as the facts on the ground was the fatalism in the air, summarized (and spread) by Ronald Reagan's line: "We fought a war on poverty and poverty won." Appearing at a conference in the early 1990s, Robert Lampman, an architect of those early antipoverty efforts, celebrated the legacy of his life's work: soaring wages, full employment, vanishing need. Then the aging eminence delivered a line from *Saturday Night Live:* "Not!"

A few years later, Lampman's punch line would no longer work. Poverty plunged. Employment surged. Crime, teen pregnancy, crack use, AIDS—all saw substantial declines. By moving poor women into the workforce, the welfare bill contributed to that progress materially. And it symbolized it powerfully. Whatever hardships the bill left untouched, whatever corners of inner-city life it may never reach, the decade renewed a forgotten lesson: that progress is possible on problems that seem impervious to change. At the conference where Robert Lampman poked fun at himself, another participant tried to ward off the gloom with lines from a Polish poet, written as Solidarity was exposing the clefts in Soviet control. "What does the political scientist know?" the poem asks.

> It doesn't occur to him
> That no one knows when
> Irrevocable changes may appear
> Like an ice floe's sudden cracks

Change "political scientist" to "poverty expert" (or reporter) and you have the feeling of the postwelfare years.

Forced by the cracking ice to discard my formula, I struggled to find a new one. The upbeat statistical reports scarcely fit the hardships before my eyes. But which revealed the greater truth? Angie's 401(k), or her drunken stock-picking session among armed boyfriends? In the trio's lives, the layers of disadvantage ran even deeper than I first glimpsed—the garnished wages, the loss of heat and lights, the fights for the last drop of milk, Kesha's weekends with a prostitute, Opal's whole life. "That was every black man's job," Jewell said about selling crack, as if to say that one thing poverty can impoverish is one's sense of possibility. And, as steady workers with above-average earnings, Angie and Jewell were unusual *successes*.

Or maybe just usual ones. In getting to know Michelle Crawford, the welfare-to-work heroine championed by Tommy Thompson, I found a similar story of work mixed with woe. Michelle, too, had made an unlikely journey off the rolls—yet she was running out of food, coping with physical attacks from a jealous man (in her case, one she had married), and panicking over a teenage son's arrest, twice, for selling cocaine. In talking about Lillie Harden, Bill Clinton had stressed how much her move from welfare to work would mean to her kids: "She looked me straight in the eye and said, 'When my boy goes to school and they say, "What does your mama do for a living," he can give an answer.'" Harden did have a straight-A daughter who went on to college. But the son that Clinton was celebrating was better known for his rap sheet than his grades. Between the time Governor Clinton first told his story and the time President Clinton revived it, the teenage Carlton Harden had already served two years for shooting at some students outside a North Little Rock high school. In the past decade, he has been arrested twenty times, for offenses ranging from disorderly conduct to possession of crack cocaine with intent to deliver; he's gone to prison on drug charges twice. "Oh boy, it almost killed me," Lillie Harden told me, speaking of her son's problems. "He got out there and act like he don't have no brain." Harden had a stroke in 2002 and wanted me to ferry a message back to Clinton, asking if he could help her get on Medicaid. She had received it on welfare, but had been rejected now, and she couldn't afford her $450 monthly bill for prescription drugs. More sad than bitter, she said of her work: "It didn't pay off in the end." I used to imagine the story someone could tell from a few scraps of Angie's life. On the job. A 401(k). What a difference it must make to the kids!

Yet Angie and Jewell worked. They worked when their whole lives seemed like tutorials in the barriers to work. They worked when they didn't have enough to eat or didn't get to sleep. They worked through ulcers and depression and back pains. They worked when Marcus shot holes in the ceiling and Ken went to jail. With little education, experience, or encouragement—they worked. If one lesson was that their misfortunes ran deeper than typically imagined, another was that their resilience ran equally deep.

Skeptics viewed the rising work rates of poor single mothers as the ephemera of the economy. "Wait until a recession," they said (at times too eagerly). Downturns always hurt the needy, and the 2001 recession did, though not as much as feared. From 2000 to 2002, the incomes of disadvantaged single mothers fell about 2 percent, after rising 17 percent over the previous six years. Child poverty rates rose by a half percentage point, less than a fifth of the average rise inflicted by the previous three recessions. The employment rates of high school dropouts held up better than those of college graduates. In part this may have reflected the shape of the recession, which spread its pain further up the income ladder than recessions often do. But it also suggested that the work habits of women like Angie and Jewell outlasted the business cycle. From 2000 to 2003, even as unemployment rates rose, the welfare rolls fell another 7 percent, which may either show the enterprise of the needy or the failure of states to serve them—and probably shows some of both.

At the peak of the Milwaukee welfare wars, I took a drive around town with one of the city's premier eccentrics, John Gardner, a school board member and lefty labor organizer, who had long called for abolishing welfare and replacing it with public jobs. While he found much to criticize in the bureaucratic blunders of W-2—"It works despite itself," he said, an enviably succinct summation—he reveled at the sight of so many poor women groping their way into jobs. He likened the postwelfare years to the aftermath of slavery, when dispossessed families roamed the countryside wondering what, besides more hunger, their newfound freedom would bring. I silently dismissed the comparison as wild hyperbole; no welfare program ever administered the lash. I dismissed it but never forgot it, since it underscores the challenge of recognizing success when it first appears, cloaked in havoc and doubt. In the case of Emancipation, the trajectory of racial progress took roughly a century to come fully into view. In their first half dozen years off the rolls, it was easy to feel like nothing had changed in Angie and Jewell's lives. But *something* had.

The country knows now what it didn't know a decade ago: that antipoverty policy can enjoy a measure of success. To borrow a diplomatic term, that ought to serve as a "confidence-building" measure that encourages additional steps. Clinton predicted that ending welfare would transform the politics of poverty, and on the surface at least it has. No one runs for office, as Reagan did, deriding Welfare Queens. "Welfare mothers make responsible employees," claimed one public-service ad—unremarkable except for the pollster who helped design it, the former Reagan aide Richard Wirthlin. When I talked to Clinton in 2004, I asked whether his prediction of a new progressive politics had proved correct. "In some ways we'll never know," he said. "Because Al Gore didn't win the White House and because the economy turned down . . . and because the whole political focus of America changed after 9/11. But I will say this . . . [George W. Bush] thought in order to win the White House he had to run as a compassionate conservative. He had to run bragging on the religious programs that help poor people and inner-city kids. And he had to go out of his way to say that he wasn't a racist." Clinton didn't note, though he might have, what a contrast that had been from the 1988 campaign of the first George Bush, whose supporters sought to mobilize racial fears with images of the black murderer Willie Horton.

Yet it's hard to picture a radically new politics of poverty when politics remains so dominated by money and the poor so lacking in power. No matter how many double shifts Angie pulled, she couldn't close the growing income gaps that increasingly define American life. The rising inequality has grown so familiar that it has lost its ability to startle. In the salad days of the 1990s, the incomes of the poorest fifth of American households rose 8 percent; the top fifth gained 40 percent; and the richest 5 percent gained 72 percent, to $434,000 a year. That meant the top 5 percent of Americans received a greater share of the national income than the bottom 60 percent combined. It may seem as though it were ever so, but that particular milestone wasn't crossed until 1997, Angie's and Jewell's first full year off the rolls. Trading welfare checks for pay stubs, they staked a moral claim to a greater share of the nation's prosperity—and entered an economy that gave the common worker proportionally less and less.

"People who work shouldn't be poor," Clinton said. They shouldn't have their lights shut off. They shouldn't run out of food. They shouldn't have their wages garnished when their ulcers bleed. But low-wage workers have vanished from a domestic agenda that's been dominated by a tax-cutting frenzy, mostly aimed at the same upper-income families who have enjoyed such outsized gains. (Congress cut *dividend* taxes.) Health care, child care, wage supplements, transportation aid—the rudiments of a package of workers' aid aren't hard to imagine. Just hard to enact, and even harder with the deficits the tax cuts helped create. Angie and Jewell finally got health insurance, through a Wisconsin program called Badger Care. In subsidizing families up to twice the poverty line, it's an admirable example of helping needy workers and one that other states should follow. But the typical state Medicaid program cuts off adults well before they reach the poverty line. The number of child-care subsidies doubled, but between 50 percent and 85 percent of eligible families still receive no help. While Angie's tax credits kept her afloat, Wisconsin's state program was unusually generous; forty states have none. At $5.15 an hour, the real value of the minimum wage is lower than in 1950 when Hattie Mae was still picking cotton.

The remarkable thing about programs of workers' aid like these is how unremarkable they are: there's nothing untested, nothing (except a minimum-wage hike) even politically controversial. The major impediment is cost. In 2001, Isabel Sawhill and Adam Thomas of the Brookings Institution came up with a plan for more child care, larger tax credits, and a $1 an hour raise in the minimum wage. They estimated it would lower the poverty rate by 2 percentage points. It would reach *20 million* families. And since all the money would go to workers, it couldn't be derided as welfare. Was it unrealistically expensive? Yes and no: at $26 billion a year, it cost less than half of what Congress spent to eliminate the inheritance tax, a benefit that almost exclusively accrues to the families of multimillionaires.

The ultimate goal isn't a safety net but a reduced need for one—to give families like Angie's a chance at real upward mobility. Elevators are harder to design than safety nets, but there are obvious places to begin. The work-first emphasis on entry-level jobs outperformed earlier programs of lengthy, up-front study. But the bias against training has probably swung too far, especially in an economy that pays the unskilled so little. An Oregon program that mixed job search and training raised earnings twice as much as those that stressed immediate work. What if Mercy Rehab (which is owned by a chain, Extendicare, Inc., with 275 facilities and revenues of nearly $2 billion) let experienced aides spend part of the week training for better jobs? What if the government subsidized the cost? Another item for the mobility agenda involves literal mobility, helping inner-city residents physically get away—to the army, to Job Corps, to better neighborhoods. The famous Gautreaux program in Chicago quietly spirited inner-city families to subsidized homes in the suburbs, where their kids went on to college at twice the rate of those who stayed behind. Its successor, Moving to Opportunity, brought families better health, less crime, and improved behavior among girls. The success of the New Hope boys shows what a difference even a few hours of the right after-school program can make. A serious attempt to help the inner-city poor would also include the men. Some experimental programs have tried to raise their earnings and strengthen their ties with their children, and mostly the results have been disappointing. But so were those of welfare-to-work programs for women a generation ago. If calls to aid the ghettos once sounded dreamy, there's a difference now: something finally worked. Or at least worked enough to encourage new attempts.

Funding for the Personal Responsibility Act expired in 2002, setting up a long-awaited reauthorization debate. There were all sorts of fights that George W. Bush could have led as a "compassionate conservative," especially with the welfare surpluses gone and state budgets reeling. He could have brought health insurance to needy workers, increased on-the-job training, or extended a hand to inner-city men. He could have offered federal money for more after-school programs. (He tried to cut them.) If he was serious about helping the working poor, he could have created subsidies for states to create tax credits like Wisconsin's. Instead, the debate that unfolded was both rancorous and obscure. Concerned that too many people on the rolls were idle, the administration sought to increase the "participation rates," the share of recipients required to perform some sort of weekly activity. (Because of adjustments for caseload reduction, most states no longer had to meet a meaningful federal standard.) Idleness was certainly one problem, and federal standards may be part of the solution. But the Bush proposal was so extreme—with new caps on education and training and a 70 percent work rate that few states could meet—it left the debate paralyzed. Arguing, rightly, that more work would require more child care, the Democrats sought more money. The value of the block grant had eroded 30 percent, but the White House was adamantly opposed. As of 2004, the issues remained unresolved, and the states were operating on short-term extensions, adding uncertainty to their fiscal woes.

For the most part, the discussion has occurred off center stage, with the country understandably focused on war and terrorism. The one Bush proposal to gain broad attention was the "marriage initiative," a plan to redirect $300 million a year of welfare money into marriage-promotion efforts, ranging from advertising campaigns to courses on budgeting and conflict resolution. Much of the Left responded with derision, and the obvious criticisms were true: it was totally untested, the decision to marry is deeply personal, some communities lack marriageable men. But similar things could have been said about teenage pregnancy, which government and civic campaigns in the 1990s helped cut by 30 percent. Rather than dismiss it, why not see it and raise it one—with an equally large "fatherhood initiative" to help inner-city men find jobs and reconnect with their kids. One congressman did push such a bill a few years ago, and he was scarcely a starry-eyed liberal: Republican Clay Shaw, the House author of the 1996 welfare bill. (To skeptical Republican colleagues he asked, "Does anyone have a better idea?") The lives of poor single mothers are too hard, the prospects for their kids too bleak, to write off the low-income family like a chunk of bad debt.

The welfare revolution grew from the fear that the poor were mired in a culture of *entitlement*—stuck in a swamp of excessive demands, legal prerogative, social due. There certainly was a culture of entitlement in American life, but it was scarcely concentrated at the bottom (as anyone following the wave of corporate scandals now knows). What really stands out about Angie and Jewell is how little they felt they were owed. They went through life acting entitled to nothing. Not heat or lights. Not medical care. Not even three daily meals. And they scarcely complained. When welfare was there for the taking, they got on the bus and took it; when it wasn't, they made other plans. In ending welfare, the country took away their single largest source of income. They didn't lobby or sue. They didn't march or riot. They made their way against the odds into wearying, underpaid jobs. And that does now entitle them to something—to "a shot at the American Dream" more promising than the one they've received.

On a frigid afternoon in December 1999, Angie followed through with her plan to put Opal out. Opal's mother took in the three older girls, and Opal and Brierra moved to a room in Bo's cousin's house. While Angie and Opal patched up their friendship, Opal's luck expired. After an early labor, she delivered her fifth daughter, Myerra, and they both tested positive for cocaine. Opal acknowledged that she was essentially homeless and had been smoking crack for a decade, and the state took the kids. Myerra left the hospital for a foster home, and Angie took legal custody of Brierra to spare her the same fate.

Losing one's kids is the ultimate sanction, the death penalty of social work. So it held out the hope of shocking Opal straight, as her other calamities had not. The court told her that to regain her girls, she had to make regular visits, find a home, complete a treatment program, and pass drug tests. She failed on every score. Then she got pregnant again. Opal did go to an outpatient program, but the boy she dubbed "Little Bo" had cocaine in his blood, and Opal seemed especially dejected when the state took him away, too. In early 2004, the state was moving to sever her parental rights.

With the loss of her kids, Opal finally lost her welfare check. She still had $5,000 a year in food stamps and, until he got caught with a stash of cocaine, she had Bo. As a repeat offender, he drew four years, leaving Opal to drift here and there, staying with whoever would have her. She has withdrawn from everyone, including me, but we did talk briefly after the birth of her son. At her request, I contacted a residential program that specialized in central city women. The director pledged to find her a spot, saying that Opal fit the profile—mid-thirties, lost kids—of many clients who turned their lives around. But Opal didn't follow through. "I guess she's just gonna be out here"—on the streets—"till somebody kill her, or she overdose." Jewell said. "Is she hurting inside? If she's alone, do she cry about it? I don't know."

W-2 remained troubled, too. As the program imploded with scandal at Maximus and Goodwill, Tommy Thompson left for Washington and a job as secretary of Health and Human Services. Having shown so little oversight of his own program, he gained oversight of the welfare system nationwide. A commission arose to study the problems he left behind, but little became of its work. From 2000 to 2003, the unemployment rate in Milwaukee surged to 9.7 percent (compared with 5.3 percent when Angie and Jewell left the rolls), and the caseload nearly doubled to nine thousand—still just a quarter of what it had been a decade earlier. The agency heads demanded more money, amid the embarrassing news that they were paying themselves up to $200,000 a year. Despite the handsome pay, half the Milwaukee agencies failed to meet the modest new performance goal—moving 35 percent of clients into jobs—and a years-long academic study found that people who entered W-2 fared no better in earnings or employment than a similar group who did not. By its very presence, W-2 served as welfare deterrent. But for the average client, its services made no difference.

Bleeding red ink, one agency (the YWCA) exited W-2, and another (UMOS) ran up multiple fines for casework failures. With only three Milwaukee agencies left, the regions were redrawn, and the Opportunities Industrialization Center—where I first glimpsed Opal spoofing the job interview—became the largest in the state. Then $270,000 of its funds were traced to the bank account of a disgraced politician. Former state senator Gary George pleaded guilty to federal conspiracy charges after acknowledging that he took the money (disguised as legal fees and routed through an attorney) while serving in a position to influence the awarding of welfare contracts. In OIC's case, those contracts totaled about $140 million. In March 2004, the OIC president, Carl Gee, was indicted for his alleged role in the kickback scheme. Gee pleaded not guilty, and other OIC officials denied any wrongdoing, but the state stationed a full-time monitor on the premises. Like a gang-ridden school, Wisconsin's largest welfare agency was being run with a cop in the hall.

Jason Turner, W-2's designer, moved on to the top welfare job in New York City and contracting problems of his own. Eager to put his stamp on the city's giant system, he had the welfare agency issue a half-billion dollars in job-placement contracts through an expedited bidding procedure. The largest single piece, more than $100 million, went to Maximus, where George Leutermann was part of a corporate team that included one or two others with ties to Turner and that critics charged had gained an inside edge. The city comptroller challenged the contracts on the grounds of "corruption, favoritism, and cronyism," and, with the process tied up in court, *The New York Times* reported that Leutermann, while seeking the New York business, had put Turner's father-in-law on the Maximus payroll. (He was a contractor on an unrelated project.) Upholding the contracts, an appeals court found that the city had shown "no evidence of favoritism" toward Maximus. But in letting family ties develop with a corporate suitor, Turner damaged his reputation and added to a controversy that shadowed the rest of his term. Amid the outcry and delay, Maximus wound up with a diminished role and was eventually eased out of the city, and Leutermann soon left the company. Turner finished four years in office that cut the rolls in half but raised, even more pointedly than in Wisconsin, the concern that his tactics—diversion and strict work rules—drove the needy away. He is now a consultant based in Milwaukee, with clients as far away as Slovakia and Israel; the latter country is setting up a version of W-2 called "Israel Works."

Farther down the bureaucratic chain, Michael Steinborn remained at Maximus, though he stopped working directly with clients. Burned out on their crises, he moved into a job trying to line up prospective employers. With his personal life in disarray, Michael saw welfare from yet another angle. He split up with his girlfriend, Jai, after they had a second child, who was born with severe medical problems and needed months of hospitalization. As a single mother with a disabled infant, Jai no longer felt able to work, and she went on W-2 herself. Michael said he felt ashamed to have his own children on welfare. But he also said the checks, with his child-support payments, helped nurture their daughter to health. "The irony kills me: I'm telling people this isn't the way, and my own family ends up on the system," he said. It was a fittingly equivocal thought from a man so ambivalent about the program he helped run.

Home life took a happier turn for Jewell and Ken. True to her word, she waited for him—for 476 days. Then on a snowy dawn in April 2000, I picked her up for a last ride to the prison, where a ponytailed man with a duffel bag walked out, smiling a hundred-watt smile. I confess I had doubts; not much I knew recommended Ken as a candidate for domesticity. But after a week in seclusion, Jewell offered an upbeat report. "It's just like it was before he went in," she said, with late-night video games and excursions with the kids.

Ken was so proud of his bricklaying certificate he unpacked it before we left the prison parking lot. Back in Milwaukee, however, he couldn't find a masonry job. Emotionally, he was in the classic ex-con's state—frustrated, vulnerable, adrift—when a friend dropped off an ounce of cocaine. The scene played out like a temptation cartoon, with an elf on each shoulder. *Take it. Don't.* Ken had pictured the moment for months and had never known what he would do. He hated being broke. He hated prison more. He gave the drugs to a friend and declared himself retired from the trade. Ken found off-and-on work disposing of hazardous waste, then took a job delivering pizzas. The money is no good, but the nightly rhythm recalls his old ways: he can roam the city, flirt with clients, and get paid in cash. He has been free for nearly four years with no arrests. "It's still in my blood," he said of the hustler's life. "But I'm trying to get it out of my blood. When you got a positive influence"—Jewell—"you can't do nothing but positive things." Jewell's conquest of Ken is the rare event of which she can say: "It's just what I hoped for."

She wouldn't say that about work. After three years on the tool-scanning line, she grew so angry at her annual raise—25 cents an hour—that she walked out of G. B. Electric and never went back. "They're making millions of dollars a day, and here we is, making $8 and $9 an hour," she said. She landed a temp job at the post office but hurt her neck and shoulder toting the mail and got fired when investigators discovered her old shoplifting conviction. Seven years after leaving the rolls, Jewell is a nursing aide again, earning $10 an hour and feeling underpaid. "I wouldn't say I like it—I just do it," she said. Still, between her earnings, food stamps, and tax credits, Jewell brings home more than $20,000 a year, and Ken makes about as much hustling pizzas—together, they have a toehold on a lower-middle-class life. With a soft spot for electronics (and payment plans), Ken bought a computer to help him write raps, and Jewell plays dominoes online; calling, I often get a message that says, "The AOL customer . . . asked that you try to reach them on their cell phone." Though she is still "scuffling" to get by, Jewell said, "I ain't scuffling like I *used* to." She said Ken's presence has helped the boys, but it hasn't been a panacea. By the eighth grade, her oldest son, Terrell, was flirting with trouble—skipping class, hanging with the wrong friends—and Jewell grew alarmed.

Despite the basic domestic contentment, one thing was missing. "That should be us," Ken said, as a couple on television cuddled their baby. Their prospects weren't good. Jewell had fibroids on her uterine tissue, and Ken had never fathered a child. So they were astonished when Jewell emerged from the bathroom with a positive pregnancy test. The fibroids brought unbearable pain, and she put off seeing a doctor for a month until she could get health insurance. The growths finally forced a risky, first-trimester operation, with a 10 percent chance of saving the pregnancy. Nearly two months of bed rest and lost wages followed—then the baby shower. Looking every bit the proud father that Jewell had pictured, Ken prowled the event with a video camera and a button that said "Dad." Kevion Quatrell Thigpen arrived in March 2002. Continuing his evolution from bad man to homebody, Ken watches his son while Jewell is at work, then leaves for his nightly pizza rounds.

Jewell still hasn't gotten a wedding ring, though she raises the subject whenever she can. "Arrrghh," Ken says in mock consternation. Despite his display of commitment, marriage seems to conjure a standard of perfection—or at least to demand more money and trust than he feels able to command. "I still think it's gonna happen," Jewell said. Given her record of beating the odds, it would be a mistake to count her out.

While Jewell's bet on romance largely paid off, Angie's bet on work did not. She stayed at Mercy, where seven years of service have made her a fixture on the ward. But despite her "workaholic" pride, her earnings stalled. Actually, they fell. After her earnings peaked at $18,500, Angie cut back to three-quarters time and averaged less than $15,000 over the next four years. Jewell, the grudging worker, earned more. Several forces tempered Angie's drive, not the least of them fatigue. "People get tired!" she said. "I'm not no machine—and even they wear out." Her decision to raise Brierra made it harder to work long hours, and Angie gave up on the nursing pool she had pursued so purposefully. Some news she welcomed contributed to her decision to cut back: after years on a waiting list, she got a Section 8 housing subsidy, which, by reducing her rent by $3,000 a year, replaced the lost wages. But the bigger brake on Angie's drive was more dispiriting: having thrown herself into work, she lost faith that hard work pays. Angie finished a computer class and applied for a promotion to a medical records job. She didn't get it. She did get her semiannual raise: nine belittling cents. She was equally indignant about its size and symbolism: it left her at $8.99 an hour, priced like a Wal-Mart sale. Wanting to tell herself she earned "nine-something," Angie demanded (and got) the extra penny, but fumed at the missing respect. "That's just like an insult—I deserve way more than that," she said. "I like the work. I like the residents. But the money's just not right."

While Angie's earnings still rank her as a welfare-to-work success, she continues to draw heavily on government support: food stamps, tax credits, housing aid, and $215 a month in "kinship care" payments for Brierra. Those programs provide more than half of her income, and she also gets subsidized child care and health insurance. She would be a lot poorer without the help, but there is a downside to the generous layering of aid: every dollar of increased earnings cuts her benefits by 85 cents. With payroll taxes, she actually loses 93 cents, making the extra effort seem pointless—a fact she intuits without fully understanding the math. While the arithmetic of Angie's situation is extreme, her broader dilemma is common: absent a dramatic increase in skills, it's hard to see how she can work her way up to a significantly better standard of living. "Just treading water," she said. "Just making it, that's all."

After a few months on the lam, Marcus did his time in jail, then spent another two years at Angie's, feeling disrespected and warring with the kids. No longer a fugitive, he wasn't quite a boyfriend, either. "Just live together, that's it—barely talk," Angie said. She put him out after she caught him smoking pot with Redd but let him return after he grew mysteriously ill. Hospitalized with several bouts of pneumonia, Marcus was a phantom presence in the house—not there, not gone, not acknowledged. Then he got in a feud with one of his sister's friends, who broke into Angie's house and dropped a car battery on his head. Marcus never fully recovered, and died four months later, at age twenty-nine. Angie speculated that Marcus had cancer, but the word on the street—and on the death certificate—was that Marcus died of AIDS. With her housing voucher, Angie moved to a larger house, where other boarders still come and go. The kids sometimes criticized her drinking, but Angie no longer talked of swearing off beer, saying, "I need my peace of mind." On a happier front, she became a surprisingly enthusiastic parent to Brierra—"surprising" because Angie seemed to have had her fill of motherhood. Once worried that she would have to keep Brierra forever, she started the process of legal adoption to make sure that she does.

Her own kids continued to struggle. Darrell suffered from mysterious seizures for which the doctors could find no cause; one of Angie's friends thought they might be psychosomatic, a lonely boy's bid for attention. Von was Angie's most promising student ("School's fun"), but in high school he fell apart. Cutting classes, defying teachers, he finished his freshman year with a grade point average of 0.2. "It was just me being a knucklehead," he said. "Just trying to follow the crowd." If ever a kid needed some distance from the ghetto, it was Von, whose cerebral streak set him apart and left him lonely. Angie viewed his acting out as an effort to establish his street bona fides. "He don't want anybody to think he's weak," she said. Repeating his freshman year, Von talked of going to college and becoming a teen counselor, but his grades continued to lag.

After years of academic failure, Redd put on a brief but revealing display of ability. Determined to get out of eighth grade, he raised a D-minus average in the fall to a B-plus in the spring, putting the lie to the summer school teacher who had labeled him a "dummy." Then he lost interest again, failing ninth grade twice and dropping out. "It was boring," he said. Hitting his middle teens, Redd shed his doughboy build and gained a new confidence and charm, which may not have been all for the best. A neighbor showed him how to steal cars, and he had just bailed out of a joy ride when the police arrested his friends, finding them with several guns. At seventeen, Redd greeted most days with a joint and though he said he hadn't sold drugs, he added, "I'm ready to get out here and sell me some. . . . I'm tired of not having no money." Hattie Mae, his grandmother, came for a visit and burst into tears. With a headful of braids and his father's soulful eyes, Redd looked just like Greg. She felt like she was losing a son all over again.

For all the boys' problems, it was Kesha who gave Angie her first gray hairs. She continued to date Jermaine, the older boy upstairs. But his sexual pursuit led her to break things off, especially after he took her to a party where the other couples were taking Viagra. "Everybody wanted to do stuff, and I was like, 'You can take me home!' " she said. With her characteristic openness and poise, Kesha said she would know when she was ready; not long after, with a new boyfriend, she decided that she was. The birth control pills that Jewell helped her get ran out, and a few months shy of her seventeenth birthday, Kesha got pregnant. The baby's father was fourteen. She broke the news at his eighth-grade graduation and scarcely heard from him again.

Knowing the struggles ahead, Angie urged her to end the pregnancy, but Kesha wouldn't hear of it. "It's wrong to kill a baby," she said. "It's just so wrong. If you're grown enough to have sex, that's on you—you gotta take responsibility." It was the subject of their angriest fight. Still seventeen, repeating the ninth grade, Kesha had a daughter: LaNayia LaCherish Jobe. She was six months younger than Angie had been when she started down the incomparably hard path of poor single motherhood. Like Angie, Kesha dropped out of school. And like Angie she moved in with a boyfriend, a sporadically employed twenty-four-year-old who lives in his mother's house. But unlike Angie, she didn't go on welfare. "That's for people who really need it," she said. "I like to earn my own money." She took a job as a checkout clerk at a grocery store and spent most of her free time at home with her boyfriend and LaNayia. By all accounts a doting mother, much less wild at nineteen than Angie had been, Kesha had a second child, Latavia.

Angie said she's over the shock of becoming a thirty-five-year-old grandmother. But the ratio of hope to defeat in her life feels like it has shifted in a downward direction. Yet, for all the turmoil and need around her, and all her pure exhaustion, she continues to mine her life for scraps of optimism and meaning. Last year, she seized a moment to herself and wrote another poem, which she called "Better Days." It honors the ancestors "who worked and cried" to get her where she is, and like many chapters in her life it ends with some unanswered questions:

Better days are here, so they say
So why am I still working, running, fighting and crying?
For my better days?
Or is it so my descendants can know of the work I'm putting in
For their better days?

TIMELINE

Early 1840s	Frank Caples, a child slave, arrives in Mississippi. He is Jewell's and Opal's great-great-grandfather and the great-great-great-grandfather of Angie's oldest kids.
1876	Frank Caples has a son named Pie Eddie Caples.
1927	Woods Eastland recruits Pie Eddie Caples to sharecrop on his Delta plantation.
1934	Woods Eastland's son, James, begins running the family plantation.
1935	President Franklin D. Roosevelt signs the Social Security Act, creating AFDC.
1937	Pie Eddie's daughter Mayola gives birth to Hattie Mae.
1939	Mayola Caples dies, leaving Hattie Mae to be raised by her grandmother, "Mama" Hattie.
1941	James Eastland, 36, is appointed to the U.S. Senate; the following year, he wins the first of his six full terms.
1950	Hattie Mae, 13, has her first child, Squeaky.
1952	Hattie Mae, 15, marries Willie Reed, with whom she moves to Missouri and later has three children.
1960	Hattie Mae, 23, leaves Willie and goes on AFDC. Soon after, she meets Isaac Johnson.
1966	Greg Reed is born to Hattie Mae Reed and Isaac Johnson.
1966	Angela Jobe is born to Roosevelt and Charity Jobe.

1967	Opal Caples is born to Hattie Mae's cousin, Ruthie Mae Caples.
1968	Jewell Reed is born to Hattie Mae Reed and Isaac Johnson.
1970	Hattie Mae leaves Isaac and joins her family in the Chicago projects.
1972	Charity and Roosevelt Jobe move to a Chicago subdivision called Jeffrey Manor as Angie, 6, is starting school.
1979	Hattie Mae and her boyfriend, Wesley Crenshaw, move to Jeffrey Manor, now troubled by gangs and drugs.
1979	Charity leaves Roosevelt and moves from Jeffrey Manor.
1982–83	Angie, visiting her father's house, begins dating Greg.
1984	Angie and Greg have their first child, LaKesha. Angie leaves high school and goes on welfare.
1986	Angie and Greg have son, Dwayne, whom they nickname Redd. About this time, Greg starts selling drugs.
1987	Angie and Greg have a third child, DeVon.
1988	Jewell gets pregnant and moves in with Angie and Greg. After her son Terrell is born in October, she begins dating Tony Nicholas.
June 1991	Greg and Tony are arrested for murder.
September 1991	Angie and Jewell move to Milwaukee.
October 23, 1991	Bill Clinton, running for president, pledges to "end welfare as we know it."
December 1991	Jewell has her second son, Tremmell.
November 1992	Bill Clinton is elected president.
June 1993	Angie has her fourth child, Darrell. Soon after, she starts a post office job that lasts a year and a half.
September 1993	Jewell's cousin, Opal Caples, moves to Milwaukee.
December 1993	Wisconsin governor Tommy Thompson signs a bill pledging to replace AFDC within six years.
June 1994	Clinton proposes a welfare bill, which never reaches a congressional vote.

November 1994	Republicans capture the House and Senate. Newt Gingrich and GOP governors agree to make welfare a block grant, with capped federal funding but expanded state autonomy.
March 1995	The House passes a welfare bill, which Clinton criticizes.
April 1995	Jason Turner, a Wisconsin welfare official, drafts a plan for a new state welfare program called W-2. Governor Thompson signs it the following year.
June 1995	Angie, Opal, and Jewell leave the house on First Street.
September 1995	The Senate passes a welfare bill, with Clinton's praise.
December 1995	Clinton vetoes the welfare bill, which is attached to a GOP balanced budget plan.
January 1996	Clinton vetoes the welfare bill, this time as a separate measure.
March 1996	Jason Turner launches a Wisconsin work program called Pay for Performance; the rolls plummet.
Spring 1996	Angie and Jewell take jobs as nursing aides; Jewell begins seeing Ken Thigpen.
Spring 1996	GOP prepares a third welfare bill, tied to a "poison pill" of Medicaid cuts to force a third Clinton veto.
July 1996	The House and Senate drop the Medicaid cuts and pass a third welfare bill.
August 22, 1996	Clinton signs a bill abolishing AFDC and creating a new program, Temporary Assistance for Needy Families, with time limits, work requirements, and increased state control.
August 1996	After eight years on welfare, Jewell leaves the rolls.
September 1996	After twelve years on welfare, Angie leaves the rolls.
December 1996	Jewell gets fired and spends most of the next year with neither welfare nor work.
Spring 1997	Angie, thriving as a worker, buys a car.
August 1997	Angie meets Marcus Robertson, who soon moves in.
September 1997	Wisconsin launches W-2 a month after Opal appears on the cover of *The New York Times Magazine* with Thompson.
November 1997	Angie's car is stolen, sending her into a downward spiral.

January 1998	Jewell goes to work at G. B. Electric.
February to May 1998	Opal quits her job and sells off her furniture to buy cocaine. Her caseworkers at the Opportunities Industrialization Center, a W-2 agency, ignore her.
March 1998	Angie is deterred from returning to welfare and finds a job at Mercy Rehab.
May 1998	Opal's mother takes her kids, as Opal, who is pregnant, moves to a crack house and continues to get welfare.
November 1998	Michael Steinborn, a new W-2 caseworker at Maximus, Inc., inherits Opal's case. Opal moves in with Angie.
December 1998	Ken Thigpen is sentenced to two years for selling cocaine. Opal gives birth to Brierra.
April 1999	Maximus transfers Opal's case to Goodwill.
April 1999	Marcus shoots up Angie's ceiling.
June 1999	Angie gets a 401(k).
July 1999	Angie stabs Marcus, but soon lets him move back in.
October 1999	W-2 wins an award from Harvard and the Ford Foundation.
October 1999	Angie starts a second job, at a nursing pool.
December 1999	Angie evicts Opal.
March 2000	Opal has a fifth child, Myerra, and admits using cocaine. The state sends the baby to foster care, and Angie takes Brierra.
April 2000	Ken Thigpen is released from prison.
Summer 2000	Legislative auditors find financial abuses at Maximus.
January 2001	Tommy Thompson takes office as secretary of Health and Human Services under President George W. Bush.
Summer 2001	Legislative auditors find financial abuses at Goodwill, which is forced out of the W-2 program.
November 2001	Kesha, 17, has a baby and drops out of high school.
March 2002	Jewell and Ken have a son, Kevion Thigpen.
Fall 2002	Redd, 15, stops going to high school.
October 2003	Marcus dies of AIDS.
March 2004	The head of the Opportunities Industrialization Center is indicted on federal kickback charges.

NOTES

SOURCES AND METHODS

In telling this story, I have relied on years of discussions with the women at its heart, Angela Jobe, Jewell Reed, and Opal Caples. Their accounts have been indispensable, but I have not relied on their memories alone. With their permission, I have also had access to their complete welfare records for the past dozen years. This archive notes every check issued, letter sent, sanction imposed, and appointment kept or missed. It also includes the quarterly earnings reports that their employers filed with the state (to track their eligibility for unemployment insurance). This trove of data produced a much more complete picture of the trio's interactions with the welfare system than I could have assembled on my own. Unless noted differently, the reader can assume that references to their welfare cases were drawn from these files. Likewise, with the permission of Angie and her children, the Milwaukee Public Schools shared a decade's worth of report cards and attendance records. All three of the main characters shared their tax returns, and they and others shared portions of diaries, letters, school essays, and the like. In addition to consulting these private materials, I have foraged along a trail of public records that runs from the nineteenth century to the twenty-first, including deeds, birth and death certificates, decennial censuses, police reports, and records in civil and criminal court proceedings.

This is a reporter's endeavor: no names have been changed, characters melded, or quotes invented. Many scenes involving Angie, Jewell, and Opal are ones I witnessed firsthand. I have reconstructed others through interviews. In some places, I have included bits of dialogue from conversations where I wasn't present; these come from accounts by the people involved and represent their words verbatim. Likewise, I occasionally use quotes to describe what someone was thinking; the words between the quotes are his or her own. For the most part, the sourcing is obvious, but in places where multiple perspectives inform complicated events, I have cited the people on whose accounts I've drawn. A large academic literature exists on the history of welfare and poverty and the performance of the current law; to embed these women's story in a broader context, I've consulted it as much as possible and cited it selectively below.

In writing about the abolition of AFDC, I had the advantage of having covered much of the story for *The New York Times,* which allowed me to talk at length with many of the main players, some of whom generously shared their files after the bill was signed. Future scholars will likely have access to new materials, as the papers of Bill Clinton and other leaders are opened to public view; my envy of them is tempered by the hope that there was something to have been gained as well from seeing things firsthand. In the interests of economy, I've offered no citations for facts and figures routinely in the public realm. Unless otherwise noted, the figures on national caseloads come from the U.S. Department of Health and Human Services. The data on Wisconsin caseloads come from the Wisconsin Department of Workforce Development. Poverty rates are calculated annually by the U.S. Census Bureau. Figures on the share of children born outside marriage are kept by the National Center for Health Statistics, which is part of the Centers for Disease Control and Prevention. People writing about welfare in these years will also find themselves consulting the *Green Book,* a statistical compilation periodically published by the Ways and Means Committee of the U.S. House of Representatives.

In analyzing how Angie's and Jewell's incomes changed as they moved from welfare to work, I wound up with more material than the text of this book could accommodate. I've posted an expanded analysis at www.jasondeparle.com, where other information about this work and the people in it can be found.

ABBREVIATIONS

ADC: Winifred Bell, *Aid to Dependent Children* (New York: Columbia University Press, 1965)
Baseline: Department of Health and Human Services, "Aid to Families with Dependent Children: The Baseline," June 1998
BLS: Bureau of Labor Statistics
CBO: Congressional Budget Office
CHIPS: Petition for Determination of Status in Need of Protection or Services
CLASP: Center on Law and Social Policy
Cong. Rec.: Congressional Record
CQ: Congressional Quarterly Weekly Report
DWD: Wisconsin Department of Workforce Development
GAO: U.S. General Accounting Office
HHS: U.S. Department of Health and Human Services
LAB: Wisconsin Legislative Audit Bureau
MDRC: Manpower Demonstration Research Corporation
MJ: The Milwaukee Journal
MJS: Milwaukee Journal Sentinel

MS: *Milwaukee Sentinel*
NYP: *New York Post*
NYT: *The New York Times*
NYTM: *The New York Times Magazine*
PPP: *Public Papers of the Presidents of the United States—William J. Clinton*
(Washington, DC: Government Printing Office)
USN: *U.S. News & World Report*
UW-M: University of Wisconsin–Milwaukee
WP: *The Washington Post*
WSJ: *The Wall Street Journal*

1. THE PLEDGE: WASHINGTON AND MILWAUKEE, 1991

3   **"We should insist":** Clinton speech in Little Rock, Oct. 3, 1991.

     "If you can work": Account of the pledge to "end welfare as we know it" comes from interviews with Bruce Reed and Stan Greenberg, Clinton's pollster; Greenberg's notes; and drafts of the Clinton speech. See also David Whitman and Mathew Cooper, *USN,* June 20, 1994.

     "fit on a bumpersticker": Memo from Bruce Reed to Bill Clinton, May 25, 1991.

4   **wanted to cancel:** Stan Greenberg diary, Oct. 19, 1991.

     no one could say who had coined it: Greenberg said he may have done so; Reed said he didn't recall. Ironically, one prominent critic of the phrase, David Ellwood of Harvard University, had used it three years earlier, saying of some welfare experiments: "It's hard to believe that this spells the end of welfare as we know it." Bob Port, *St. Petersburg Times,* Nov. 21, 1988.

     New Covenant: Spencer Rich, *WP,* Oct. 24, 1991.

     "Pure heroin": Campaign memo from Celinda Lake, Oct. 1, 1992.

     "guiding star": Jason DeParle, *NYT,* May 8, 1994.

     "Greyhound therapy": Paul Peterson and Mark Rom, *Welfare Magnets: A New Case for a National Standard* (Washington, DC: Brookings Institution, 1990), 25.

6   **Twelfth and Vliet:** Carlen Hatala, City of Milwaukee Historic Preservation Commission, interview by the author. The department store was Schuster's.

7   **Cuomo struck back:** Joe Klein, *New York,* Nov. 18, 1991.

     Clinton feared Duke: Greenberg diary, Oct. 20, 1991.

8   **"half this election," "major deal":** Greenberg diary, Dec. 1, 1991.

     "The welfare message": Memo from Celinda Lake to Stan Greenberg, undated.

     "single most important," voters "stunned"; Stan Greenberg, "Bill Clinton: New Hampshire, Exploratory Focus Groups," Sept. 27, 1991, 8.

8 **"taken aback":** Greenberg memo to Clinton, March 7, 1992, 3.
"The strongest media": Greenberg memo to Clinton, March 2, 1992, 4.
"No other message": Greenberg memo to Clinton, April 22, 1992, 4.
Democratic convention: Greenberg memo to Clinton, July 19, 1992, 6.
Most effective answer: Greenberg memo to Clinton, Aug. 18, 1992, 2.

9 **"Get a job":** Bush in Riverside, California, July 31, 1992. Clinton wasn't the first Democrat to get to Bush's right on welfare. In a 1970 Senate race, Lloyd Bentsen attacked Bush for voting for Nixon's Family Assistance Plan; in a statewide advertising campaign, Bentsen, who won, told Texas voters that a vote for Bush was "a vote for big welfare." Jonah Martin Edelman, " The Passage of the Family Support Act of 1988 and the Politics of Welfare Reform in the United States" (PhD dissertation, Balliol College, Oxford University, 1995), 211.

14 **"Biological as it gets":** Though Angie and Opal aren't related, Greg Logan, the father of Angie's first three children, is Opal's second cousin.

15 **children "sleeping on grates":** Moynihan, 104th Cong., 1st sess., *Cong. Rec.* 141 (Sept. 5, 1995): S 12705.
"greatest social policy": Thompson, HHS press release, Feb. 4, 2002.
"greatest advance . . . since capitalism": Editorial, *WSJ,* April 2, 2004.

16 **racial composition:** Nationally, in 1991 the rolls were 38 percent white, 39 percent black, and 17 percent Hispanic. *1993 Green Book,* 705.
nearly 70 percent of the city's caseload: John Pawasarat and Lois M. Quinn, "Demographics of Milwaukee County Populations Expected to Work Under Proposed Welfare Initiatives" (University of Wisconsin–Milwaukee, Employment & Training Institute, Nov. 1995), 1, 26.
six times as likely: In 1991, 2.3 percent of whites received Aid to Families with Dependent Children, compared to 15.5 percent of blacks and 9.3 percent of Hispanics. (Unpublished analysis by Wendell Primus, U.S. Congress Joint Economic Committee.)
nearly seven of ten long-term: Greg Duncan of Northwestern University calculated the number from the Panel Study of Income Dynamics, a longitudinal study of nearly eight thousand families. He defined "long term" as any recipient who, upon enrolling in AFDC, received payments in sixty of the following eighty-four months; among people in that category, 68 percent were black. Communication with Duncan by author.

2. THE PLANTATION: MISSISSIPPI, 1840–1960

20 **Percy kept her from being run out:** Hortense Powdermaker, *Stranger and Friend* (New York: W. W. Norton, 1966), 129.
"Negroes are innately inferior" to **"there may be good":** Hortense Powdermaker, *After Freedom* (1939; repr., Madison: University of Wisconsin Press, 1993), 22–23.

21   **"capable of being mobilized"** to **"it is more or less assumed":** Powdermaker, *After Freedom,* 68, 69, 208, 363.

    welfare didn't exist: Powdermaker started her fieldwork in 1932; Aid to Dependent Children (later renamed Aid to Families with Dependent Children) was created in 1935 and didn't reach the rural South for years.

    "Every aspect of underclass culture": Nicholas Lemann, "The Origins of the Underclass," *The Atlantic,* June 1986, 35.

    In the exchanges that followed: Part of the controversy stemmed from Lemann's argument that there was a "strong correlation" between sharecropper experience in the South and underclass status in the North. Demographers have failed to show that sharecroppers fared worse than other black migrants (perhaps because the data are poor), and Lemann dropped the word *correlation* from *The Promised Land,* his acclaimed book on the black migration. There he presents the sharecropper thesis in a more diffuse form, arguing simply that black sharecropper society "was the equivalent of big-city ghetto society today in many ways." *The Promised Land: The Great Black Migration and How It Changed America* (New York: Knopf, 1991), 31.

22   **James Eastland took over:** *Current Biography,* vol. 10 (New York: H. W. Wilson Company, 1949), 184.

23   **Pie Eddie Caples arrived in 1927:** Interviews with Mack Caples (his son), Ruth V. Caples (his daughter-in-law), and Virginia Caples (his granddaughter).

    Pie Eddie Caples's wives: Interviews with Mack Caples and Ruth V. Caples, along with decennial census records, identify three wives: Virgie Caples, Alice Caples, and Hattie Chapman Caples. An 1892 marriage certificate shows an earlier union to Savanah Watson Caples. Divorce papers in the Scott County, Miss., courthouse list Eastland & Nichols as his lawyers in his 1923 divorce from Alice. The Eastland in the law firm was Woods's brother Oliver, supporting Mack Caples's recollection that his father, Eddie, had ties to the Eastland family before moving to the Delta. (See main text page 28.)

    labor killed her: Mayola Caples's death certificate, April 10, 1939.

    Samuel Caples arrived in about 1843: The 1840 census has him still living in Fayette County, Alabama, a fifty- to sixty-year-old man with seven slaves. By 1843, he and his slaves appear on the tax rolls of Scott County, Mississippi. He is identified as a tavernkeeper in a genealogical reference book, *Looking Back: Fayette County, Alabama, 1824–1974* (Fayette, AL: Fayette County Historical Society, 1974), Part III, 68. Frank Caples's age can be deduced from the 1855 loan agreement (see below) that lists him as about twenty years old.

24   **"detestable":** John Chester Miller, *The Wolf by the Ears: Thomas Jefferson and Slavery* (New York: Free Press, 1977), 7.

24   abandoned life in middle Tennessee: In tracking Samuel Caples, I got help from two members of his descended family, Joyce McFarland and Kathe Hollingshaus. Their records show him as a "bondsman" in a Wilson County, Tenn., marriage in 1806 and selling land in Lincoln County, Tenn., in 1815 and 1821. The 1830 census places him in Fayette County, Alabama. A surviving log of a dry-goods store there shows him sending someone named Frank, presumably Hattie Mae's great-grandfather, to buy pins and tumblers on credit.

25   "my Negro boy Hyram": Bill of Sale, Samuel Caples to Bird Saffold, Jan. 1, 1849, on file at Scott County, Miss., Courthouse, Deed Book E, 38. The clerk of probate court who witnessed the sale happened to be Alfred Eastland, Senator James Eastland's great-great-grandfather.

"Caples has this day executed": Mortgage, Samuel Caples to A. J. Wright, April 17, 1855, on file at Scott County Courthouse, Deed Book F, 585–86.

Jefferson Davis Caples: He is listed as eight years old on the 1870 census.

joined a local militia: Service records at the Mississippi Department of Archives and History list Caples in "Capt. Thacker Vivion's Company, Mississippi Cavalry," a unit of volunteers whose members were all over fifty.

"ten miles of negros" to "hegira": Margie Riddle Bearss, *Sherman's Forgotten Campaign: The Meridian Expedition* (Baltimore: Gateway Press, 1987), 238–40.

26   lost the homestead and family left: Tax sale recorded in *Newton Weekly Ledger,* May 16, 1872, and referenced in Jean Strickland and Patricia Nicholson, *Newton County, Mississippi Newspaper Items 1872–1875 & W. P. A. Manuscript* (Moss Point, MS: self-published, 1998), 12; Arkansas, interviews with Kathe Hollingshaus and Joyce McFarland.

policemen, letter carriers, and "eliminate the nigger": Neil R. McMillen, *Dark Journey: Black Mississippians in the Age of Jim Crow* (Urbana: University of Illinois Press), 1989, 5, 43.

In 1876, Frank had a son: The 1890 Enumeration of Educable Children for Newton County, on file at the Mississippi Department of Archives and History (microfilm #14292) lists Eddie Caples as fourteen years old.

Oliver Eastland launched a plantation: Dan W. Smith Jr., "James O. Eastland: Early Life and Career, 1904–1942" (master's thesis, Mississippi College, 1978), 7.

27   mob death every 5.5 months: James C. Cobb, *The Most Southern Place on Earth: The Mississippi Delta and the Roots of Regional Identity* (New York: Oxford University Press, 1992), 114.

What prompted the dispute: White newspapers reported that Holbert was being evicted for harassing another worker over a woman. A black publication argued that "Holbert had persuaded a Negro whom Eastland held in involuntary servitude" over a debt "to leave the white planter." "The Doddsville Savagery," *The Voice of the Negro* 1, no. 3 (March 1904): 81. I am grateful to Todd Moye for pointing out these competing accounts.

27   **Holbert's "young master":** The Memphis *Commercial Appeal*, Feb. 4, 1904, which reported that the posse pursuing Holbert and his wife was "determined to burn the wretches at the stake."
  "The blacks were forced": *Vicksburg Evening Post*, Feb. 13, 1904.

28   **"intention of W. C. Eastland":** *Commercial Appeal*, Feb. 8, 1904.
  swept from the courthouse: New Orleans *Daily Picayune*, Sept. 22, 1904.
  named for his slain brother, James: Although the Holbert lynching is often cited as a particularly gruesome example of the practice, its link to the Eastland family was largely forgotten at the height of Senator James Eastland's power, which is odd, since Eastland attracted a scathing liberal press.
  civil rights bills went to die: Robert G. Sherrill, "James Eastland: Child of Scorn," *The Nation,* Oct. 4, 1965, 194.
  "Mr. Woods" persuaded: Interview with Mack Caples.

29   **eight in ten, "congenitally lazy":** Powdermaker, *After Freedom*, 86, 88.
  fell from a roof and died: Interview with Mack Caples; Ed Caples death certificate, Dec. 6, 1930.
  drew her name: Oddly, at her birth, Hattie Mae was named Robert, for her father, Robert Logan. She grew up known as Hattie Mae, after her grandmother, but she didn't make the legal switch until the 1980s.
  children that Pie Eddie left behind: Stories of Frank, Lula Bell, Pop, Vidalia, 'Lij, Wiley, and Will Caples from interviews with Hattie Mae Crenshaw, Mack Caples, Ruth V. Caples, and Virginia Caples.

31   **the Eastlands' cook:** Interviews with Hattie Mae Crenshaw and Ruth V. Caples. Woods Eastland, Senator James Eastland's son, was six when Mama Hattie died in 1951 but told me he recalls seeing a picture of himself as a young child with a housekeeper or cook named Hattie Mae.
  "I was the troublemaker": Hattie Mae left the Eastland plantation for good smuggled out on the floor of a car; she had gotten some new dresses from a black boyfriend, but the wife of a white plantation boss, assuming only a white man could afford such goods, accused her of sleeping with her husband.

32   **Woods Eastland persuaded his friend:** Chris Myers, "Delta Obsession, World Power" (chapter in forthcoming PhD thesis), 21; Smith, "James O. Eastland," 37–39.
  the price of cottonseed: Myers, "Delta Obsession, World Power," 24–26; Smith, "James O. Eastland," 48–54.
  James Eastland helped kill FEPC: Chris Myers, "Reconstruction Revisited: James O. Eastland, Germany, and the Fair Employment Practices

Commission, 1945–1946," forthcoming in 2004, *Journal of Mississippi History.*

32 **"an inferior race":** 79th Cong., 1st sess., *Cong. Rec.* 91 (June 29, 1945): S 7000.

"mental level": Robert Sherrill, *Gothic Politics in the Deep South: Stars of the New Confederacy* (New York: Grossman, 1968), 211.

"pro-Communist" decision: Patricia Webb Robinson, "A Rhetorical Analysis of Senator James O. Eastland's Speeches, 1954–1959" (master's thesis, Louisiana State University, 1976), 29.

33 **J. W. Milam:** After his acquittal in the Till case, Milam said, "I just decided it was time a few people got put on notice. . . . Niggahs ain't gonna vote where I live. . . . They ain't gonna go to school with my kids." Cobb, *The Most Southern Place on Earth,* 219.

"far more dismaying phenomenon": *Time,* March 26, 1956, 26.

alter its way of life: For a fuller account of both the mechanical cotton-picker and the far-reaching effects of the black migration on American life, see Lemann, *The Promised Land,* from which I've drawn the references to fifty field hands, the Citizens Council's tickets, the quadrupling of wages, and the movement of five million southern blacks: 5, 95, 41, 6.

34 **"dean of Mississippi":** My interviews with Virginia Caples took place in the summer and fall of 2000 on the Eastland plantation, where her mother and her uncle Mack still lived. Virginia Caples was measured in her critique of plantation life, but she grew angry when her brother suggested that James Eastland had financed her education by loaning their father the money and forgiving the loan. "Senator Eastland didn't help my father do anything," she said. "Anything he did, my father earned ten times over. Anything Eastland had, my father and Uncle Mack helped him get."

35 **"twelve-year-olds having babies":** The line was part of Gingrich's stump speech in the mid-1990s; Katharine Q. Seelye, *NYT,* Oct. 27, 1994.

37 **midnight raid:** Under so-called man-in-the-house rules, a boyfriend, even the most casual one, could have been deemed a substitute father, rendering the family ineligible for aid.

3. THE CROSSROADS: CHICAGO, 1966–1991

38 **60 percent of manufacturing jobs:** William Julius Wilson, *When Work Disappears: The World of the Urban Poor* (New York: Knopf, 1996), 30.

Henry Horner Homes et al.: Lemann, *The Promised Land,* p. 92.

39 **rolls quadrupled:** From 984,000 cases in 1964 to 3.97 million in 1990. (Baseline, table 2.1.)

"social pathologies": William Julius Wilson, *The Truly Disadvantaged: The Inner City, the Underclass, and Public Policy* (Chicago: University of Chicago Press, 1987), vii.

39   **underclass:** Erol R. Ricketts and Isabel V. Sawhill proposed a four-part definition of underclass neighborhoods, as those with high levels of high school dropouts, nonworking men, welfare recipients, and single mothers. In 1980, 1 percent of the population lived in such census tracts. The difficulties of codification can be seen, however, in the case of Jeffrey Manor, the rough neighborhood where Angie and Jewell grew up; it fits only one of the four criteria—single-parent families. Ricketts and Sawhill, "Defining and Measuring the Underclass," *Journal of Policy Management and Analysis* 7, no. 2 (1988): 316–25.

41   **Levi Gillespie:** The 1880 Census lists Levi Gillespie, seven, as the son of Alfred Gillespie, forty-one, and his wife, Ella, twenty-seven.

contract to buy 110 acres: Deed on file at Monroe County Courthouse, Trust Book 1-Q, 167. The land was purchased on Nov. 24, 1941, and transferred to Levi's son Henderson for $1 on Jan. 25, 1954. Charity Scott said she grew up hearing "Papa Levi," her grandfather, urge his family to own land, warning that sharecroppers would always be in debt.

poorer, more troubled family: Angie and her mother both have a hazy, negative view of Roosevelt's family background. About Roosevelt's father, Charity said: "He might a got killed or just walked away—they don't know what happened." Angie recalls visiting the Mississippi Jobes as a child and encountering her first outhouse.

found out she was pregnant: Interview with Charity Scott.

42   **"My mother is the nicest":** Charity kept the May 6, 1980, essay, in which Angie describes her as the ultimate role model: "She is always telling me how much she loves me but she doesn't have to tell me because I can see it. I say if she didn't love me she wouldn't be out there working herself half to death trying to give me the best in life."

44   **signature of Joseph Merrion:** Interviews with his son, Jack Merrion, and grandson, Ed Merrion. Merrion built Jeffrey Manor shortly after serving as president of the National Association of Homebuilders.

1968 graduates of Luella: See www.netaxs.com/~jeff/luella.html (accessed May 25, 2004); also, Marja Mills, *Chicago Tribune,* Dec. 3, 1989.

whites fought housing integration: One of the most infamous battles was fought just a few blocks south of Jeffrey Manor, at Trumbull Park Homes, where the arrival of a single black family in white public housing set off a huge riot.

race of Luella students: Chicago Public Schools, annual student racial surveys, 1968–71.

45   **demographics of Jeffrey Manor:** The data cover Census Tract 5103 for 1980 and were supplied by Chuck Nelson and Marie Pees of the Census Bureau.

46   **"crossroads" to "merge styles":** Mary Pattillo-McCoy, *Black Picket Fences: Privilege and Peril Among the Black Middle Class* (Chicago: University of Chicago Press, 1999), 6, 11, 119. Elizabeth Fenn of Duke University points out to me that crossroads also had special meaning in black folklore, as dangerous, exciting places populated by badmen and tricksters.

46 **"any way any day":** Mary E. Pattillo, "Sweet Mothers and Gangbangers: Managing Crime in a Black Middle-Class Neighborhood," *Social Forces* 76, no. 3 (March 1998): 753.

a third in female-headed households: 1980 Census, Tract 5103.

statistical risks of single-parent homes: One example of the large social science literature is Sara McLanahan and Gary Sandefur, *Growing Up with a Single Parent: What Hurts, What Helps* (Cambridge, MA: Harvard University Press, 1994).

"I wanted to join": Pattillo-McCoy, *Black Picket Fences*, 145.

47 **beginning of the end:** Charity said that she prayed at length about her marriage. Then "the Lord just laid it out for me. 'Well, you're paying the house note; you're buying the groceries.' I was the one sending them to private school. What did I need him for? The next day I was at the lawyer's office, after saying 'thank you Lord' all night long." The property settlement gave Charity the "encyclopedia set," "china set with glasses," and "library books for Angela"; Roosevelt drove off with a late-model Lincoln and three other cars. Settlement agreement Feb. 4, 1981, *Charity Jobe v. Roosevelt Jobe,* case #80-4683, Circuit Court of Cook County, Illinois. I am grateful to Margaret Stapleton for her research assistance.

48 **psychologist:** Interviews with Angie Jobe, Rodger Scott, and Charity Scott.

50 **"Dear Diary"** to **"Little tiny feet":** Angie wrote these diary entries in 1983 and 1984 and read portions of them to me.

52 **switchblade:** Interviews with Angie Jobe and Rodger Scott.

53 **Angie still had welfare:** While the Chicago welfare office never asked Angie or Jewell to work or go to school, they did each enroll in a trade school on their own. Jewell signed up to be a dental hygienist, and Angie took a business school course. ("I got tired of working for chicken joints.") Neither finished, and Jewell wound up with an unpaid student loan for which bill collectors were still chasing her ten years later.

Terrance got twenty years: The long sentence, imposed by a federal judge in 1997, was required under mandatory sentencing laws, since Terrance had a prior drug conviction.

55 **Hattie Mae's children:** Mary, Gwen, and Jewell all became teen welfare mothers, but Mary quickly left the rolls. She worked her way through community college, eventually married, and landed a lower-lever managerial job at a Chicago hospital. In part, she credits her aspirations to the time she spent with Hattie Mae's father, Robert Logan, who reconnected with the family during her adolescence. (Jewell, fourteen years younger, knew him much less well.) "His side of the family was different," Mary said. "They were about education, schools, good jobs, having things." She

said her stepmother's family, whom Jewell likewise didn't know, played a similar role. Of Hattie Mae's sons, Squeaky was murdered, Terry is mostly out of touch with the family, and Greg and Robert both went to prison for violent crimes. But her second son, Willie, works with computers at DePaul University and his daughter Twanda recently graduated from Illinois State University.

55 **police catching on:** Arrests occurred on July 24, 1989, Nov. 30, 1989, Feb. 20, 1990, and Dec. 6, 1990.

"His Tendency to Project Blame": Notes of probation officer from Oct. 4, 1990, filed in *People vs. Gregory Reed*, case #91CR-16373, Circuit Court of Cook County, Illinois.

56 **a wild shooting:** The murder of fourteen-year-old Kathryn Miles is from interviews with Hattie Mae Crenshaw, Angie Jobe, and Jewell Reed, as well as the record in *People vs. Reed*, which includes the confessions of Greg Reed, Tony Nicholas, and David Washington.

4. THE SURVIVORS: MILWAUKEE, 1991–1995

58 **"Where Have All the Houses":** *MJS,* March 21, 1999.

fifteen thousand drawing checks: Author's communication with John Pawasarat, UW-M.

Angie's check rose: Angie's total monthly benefits rose 26 percent, from $709 in Chicago to $896 in Milwaukee. (AFDC rose from $373 to $617, while food stamps fell from $336 to $279.) Jewell's total package rose 41 percent, from $415 in Chicago to $586 in Milwaukee. (AFDC went from $286 to $496, in part due to a pregnancy allowance, while stamps fell from $147 to $90.)

59 **"only thing that has kept":** John Gurda, *The Making of Milwaukee* (Milwaukee: Milwaukee County Historical Society, 1999), 363.

"Shame of Milwaukee": *Time,* April 2, 1956.

time limits on public housing: After leaving office in 1960, Frank Zeidler produced a 1,022-page typescript, which awaits some future historian of urban change. In it, he writes that he stepped down after three terms because the "issue of my being too friendly to Negroes was again going to be raised" and tells of Alderman Milton J. McGuire calling for time limits on public housing. Frank P. Zeidler, "A Liberal in City Government: My Experiences as Mayor of Milwaukee" (typescript, Milwaukee Public Library), ch. 2, 59; ch. 4, 417.

60 **blacks composed 3 percent:** Gurda, *The Making of Milwaukee,* 361.

benefits not much different: In 1951, Wisconsin's average monthly benefit was slightly higher than that of its neighbors—$99 versus $96 in Illinois and $91 in Minnesota. (*Social Security Bulletin,* April 1951, table 13.) In 1967, it was lower: $175 in Wisconsin versus $178 in Minnesota and $195 in Illinois. (Department of Health, Education and Welfare, *Public Assistance Statistics,* June 1967, table 6.)

60   **if Wallace left Alabama:** Frank A. Aukofer, *City with a Chance: A Case History of the Civil Rights Revolution* (Milwaukee: Bruce Publishing, 1968), 56.

rock-throwing crowds: Ibid., 111–12.

welfare battle in 1969: benefit cut: *MJ,* Sept. 14, 1969; occupation of the Capitol: *MJ,* Sept. 30, 1969; antifornication laws, 22 cents a meal: *MJ,* Sept. 18, 1969; gorillas: *MJ,* Sept. 30, 1969.

61   **benefits more than doubled:** For a family of three, they rose from $184 in 1970 to $444 in 1980. *1993 Green Book,* 667.

Caseloads tripled: Excluding the small number of two-parent cases, the AFDC rolls rose from 23,000 cases in 1970 to 72,000 in 1980. Peter Tropman, "Wisconsin Works" (briefing paper for Gov. Anthony Earl, circa 1986).

among the lower forty-eight: *1993 Green Book,* 666–67.

hedge against violence: In calling for the restoration of the 1969 cuts, the Madison newspaper warned, "Unless we can figure out an economic system that will eliminate hunger in one of the world's most affluent nations, we are going to be faced with a radicalized poor who will demand a revolution." *The Capital Times,* May 12, 1971.

54 percent higher than Illinois: *1993 Green Book,* 666–67.

"relatively small," nearly half: Wisconsin Expenditure Commission, "Report of the Welfare Magnet Study Committee," Dec. 1986, 5, 104.

21 percent of Milwaukee applicants: "Prior Residence of Wisconsin Newly Opened AFDC Cases" (computer printout, prepared by Ed Mason and Chuck Brassington, Wisconsin Department of Health and Social Services, June 1991), copy provided by Gerald Whitburn. Of 695 new Milwaukee cases, 144 had come from out of state within the previous three months.

fastest-growing ghetto: Interview with Paul A. Jargowsky.

census tracts tripled: Paul A. Jargowsky, *Poverty and Place: Ghettos, Barrios, and the American City* (New York: Russell Sage Foundation, 1997), 225.

from 1 percent to 10 percent: Data provided to author by Jargowsky.

62   **half the black population:** Peter Tropman, "Wisconsin Works," 2. Tropman, a state welfare official, reported that 42 percent of Milwaukee's blacks were on AFDC and 7 percent on general relief, a state and local program.

lost manufacturing jobs: Julie Boatright Wilson, "Milwaukee: Industrial Metropolis on the Lake" (working paper, Wiener Center, Kennedy School of Government, Harvard University, April 1995), section IV, 2.

"Go back to Illinois": *Kenosha News,* March 16, 1986.

advisers to the Democratic governor: One of them, Peter Tropman, wanted to call the new program "Wisconsin Works," as Tommy Thompson named his a decade later.

62   **"two-bit hack," bra size:** Matt Pommer, *The Capital Times*, July 13, 1998.

"make Wisconsin like Mississippi": Norman Atkins, *NYTM*, Jan. 15, 1995.

64   **"baby killer":** Milwaukee was the site of large antiabortion protests in 1992, with more than one thousand arrests in four months. Tina Burnside, *MS*, Oct. 7, 1992.

66   **Angie reported the job:** Caseworkers had access to the quarterly earnings reports that employers file with state labor departments. But the records could lag as much as six months from an employee's starting date, and officials typically made criminal referrals for fraud only after discovering more than $3,000 of welfare or food stamp overpayments. Interview with Debra Bigler, Milwaukee County Department of Human Services. In practice, caseworkers sometimes ignored small amounts of unreported earnings, since recouping welfare overpayments could be a hassle.

for every $100: In the six months after she reported the job, Angie earned an average of $986 a month. But her AFDC and food stamps fell by $599, and she paid $75 in payroll taxes. That is, she effectively kept about $312, or 32 percent. That does not add in tax credits, but it doesn't subtract work expenses, either. Author's calculation based on 1994 monthly earnings reports.

68   **Hattie Mae's boyfriend, Wesley:** Although she and Wesley are now married, Hattie Mae said of his relationship with her kids: "If Wesley had been the type of father, man, he should have been and helped me to raise them, maybe—I'm saying maybe—some of the things that happened could have been prevented with Greg." Wesley told me he traced his anger to growing up black in the Delta, where a white boycott cost his father his dry-cleaning business after his father called for school desegregation. "I have a lot of hate and I'll always have a lot of hate," he said. "Hatred will not let you forget where you came from."

69   **battery:** Jewell, who had just turned eighteen, pleaded guilty and was sentenced to a year of supervision by the social services department.

Tony's drug problem; errant bullet: The presentencing report in the murder case says "he was snorting heroin and was spending up to $200 per day on the drug. . . . He did state . . . that he was under the influence of heroin at the time" of the shooting. A forensics expert identified the bullet as coming from Tony Nicholas's gun. In his closing argument, the prosecutor highlighted Tony's confession that he joined the plot after one of the coconspirators promised to fix his car: "He wanted used car parts to kill." *People vs. Antonio Nicholas*, case #91CR-16373, Circuit Court of Cook County, Illinois.

70   **self-efficacy:** See also Toby Herr and Suzanne L. Wagner, "Self-Efficacy as a Welfare-to-Work Goal: Emphasizing Both Psychology and Economics in Program Design" (Chicago: Project Match, Feb. 2003).

As bureaucratic runarounds go: Eight weeks after Jewell signed up for the course, her caseworker noted in the file that a letter had been sent, telling Jewell the course "has been placed on hold." Jewell said she never got the letter.

72   **"tax-free cash income alone":** While the Reagan story is sometimes called "apocryphal," he was referring to an actual case, albeit an atypical one whose known facts he exaggerated. The case involved a Chicago woman named Linda Taylor, whom an investigator initially described as having eighty aliases and a welfare income of $150,000; she was convicted of a more modest crime—using four aliases to steal $9,800. Reagan also told a New Hampshire audience that by moving to public housing in East Harlem, "you can get an apartment with eleven-foot ceilings, with a twenty-foot balcony, a swimming pool, laundry room, and play room." "'Welfare Queen' Becomes Issue in Reagan Campaign," *NYT*, Feb. 15, 1976; "Chicago Woman Sentenced in Welfare Fraud Cases," *NYT*, May 13, 1977.

73   **"We have been studying":** McLanahan and Sandefur, *Growing Up with a Single Parent*, 1–2.

74   **commit crimes:** Cynthia Harper and Sara McLanahan, "Father Absence and Youth Incarceration," *Journal of Adolescence*, forthcoming.

Tony's father: His presentencing report presents Tony Nicholas as another working mother's son disadvantaged by the absence of a father: "Deft. said his father was a heavy drug and alcohol abuser. Antonio stated he did not have much contact with his father. . . . Defts mother works as a secretary." *People vs. Nicholas*, case #91CR-16373, Circuit Court of Cook County, Illinois.

fatherhood in sharecropping society: In citing the disproportionate success she enjoyed, Virginia Caples, the university dean, cited two factors: her mother's stress on education and the presence of a stable father in the home. "My father was the centerpiece of the extended family," she said, in contrast to her uncles who "moved hither or yon—they would be lost for two, three years. . . . I'm not speaking in disparaging tones, but my father's brothers, you know, if it's a skirt tail they wanted to follow it. . . . They didn't seem to have that sense that 'I have five kids here and I need to do something for them.'" In tracing the Caples family history, I found many examples of hardworking mothers; this was a rare example I encountered of stable fatherhood.

"Often there is no man": Powdermaker, *After Freedom*, 146.

"America's biggest problem today": Clinton, speech to National Governors Association, Feb. 2, 1993.

75   **"fantastic campaign issue," one observer:** DeParle, *NYT*, Oct. 20, 1994.

75   **reason to be skeptical:** For the early Thompson record, see Michael Wiseman, "State Strategies for Welfare Reform: The Wisconsin Story," *Journal of Policy Analysis and Management* 15, no. 4 (1996): 515–46.

76   **campaign driver:** Tommy G. Thompson, *Power to the People: An American State at Work* (New York: HarperCollins, 1996), 42.

    Learnfare failed to boost: John Pawasarat, Lois M. Quinn, and Frank Stetzer, "Evaluation of the Impact of Wisconsin's Learnfare Experiment on the School Attendance of Teenagers Receiving Aid to Families with Dependent Children" (Employment & Training Institute, UW-M, Feb. 1992). Some Learnfare critics warn the program can actually reduce parental control, since it gives rebellious teenagers power over their mothers' checks.

    Thompson attacked researchers: Amy Rinard, *MS*, March 11, 1992.

    the new analysts found: LAB, "An Evaluation of the Learnfare Program: Final Report," April 1997, 4.

    hand over work program data: Dave Daley, *MJ*, Sept. 24, 1992.

    published anyway: John Pawasarat and Lois M. Quinn, "Wisconsin Welfare Employment Experiments: An Evaluation of the WEJT and CWEP Programs" (Employment & Training Institute, UW-M, Sept. 1993). While Thompson accused the evaluators of slanting the data, an internal memo later surfaced arguing that the Thompson administration had done so itself. After collecting data on the program, a state researcher, Neil Gleason, complained the numbers in the state's published report "were taken so out of context that their meaning was reversed." Contrary to the state's claims of success, he wrote, the program had made families "less likely to leave AFDC" and had "increased AFDC costs." Memo from Neil Gleason to Fred Buhr, Aug. 18, 1988, provided to author by John Pawasarat. See also, Gregory D. Stanford, *MJ*, Oct. 13, 1993.

    White House event: It was held on April 10, 1992.

    point man on polling: Interview with Gerald Whitburn.

77   **percentage in welfare-to-work:** *1994 Green Book*, 357–59.

    pipeline to federal aid: See Wiseman, "State Strategies for Welfare Reform," 524–25; Mark Greenberg, "Issues in Establishing a Distribution Formula for a Cash Assistance Block Grant" (CLASP, July 1995), 5–6. As Greenberg notes, if Wisconsin saved the feds money by cutting its grants to $517, imagine how much Mississippi saved by paying $120. Curious about the other $70 million, John Pawasarat of UW-M wrote federal officials asking how the figure was calculated. The response acknowledged they knew of no objective reason for giving Wisconsin the money: "No documentation can be found describing the basis for determining the specific amounts agreed upon." (Letter from Laurence J. Love, Acting Assistant Secretary for Children and Families, HSS, July 21, 1993.)

77   **Norquist called for repealing:** John O. Norquist, "The Future of America's Cities" (lecture, New York City, Nov. 12, 1990).

78   **Riemer responded with a plea:** My account of the Democrats' dare to abolish AFDC is drawn from interviews with John Gard, Walter Kunicki, John Norquist, David Riemer, Antonio Riley, Tommy Thompson, and Gerald Whitburn, as well as extensive notes kept by Riemer.
      Thompson chewed out Whitburn: Interview with Gerald Whitburn.
      "a filet mignon": DeParle, *NYT,* Oct. 20, 1994.

79   **"They trade food stamps"** to **"survival demands":** Carol Stack, *All Our Kin* (1974; repr., New York: Basic Books, 1997), 32, 43, 124.

80   **"Ms. Caples had minimal":** CHIPS, Wisconsin Circuit Court Children's Division, March 13, 2000.
      investigator let the matter drop: Ibid.
      Robert knocked down Felmers Chaney: Interviews with Jewell Reed, Angie Jobe, and Felmers Chaney.

5. THE ACCIDENTAL PROGRAM: WASHINGTON, 1935–1991

85   **AFDC:** The program became Aid to *Families* with Dependent Children because grants were extended to adults. That happened in 1952, though the name change followed a decade later.
      farmed them out: Linda Gordon, *Pitied But Not Entitled: Single Mothers and the History of Welfare, 1890–1935* (Cambridge, MA: Harvard University Press, 1994), 256–57.

86   **Mothers' pensions, "gilt-edged widows":** Winifred Bell, *Aid to Dependent Children* (New York: Columbia University Press, 1965), 3–12.
      "release from the wage-earning role": 1935 Report of the Committee on Economic Security; quoted in Jonah Martin Edelman, "The Passage of the Family Support Act of 1988 and the Politics of Welfare Reform in the United States" (PhD dissertation, Balliol College, Oxford University, 1995), 24. Edelman's unpublished dissertation is an especially rich source of information on the history and politics of AFDC.
      "I can see the careworn": Gordon, *Pitied But Not Entitled,* 254–55.
      96 percent white: Bell, *ADC,* 9.
      Southern members of Congress: Frances Fox Piven and Richard Cloward, *Regulating the Poor: The Functions of Public Welfare* (1971; repr., New York: Vintage, 1993), 115–16; Gordon, *Pitied But Not Entitled,* 284–85. Gordon writes, "the fate of ADC was defined by the Civil War and Reconstruction," in that it was shaped by a Southern white political elite eager to preserve cheap black labor and hostile to federal authority.
      "No other federal": Edwin Witte, "A Wild Dream or a Practical Plan?" in Robert J. Lampman, ed., *Social Security Perspectives: Essays by Ed-*

win E. Witte (Madison: University of Wisconsin Press, 1962), 6–7; cited in Edelman, "Family Support Act," 21.

87   **Negro quotas:** Bell, *ADC*, 35.

Myrdal wondered, "discrimination against Negroes": Gunnar Myrdal, *An American Dilemma: The Negro Problem and Modern Democracy* (1944; repr., New York: Pantheon, 1972), 359–60.

Mary S. Larabee: Bell, *ADC*, 34–35.

covering about 2 percent: Vincent J. Burke and Vee Burke, *Nixon's Good Deed: Welfare Reform* (New York: Columbia University Press, 1974), 9.

predominately white program: From 1937 to 1940, blacks composed 14 to 17 percent of the caseload. Bell, *ADC*, 34.

caseloads nearly tripled: From 274,000 cases in 1945 to 745,000 in 1960. Piven and Cloward, *Regulating the Poor,* appendix table 1.

widows, broken families: Edelman, "Family Support Act," 25.

40 percent black: Martin Gilens, *Why Americans Hate Welfare: Race, Media, and the Politics of Antipoverty Policy* (Chicago: University of Chicago Press, 1999), 106.

Pensions carefully policed: Even in 1914, a prominent social worker, Homer Folks, warned that "to pension desertion or illegitimacy would, undoubtedly, have the effect of a premium upon these crimes against society." Bell, *ADC*, 7.

88   **"founding document":** Mickey Kaus, *The End of Equality* (New York: Basic Books, 1992), 110.

caseloads more than quadrupled: From 745,000 cases in 1960 to 3.12 million in 1973. Piven and Cloward, *Regulating the Poor,* appendix table 1; Baseline, table 2.1.

"Animals shouldn't live in such": Bell, *ADC*, 103.

90 percent of blacks poor; Eastland's cotton subsidies: Nick Kotz examined the living conditions on the Eastland plantation in a four-part series for the *Des Moines Register and Tribune,* Feb. 25–28, 1968, from which this information comes. See also Kotz, *WP,* July 5, 1971.

89   **Ralph Abernathy:** Burke and Burke, *Nixon's Good Deed,* 44.

turning people away, half the eligible: Piven and Cloward, *Regulating the Poor,* 219.

of the 23,000 children purged: Bell, *ADC*, 137.

"a substitute father" to "grocers": *King vs. Smith,* 392 U.S. 309 (1968).

"workers began focusing": Cloward quote and background on welfare rights movement from interviews with Richard Cloward and Frances Fox Piven. In a sign of how quickly the spirit of the times changed, Cloward's proposal for Mobilization for Youth, the program that launched the welfare-rights age, included a boilerplate pledge to *cut* the welfare rolls. See also DeParle, *NYTM,* Dec. 29, 1998, and Frances Fox Piven and Richard A.

Cloward, *Poor People's Movements: Why They Succeed, How They Fail* (1977; repr., New York: Vintage, 1979), 264–361.

89 **"argued and cajoled":** Piven and Cloward, *Regulating the Poor,* 291.

90 **"massive drive to recruit the poor":** *The Nation,* May 2, 1966.

age of the welfare radical: Nick Kotz and Mary Lynn Kotz: *A Passion for Equality: George Wiley and the Movement* (New York: W.W. Norton, 1977), 40 cities, 307; Harassment, 234; Korvettes, 236; "brood mares," 251.

"people who lay about": Daniel Patrick Moynihan, *The Politics of a Guaranteed Income: The Nixon Administration and the Family Assistance Plan* (New York: Random House, 1973), 523.

iron his shirts: James T. Patterson, *America's Struggle Against Poverty 1900–1994* (Cambridge, MA: Harvard University Press, 1994), 194.

"jobs that pay ten thousand," "You can't force me": Burke and Burke, *Nixon's Good Deed,* 162.

New York City caseload doubled: From 502,000 recipients (as opposed to cases) in 1966 to 1.1 million in 1972, NYC, Human Resources Administration.

91 **"my department of health":** Burke and Burke, *Nixon's Good Deed,* 44.

"the days of the dole": Kaus, *The End of Equality,* 113.

one of every nine kids: Burke and Burke, *Nixon's Good Deed,* 9.

a third of children, 80 percent of black children: Daniel Patrick Moynihan, "Social Justice in the Next Century," *America,* Sept. 14, 1991, 134–35.

Merle Haggard: "Working Man Blues" reached number 1 in 1969.

average package of cash and food stamps: In 1972, a mother of two received an average of $10,370 (*1993 Green Book,* 1253, expressed in 1992 dollars); the poverty threshold in 1992 was $11,304 (Census Bureau); benefits for subsequent years in *1993 Green Book,* 1248–53.

92 **one in ten worked when AFDC started:** Kaus, *The End of Equality,* 111.

half worked by the mid-1970s: For mothers of minor children, the labor force participation rate (the share working or looking for work) was 49 percent in 1976 and 51 percent in 1977. Data provided to the author by Howard Hayghe, BLS.

triple the cost, 15 percent of domestic: Calculations by Adam Carasso of the Urban Institute, based on 1990 data.

school lunches, subsidized housing: *1993 Green Book,* p. 1604. The share with subsidized housing ranged from 19 percent in 1987 to 35 percent in 1990.

view in Jacksonville: Interview with Mark Greenberg. The case of Alice Roberts, the food stamp recipient arrested for fraud, wound up in the Fifth Circuit Court of Appeals, which barred the indiscriminate investigations. Quoting from a congressional report accompanying the food stamp law, the court warned of "the need to protect needy individuals

from having their privacy bartered away in order to assuage their hunger."
Roberts vs. Austin, 632, F2nd, 1202 (5th Cir. 1981), 9.

93 *half* **the black women:** Lawrence Mishel, Jared Bernstein, and Heather Boushey, *State of Working America 2002–03* (Ithaca, NY: ILR Press), 136.
problems that could interfere: Krista K. Olson and LaDonna Pavetti, "Personal and Family Challenges to the Successful Transition From Welfare to Work," The Urban Institute, May 17, 1996.

94 **Carter was appalled:** Laurence E. Lynn Jr., and David deF. Whitman, *The President as Policymaker: Jimmy Carter and Welfare Reform* (Philadelphia: Temple University Press, 1981), 88.
"Middle East": Joseph A. Califano Jr., *Governing America: An Insider's Report from the White House and the Cabinet* (New York: Simon & Schuster, 1981), 321.
slum and ghetto census tracts: Jargowsky, *Poverty and Place,* 35–41. Of the five million people who lived in high-poverty census tracts, 80 percent were members of racial minorities.
the disaster brought journalists: See Ken Auletta, *The Underclass* (New York: Random House, 1982); staff of the *Chicago Tribune, The American Millstone: An Examination of the Nation's Permanent Underclass* (Chicago: Contemporary Books, 1986); Leon Dash, *When Children Want Children: An Inside Look at the Crisis of Teenage Pregnancy* (1989; repr., New York: Penguin Books, 1990); Bill Moyers, "The Vanishing Family—Crisis in Black America," CBS, Jan. 25, 1986.

95 **"blaming the victim":** The phrase was coined by the psychologist William Ryan as part of his critique of the Moynihan report; see Ryan, *Blaming the Victim* (New York: Pantheon, 1971).
the Moynihan report: See Lee Rainwater and William L. Yancey, *The Moynihan Report and the Politics of Controversy* (Cambridge, MA: MIT Press, 1967), esp. 51, 75; also Lemann, *The Promised Land,* 171–76.
poverty academics: For an expanded discussion of academic research on poverty following the Moynihan report, see Alice O'Connor, *Poverty Knowledge: Social Science, Social Policy, and the Poor in Twentieth-Century U.S. History* (Princeton, NJ: Princeton University Press, 2001), especially chapters 8 and 9.

96 **"slavefare":** Edelman, "Family Support Act," 254, quoting Rep. Augustus Hawkins of California.
"lives of large numbers": Charles Murray, *Losing Ground* (New York: Basic Books, 1984), 229. Presciently, Murray foresaw a large element of his appeal. "Why can a publisher sell it?" he wrote in his book proposal. "Because a huge number of well-meaning whites fear that they are closet racists, and this book tells them they are not. It's going to make them feel better about things they already think but do not know how to say." DeParle, *NYTM,* Oct. 9, 1994. The film, *With Honors,* was released in 1994.

97 **reigning explanation:** William Julius Wilson, *The Truly Disadvantaged: The Inner City, the Underclass, and Public Policy* (Chicago: University of Chicago Press, 1987).

"Our goal": Mickey Kaus, "The Work Ethic State," *The New Republic,* July 7, 1986, 31.

"the ghetto-poor culture": Kaus, *The End of Equality,* 129.

98 **including Arkansas:** The Arkansas WORK program began in October 1982 under Governor Frank White. Having lost to White in 1980, Bill Clinton was reelected in Nov. 1982 and continued the program.

half the mothers of preschool: For women with children under six, the labor force participation rate was 50.5 percent in 1983. Data provided to the author by Howard Hayghe, BLS.

groundbreaking study: Mary Jo Bane and David T. Ellwood, "The Dynamics of Dependence: The Route to Self-Sufficiency," Report to HHS, 1983.

nine programs raised employment and earnings: Summarized in Edelman, "Family Support Act," 102. The modesty of some of the gains can be seen in the data on Arkansas, which raised the average recipient's earnings by a total of $78 over six months. Judith M. Gueron, "Reforming Welfare with Work" (Occasional Paper 2, Ford Foundation Project on Social Welfare and the American Future, 1987), 17.

99 **"viable solution":** Edelman, "Family Support Act," 104.

Reagan task force and events leading to the 1988 bill: Ibid., 100–147, 161, 262, 217.

6. THE ESTABLISHMENT FAILS: WASHINGTON, 1992–1994

101 **never met anyone on welfare:** Interview with Bruce Reed.

prosperous family: Interviews with Bruce Reed, Mary Lou Reed (his mother), and Tara Reed (his sister).

six times as many: In 1990, Idaho's average caseload was 6,100, and Milwaukee's was 36,200.

"We should invest": Clinton speech to Democratic Leadership Council in Cleveland, May 6, 1991.

"build a mad as hell": Reed memo to Bill Clinton, May 25, 1991.

"off the welfare rolls": Clinton speech in Little Rock, Oct. 3, 1991.

a half dozen drafts, The next morning: Interviews with Bruce Reed and Stan Greenberg.

103 **paper elaborated:** The paper, "Reducing Poverty by Replacing Welfare," was later printed in Mary Jo Bane and David T. Ellwood, *Welfare Realities: From Rhetoric to Reform* (Cambridge, MA: Harvard University Press, 1994), 143–62; it grew from David T. Ellwood, *Poor Support: Poverty in the American Family* (New York: Basic Books, 1988).

"end to welfare as we know it": Bill Clinton speech at Georgetown University, Oct. 23, 1991.

104   **"spending even more":** Clinton, interview by Paula Zahn, *CBS This Morning,* Nov. 14, 1991.

"skepticism about spending": Greenberg memo to Clinton, Aug. 16, 1992.

Among those unsettled: Interview with David Ellwood, DeParle, *NYTM,* Dec. 8, 1996.

met in passing: Ellwood tells the story of reintroducing himself to Clinton at a governors' meeting in the summer of 1991. Clinton lit up and told Ellwood he was carrying one of his papers. "Look, I've got it right here— all marked up," Ellwood recalls Clinton saying. Then fishing the paper from a notebook, Clinton said, "Oh wait, this is Hillary's copy." While the encounter fortified Ellwood's sense of Clinton's seriousness, it may also have laid a groundwork for subsequent disappointments; at their first White House meeting on welfare, Clinton passed a note to an aide suggesting he had Ellwood confused with his father, Paul Ellwood, a prominent health-care expert. (On the confusion with Paul Ellwood, see Whitman and Cooper, *USN,* June 20, 1994.)

klieg lights: 1992 interview with David Ellwood, in which he called child support assurance (a welfare *expansion* that Clinton had never mentioned) "the single most important" part of his plan and said of time limits, "You can do that last."

"We simply do not have": David T. Ellwood, "Major Issues in Time Limited Welfare" meeting (background paper prepared for meeting at the Urban Institute, Dec. 2, 1992), 20, 24.

"Vacuous and incendiary": David T. Ellwood, "From Social Science to Social Policy: The Fate of Intellectuals, Ideas, and Ideology in the Welfare Debate in the Mid-1990s" (lecture, Northwestern University, Jan. 9, 1996), 11.

105   **nearly 3 million:** Mark Greenberg, "The Devil Is in the Details: Key Questions in the Effort to 'End Welfare As We Know It,'" CLASP, July 1993, 11.

106   **cut the rolls 2 percent:** Stephen Freedman and others, "The GAIN Evaluation: Five-year Impacts on Employment, Earnings, and AFDC Receipt" (Working Paper 96.1, MDRC, July 1996), table 1.

By just mailing checks: Cost estimates come from CBO, "The Administration's Welfare Reform Proposals: A Preliminary Cost Estimate," Dec. 1994, and interviews with its coauthor John Tapogna.

The politics were hard: Early in their tenure, Ellwood and Reed convened a meeting of Democratic experts, many veterans of President Carter's failed reform. A sampling of their advice: "Start small." "Don't go national." "Be modest in goals and rhetoric." "A quarter of a loaf isn't so bad." "The planets could not be more misaligned. "What you want to do might be impossible." (Notes of one participant.)

106   **visited some Democrats:** McDermott, *USN,* June 20, 1994, 31; interviews with Robert Matsui and Harold Ford.

Children's Defense Fund opposed JOBS: Those wondering whether Clinton would really end welfare noted that his first stop in Washington as president-elect was a Children's Defense Fund event. For CDF's opposition to the Family Support Act, see letter from Marian Wright Edelman, the group's founder, on Sept. 28, 1988; cited in 100th Cong., 2nd sess., *Cong. Rec.* 134 (Sept. 30, 1988): H 9103.

107   **"clatter of campaign promises":** Pear, *NYT,* Jan. 15, 1993. Others voicing doubts included the housing secretary, Henry Cisneros ("I'm not a believer in artificial deadlines of that nature") and the domestic policy adviser, Carol Rasco (she warned workfare jobs would have to be part of a meaningful "piece on a career ladder. . . . I feel very strongly about that"); DeParle, *NYT,* June 21, 1993. Ellwood's deputy, Wendell Primus, was an ardent safety-net defender as a congressional aide; testifying a few months into office, he called for postponing a work rule already on the books; David E. Rosenbaum, *NYT,* May 5, 1993.

"break the culture": Clinton speech to American Newspaper Publishers Association, New York, May 6, 1992.

"punish the kids": Interview with Bill Clinton, Feb. 24, 1992.

JOBS Plus: "If you've done that, you've done a great thing," Moynihan told Reed, referring to an expanded JOBS program; interview with Bruce Reed.

a dyspeptic skeptic: "Need I say there is *no* commitment the campaign made that will so easily come to ruin," Moynihan wrote to Vernon Jordan, the head of the Clinton transition team, speaking of the pledge to end welfare. He was pushing an aide, Paul Offner, for a welfare job that instead went to Mary Jo Bane, a New York state official (and former Harvard professor), with whom he had clashed. The rebuff did nothing to ease Moynihan's distrust of the administration, which may have deepened when an anonymous Clinton aide told *Time,* "We'll roll right over him." (Moynihan letter to Jordan, Nov. 11, 1992; *Time,* Feb. 1, 1993.)

"I'll look forward": David T. Ellwood, "Welfare Reform As I Knew It," *The American Prospect,* May–June, 1996.

108   **an affluent childhood:** Interviews with David Ellwood, Ann Ellwood (his mother), Deborah Ellwood (his sister), Marilyn Ellwood (his wife), and Paul Ellwood (his father); see also DeParle, *NYTM,* Dec. 8, 1996.

putting health care before welfare: As a newcomer to Washington with few ties to the Hill, Clinton also may have hoped that starting with a health-care bill that Democrats wanted (as opposed to a welfare bill they disliked) would help him avoid Jimmy Carter's troubled relations with Congress.

109   **"Let 'em rip":** Clinton to leaders of welfare task force, June 18, 1993; interview with Bruce Reed. During my interviews with Reed, he sometimes consulted his records of meetings; any direct quotations of Clinton (or others) sourced to Reed stem from these written materials, rather than from his memory alone.

110 **Ellwood joined the effort:** Interviews with Ellwood and Bob Greenstein of the Center on Budget and Policy Priorities, who played an important behind-the-scenes role. Spotting the shortfall in the EITC, Greenstein sent a confidential memo to Melanne Verveer in Hillary Clinton's office. Mrs. Clinton passed it on to the president, who ordered the problem fixed. Among other things, the incident showed the rarefied access advocates like Greenstein momentarily enjoyed after twelve years of GOP control.
Clinton at his seductive best: Interviews with Bruce Reed, David Ellwood, and Judith Gueron.

111 **"that goddam task force":** Interview with Daniel Patrick Moynihan.
"destructive element": Interview with Bruce Reed.
"What kind of program": Interview with Wendell Primus.
"only reasonable reaction": Interview with David Ellwood.

112 **Riverside had raised earnings:** After two years, the counties that emphasized education and training raised their participants' earnings by 17 percent; Riverside's increase was 53 percent. For those who see this as complete vindication of the work-first model, several qualifications are worth noting. Even in Riverside about 60 percent of the participants got some education or training. Plus, the differences between Riverside and its rivals diminished with time, consistent with the notion that education is a long-term investment; over five years, recipients in Butte County earned more. And earnings in all sites remained low, on average just $3,800 in the fifth year. See Freedman and others, "The Gain Evaluation," table 1. See also Julie Strawn, "Beyond Job Search or Basic Education: Rethinking the Role of Skills in Welfare Reform," CLASP, April 1998.
"bag lady," "work is education": DeParle, *NYT,* May 16, 1993.
"Work organizes life": Clinton at Church of God in Christ, Memphis, Nov. 13, 1993, *PPP-1993,* vol. 2, 1985.
Lillie Harden: See, for instance, Clinton's State of the Union Address, Jan. 25, 1994 (*PPP-1994,* vol. 1, 129), where he told her story without using her name.
"My *life*": Interview with Bill Clinton, Jan. 30, 2004.

113 **task force sent him:** Working Group on Welfare Reform, Family Support, and Independence, "Draft Discussion Paper," Dec. 2, 1993.

114 **"You let loose":** Interview with Daniel Patrick Moynihan.
first showy move: Florida, with a Democratic governor, passed a time-limit bill first, in April 1993, but Thompson's move in May was much more public and political. Winking at those in the know, his handouts argued for time limits by citing the Bane-Ellwood data on dependency.

114   **"meaningful community service":** Gov. Bill Clinton and Sen. Al Gore, *Putting People First: How We Can All Change America* (New York: Times Books, 1992), 165.

      Clinton gave the green light: Interview with Bruce Reed.

      an "untested" idea: E. Clay Shaw, Nancy L. Johnson, Fred Grandy, "Moving Ahead: How America Can Reduce Poverty Through Work," June 1992, iii.

      "You can cut them off": Rep. Rick Santorum at press conference, Nov. 10, 1993.

115   **Rector was raised:** Interview with Robert Rector.

      Jacuzzis: DeParle, *The Washington Monthly* (July/Aug. 1991): 51–54.

      "way to 'end welfare'": Rep. Jim Talent, press release, April 27, 1994.

116   **"realm of politics":** Memo from William Bennett, Jack Kemp, and Vin Weber, Empower America, April 13, 1994.

      the "stench": DeParle, *NYT,* May 12, 1994.

      "I am impelled": Henry Aaron to Ellwood, Jan. 14, 1994.

117   **"White House Seeks":** DeParle, *NYT,* Jan. 5, 1994.

      "boob bait": Deborah Orin and Christopher Ruddy, *New York Post,* Jan. 7, 1994. While Moynihan's erratic behavior had many causes, his consumption of alcohol (an intermittent topic of conversation among his admirers and his critics) may have been among them. The night he told me "I talk too much," I had reached him at home, where he sounded like he'd been drinking.

      "Many are willing": Ellwood, *Poor Support,* 241.

      "If you don't put money": Clinton speech in Jonesboro, Georgia, Sept. 9, 1992.

118   **"things so much closer":** Interview with Bruce Reed.

      This was a bind: For details on the attempt to finance the Clinton plan, see author's 1994 articles in the *NYT* on Feb. 13, 22, and 25; March 3, 10, 21, and 23; April 5; May 9, 16, and 19; and July 15.

      "There simply is no money": Ellwood, "From Social Science to Social Policy," lecture, Jan. 9, 1996, 1.

      "Tim Valentine problem": Interviews with Bruce Reed and David Ellwood.

119   **glassy-eyed look:** Robert Reich, *Locked in the Cabinet* (New York: Knopf, 1997), 156.

      "the most negative": DeParle, *NYT,* May 9, 1994.

      8 percent: DeParle, *NYT,* June 15, 1994.

      slow the rate of growth: CBO, "The Administration's Welfare Reform Proposals," Dec. 1994, 10.

120   **Rector made his case:** Robert Rector, "Welfare Reform, Dependency Reduction, and Labor Market Entry," *Journal of Labor Research* 14, no. 3 (Summer 1993): 283–97.

120   **more rigorous studies:** The leading study of work (as opposed to education or job-search) programs was Thomas Brock, David Butler, and David Long, "Unpaid Work Experience for Welfare Recipients: Findings and Lessons from MDRC Research," MDRC, Sept. 1993. It examined programs in San Diego, Chicago, and West Virginia and concluded, "It is not clear from the limited evidence that unpaid work experience leads to reductions in welfare receipt or welfare payments," 3.
      "self-limiting expertise": Interview with John Tapogna.
      "there go the Wright brothers": Interview with Robert Rector.
      $5 billion short: CBO, "The Administration's Welfare Reform Proposals," Dec. 1994, 2.

121   **Clinton on both sides:** "something at the end of the road," Clinton remarks in Kansas City, June 14, 1994, *PPP-1994*, vol. 1, 1078; "You're not eligible," Clinton exchange with reporters, June 15, 1994, *PPP-1994*, vol. 1, 1083.
      "I wasn't pleased": Ben Wattenberg, *New York Post*, Nov. 3, 1995.
      action was deferred: Clinton grasped the point that the future impact of a welfare bill was hard to predict, cautioning the cabinet on March 22, 1994, that "things depend entirely on how the welfare bureaucracy responds." Interview with Bruce Reed.
      "hope and structure": Clinton remarks in Kansas City, June 14, 1994.

122   **turned Ellwood into a piñata:** DeParle, *NYT*, July 31, 1994.

7. REDEFINING COMPASSION: WASHINGTON, 1995

123   **"viciously hateful," "totally sick":** DeParle, *NYTM*, Jan. 28, 1996, 48.
      declined Clinton's call: Maureen Dowd, *NYT*, Nov. 10, 1994.
      "the real Reagan revolution": Memo from Ron Haskins to Bill Archer, Nov. 14, 1994.

124   **"it was too radical":** Interview with Newt Gingrich.

125   **"couldn't spell AFDC":** Interview with Ron Haskins.
      " 'We're not talking theory' ": Interview with Newt Gingrich.
      would have lost $11 billion: From 1989 through 1993, the federal government spent $63 billion on AFDC; had spending been frozen in 1988, the five-year total would have been $52 billion; *1996 Green Book*, 459. One reason Republicans had dismissed block grants the previous year, Rep. E. Clay Shaw Jr. told me, was that "we were afraid the governors would fight us." As governor in 1988, Bill Clinton opposed them. (See text, p. 99.)
      "resist publicly": Memo from Henick to Haley Barbour, Nov. 11, 1994.
      "burdensome unfunded mandate": George A. Voinovich, "The Need for a New Federalism: A State-Federal Legislative Agenda for the 104th Congress" (paper circulated at Republican Governors Association, Nov. 1994), 7.

126 **"I couldn't understand":** Interview with Ari Fleischer.

"come in on bended knee": A participant's notes from meeting with Thompson, Dec. 8, 1994.

meeting of Republican Governors: Interviews with Sheila Burke, Don Fierce, Chris Henick, Gerald Miller, LeAnne Redick, and others on background.

"spleen-venting": Memo from Chris Henick to Haley Barbour and others, Oct. 4, 1994.

"We are willing to accept": Letter from Engler, Weld, and Thompson to Rep. Clay Shaw, Dec. 12, 1994.

127 **child welfare systems:** Memo from Ray Scheppach, National Governors Association, to governors Thompson, Engler, and others, April 7, 1995.

average state had just 13 percent: *1996 Green Book,* 427.

Rector feeling bilious: "panhandlers": Rector, *National Review,* April 17, 1995; "sluggards," editorial, *National Review,* Feb. 6, 1995; "obstacles," Judith Havemann, *WP,* Feb. 19, 1995.

"always been irritating": Interview with Newt Gingrich.

"starve children": Dan Balz, *WP,* Jan. 9, 1995.

"A major embarrassment": *Charleston Gazette,* Feb. 14, 1995.

128 **twenty states wouldn't have to run a work program:** Temporary Assistance for Needy Families Program: Fourth Annual Report to Congress, May 2002, table 3:1:a.

Rector hatched the idea: Interviews with Robert Rector and Ron Haskins.

129 **"You cannot sustain":** Interview with Newt Gingrich.

$65 billion cut: Sharon Parrott, "Cash Assistance and Related Provisions in the Personal Responsibility Act," Center on Budget and Policy Priorities, April 6, 1995, 3.

130 **Democrats reacted:** "Make Americans Hungry," Rep. Harold Volkmer in *CQ,* March 11, 1995, 758; Rep. Major Owens in Robert Pear, *NYT,* March 23, 1995; Rep. John Lewis in Mary McGrory, *WP,* April 2, 1995.

"not trying to get people entitled": Robert Pear, *NYT,* March 9, 1995. The word does have unfortunate connotations, suggesting entitlements are by nature permissive. But in this context, "entitlement" refers only to the funding structure. A strict work program that cuts off recipients who fail to work could still be an entitlement, as long as those who do follow the rules are guaranteed the aid. The conflict between the word's formal and informal meanings was a source of constant confusion.

131 *The less we spend:* GOP senator Phil Gramm put on a particularly bald display of the New Compassion while campaigning before the Iowa caucuses in 1996. Around Washington, the Texan liked to say he was so tough he kept his heart in a jar, but when I asked why he wanted to end welfare, he said of recipients: "Because ahh *luvvvv* 'em!"

131 **"Orwellian perversion":** Interview with Daniel Patrick Moynihan.

132 **"I thought we'd be in more trouble":** Interview with Gingrich.

generous people have stopped: Murray, *Losing Ground*, p. 236.

Shechtman: DeParle, *NYTM*, Jan. 28, 1996.

thirteen "power phrases," "Rep. Dunn": The Wirthlin Group, "Pulseline Research on Welfare Reform Conducted on Behalf of the Republican National Committee & the National Republican Congressional Committee," March 1995, 3, 8.

dystopian future: *The Bell Curve* (coauthored with Richard Herrnstein) also marked a shift in Murray's treatment of race. When he first proposed ending welfare in *Losing Ground*, Murray took pains to stress his color-blind views. "It makes no difference whether Harold is white or black," he wrote, in his famous parable about the welfare couple Harold and Phyllis (p. 162). The main furor in *The Bell Curve* (New York: Free Press, 1994), however, was its stress on black-white differences in intelligence scores and especially his speculation about whether a genetic element was in play.

list of horrifying stories: Dick Armey, "Welfare Reform Debate Information," March 16, 1995.

133 **alligators and wolves:** 104th Cong., 1st sess., *Cong. Rec.* 141 (March 24, 1995): H 3766 (alligators), H 3722 (wolves).

After decades of predictable: Ford and Shaw traded barbs on Feb. 15, 1995, in the Ways and Means subcommittee on welfare.

134 **"Newt Gingrich believed":** Interview with Bill Clinton, Jan. 30, 2004.

Shays told his wife: Interview with Christopher Shays.

"My hero is Newt Gingrich": Christopher Shays press conference, Nov. 17, 1995.

135 **"fast-forward":** Dick Morris, *Behind the Oval Office: Getting Reelected Against All Odds* (1997; repr., Los Angeles: Renaissance Books), 37.

"get welfare off": Interview with Doug Schoen.

"strategic mistake": Mickey Kaus, "They Blew It," *The New Republic*, Dec. 5, 1994.

"I should have done welfare": Joe Klein, *The Natural: The Misunderstood Presidency of Bill Clinton* (New York: Doubleday, 2002), 81.

"It wasn't really until the summer": Interview with Dick Morris.

"liberate" the poor: Clinton State of the Union Address, Jan. 24, 1995, *PPP-1995*, vol. 1, 79; remarks at White House, Jan. 28, 1995, *PPP-1995*, vol. 1, 108; remarks at Democratic Governors Association dinner, Jan. 30, 1995, *PPP-1995*, vol. 1, 123.

Lillie Harden: Clinton remarks to National Association of Counties, March 7, 1995, *PPP-1995*, vol. 1, 321.

"I still hope it will be the basis": Clinton remarks to NACO, March 7, 1995, *PPP-1995*, vol. 1, 317.

136 **"I wasn't pleased":** *New York Post*, Nov. 3, 1995.

136   **"I loved block grants":** Clinton remarks to Florida Legislature, March 30, 1995, *PPP-1995,* vol. 1, 422.

    "It is not fair": Ibid., p. 423.

    If "these people can't find jobs": Clinton radio address, April 8, 1995, *PPP-1995,* vol. 1, 492.

    praised bills without last-resort jobs: Clinton radio address, Sept. 16, 1995, *PPP-1995,* vol. 1, 1305.

    answer "yes and no": Talking Points on Welfare Reform, Nov. 13, 1995, author's files.

    Modified Madman: Interview with Bruce Reed.

    didn't think the entitlement meant much: Interviews with Dick Morris, Bruce Reed, and Bill Clinton, who told me, "I didn't have a problem with block-granting to the states because we had already de facto done that" given the wide variation in state benefit levels; Jan. 30, 2004.

    obscure tool of child support: Clinton radio address, March 18, 1995, *PPP-1995,* vol. 1, 373.

    polled well: Interview with administration official on background.

    "In no time in recent": Donna E. Shalala, Memorandum to the President, Jan. 19, 1995. Labor Secretary Robert Reich, an opponent of the bill, was another cabinet member impatient with Clinton's stance. "The big strategic error was to let things drift initially and not to signal what was acceptable and what wasn't," he told me. "Everything from that point on was about reducing the abomination."

137   **"only from the right":** Dick Morris memo to Bill Clinton, Feb. 17, 1995, excerpted in Morris, *Behind the Oval Office,* 353.

    Panetta: Interview with Leon Panetta.

    moment of subtle revelation: Reuters, May 23, 1995; interview with Ginny Terzano.

8. THE ELUSIVE PRESIDENT: WASHINGTON, 1995–1996

138   **Moynihan assured:** In an interview, Paul Offner, Moynihan's main welfare aide, said: "Dole and Packwood were probably his two closest friends on the Finance Committee. He thought there was no way in the world Dole was going to go along with this stuff. I think Moynihan was really blind-sided by those guys, whom he had such respect for, that they would fall in behind Gingrich. . . . They shut him out just as tight as could be."

    affection Dole felt for the governors: Unlike Clinton, who portrayed his politicking as the essence of high-mindedness, Dole had an endearing habit of broadcasting his ulterior motives. He boasted his plan had the support of governors in New Hampshire, Iowa, and Arizona—"to name a few primary states." *CQ,* Aug. 12, 1995, 2444.

139   **only speech published:** Daniel Patrick Moynihan, "Congress Builds a Coffin," *The New York Review of Books*, Jan. 11, 1996.

"Nothing I did connected": Daniel Patrick Moynihan, *Miles to Go: A Personal History of Social Policy* (Cambridge, MA: Harvard University Press, 1996), 36.

drove other problems: Moynihan wrote, "From the wild Irish slums of the 19th-century Eastern Seaboard to the riot-torn suburbs of Los Angeles, there is one unmistakable lesson in American history: A community that allows a large number of young men to grow up in broken families, dominated by women, never acquiring any stable relationship to male authority, never acquiring any rational expectations about the future—that community asks for and gets chaos. Crime, violence, unrest, disorder—most particularly the furious, unrestrained lashing out at the whole social structure—that is not only to be expected; it is very near to inevitable." (*America*, Sept. 18, 1965, and repeated in *America*, Sept. 14, 1991)

"To ask questions": Mickey Kaus, a trenchant Moynihan observer, cites this quote in a book review in *The Washington Monthly*, Sept. 1986. The original is from Daniel Patrick Moynihan, *Family and Nation* (1986; repr., New York: Harcourt, Brace, Jovanovich, 1987), 187.

"grown more perplexed": 104th Cong., 1st sess., *Cong. Rec.* 141 (Dec. 21, 1995): S 19089.

gloom about the welfare poor: "paupers," Moynihan, letter to the editor, *NYT*, Dec. 26, 1991; "failed persons," Mickey Kaus, *NYT*, Nov. 19, 1996. At times, Moynihan wondered aloud whether the underclass had a biological basis in the falling age of female puberty. "You could find yourself talking about speciation here," he said in Senate hearing, a comment at once opaque and degrading (Senate Finance Committee, July 13, 1994). Once when an aide referred to welfare "clients," Moynihan flew into a rage: *Clients* pay and command respect! These are *recipients;* they take what they get.

140   **"I just do":** Robin Toner, *NYT*, June 18, 1995.

ragged childhood: Moynihan made his hard-knocks past part of his political persona, but one knock he rarely mentioned was his own family's stay on welfare. His father abandoned the family when he was ten, and his mother went on public aid before seeking refuge in a brief, unhappy second marriage to a well-to-do man. As a 1994 profile in *Vanity Fair* reported: "He doesn't talk about what happened. Even his daughter says she knows only the sketchiest outlines of the story." Elise O'Shaughnessy, *VF*, May 1994; see also Douglas Schoen, *Pat: A Biography of Daniel Patrick Moynihan* (New York: Harper & Row, 1974), 10–11.

"I write to plead": Letter from Offner to Moynihan, April 21, 1995.

"ruinous": Judith Havemann and John Harris, *WP*, June 15, 1995.

141 **"filibuster it"**: Robert Pear, *NYT*, June 16, 1991.
bill's preamble: DeParle, *NYTM*, Nov. 12, 1995, 35.

142 **"These moves"**: Interview with Robert Rector.
Senate allies: Faircloth, Judith Havemann, and John Harris in *WP*, June 15, 1995; Ashcroft in Robert Pear, *NYT*, Aug. 20, 1995; Gramm on CBS, *Face the Nation*, Aug. 6, 1995.
"jump ball": *CQ*, Aug. 12, 1995, 2444.

143 **"sleeping on grates"**: 104th Cong., 1st sess., *Cong. Rec.* 141 (Sept. 6, 1995): S 12705.
"I cannot believe": Clinton news conference, Aug. 10, 1995, *PPP-1995*, vol. 2, 1245.
"[b]rag about cuts": Morris, *Behind the Oval Office*, 467. Morris told me he had been polling to see what message might win public support for a veto and found none.
Democrats demanded $3 billion: Interviews with Grace Reef, Laurie Rubiner, Cynthia Rice, and Helen Blank.
Dole, Dodd: In 104th Cong., 1st sess., *Cong. Rec.* 141 (Sept. 14, 1995): S 13581.

144 **"wisdom and courage"**: Clinton radio address, Sept. 16, 1995, *PPP-1995*, vol. 2, 1366.
high fives in the West Wing: Alison Mitchell, *NYT*, Nov. 20, 1995.
open letter: Marian Wright Edelman, *WP*, Nov. 3, 1995.
encyclopedia entry: DeParle, *NYTM*, Dec. 17, 1995.
Primus revived: Interview with Wendell Primus. The study appears in 104th Cong., 1st sess., *Cong. Rec.*, 141 (Nov. 1, 1995): S 16466.
"Clinton's tendency": Interview with Donna Shalala.

145 **"right kind" of reform**: Clinton radio address, Sept. 16, 1995, *PPP-1995*, vol. 2, 1366.
"stick of dynamite": Interview with Wendell Primus.
nonexistent study: Elizabeth Shogren, *Los Angeles Times*, Oct. 27, 1995; also interviews with Wendell Primus, Bruce Reed, Donna Shalala, and Melissa Skolfield.
"may have to accept": Mike McCurry, White House briefing, Nov. 9, 1995.

146 **"This is petty"**: David Maraniss and Michael Weisskopf, *"Tell Newt to Shut Up!"* (New York: Touchstone, 1996), 152.
job-approval rating: George Hager and Eric Pianin, *Mirage: Why Neither Democrats Nor Republicans Can Balance the Budget, End the Deficit, and Satisfy the Public* (New York: Times Books, 1997), 269.
Gingrich sobbed: Maraniss and Weisskopf, *"Tell Newt to Shut Up!"* 1.

147 **"I've got a problem," Leave It to Beaver**: Ibid., 182, 190.
Clinton had a problem: Trent Lott, the second-ranking Senate Republican, sent around a bulletin asking, "Why take BC off the welfare hook?"

(*FaxNet,* Feb. 1, 1996), and the Republican National Committee began airing ads attacking Clinton's failure to end welfare.

147 **"All of us are here":** Ron Haskins, "A Potential Welfare Reform Agenda for the Second Session" (background paper for GOP members of the Ways and Means welfare subcommittee), Feb. 26, 1996, 1, 3. Ari Fleischer also worked to jump-start a bill, as did Mickey Kaus, who met with potential funders in the hopes of starting a nonprofit group to lobby for welfare legislation. Instead, he took on an informal role of ferrying messages between Haskins and Bruce Reed and working the press.

"politics were quite ravishing": Interview with Clay Shaw.

148 **block grant Medicaid:** In her memoir, Hillary Clinton wrote: "I made clear to Bill and his policy advisers in the West Wing that if I thought they were caving in . . . I would publicly oppose it . . . I would speak out against any bill that did not provide heath [*sic*] care through Medicaid." *Living History* (New York: Simon & Schuster, 2003), 326, 367.

Emphasize "the tragedy of welfare": Rep. Jennifer Dunn, Memorandum to GOP Welfare Reform Working Group, April 24, 1996.

"We're not going to give" to **"This is nuts!":** Notes from meeting of Ways and Means Republicans, June 12, 1996. A turning point in rank-and-file sentiment occurred on June 21, 1996, at a meeting of the whole House GOP. The Medicaid block grant was still in the bill, but the comments of Rep. Tillie Fowler of Florida brought rousing support for dropping it. She said her constituents weren't sure what Medicaid was; they confused it with Medicare. "But *welfare*—that they know! We have to pass that bill!" (Interviews with Tillie Fowler and Dave Camp.)

What finally swayed: Interviews with Newt Gingrich and Jimmy Hayes.

149 **"We thought we would cause a split":** Interview with Gingrich.

"Moot": Clinton exchange with reporters, Jan. 30, 1996, *PPP-1996*, vol. 1, 116.

"good bill": Clinton remarks to the National Governors Association, Feb. 6, 1996, *PPP-1996*, vol. 1, p. 177.

"all any American": Ibid.

spokesman criticized: Mike McCurry, White House briefing, Feb. 7, 1996.

praised a protest against time limits: Clinton remarks in radio address and exchange with reporters, June 1, 1996, *PPP-1996*, vol. 1, 848.

called for "tough time limits": Clinton remarks to the American Nurses Association, June 18, 1996, *PPP-1996*, vol. 1, 925.

negotiator uses ambiguity: Speaking to the NGA, Clinton called the latest bill "a real turning point" on July 16, 1996, but reversed himself a week later, dismissing it with a cornpone quip: "You can put wings on a pig but you don't make it an eagle." (Clinton remarks to the NGA, July 16,

1996, *PPP-1996*, vol. 2, 1129; remarks in Sacramento, July 23, 1996, *PPP-1996*, vol. 2, 1187.

149   **"Government's going to have to train everybody":** Clinton interview with Tom Brokaw, *NBC Nightly News*, Dec. 3, 1993.

"build a jobs program": Ibid.

"I don't think it's a good idea to say 'You can stay on welfare two years'": Clinton interview with the New Jersey media in Hackensack, March 11, 1996, *PPP-1996*, vol. 1, 419. In my 2004 interview with Clinton, he repeated his misgivings about time limits: "I think having a five-year lifetime limit, plus the cutoff after a certain time for able-bodied people, ignores the impact of having a sustained recession."

150   **"I say 'tough on work, yes'":** Clinton remarks to the NAACP, July 10, 1996, *PPP-1996*, vol. 2, 1106.

"We regret that there will be a certain negative side": Interview with Clay Shaw.

"I don't think it's a good thing to hurt children": Clinton interview with the New Jersey media in Hackensack, March 11, 1996, *PPP-1996*, vol. 1, 419.

"Bill Clinton just did this for the ninety-six election!": Interview with Bill Clinton, Jan. 30, 2004. The other Clinton quotes explaining his thinking come from the same interview.

"We've got to rebuild our political life": Clinton at Georgetown University, Oct. 23, 1991.

151   **"children are blown to the winds":** 104th Cong., 1st sess., *Cong. Rec.* 141 (Dec. 12, 1995): S 18436.

Clinton's 1993 homily: Clinton at Church of God in Christ, Memphis, Nov. 13, 1993.

Dick Morris plied him: Interviews with Morris, Bill Clinton, and Leon Panetta.

country would do more for the poor: Hillary Clinton makes the same argument in her memoir: "We also hoped to persuade the American public, now that the old welfare system had been replaced, to address the greater problem of poverty and its consequences. . . . I hoped welfare reform would be the beginning, not the end, of our concern for the poor." *Living History*, 369–70.

152   **"After I sign my name to this bill":** Clinton remarks in the Rose Garden, Aug. 22, 1996, *PPP-1996*, vol. 2, 1326.

three-point deficit, "veto would be a disaster": Morris, *Behind the Oval Office*, 596.

Hillary Clinton's signals: Interviews with Donna Shalala and Doug Besharov; Morris, *Behind the Oval Office*, 300; Hillary Clinton, *Living History*, 369.

Hillary Clinton was out of town: Hillary Clinton's role in the welfare bill has been the subject of great speculation and modest mystery. Her one-time ally, George Stephanopoulos, wrote: "In my last few phone calls with the first lady, I could tell she preferred a veto." *All Too Human* (New York: Little, Brown, 1999), 419. Joe Klein, a perceptive Clinton watcher, wrote: "Most of the President's staff, including his wife, were opposed." (*The Natural*, 151.) One White House aide told me he got a phone call from her shortly after the president endorsed the bill, in which she said something like: "Those of us who are opposed to it have to keep on fighting." But Melanne Verveer, her close aide and friend, told me: "If she were writing the bill, she might have nuanced it differently. But she was not opposing." Verveer said Clinton talked admiringly of a single mother she had met, who worked as an all-night waitress to stay off public aid. Verveer recalls Mrs. Clinton asking something along the lines of "How do you face a woman like that and not have others do the same?" Welfare, Verveer said, was "like a double standard for her." Bruce Reed said, "I had the sense that she was for it, or at least not against it. I had always been of the opinion that she was much more conservative on these issues than people thought. Her staff wasn't involved."

Certainly, like any politician, she was adept at letting different people hear what they wanted to hear. In 1996 with her liberal allies enraged, she had a motive to seem opposed. Now that she's an elected official, referring to a popular law, she has a motive to look like she was for it all along. But whether she was actively for it, or merely neutral, there's no evidence that she tried to stop the president from signing it. *Why* she lent it at least passive support is a separate question. The interesting thing about the account in her memoir is that it makes no attempts to hide the political considerations. Of critics like her old friend Marian Wright Edelman, she wrote: "They didn't have to negotiate with Newt Gingrich and Bob Dole or worry about maintaining a political balance in Congress." (*Living History*, 369.)

153   **Clinton turned red with indignation:** My account of the July 31, 1996, meeting comes from interviews with Henry Cisneros, Leon Panetta, Bruce Reed, Robert Reich, Donna Shalala, and George Stephanopoulos; Reich told me: "I began to suspect halfway through the meeting that it was not a sincere meeting. It was a show meeting. He wanted to show people he was sincere about their concerns, but he had already made up his mind." In an e-mail, Elaine Kamarck told me: "I was called in at the last minute by [Vice President Al] Gore personally, who said that Clinton had asked me to be there since he wanted some more people in the room who would argue in favor of the bill. I took it as a sign he'd made up his mind already."

Incensed at the budget cuts: Having agreed to give Clinton a third bill, the Republicans did what they could to maximize the political pain. In a memo to Gingrich, his legislative aide Jack Howard wrote: "I believe the

White House will sign just about anything we send them, so we should make them eat as much as we can" (memo, July 25, 1996).

153   **most cabinet members opposed:** One surprisingly strong argument for signing came from the Commerce secretary, Mickey Kantor, who had started his career as a legal aid lawyer; he argued to Clinton that the system was doing more harm than good. For the Ellwood op-ed opposing the bill, see *NYT*, July 22, 1996.

154   **Roosevelt had abolished:** The FDR story, which caught Clinton's notice, was part of the unusual campaign by Mickey Kaus, who was operating in the hybrid status of journalist and policy advocate. Kaus had called Reed from Los Angeles the night before the meeting and told him of FDR's end-welfare moment, which he had gotten from William Leuchtenburg's history, *Franklin D. Roosevelt and the New Deal, 1932–1940* (New York: Harper & Row, 1963). Reed asked him to fax the relevant pages. After racing around town in search of a copy, Kaus found one at Borders and got the passage to Reed at about midnight eastern time. It describes Roosevelt's decision to shut down the Civil Works Administration, a precursor to the WPA that had employed 4.5 million people in the winter of 1933–34. Leuchtenburg writes: "Alarmed at how much CWA was costing, Roosevelt ended it as quickly as he could. He feared he was creating a permanent class of reliefers whom he might never get off the government payroll." Leuchtenburg quotes Roosevelt telling his aides: "Nobody is going to starve in the warm weather." (See pp. 122–25.) In calling Clinton's attention to the story, Kaus said he was trying to make three points: (1) presidents used to do big, bold things; (2) it's impossible to overhaul welfare while holding every recipient harmless; (3) Clinton needed to "generally harden his heart" and accept that big policy changes toward the poor carry some costs.

  "I want to sign this bill": Three Clinton welfare aides resigned in protest: Mary Jo Bane, Wendell Primus, and Peter Edelman, who aired his criticisms in a widely read article in *The Atlantic* (March 1997) called "The Worst Thing Bill Clinton Has Done."

9. THE RADICAL CUTS THE ROLLS: MILWAUKEE, 1995–1996

159   **penalty amounted to 6 percent:** Without the penalty, Jewell was getting $517 in AFDC and $340 in food stamps, for a total of $857. The penalty cut her cash to $440 but raised her food stamps to $363, for a total of $803.

160   **makings of a dumb-criminal joke:** Interviews with Opal Caples and Jewell Reed, and arrest report, Nov. 3, 1995.

161   **Milwaukee's economy:** From 1990 to 1994, the average unemployment rate in Milwaukee was 6.3 percent; by comparison, it was 12.3 percent in Detroit, 11.8 percent in Cleveland, and 8.8 percent in Chicago.

161   **right-wing idealist:** Interviews with Jason Turner; see also DeParle, *NYTM*, Aug. 24, 1997, and *NYTM*, Dec. 20, 1998.

162   **"It's work that sets you free!":** Robert Polner, *Newsday*, June 28, 1998.
welfare article: "How It Pays to Be Poor in America," *USN*, Nov. 1, 1965.

163   **robbed at gunpoint:** The second robbery occurred in Houston, where Turner was driving a cab on a college break.

165   **the statewide caseload had already fallen:** Some key caseload figures are these: 98,300 when Thompson took office (Jan. 1987); 81,300 when Turner arrived (April 1993); 31,500 when the transition to W-2 began (Sept. 1997); 13,400 when the transition to W-2 ended (March 1998); and 6,700 when Thompson left office (Jan. 2001). Turner took a lead role in designing W-2 but left the state government in the spring of 1997, so he played no role in running it.

While the caseload declines were extraordinary by anyone's accounting, these official data do modestly overstate its extent. Through 1996, AFDC included about 10,000 "child only" cases, in which the adult was not part of the case (often, for instance, a grandmother caring for a grandchild). With the conversion to W-2 in 1997, the state shifted those cases into two new programs, separate from W-2. So part of what appears as a welfare decline was really just a reshuffling of the existing caseload. By the state's official count, the rolls dropped 93 percent during Thompson's four terms (from 98,300 to 6,700). If one added back the child-only cases (as an apples-to-apples comparison should), the decline would equal 84 percent. For simplicity's sake (and because the child-only figures are unreliable for certain months), I use the official state numbers throughout the text unless otherwise noted.

recipients placed in jobs rose: Jason Turner, "Performance Contracting in Wisconsin" (unpublished paper, circa 1997), 2.

Oregon diversion program: Interviews with Jason Turner and with Verl T. Long and Sandy Steele, of the Oregon Department of Human Services; *AFSelf-Sufficiency* (newsletter, Division of Adult and Family Services, Dec. 1993), 6.

166   **case openings fell by a third:** Statewide, the annual number of case openings fell from 37,000 in 1995 to 24,200 in 1996. The decline was 21 percent in Milwaukee and 45 percent in the rest of the state. Author's analysis of DWD data.

The Emergency Work Program: Interview with Bill Biggs; testimony of Norman G. Angus, Director of Utah State Department of Social Services before the U.S. Senate Finance Committee, Sept. 1985.

167   **Utah caseload fell nearly 90 percent:** Frederick V. Jansen and Mary Jane Taylor, "Emergency Welfare Work and Employment: An Independent Evaluation of Utah's Emergency Work Program," June 13, 1991, 4. Three months after leaving the rolls, 76 percent of program participants were employed.

167 **Milwaukee's caseload collapsed:** In the two years beginning in March 1996, the Milwaukee caseload fell from 33,700 to 11,500. Outside Milwaukee, it dropped from 29,000 to 2,000. The total number of Milwaukee recipients, as opposed to cases, fell by 60,000 in a city of 611,000 residents. (As noted above, these official figures on caseload decline would look a bit smaller if they properly accounted for child-only cases.)

168 **nearly a third had jobs:** John Pawasarat and Lois M. Quinn, "Demographics of Milwaukee County Populations Expected to Work Under Proposed Welfare Initiatives" (UW-M, Employment & Training Institute, Nov. 1995), 33.

"pogs": Scott Sloan, *Shepherd Express,* July 10, 1997.

169 **sanctions rose a dozenfold:** In 1993, Turner's first year in Wisconsin, Milwaukee sanctioned about 360 people a month. (See State of Wisconsin, *JOBS Annual Report,* Dec. 1994, 60.) In the spring of 1996, under Pay for Performance, monthly sanctions averaged about 4,200. (Author's 1997 communication with Eva J. Davis, Milwaukee County Department of Human Services.) The penalties rose not only because of the default mechanism, of course, but also because the program had tougher rules with which few people would or could comply.

Congressional investigators: GAO, "States' Early Experience with Benefit Termination," May 1997, 7.

170 **homeless families, Ramon Wagner:** DeParle, *NYT,* May 7, 1997.

10. ANGIE AND JEWELL GO TO WORK: MILWAUKEE, 1996–1998

175 **difficult, dangerous work:** From 1995 to 1999, an average of 15.4 percent of nursing home workers were injured each year; among coal miners, the number was 7.6 percent (Bureau of Labor Statistics). In 1998, nursing aides earned an average of about $7.50 an hour, while coal miners earned $19.17. (The nursing aide figure is from author's communication with Joshua Wiener, Urban Institute; coal miners' data is from BLS.) Data on back injuries and rise in injury rates is from "Caring till It Hurts," Service Employees International Union, 1997, 2, 5. For turnover rates, poverty rates, and health insurance, see testimony of William A. Scanlon of the GAO before the Senate Finance Committee, May 17, 2001, 12–13.

176 **caregivers' role and background on nursing homes:** Interviews with Judith Feder, Robert Friedland, Robyn Stone, and Josh Wiener.

178 **650 Chicago workers:** Timothy M. Smeeding, Katherin Ross Phillips, and Michael O'Connor, "The EITC: Expectation, Knowledge, Use, and Economic and Social Mobility," *National Tax Journal* (Dec. 1, 2000).

180 **Bel Air turnover rate:** The annual turnover rate among Bel Air nursing aides was 144 percent versus a statewide average of 69 percent. *1999*

Consumer Information Report, Wisconsin Department of Health & Family Services, 6.

182 **probation officer noted:** J. Mulcrone, pretrial investigation in 93-CR 24020-02, filed Jan. 4, 1994, Circuit Court of Cook County.

186 **the kids' school absences rose:** Kesha's absentee rate rose from 19 percent when Angie was on welfare to 33 percent after she left the rolls. Redd's went from 27 percent to 29 percent, and Von's from 16 percent to 19 percent. The data cover the eight school years beginning in 1991–92; Kesha's eighth-grade attendance records are missing. (Author's analysis of attendance records supplied by Milwaukee Public Schools.)

190 **"Leaving welfare is a process":** Toby Herr and Robert Halpern with Aimee Conrad, "Changing What Counts: Re-thinking the Journey Out of Welfare" (Project Match, April 1991), 10.

191 **work despite multiple barriers:** One major study of W-2 bore out Herr's view that people with barriers can work. "Contrary to what one might expect, sample members who had at least a high school diploma were no more likely to have been employed than those who had not graduated from high school." People with high school diplomas did earn more. Irving Piliavin, Amy Dworsky, and Mark E. Courtney, "What Happens to Families Under W-2 in Milwaukee County, Wisconsin? Report from Wave 2 of the Milwaukee TANF Applicant Study," Chapin Hall Center for Children at the University of Chicago and Institute for Research on Poverty, University of Wisconsin, Madison, Sept. 2003, 58.

192 **$8,100:** See Maria Cancian and others, "Before and After TANF: The Economic Well-Being of Women on Welfare" (Institute for Research on Poverty, Special Report no. 77, May 2000), table 8. Among former recipients who worked, average earnings were $10,300. But only 79 percent worked. Counting all former recipients, employed and unemployed, lowers the figure to $8,100. (All figures, including Jewell's, in 1998 dollars.)

193 **Jewell took her in:** One peculiarity of the trio's experiences in the post-welfare years is that they each had a prostitute move in with them. After Ken's teenage associate left Jewell's, she stayed with Angie. The girl's sister, who was also occasionally employed as a sex worker by Ken, stayed with Opal and helped take care of her kids.

194 **two-week manhunt:** See *MJS,* Feb. 11, 12, 20, 21, and 26, 1998.
loaded rifle, $400 of cocaine: Arrest report, Sept. 19, 1998, on file in *State vs. Kenyatta Thigpen,* 98CF005103, Milwaukee County Circuit Court.
one house arrest per house: Actually, there is no ban on two accused felons sharing a residence on house arrest; decisions are made case by case.

11. OPAL'S HIDDEN ADDICTION: MILWAUKEE, 1996–1998

196 **cut Milwaukee's rolls by a third:** The city's caseload fell from 33,700 in March 1996, at the start of Pay for Performance, to 23,300 in July 1997.
more than half the caseload untouched: Of 55,000 cases statewide in June 1996, for instance, 20,400 were enrolled in welfare-to-work activities; author's communication with Paul Saeman, DWD.
sightings of "Maria!": At a motivation class in 1997 the instructor asked students for examples of how the program had helped. I thought: interview skills? self-esteem? A hand flew up: "It really helped me with the interview for *Dateline NBC!*"

197 **social work as farce:** OIC also marched Opal through something called the Harrington-O'Shea Career Decision-Making® System Revised, a list of ninety-six like-dislike questions compiled by two Boston psychologists. Opal reported that she would like to "write a novel," "perform scientific studies," or serve as "a mayor or senator." She would not like to "drive a large truck" or "carve animals out of wood." With that, the test detected an interest in social issues and suggested a future as a dean of students or probation officer. Opal wrote that she'd rather be a chemist.

201 **Robert Lee's arrests:** Interviews with Opal, Chicago court records.

202 **crack's American debut:** Michael Agar, "The Story of Crack: Towards a Theory of Illicit Drug Trends," *Addiction Research and Theory* 11, no. 1 (2003): 3–29; see also the history of crack on the Web site of the Drug Enforcement Administration.
"I could do anything": "My Secret Addiction," *Ladies' Home Journal,* Nov. 1994, 162.
behavior of addicts: Interviews with Ric Curtis, Francine Feinberg, Jerome Jaffe, George Koob, Michael Massing, Thomas McLellan, Anne Paczesny, Luigi Pulvirenti, and Pat Tucker. Also helpful is the 1998 Bill Moyers series on PBS, *Close to Home,* available at http:www.pbs.org/wnet/closetohome/home.html (accessed May 26, 2004).
paradigmatic cocaine experiment: Michael A. Bozarth and Roy A. Wise, "Toxicity Associated with Long-term Intravenous Heroin and Cocaine Self-Administration in the Rat," *Journal of the American Medical Association* (1985): 81–83.

206 **poor record of leading to employment:** Brock, Butler, and Long, "Unpaid Work Experience for Welfare Recipients," 3. One reason the early experiments failed to predict the later plunge of the rolls may have to do with scale; the declines came in part from changes in street and bureaucratic culture, which don't occur until the new rules are broadly applied.

207 **unusually generous:** Shortly before the program began, Tommy Thompson (who was first elected promising benefit cuts) pushed through a 20 percent hike, raising the community service jobs to $673 a month. In

doing so, he overrode the objections of his aides and Republicans in the legislature. "It's brought in a lot of opponents and advocates to help make the system work," he said. Thompson's politically savvy move was one example of the kind of positive political dynamic Clinton had hoped the welfare bill would encourage. At the same time, W-2 drew some criticism on the Left for abandoning the practice of paying more to larger families. AFDC paid $440 a month to a mother with one child, and additional children raised the figure to $517, $617, and $708, up to $963 for a mother of ten. In paying a flat $673, the CSJs amounted to a pay raise for anyone with three kids or less—about 90 percent of the caseload. However, a few women with very large families lost significant ground.

207 **preview of W-2:** DeParle, "Getting Opal Caples to Work," *NYTM,* August 24, 1997.

12. HALF A SAFETY NET: THE UNITED STATES, 1997–2003

208 **Nine out of ten:** For jobs and children, *1996 Green Book,* 473; for fathers and education, interview with Donna Pavetti.

"God, not government": Joe Loconte, *WSJ,* Oct. 6, 1995.

209 **"The debate is over":** Clinton, remarks in St. Louis, Aug. 12, 1997, *PPP-1997,* vol. 2, 1087.

Rudolph Giuliani planned: Robert Polner, *Newsday,* May 12, 1998.

"Life works if you work": Thomas L. Gais and others, "Implementation of the Personal Responsibility Act of 1996," in Rebecca Blank and Ron Haskins, eds., *The New World of Welfare* (Washington, DC: Brookings Institution Press, 2001), 46.

About three-quarters made applicants look: Pamela A. Holcomb and Karin Martinson, "Putting Policy into Practice," in Alan Weil and Kenneth Finegold, eds., *Welfare Reform: The Next Act* (Washington, DC: The Urban Institute, 2002), 9. They found diversion programs in thirteen of seventeen sites studied.

210 **"culture of improper deterrence":** Shortly after becoming the New York City welfare commissioner, Jason Turner began converting the city's thirty-one welfare offices into so-called "job centers," with a heavy stress on diverting would-be applicants. City officials said that front-line workers merely were supposed to make sure that applicants had considered alternatives to welfare, like using food banks or soup kitchens. But city workers often refused to give out applications during a person's first visit to the office, in violation of the law; they did so not only for cash aid but for Medicaid and food stamps, too. While the city called such incidents isolated, District Judge William H. Pauley III found "system-wide failures" and wrote that the "evidence indicated that job centers were failing to timely process applications . . . erroneously denying food stamps and

Medicaid applications, [and] failing to allow individuals to apply for benefits on their first visit to a job center." Turner may not have helped his cause when he said in a deposition, "We acted first and worried about the consequences later." One of the plaintiffs was a homeless woman, pregnant with twins, who was skipping meals as she waited more than a month for food stamps. *Lakisha Reynolds vs. Rudolph Giuliani,* U.S. District Court, Southern District of New York, July 21, 2000.

210 **two-thirds of adults lost Medicaid:** Pamela Loprest, "How Are Families that Left Welfare Doing? A Comparison of Early and Recent Welfare Leavers," The Urban Institute, B-36, April 2001, 5. The data covers 1997, a low point in the health insurance story, which made modest improvements with time. The share of former recipients with Medicaid or other subsidized insurance rose from 36 percent in 1997 to 48 percent in 2002, in part because states did a better job of enrolling eligible families and in part because of the new state Children's Health Insurance Program, which in some states covered adults, too. (2002 data from author's communication with Loprest.) **Among children eligible for food stamps:** Bob Greenstein and Jocelyn Guyer, "Supporting Work through Medicaid and Food Stamps," in Blank and Haskins, eds., *The New World of Welfare,* 347.

211 **three-quarters had full-family sanctions, half-million cut off:** Dan Bloom and Don Winstead, "Sanctions and Welfare Reform," in Isabel V. Sawhill and others, *Welfare Reform and Beyond: The Future of the Safety Net* (Washington, DC: Brookings Institution, 2002), 50–51. Some of those penalized ignored their assignments because they already had jobs. But on average, they had less education, less work experience, and more problems with domestic violence and physical and mental health than did other people leaving the rolls. They also wound up with lower employment rates. While sanctioned families can return to the rolls, often after a waiting period, the overwhelming majority do not. See also LaDonna Pavetti and Dan Bloom, "State Sanctions and Time Limits," in Blank and Haskins, *The New World of Welfare,* 261.
a third of New York City's caseload: Interviews with Seth Diamond, Swati Desai, NYC Human Resources Administration.

212 **Utah found half had problems:** DeParle, *NYT,* June 30, 1997.
thirty-three states spent more on child care: Mark H. Greenberg, CLASP, testimony before U.S. Senate Committee on Finance, March 19, 2002. Wisconsin spent *four* times as much on child care as it did on cash benefits.

213 **earnings disregards:** Wisconsin was the rare state that did *not* let recipients keep at least part of their checks once they got regular jobs.
collecting child support: Analysis of HHS data by Vicki Turetsky of CLASP. From 1996 to 2002, the share of child-support cases in which the government made a collection rose from 20 percent to 49 percent.

213 **half the adults, 30 percent of kids were uninsured:** Bowen Garrett and John Holahan, "Welfare Leavers, Medicaid Coverage, and Private Health Insurance," The Urban Institute, B-13, March 2000, 3.

eligibility for SCHIP and Medicaid: Author's communication with Edwin Park, Center on Budget and Policy Priorities.

37 percent adults uninsured: Author's communication with Pamela Loprest of the Urban Institute, who derived the data from the National Survey of America's Families.

mother of two leaving welfare: David T. Ellwood, "Anti-Poverty Policy for Families in the Next Century: From Welfare to Work—and Worries," *Journal of Economic Perspectives* (Winter 2000): 187–98.

214 **seven states cut the rolls by three-quarters:** It depends upon what years you choose, but from January 1993 to June 2000, they are Colorado, Florida, Idaho, Mississippi, Oklahoma, Wisconsin, and Wyoming.

states with more unemployment: Robert E. Rector and Sarah E. Youssef, "The Determinants of Welfare Caseload Decline," The Heritage Foundation, May 11, 1999.

prominent economists: June E. O'Neill and M. Anne Hill, "Gaining Ground? Measuring the Impact of Welfare Reform on Welfare and Work" (Manhattan Institute, July 2001); Rebecca M. Blank, "Declining Caseloads/Increased Work: What Can We Conclude About the Effects of Welfare Reform?" *Economic Policy Review* (Federal Reserve Bank of New York, Sept. 2001), table 2.

215 **Creek County:** Dana Milbank and Christopher Georges, *WSJ*, Feb. 11, 1997.

white families left faster, blacks and Hispanics outnumbered: DeParle, *NYT*, July 27, 1998; "Temporary Assistance for Needy Families Program: Fourth Annual Report to Congress," May 2002, ch. X, 190.

$59 billion more: Douglas J. Besharov and Peter Germanis, "Toughening TANF: How Much? And How Attainable?" University of Maryland School of Public Affairs, Welfare Reform Academy, March 23, 2004, 53.

216 **state spending, New York to New Mexico:** DeParle, *NYT*, August 29, 1999.

trip to the Delta: DeParle, *NYT*, Oct. 16, 1997.

217 **factors that shape state policy:** Joe Soss and others, "Setting the Terms of Relief: Explaining State Policy Choices in the Devolution Revolution," *American Journal of Political Science* 45, no. 2 (April 2001): 378–95

218 **Oregon presented a contrasting view:** DeParle, *NYT*, Nov. 20, 1997.

talk of childhood molestation: DeParle, *NYT*, Nov. 28, 1999.

220 **twenty states met the work rate:** HHS, Office of Family Assistance, "TANF Work Participation Rates, Fiscal Year 2002," April 25, 2003.

states reported that 61 percent: "Welfare Reform Reauthorization: State Impact of Proposed Changes in Work Requirements, April 2002

Survey Results," National Governors Association/American Public Human Services Association, 7.

13. W-2 BUYS THE CRACK: MILWAUKEE, 1998

223 **Opal admitted using cocaine:** Interviews with Opal Caples and Darlene Haines.

forgery: *State vs. Darlene Haines,* Case #2001CF000403, Milwaukee County Circuit Court; interview with Megan Carmody, assistant district attorney.

224 **Opal's collapse:** Interviews with Opal Caples, Jewell Reed, and Kenny Gross.

226 **failed to pick up the girls:** On April 15, 1998, someone filed a child-welfare complaint warning, "Ms. Caples had a cocaine addiction and had abandoned all her children at day care while on a crack binge." (CHIPS petition, March 13, 2000, 2.)

caseworker knew nothing of her addiction: Opal's computerized case notes, instantly available to any caseworker, contained three references to drug use over the previous eighteen months. There is "a conflict with her . . . treatment" (Aug. 19, 1996); she is "attending her treatment program" (Sept. 12, 1996); and "[s]he has just completed . . . her treatment program" (Dec. 23, 1996).

222 **Sonya Gordon:** In an interview, Gordon explained she was a "retention specialist," whose job was to prepare the case for the "AODA"—alcohol and other drug abuse—"specialist" by talking to Opal and her former employer about why she had lost her job. She spoke to neither. An additional note of folly entered the case when another OIC worker gave Opal a $400 "job access loan" under a program meant to help workers keep their jobs. "You really don't qualify for it if you're not working," Opal said. "It wasn't hard. I just went in and filled out my papers."

229 **an investigator arrived:** Interview with Opal Caples; CHIPS petition, March 13, 2000, 2. The investigation was triggered when Opal left the girls at day care, but a month passed before the social worker arrived.

"The unborn child": Sam Martino, *MJS,* June 17, 1998.

14. GOLF BALLS AND CORPORATE DREAMS: MILWAUKEE, 1997–1999

230 **"The Company's services":** Maximus, Inc., 1997 Form 10-K, Securities and Exchange Commission.

welfare cartel: In describing the agencies' cooperative spirit, the consultant, George Gerharz, told me: "This is the biggest small town in America—you don't screw each other."

230 **Goodwill Industries:** It ran the program through a subsidiary, Employment Solutions, Inc., which operated two Milwaukee regions and was therefore the state's largest W-2 agency. The agency run by the YWCA was called YW Works.

231 **Maximus thought to have an edge:** The Wall Street firm Donaldson, Lufkin & Jenrette, for instance, credited the bill with "creating vast opportunities for the private sector" and called Maximus "ideally positioned to benefit from the expected surge in outsourcing." (Maximus, Inc., Company Report, DL&J, Aug. 22, 1997, 14, 1.)

Mastran's stake: Adam Cohen, *Time*, March 23, 1998.

Maximus had to start from scratch: Among those Maximus employees who spoke on the record were Jose Arteaga, Keith Garland, Mona Garland, George Leutermann, David Mastran, Bridgette Ridgeway, and Michael Steinborn.

232 **"plan to replicate":** Pete Millard, *Milwaukee Business Journal*, July 7, 1997.

employees would pose: When CNN called to ask if the program offered clients tax advice, Maximus staged a class for the cameras. Keith Garland, the Maximus manager who conducted it, told me, "that's the only workshop I've ever done."

Nightline: Transcript, *ABC News*, Sept. 4, 1997.

233 **up to "thirty hours":** Even Jason Turner, who designed W-2 (and then left the state government), was unaware of the "up to" codicil until I pointed it out to him. "That wasn't the original plan," he said. "The counties were definitely not allowed to put people in twenty hours—that definitely wasn't permissible." Jean Shiel, the official who wrote the manual, said the language was meant to offer "a little bit of flexibility, but not much—we still emphasized it was thirty hours of work."

"limbo": Memorandum from Mona Garland to George Leutermann, March 3, 1998.

"[M]any job seekers": E-mail from Mona Garland to Jose Arteaga, April 30, 1998.

"The no-show rate": E-mail from Paula Lampley to Mona Garland, Oct. 29, 1997.

"Northwestern Mutual": E-mail from Mona Garland to caseworkers, March 24, 1998.

"virtually no referrals": E-mail from Steve Perales to Mona Garland, Feb. 11, 1998.

234 **more than twice as many:** "Distribution of Caseloads by FEP For the Week Ending June 5, 1998," data supplied by DWD at author's request.

13 Feps, needed 28: Mona Garland memo to Steve Perales, Jan. 14, 1998.

Sixty-seven percent had no work assignments: The comparable figures were 15 percent at Employment Solutions (Region 4); 21 percent at

Employment Solutions (Region 5); 33 percent at YW Works and OIC; and 52 percent at UMOS. The statewide average was 38 percent. "Full Participation Exceptions (740RC Report)," DWD, June 26, 1998.

234 **46 percent with no assignment:** E-mail from Jose Arteaga to four Maximus managers, Sept. 28, 1998.

"[O]ur dismal performance": George Leutermann memo to Mona Garland, June 30, 1998.

236 **W-2 Provides the Jobs:** The other tier on the W-2 ladder, rarely utilized, involved "Trial Jobs," in which the state used the welfare grant to subsidize work with a private employer. In January 2000, the breakdown of assignments statewide was 51 percent in Community Service Jobs; 35 percent in W-2 Transitions; 1 percent in Trial Jobs; and 13 percent on three months of paid maternity leave.

238 **"professional work environment":** Maximus, 1997 Form 10-K, 2.

Maximus work atmosphere: gambling jags and screensaver, interviews with Michael Steinborn; "off the deep end," e-mail from George Leutermann to Mona Garland, Feb. 23, 1998; "Marine combat veteran," e-mail from Maximus employee to his supervisor, Feb. 17, 1998; "Monkey Ass away," memo from Paula Lampley to Phyllis Kirk, Aug. 31, 1998; sex-and-drug peddling scheme, e-mail from Christine Brost to Steve Perales, March 17, 1998 and from interviews with Keith Garland and George Leutermann, who confirmed the credibility of the allegations; "dumb-ass . . . should have paid," a Maximus employee on the condition of anonymity.

239 **practiced what he preached:** Leutermann's wife, Barbara, ran literacy classes; his son, George Jr., had a summer job; his niece, Twila Hatzinger, worked in PR; his girlfriend was a senior manager; and her mother supervised receptionists. The "rumors and soap operas" memo is dated June 9, 1998. The talk of Leutermann's affair was so widespread it reached David Mastran, the CEO, who later said in an interview he considered it "a firing offense" but lacked evidence at the time; given the program's other problems, he said, it was a "peripheral issue in a bigger storm." Leutermann, in an interview, didn't deny the relationship with his subordinate (he is listed on a birth certificate as the father of her child) but said she was hired on merit. "She was basically a brilliant person," he said. Likewise, he said, "My wife was hired not because she was my wife but because she had a master's degree in computer education. . . . We didn't just hire people because they were relatives."

"more than its share of complaints": E-mail from David Mastran to George Leutermann and others, May 25, 1999; the Swann report, marked in a cover note as a "draft," is dated June 1, 1999, and was circulated to the senior corporate management.

"living a double life": Judge Diane S. Sykes, May 1, 1995; transcript of sentencing in *Wisconsin vs. Corey Daniels,* case #F-950959, Milwaukee

County Circuit Court, 14. At a trial that largely pitted his word against theirs, Daniels was acquitted of extorting money from Maximus clients. "I was a little, I wouldn't say surprised, but I wasn't sure I was going to come out of there with any acquittal," his attorney, Douglas Pachucki, told me.

242 **$300-a-day habit:** Opal Caples, CHIPS petition, March 13, 2000, 2.

243 **Maximus went on a grander binge:** Unless otherwise noted, spending details come from LAB, "Administration of the Wisconsin Works Program by Maximus, Inc.," and accompanying letter of transmittal, July 28, 2000. In yet another instance of governmental disarray, the audit citing program abuse was addressed to state senator Gary R. George, who later pleaded guilty to federal conspiracy charges after receiving kickbacks from OIC.

Maximus agreed to repay: DWD news release, Oct. 13, 2000.

244 **"I have permission":** 1998 interview with George Leutermann.

a $60,000 PR chief: Interview with Bridgette Ridgeway. One of the smiling kids in the Maximus ads was her son, for which he was paid a shoot fee. "The W-2 families didn't want to participate," she said.

Leutermann covered the bases: The fuller list of Maximus donations includes African World Festival ($5,000); Bastille Days Festival ($5,000); Black Education Hope Fund ($3,875); Black Excellence Awards ($500); The Charlie Lagrew Fiddle and Jig Contest at Indian Summer Festivals ($2,500); Juneteenth Day Street Festival ($1,100); Mary Church Terrell Club ($3,350); Milwaukee Minority Chamber of Commerce ($1,000); Milwaukee Urban League ($2,750); NAACP ($1,000); Project Equality of Wisconsin ($1,700), Spirit of Truth Worship Center ($2,000); Friends of Women's Studies ($500). (LAB audit, July 28, 2000.)

245 **golf balls:** The golf balls, though not in the auditors' reports, were cited by an anonymous Maximus employee interviewed by *The New York Times* and became a shorthand for the spending spree; Nina Bernstein, *NYT*, Feb. 22, 2000.

"sad or dark tones": Memo from Randle Jackson, Sykes Communications, May 19, 1998, in author's files.

Melba Moore: David Mastran, the Maximus CEO, defended the Moore concert as an example of the kind of unconventional activity privatization was meant to foster. "We were told, 'You guys in the private sector can do things that we can never do—we want you to think outside the box,'" he said in an interview. "Well, maybe it was stupid . . . [but] I thought it was a great idea." While legislative auditors found fault with it, he said, a state welfare official had given verbal approval ahead of time.

"painted from Day One": Interview with George Leutermann.

payment to Thompson's cronies: The consultants were Phil Prange, a longtime Thompson campaign fundraiser, and John Tries, a former cabi-

net member. While the consultants' invoices were not directly charged to
W-2, state law allowed Maximus to recoup $8,500 in corporate overhead
said to relate to their work. Steven Schultze, *MJS*, Aug. 15 and Oct. 14,
2000.

245   **"on the lops"**: Memo from Leutermann to Holly Payne, July 7, 1998.
For advice on how to work the convention, Leutermann also hired a publicist named Julie Jensen, whose husband, Scott, happened to be the Republican Speaker of the Assembly until his indictment a few years later
on political corruption charges. Memo from Julie Jensen to Leutermann,
May 20, 1998.

246   **"My department bought"**: Interview with Bridgette Ridgeway.
    OIC to Employment Solutions: LAB, "Administration of the Wisconsin Works Program by Employment Solutions Inc., and Other Selected
Agencies," Feb. 16, 2001.
    her own "vigilant efforts": Stewart resigned under fire three weeks
later, but her successor, Jennifer Reinert, continued to defend Maximus.
While auditors concluded that Maximus had overcharged the state
$500,000, they also said the company failed to claim $1.6 million to which
it was entitled—its disarray had cost it $1.1 million. Citing that finding,
Reinert said of Maximus: "They were as much victims of sloppy bookkeeping as we were." Steve Schultze, *MJS*, Oct. 14, 2000.
    78 percent failed: Memo from George Leutermann to Holly Payne,
Oct. 11, 1998.

247   **attendance at MaxAcademy**: Interview with Keith Garland.
    Maximus reduced payments: LAB, "Wisconsin Works (W-2) Program:
An Evaluation," April 2001, 54–55. Statewide, only 4 percent of the caseload suffered full sanctions.
    move away from Jason Turner's theory: The subtle philosophical shift
even found doctrinal expression when the state scrapped a controversial
policy known as "Light Touch." Reflecting Turner's zeal for deterrence,
the policy told caseworkers to offer "only as much service as an eligible
individual asks for or needs" rather than "every support available." In practice, the vague dictum encouraged caseworkers to withhold information
about Medicaid and food stamps—both federal entitlements—and the
food stamp rolls fell faster in Wisconsin than in any other state. Under fire
from two federal investigations, the Thompson Administration eased its
deterrence efforts. In 2002, Thompson's Republican successor, Scott Mc
Callum, formally canceled "Light Touch," and by 2004, under a Democratic governor, Jim Doyle, the original W-2 philosophy had shifted 180
degrees. While Turner called for "securing the front door," the new program manual advised, "W-2 shall be participant friendly."

248   **just type something in the system**: In another sign of the distance between W-2 theory and practice, Turner was unaware that the policy man-

ual allowed caseworkers to write employability plans and put them in the mail. "Is that what some of them were doing?" he said. "Making something up and putting them in the mail—that's crazy. That's not how it's supposed to happen. Oh shit, that's a surprise to me."

248   **the award administrators:** The Ford/Harvard evaluation shows how hard it is for outsiders to know what's really happening inside a program, and by extension how little reliable information there may be about welfare programs nationwide. To assess W-2, the Innovations program sent a respected researcher, Julie Boatright Wilson, on a two-day visit to Wisconsin. Wilson, a former New York state official, is a lecturer at the Kennedy School, and she had written a detailed economic and demographic study of Milwaukee. That is, she arrived with an experienced eye. In a whirlwind visit, she interviewed seventy-five to one hundred people, including George Leutermann, Paula Lampley, and Becky Redmond, the MaxAcademy speaker featured on *Nightline*. "I was struck by the extent to which the front-line workers believe in the program," she wrote in a confidential report. Citing W-2's "institutional culture" as its greatest strength, she praised caseworkers for their "problem-solving" and their "can-do attitude" and the state for "monitoring outcomes rather than process." Among her concerns was that the program might have too many people in community service jobs.

249   **"a pitch man":** Pete Millard, *Milwaukee Business Journal,* Feb. 14, 2000. Leutermann's problems began at the beginning of 2000 when Mona Garland, the manager he had blamed for the early casework problems, quit and filed a racial discrimination complaint with the Equal Employment Opportunity Commission. David Mastran, the Maximus CEO, told me the company paid to settle her case and those of four other Milwaukee employees. Garland also strafed the company in the press, calling its presence in Milwaukee a "travesty." Soon after, the New York City comptroller, Alan Hevesi, challenged the company's $100 million deal, saying that Maximus had gained an unfair political advantage in the contracting process. With that, storms were under way in both cities, with Leutermann caught in both. He stopped running the W-2 program in the summer of 2000 and left the company in 2001.

When I talked to Mastran, he offered what he called a "Yogi Berra" defense of the company's problems. "We made mistakes," he said, "but we didn't do anything wrong." That is, he conceded the problems in personnel ("In all our projects, we never had personnel problems like we had up there—it was out of control") and accounting ("guilty of being inept"), but stressed that none of its transgressions had reflected a conscious attempt to defraud the state. "I don't say we were looked at with a microscope," he said. "We were looked at with a proctoscope. And no one indicted us." In part, he blamed the problems on growing pains ("It's night and day now"); in part, on the lack of state oversight; and in part on Leutermann ("His head got too big"). He also argued that for all its problems Maximus performed as well as or better than the competition and sent along some data to make his case. The data covered later years, but my subjective sense is that he's probably right when he says, "relatively speaking, we were a top performer" from the start; on the surface the only place that elicited more confidence was YW Works. The numbers he sent showed the agencies with fairly similar outcomes, which is consistent with my sense that the operational differences between them were minor. To the extent W-2 "worked," it seemed to do so more as a general welfare deterrent than as a service delivery machine.

249 **Kenny resisted Opal's claims:** The following year, Kenny failed to appear at a paternity hearing, and the court issued a default judgment, naming him the father.

15. CASEWORKER XMI28W: MILWAUKEE, 1998–2000

253 **clients liked Michael:** Interviews with clients Shelley Block, Opal Caples, Juanita Dotts, Dinah Doty, Kim Hansen, Angiwetta Hills, Melina Scott, and Angela Wilkerson.

254 **"More of the success":** Jason Turner and others, "Wisconsin Works: Draft, April 1995," proposal to Secretary Carol Skornicka, 30–31.

Pathways: Suzanne L. Wagner, Charles Chang, and Toby Herr, "An Unanticipated Story of Caseload Declines: The First Two Years of the Pathways Case Management System in Oswego County, New York" (Chicago: Project Match, July 2002). Despite the shortage of personalized attention, people leaving the rolls often say they were treated fairly—in one Wisconsin survey, for instance, the ratio was 67 percent yes versus 32 percent no. DWD, "Survey of Those Leaving AFDC or W-2: January to March 1998: A Preliminary Report," Jan. 13, 1999, 11.

one in five changed regions: Caseload analysis from DWD, supplied at author's request.

255 **Wisconsin bureaucracy celebrated:** One prominent W-2 supporter, the political scientist Lawrence M. Mead, called the Wisconsin administrators "quite literally world statesmen and stateswomen" who exemplify "their state's intense faith in the public enterprise." Lawrence M. Mead, *Government Matters: Welfare Reform in Wisconsin* (Princeton, NJ: Princeton University Press, 2004), xi.

260 **refer to a more specialized:** It turned out that by moving to a shelter, Michael's client left the Maximus region, so her case was transferred to another agency. Checking CARES a few months later, Michael saw nothing that indicated her new caseworker knew she was using drugs.

"always gonna be in the gutter": Interview with Jai Marin.

16. BOYFRIENDS: MILWAUKEE, SPRING 1999

264   **three-quarters worked** to **thirty-five hours a week:** Gregory Acs and Pamela Loprest, with Tracy Roberts, "Final Synthesis Report of Findings from ASPE Leavers' Grants" (Washington, DC: The Urban Institute, Nov. 27, 2001), Executive Summary; hereafter "ASPE Leavers Study."

    employment rates of never-married mothers: They grew from 44 percent in 1992 to 66 percent a decade later. Gary Burtless, "The Labor Force Status of Mothers Who Are Most Likely to Receive Welfare: Changes Following Reform," Brookings Institution Web site, March 30, 2004; for employment trends, see also Rebecca M. Blank and Lucie Schmidt, "Work, Wages, and Welfare," in Blank and Haskins, eds., *The New World of Work,* 70–102.

265   **"Work organizes life":** Clinton at Church of God in Christ in Memphis, Nov. 13, 1993, *PPP-1993,* vol. 2, 1985.

    Michelle Crawford: DeParle, *NYT,* April 20, 1999.

    "Ending of the Black Underclass": Mickey Kaus, "A Response to My Critics! The case for optimism about the underclass," www.kausfiles.com (accessed Nov. 8, 1999).

266   **Samuel Brown:** Carl Baehr, *Milwaukee Streets: The Stories Behind Their Names* (Milwaukee: Cream City Press, 1995), 33.

    a gang of boys: The killing was the subject of dozens of articles in Milwaukee and beyond, starting with Leah Thorsen, *MJS,* Oct. 1, 2002.

267   **incipient investigation fizzled:** Opal's case file paints a less-than-vigilant picture of the child welfare bureaucracy. It notes that "Ms. Caples admitted to the hospital staff that she had a $300.00 a day cocaine habit and . . . that she had been bingeing two to three days at a time while staying at drug houses." A social worker met her at Angie's on Jan. 8, 1999, "but as of January 20, 1999, Ms. Caples had moved" and attempts "to locate Ms. Caples in February of 1999 were unsuccessful." CHIPS petition, March 13, 2000, 2.

270   **only half of young black men had jobs:** Harry J. Holzer and Paul Offner, "Trends in Employment Outcomes of Young Black Men, 1979–2000" (Institute for Research on Poverty: Discussion Paper 1247-02, Feb. 2002), table 1. The number fell from 59 percent in 1989 to 50 percent in 1999 before bouncing back to 54 percent in 2000, still far below its historical level at the peak of a business cycle.

    black men in Milwaukee: David J. Pate Jr. "An Ethnographic Inquiry into the Life Experiences of African American Fathers with Children on W-2," in Daniel R. Meyer and Maria Cancian, *W-2 Child Support Demonstration Evaluation: Report on Nonexperimental Analyses* (Madison: Institute for Research on Poverty, March 2002), 2:29–118.

    write their own obituaries: DeParle, *NYT,* Sept. 11, 1999.

271   **If working mothers:** Interviews with Marcus Robertson, Mary Williams.

Someone Hug Me: Darrell's first report cards showed a dismayingly familiar picture of uncultivated potential. "Darrell is such a joy to have in class. He works hard and does very well with others," wrote one teacher. But she pleaded: "Mom & Dad please help Darrell get to school." Another teacher warned: "Darell [sic] is having difficuties [sic] with all subject areas."

17. MONEY: MILWAUKEE, SUMMER 1999

282   **Had she stayed on welfare:** If Angie had gone on W-2 in 1999, she would have gotten $673 a month in cash and $417 in food stamps, or $13,080 a year. Expressed in 2003 dollars, the measure I use throughout this chapter unless otherwise noted, that's $14,400.

283   **how Angie's finances worked:** "On welfare" refers to Angie's last four-full years on AFDC, 1992 through 1995. "Off welfare" covers her first three years after leaving, 1997 through 1999. She left midway through 1996, making it a unique year that I placed in neither category. Earnings records are from tax returns and the state wage files kept to track eligibility for unemployment insurance; cash and food stamp figures come from state records. Angie's 1992 and 1993 earnings are estimates based on partial data; all other figures are actual. The numbers have been adjusted for inflation and expressed in constant 2003 dollars.

One thing to notice is that even when Angie was on AFDC, her welfare check accounted for only 38 percent of her income. Another 29 percent came from earnings (after taxes); 22 percent from food stamps; and 11 percent from tax credits. If that suggests she wasn't as "dependent" on AFDC as she seemed, it also explains why taking it away may do less, for good or ill, than either side assumed. A fuller picture of Angie's finances would have to quantify the contributions of boyfriends and relatives, which other research suggests typically add another 15 to 20 percent, further diminishing the role of AFDC. (See Kathryn Edin and Laura Lein, *Making Ends Meet* [New York: Russell Sage Foundation, 1997], 44.) Another thing to keep in mind is that Angie's monthly income was less stable than these multiyear averages suggest. Both of her peak-income years—$26,000 at the post office in 1994 and $27,400 at the nursing pool in 1997—were followed by years with steep losses. Her income fell nearly a third in 1995, when she got discouraged and quit, and by 20 percent in 1998, after her car got stolen. That is, the anxiety of living on sums like these is even greater than the numbers suggest. For more financial data see www.jasondeparle.com.

Jewell's earnings rose *sixfold*: Her box score looked like this:

	ON WELFARE	OFF WELFARE
Earnings	$1,900	$12,700
Tax credits	700	4,000
Payroll taxes	(-100)	(-1,000)
AFDC	7,800	0
Food stamps	4,400	900
TOTAL	$14,700	$16,600

Jewell's 1994 earnings and tax credits are estimates; all other numbers are actual. Amounts expressed in 2003 dollars.

283   **monthly earnings reports:** The state stopped requiring the reports in August 1997, a month after Jewell lost her stamps.

284   **earnings may grow with time:** For a later look at the finances of Angie and Jewell, see pages 403 and 404.

Angie earned at least 50 percent more: In her first three years off welfare, Angie's earnings averaged more than $16,100 a year. By contrast, a typical woman leaving the Wisconsin rolls earned between about $9,000 and $10,400, as discussed on page 286. Angie's first two jobs, at Clement Manor and Mercy Rehab, paid hourly wages of $8.33 and $7.46 (in 2003 dollars), placing her squarely in the middle of former recipients nationwide; her annual earnings were higher than average only because she worked more steadily.

case for encouragement: From 1994 to 2001, annual earnings among the poorest half of single mothers rose from $4,500 to $8,800; earnings among the poorest quarter rose from $1,500 to $3,900. Total income grew more modestly, rising 32 percent to $17,000 for the poorest half and rising 16 percent to $10,000 among the poorest quarter. Over the same years, hourly wages for women at the 20th percentile rose by 14 percent, to $7.79. (Author's communication with Jared Bernstein of the Economic Policy Institute.)

As for former recipients, Acs and Loprest found them earning about $8.25 an hour; Elise Richer and two colleagues produced an estimate of $8.20; Ron Haskins came up with about $7.50 (all in 2003 dollars). Converting a midpoint estimate of $7.85 back into late-nineties dollars suggests the average leaver earned about 35 percent above the minimum wage. (Acs and Loprest, "ASPE Leavers Study," table 3; Elise Richer, Steve Savner, and Mark Greenberg, "Frequently Asked Questions About Working Welfare Leavers," CLASP, Nov. 2001, 13; Ron Haskins, "Effects of Welfare Reform on Family Income and Poverty," in Blank and Haskins, *The New World of Welfare*, 109.)

285   **poverty rates plunged:** Among children, the poverty rate fell from 21.8 percent in 1994 to 16.3 percent in 2001; among blacks, from 30.6 percent to 22.5 percent; among Hispanics, 30.7 percent to 21.4 percent; and

among people living in single-mother homes, from 38.7 percent to 28.6 percent. In 2003, the poverty threshold was $12,682 for a mother with one child; $14,824 for a mother of two; $18,725 for a mother of three; and $21,623 for a mother of four.

285 **"first recovery in three decades"**: Clinton interview with five reporters from *The New York Times,* Nov. 30, 2000.

286 **a third held jobs:** Acs and Loprest, "ASPE Leavers Study," Executive Summary and table 3.3.

average earnings: $9,000 and $12,000, Acs and Loprest, "ASPE Leavers Study," table 3.5. (The $9,000 includes an adjustment to account for non-workers.) $14,500 comes from the same study, table 3.7. All figures expressed in 2003 dollars.

Wisconsin earnings growth, three-year mean: Maria Cancian and others, "Before and After TANF: The Economic Well-Being of Women Leaving Welfare" (Madison: Institute for Research on Poverty, Special Report, no. 77), May 2000, table 8; figures in 2003 dollars.

poor people even poorer: The Cancian study examined eight thousand families who left the rolls in late 1995, just before Angie and Jewell. Over the next year, they gained $2,900 in earnings and tax credits but lost $5,500 in cash and food stamps. That reduced their total income from $13,600 on aid to $11,000 off it. (Ibid., fig. 2, in 2003 dollars.) The study appeared six months after W-2 won the Innovations Award and received almost no attention.

extreme poverty: Sheila R. Zedlewski and others, "Extreme Poverty Rising, Existing Government Programs Could Do More," Urban Institute, April 1, 2002; they use an alternate definition of poverty that includes food stamps.

***Spending* among the very poor:** Ron Haskins, "Effects of Welfare Reform," in Blank and Haskins, *The New World of Welfare,* 116–19.

287 **about 7 percent grew poorer:** Analysis of Census Bureau data by Wendell Primus; Christopher Jencks and Joseph Swingle find the tipping point somewhere between the 5th and 10th percentile in "Without a Net," *The American Prospect,* Jan. 3, 2000.

basic necessities: Shortages of food, rent, Acs and Loprest, "ASPE Leavers Study," tables 6.2–3; half uninsured, Bowen Garrett and John Holahan, "Welfare Leavers, Medicaid Coverage, and Private Health Insurance," The Urban Institute, B-13, March 2000.

Michigan families: Sheldon Danziger and others, "Does It Pay to Move from Welfare to Work?" *Journal of Policy Analysis and Management* 21, no. 4 (2002): 671–92.

depleted cupboards: While I regularly encountered food shortages in my travels in Milwaukee, surveys by the United States Department of Agriculture indicated that food hardships declined in the late 1990s among the broader population, for some groups dramatically. One report found: "the prevalence of children's hunger declined by about half, from 1.1 percent of all households with children in 1995 to 0.6 percent in 1999." It's possible, of course, for both "food insecurity" and outright "hunger" (two different measures) to be declining yet still common among former welfare recipients. Mark Nord and Gary Bickel, "Measuring Children's Food Insecurity in U.S. Households, 1995–99," Economic Research Service, USDA, *Food Assistance and Nutrition Research Report*, Number 24, April 2002, Abstract.

288 **persistence of hardship:** Heather Boushey and others, *Hardships in America: The Real Story of Working Families* (Washington, DC: Economic Policy Institute, 2001), esp. table 4.

fewer than one in ten reach twice the poverty line: Maria Cancian and Daniel R. Meyer, "Alternative Measures of Economic Success Among TANF Participants," July 2003, table 2 (most but not all the of the families they surveyed had left the rolls).

most never will: Among former AFDC families, the share with incomes above 200 percent of the poverty line was 12 percent in the first year, 27 percent after five years, and 33 percent after ten years. Daniel R. Meyer and Maria Cancian, *Journal of Applied Social Sciences* 25, no. 1 (Winter/Fall 2000–2001).

poverty status of Angie and Jewell: These numbers include food stamps and tax credits, which the official numbers omit. Angie's peak year rose from 121 percent of the poverty line on welfare to 127 percent off it— hardly any difference. Likewise, Jewell's rose from 117 percent on welfare to 121 percent off it. She did, however, experience more income fluctuation after leaving welfare. In her first full year off the rolls, when she mostly went jobless, her income fell to a new low of 54 percent of the poverty line.

289 **What Angie really lived on:** In her first three years off welfare, Angie's annual earnings after payroll taxes averaged $14,850 (in 2003 dollars), or $1,238 a month. To show how this fit her 1999 expenses on Brown Street, I converted it into 1999 dollars; that leaves her with monthly take-home pay of $1,121.

optional necessity: Angie's phone had long been cut off, but I had one installed in the summer of 1999, to make it easier to reach her.

291 **she earned $7.82:** That was her nominal wage in the spring of 1999, her third year off the rolls; the equivalent in 2003 dollars is $8.64.

292 **Michael didn't know Opal used drugs:** Along with notes from previous caseworkers indentifying her drug use, Michael had Opal's latest assessment test, which identified "substance use" as among her likely "work barriers." "To be honest, I don't pay any attention to it," Michael said. "I'm more interested in my interaction with them."

294 **nonmarital births:** From 1995 to 2002, the share of children born outside marriage dipped among blacks (from 69.9 percent to 68.2 percent), while it rose among Hispanics (from 40.8 percent to 43.5 percent) and whites (from 21.2 percent to 23.0 percent). Because of changes in reporting techniques in California, Michigan, and Texas, it's impossible to say when the national rate first slowed. The official numbers show a decline between 1994 and 1995, but most researchers think the trend lines changed a few years earlier.

294   **fewer children with lone single mothers:** Gregory Acs and Sandi Nelson, "Changes in Family Structure and Child Well-Being: Evidence from the 2002 National Survey of America's Families" (paper for University of Michigan, National Poverty Center), Aug. 15, 2003, table 3.

295   **more black children with married parents:** Wendell E. Primus, "Child Living Arrangements by Race and Income: A Supplementary Analysis," Center on Budget and Policy Priorities, Nov. 19, 2001, table 5. Since Primus had resigned from the government to protest the welfare bill, his public comment about an earlier version of this paper was widely noted: "In many ways, welfare reform is working better than I thought it would. . . . Whatever we have been doing over the last five years, we ought to keep going." With his willingness to reexamine a strongly held position in light of new evidence, Primus showed admirable intellectual integrity. (See Blaine Harden, *NYT,* Aug. 12, 2001.)

  no obvious policy pattern: While doing little about welfare, the District of Columbia cut the share of children born outside marriage by 18 percent (68.8 percent in 1994 to 56.6 percent eight years later). Over the same years, as Wisconsin led the drive to end welfare, the share of its children born outside marriage rose 10 percent (from 27.2 percent to 30.0 percent). Nationally, the average rose 4.3 percent (from 32.6 percent in 1994 to 34 percent in 2002). (Author's communication with Stephanie Ventura, National Center for Health Statistics.)

296   **"$8.25 an hour":** The equivalent in 2003 dollars is $9.11.

18. A SHOT AT THE AMERICAN DREAM: MILWAUKEE, FALL 1999

308   **William Martin's performance bonuses:** LAB, audit of Employment Solutions, Inc., Feb. 16, 2001, 7.

  Martin's total salary: Steve Schultze, *MJS,* Feb. 28, 2001.

  staff parties to $160,000 in unallowable costs: LAB audit, 2–5, appendix 1.

  "FBI investigation": Steve Schultze, *MJS,* June 23, 2001. No charges were filed as a result of the alleged investigation, which the FBI did not publicly confirm.

  "bumbling rather than trickiness": Steve Schultze, *MJS,* June 8, 2001. David Mastran, the Maximus CEO, chose nearly the same words when describing the company's problems to me: "It was clearly ineptness on our part and lack of guidance on the state's part, rather than any mal intent." Once heralded as exemplars of efficiency, in other words, the state's two leading privatized agencies defended themselves by citing their own incompetence.

311   **benefits to *younger* children:** Johannes Bos and others, "How Welfare and Work Policies Affect Children: A Synthesis of Research," MDRC, March 2001, ES-4.

adolescents in Minnesota, Canada, and Florida: Jennifer L. Brooks, Elizabeth C. Hair, and Martha J. Zaslow, "Welfare Reform's Impact on Adolescents: Early Warning Signs," Child Trends, July 2001.

"dogs that didn't bark": Greg J. Duncan and P. Lindsay Chase-Lansdale, "Welfare Reform and Children's Well-Being," in Blank and Haskins, *The New World of Welfare,* 407.

"children of current and former recipients": Kathryn Tout, Juliet Scarpa, and Martha J. Zaslow, "Children of Current and Former Welfare Recipients: Similarly at Risk," Child Trends, March 2002.

"environments changed little": Bruce Fuller and others, "New Lives for Poor Families? Mothers and Young Children Move Through Welfare Reform," The Growing Up in Poverty Project—Wave 2 Findings, ES, 2.

312   **New Hope had little impact on family life:** Hans Bos and others, "New Hope for People with Low Incomes: Two-Year Results of a Program to Reduce Poverty and Reform Welfare," MDRC, 1999, tables 5.7, 6.1–6.3, 6.6–6.12. The evaluators concluded: "theory envisions that a program such as New Hope might have many more impacts than in fact emerged" (ch. 6, 14). By the five-year follow-up study, the depression rate among New Hope parents had slightly improved. Still, it remained high and was the only one of ten psychosocial measures in which researchers saw any improvement. Once again, they wrote, "the program had few impacts on the well-being of parents and families." Aletha C. Huston and others, "New Hope for Families and Children: Five-Year Results of a Program to Reduce Poverty and Reform Welfare," MDRC, June 2003, 89.

one outstanding finding: After two years, teachers ranked the New Hope boys as better behaved and more academically skilled than members of a control group, and the boys themselves were more likely to say they expected to attend college. The statistical magnitude was roughly equivalent to adding 100 points to an SAT score (Bos and others, table 7.2). Many of the positive effects for boys continued after five years (Huston and others, 146–59, 169).

314   **Lisa moved back:** After four years away, she was startled by the new hassle of getting a welfare check; she gave up and moved in with an old boyfriend, but not before spending two months crowded in at Angie's and Jewell's.

321   **earned about $18,500:** In 1999, Angie's nominal earnings were $16,800; the equivalent in 2003 dollars is $18,500.

EPILOGUE: WASHINGTON AND MILWAUKEE, 1999–2004

324   **"What does the political scientist":** The 1981 poem by Artur Miedzyzrecki was read by the political scientist Hugh Heclo at a conference at the University of Wisconsin in May 1992.

attacks from a jealous man: Donald Crawford described himself as an aspiring minister, but he was also a recovering addict who had been arrested a few years earlier for his role in torturing a man he suspected of stealing his drugs. Twice in the year before Michelle addressed the legislature, he had been led away in handcuffs for striking her; once, she had been arrested for hitting him and threatening him with a knife. DeParle, *NYT,* April 20 and Dec. 30, 1999.

Lillie Harden: Bill Clinton met her in Arkansas in 1986, and brought her to speak to the National Governors Association later that year. He retold her story often but didn't see her again until 1996, when she stood beside him in the Rose Garden as he talked about her inspired son and signed the new law. As he continued to tell the story during the 1996 campaign, the *Arkansas Democrat Gazette* published a Harden profile. It said Clinton had "bungled the resumes" of her four kids (one, whom Clinton had described as "studying to be a doctor," was working as a garbage collector); cited Carlton Harden's teenage imprisonment; and noted that during the years in which Clinton described Harden as an emblem of postwelfare success, she had gone back on welfare several times. (Frank Wolfe, *Arkansas Democrat Gazette,* Oct. 27, 1996.) In *My Life,* his memoir, Clinton called the story of Harden and her son "the best argument I've ever heard for welfare reform." He added: "I had been working on welfare reform for more than fifteen years. But I didn't consider it a Democratic issue. Or even a governors' issue. Welfare reform was about Lillie Hardin [*sic*] and her boy" (330).

When I talked to Harden, she seemed of two minds about whether working mothers have the ability to inspire their kids. She retold the story of Carlton saying, "Mama, I'm so proud of you," and warned that when mothers "sit around at home and don't do nothing it takes an effect on children." But later in the conversation she said, "Most of the time, these kids don't care about whether you work or scrape to take care of them. They just feel like it's something you have to do."

325   **the story someone could tell:** As too-tidy symbols of success, Crawford and Harden were scarcely unique. I was driving across Wisconsin with Jason Turner one day when he began raving about a woman named Jackie Muriel. As one of the first people off W-2, Muriel was the subject of a long profile in the *Milwaukee Journal Sentinel* that noted a moment in which she had run short on toilet paper. In the past, she had just resorted to theft, but this time she demurred, and Turner attributed the decision to the morally uplifting powers of work. "I was high on life for a week after I read that," Turner said. "It showed you that the system had the capability of transforming someone's life." A few months later, Muriel was in jail, and she went on to lose her kids. (Joel Dresang and Crocker Stephenson, *MJS*, May 18 and Sept. 28, 1997.) Another *Journal Sentinel* story making the rounds relied on a few Milwaukee bus drivers to argue that "a startling change" was under way in the city's poor neighborhoods. "I see more people with kids early in the morning," said one driver, William Love. Another, Pearlie Duncan, said, "You can look into their eyes; they're happy. The eyes tell no lies." A gift from the quote gods if ever there was one, "the eyes tell no lies" appeared in Thompson's application for the Harvard-Ford Foundation award, and Clinton cited the bus story in a radio address. Though I missed Duncan, I spent a morning riding the bus with William Love, whose fame as a social critic was news to him. As we rode around the central city, he said, "I can't say I see a noticeable change" from the welfare years. Then he thought of one: he owned some inner-city houses and had more tenants behind on their rent. (Michele Derus, *MJS*, June 28, 1998.)

For another cautionary welfare-to-work tale, see Peter Boyer's article in *The New Yorker* about the six-year-old Flint, Michigan, boy who took a gun to school and shot and killed a five-year-old girl. In the deluge of coverage, some noted that the little girl's mother, Veronica McQueen, was a welfare-to-work success. But so was the mother of the six-year-old gunman. Tamarla Owens was working not one but two jobs, and gone ten hours a day. Despite her long hours, she had gotten evicted, and sent her son to live with her drug-dealing brother, where he found the loaded gun. (Peter Boyer, *The New Yorker,* July 3, 2000.) In the recent literature of the ghetto, there is one role-model mother who stands out above the others, propelling her son to the Ivy League. But as Ron Suskind tells the story in his book *A Hope in the Unseen,* the moral isn't as clean as it might appear. When explaining what helped her son succeed, Barbara Jennings partly credited a decision she made when her son, Cedric, was two: she quit her job and went on welfare, so they could spend more time together. She lost income but gained time, and they spent it at church, libraries, and museums. In the preschool years, she explained, "a child either gets the love he needs or he doesn't." Then she went back to work. (New York: Broadway Books, 1998, 31.)

325 **incomes of disadvantaged single mothers:** Jared Bernstein of the Economic Policy Institute examined the incomes of all single mothers below twice the poverty threshold. From 1994 to 2000, their incomes rose 17 percent to $16,300, before surrendering 2 percent of the gains over the next two years. Bernstein, "Single Mothers Lose Ground in Weak Labor Market," EPI Web site, May 19, 2004. When I talked to Clinton, he, too, noted that the recession's effect on poor single mothers had been milder than feared: "The assumption was that since the welfare people were hired during the expansion, when the economy turned down, they'd be the first ones laid off, and that's not necessarily what's happened."

325 **child poverty rates:** Analysis by Gary Burtless of the Brookings Institution (presented at a briefing, Sept. 26, 2003).

employment of high school dropouts: Jared Bernstein and Lawrence Mishel, "Labor Markets Left Behind," Economic Policy Institute, Briefing Paper, Sept. 2003, 8–10.

unemployment rose: From 4.0 percent in 2000 to 6.0 percent in 2003.

326 **"works despite itself":** Gardner, who has spent more than two decades living and working in the central city of Milwaukee, said of W-2: "It is demonstrably, radically, unequivocally better than the old AFDC system, because it doesn't pay you not to work. And it's been implemented as badly as is humanly possible. . . . The moral is the right thing done badly is much better than the wrong thing, even when done well. . . . It is just staggering to me how many uneducated poor folks who I really didn't expect to work, are working."

327 **"compassionate conservative":** In noting that George W. Bush took pains "to say that he wasn't a racist," Clinton added: "Based on his appointments in Texas and his appointments in the White House, he's not. The only really unforgivably racist thing he's done is let his people call the white voters in South Carolina in the primary and tell them John McCain had a black baby. . . . But he has governed, at least, without apparent racial discrimination." The reference was to a phone campaign by anonymous Bush supporters, who spread the rumor that McCain's adopted Bangladeshi daughter was his illegitimate black child. The Bush campaign said it had nothing to do with the calls.

rising inequality: Data are from CBO, "Effective Federal Tax Rates, 1997–2000," Aug. 2003, table B1-C.

tax-cutting frenzy: *The Wall Street Journal* editorial page went as far as calling women like Angie and Jewell—people too poor to pay income taxes—"lucky duckies." Grover Norquist, Washington's leading antitax operative, told Terry Gross of the public radio show *Fresh Air* that inheritance taxes reflected the "morality of the Holocaust." (*WSJ*, Nov. 20, 2002; *Fresh Air,* Oct. 2, 2003.)

Medicaid eligibility: Matthew Broaddus and others, "Expanding Family Coverage: States' Medicaid Eligibility Policies for Working Families in the Year 2000," Center on Budget and Policy Priorities, Feb. 13, 2002.

child-care subsidies: Jennifer Mezey, Mark Greenberg, and Rachel

Schumacher, "The Vast Majority of Federally Eligible Children Did Not Receive Child Care Assistance in FY 2000," CLASP, Oct. 2, 2002.

327   **tax credits:** Nicholas Johnson, "A Hand Up: How State Earned Income Tax Credits Help Working Families Escape Poverty in 2001," Center on Budget and Policy Priorities, Dec. 2001.

328   **At $5.15 an hour:** The 1950 minimum wage of seventy-five cents is worth $5.85 in 2004 dollars, 70 cents more than today's minimum.

program of workers' aid: Isabel Sawhill and Adam Thomas, "A Hand Up for the Bottom Third: Toward a New Agenda for Low-Income Working Families," Brookings Institution, May 2001.

Oregon program: A study called the National Evaluation of Welfare to Work Strategies (NEWWS) examined 11 sites nationwide. Programs that stressed basic education achieved a five-year earnings gain of 7 percent. Job-search programs gained 12 percent. But with a "mixed-services" strategy of job search and training, Portland, Oregon, topped the list with a gain of nearly 25 percent. Nan Poppe, Julie Strawn, and Karin Martinson, "Whose Job Is It?" in Bob Giloth, ed., *Workforce Intermediaries for the 21st Century* (Philadelphia: Temple University Press, 2003), 39.

physically get away: For Gautreaux, see James E. Rosenbaum, "Changing the Geography of Opportunity by Expanding Residential Choice: Lessons from the Gautreaux Program," *Housing Policy Debate,* vol. 6, 1995, 231–69. For Moving to Opportunity, see Jeffrey R. Kling and Jeffrey B. Liebman, "Experimental Analysis of Neighborhood Effects on Youth," unpublished paper, May 2004.

329   **"marriage initiative":** When I talked to Clinton, he said: "If they shuffle a bunch of money to their political supporters and don't do anything but pontificate at people, well, I don't think it will have much impact. On the other hand, I think the central insight that children will be better off with two parents than one is true. . . . I didn't have any problem with him wanting to spend some money to help people build strong marriages and take care of kids." He suggested that Democrats support the initiative on the condition that some of the money be used to expand welfare eligibility and training for two-parent families, to keep more fathers in the home.

330   **Opal acknowledged crack use:** CHIPS petition, March 13, 2000.

331   **$200,000 a year:** Meg Kissinger, *MJS,* July 15, 2003.

half failed the performance goals: To succeed, agencies had to place 35 percent of their recipients in jobs. Maximus recorded a job-placement rate of 35.54 percent; YW Works had 35.25 percent; OIC had 28.55 percent; and UMOS had 24.38 percent. (Felicia Thomas-Lynn, *MJS,* July 31, 2003.)

332   **people in W-2 fared no better:** Irving Piliavin, Amy Dworksy, and Mark E. Courtney, "What Happens to Families Under W-2 in Milwaukee County, Wisconsin? Report from Wave 2 of the Milwaukee TANF Appli-

cant Study," Chapin Hall Center for Children at the University of Chicago and Institute for Research on Poverty, University of Wisconsin, Madison, Sept. 2003, 43–58.

332   **Bleeding red ink:** The financial problems arose at YW Works, which had struck me as the most competent and creative of the five agencies. Its clients included Michelle Crawford, the woman whom Tommy Thompson had invited before the legislature, and the Y's handling of her case was one of the most skillful I've seen. Her caseworkers arranged for months of psychological counseling to address her depression, then put her through an on-the-job training program at a plastics factory the Y bought for that purpose. "They were like a family to me," Crawford said. But the factory failed in the recession, and the Y's longtime director, Julia Taylor, moved on, trailing board criticisms of her financial stewardship; in another venture, she used much of the agency's W-2 profits to create an unsuccessful software company in which, as a member of its two-person board of directors, she gave herself stock options. (See Bruce Murphy, *MJS*, May 30, 2004.) The penalty was assessed against the United Migrant Opportunity Society, after an audit found it had mishandled 86 of 110 cases. It was imposed in 2003 by a new Democratic governor, James Doyle. The original W-2 law allowed the state to penalize the agencies $5,000 for any instance of a "failure to serve" a client. But under Thompson and his Republican successor, Scott McCallum, no penalties were ever assessed.

"no evidence of favoritism": While a state appeals court rejected Comptroller Alan Hevesi's charges of "corruption," elements of the Maximus deal were cozy in a way that invited public distrust. Turner recruited a friend from Milwaukee, Tony Kearney, to work as a consultant on an ostensibly separate project, a "faith-based" initiative that tried to reach troubled recipients through the churches. But Kearney was also a consultant for Maximus, and his city work had him meeting with some of the same groups against whom Maximus would bid; some of them worried he was using his access to gather information about their proposals. Another element involved the role of Richard Schwartz, a former top aide to Mayor Rudolph Giuliani. In leaving City Hall, he founded a for-profit company, Opportunity America, to provide welfare-to-work services. The Maximus proposal pledged to give Schwartz a $30 million subcontract, which critics called a further way of seeking favor with the Giuliani administration. Turner had previously done some consulting work for Schwartz. In addition, *The Village Voice* later reported that, while seeking Turner's business, Leutermann also agreed to a request from Turner's wife, Angie, to contribute up to $60,000 to an abstinence program she had designed for the Milwaukee public schools. (She sought support from all five W-2 agencies, Turner told me, and Maximus and OIC agreed.)

When I asked Turner about the contracting dispute, he dismissed the criticisms as unfair attacks by interests wedded to the city's status quo. While he designed the bid process, he said, he didn't choose the seventeen vendors and therefore couldn't have favored Maximus or Schwartz even had he wanted to. He did say he hoped the process would bring in some for-profit companies, since he thought they would be more efficient. (At the time Maximus won the New York contract, its problems in Milwaukee were largely unknown.) Turner also stressed that multiple agencies—including the Manhattan district attorney and federal prosecutors—had investigated his conduct without finding any wrongdoing. The city conflict-of-interest board also found no breach of rules in the hiring of Turner's father-in-law. But it fined him $6,500 for two unrelated ethics violations: renting an apartment from a subordinate and having his city assistant help him for a few hours with a private consulting job. Leaving the welfare business, Schwartz sold his company to Maximus for $780,000 and became the editorial page editor of the *New York Daily News*.

334   **more than $20,000 a year:** For those betting that incomes of former welfare families will improve with time, Jewell's case is encouraging. She did much better in her second four years off the rolls than she did in her first three. She worked more regularly, at a rising wage, so her earnings in the second period rose 30 percent. She also straightened out her problems with the food stamp office (and, after having another child, spent six months getting W-2). Compared with her first years off the rolls, her total income grew nearly 40 percent, and she got out of poverty. The updated box score (in 2003 dollars) looks like this:

	FIRST 3 YEARS OFF WELFARE	NEXT 4 YEARS
Earnings	$12,700	$16,500
Tax credits	4,000	5,000
Payroll taxes	(-1,000)	(-1,300)
W-2	0	1,000
Food stamps	900	1,600
	$16,600	**$23,000**
% of poverty line	**93%**	**122%**

While the trend line is positive, on her own, Jewell is still in that near-poverty zone, in which material hardships abound. Or she would be if she were all alone. Counting Ken's income brings them to something like 185 percent of the poverty line, the level at which families usually start to feel better off. It's another bit of evidence pointing to the importance of men.

lower-middle-class life: The average married couple with kids has an annual income of about $65,000. With approximately $40,000 combined,

Jewell and Ken would rank at about the 25th percentile. (Author communication with Ed Welniak, Census Bureau.)

336 **"the money's just not right":** Here's Angie's updated box score (in 2003 dollars):

	FIRST 3 YEARS OFF WELFARE	NEXT 4 YEARS
Earnings:	$16,100	$14,900
Tax credits:	5,600	5,700
Payroll taxes:	(-1,200)	(-1,100)
W-2:	0	0
Food stamps:	4,400	4,600
Kinship care	0	2,400
	$24,900	**$26,500**
% of poverty line	**115%**	**116%**

Angie's summary—"just treading water"—is apt. Her earnings declined 7 percent, but her public subsidies grew, especially the kinship care payments for taking in Brierra. (In the old days, these were part of AFDC, so technically the household would have been back on the welfare rolls.) The payment raised her total income, but with Brierra her family size grew, so in relationship to the poverty line, Angie's circumstance hardly changed. She went from 103 percent of poverty (on welfare) to 115 percent (newly off) to 116 percent (in the next four years). On most days, it wasn't enough for her to notice the change.

ACKNOWLEDGMENTS

In doing this work, I've accumulated more debts than I can fully acknowledge, but it's gratifying to begin. This book wouldn't exist without *The New York Times*, which for more than a decade has let me go where I want and write what I wish about welfare and poverty. In an age of tight newsroom budgets, the *Times*'s commitment to a poverty beat is, in the literal sense, extraordinary. Joe Lelyveld, the executive editor through most of my tenure, made me feel empowered from the start, while Jack Rosenthal of the *Times Magazine* and Dean Baquet of the national desk—great editors and friends—offered extravagant support. Joe and Bill Keller let me spend a year in Milwaukee writing about welfare and also agreed to the leave with which I started the book. Howell Raines generously extended it, and Bill Keller, now the executive editor, patiently extended it again. Jon Landman has been a source of friendship and counsel since the day I walked in the door, and Gerry Marzorati helped make a magazine writer out of me. Other current or former employees of the *Times* to whom I'm indebted include Soma Golden Behr, Nicole Bengiveno, Doug Frantz, George Judson, Adam Moss, Matt Purdy, Andy Rosenthal, Bill Schmidt, and Arthur Sulzberger Jr.

Just as crucially, this book wouldn't exist without Angela Jobe, Jewell Reed, and Opal Caples, who along with their families have taught me a great deal about welfare and poverty and also about resilience. Kesha, Redd, and Von Jobe were always welcoming, and I'm grateful for the goodwill of Marcus Robertson, Kenny Gross, and especially Kenyatta Thigpen, a frank and articulate narrator of his past. In pointing me toward the Eastland plantation, Hattie Mae Crenshaw, Jewell's mother, gave this work a vital context. Listening to her tell her life story has been one of the great pleasures of my reporting career. Jewell's sister and niece, Mary Reed-Flowers and Monica Reed, greeted me warmly in Chicago and in subsequent interviews. Virginia Caples arranged two visits to the Eastland plantation and introduced me to her uncle, Mack Caples, Pie Eddie's son and a living link to the family's past. In the summer of 2000, Angie, the kids, and I made the drive from Milwaukee to Egypt, Mississippi, for her family's annual reunion, where Charity and Rodger Scott, Angie's mother and stepfather, greeted me as though I were real family. They've shown nothing but patience with my project ever since, even when it resurrected painful events in their past. Another person to whom I owe special thanks is Michael Steinborn, whose empathy and perseverance brightened an otherwise disheartening picture of the welfare bureaucracy. The relationship between a reporter and his subjects involves an odd mix of closeness and distance—closeness while gathering the material, distance while processing it. Virtually everyone listed above went through this cycle multiple times as I realized how much I still needed to understand and returned with more questions. They bore up with grace, for no reward other than my interest and gratitude. My interpretation of their lives is mine alone, offered in the reporter's vague faith that an important story, properly told, can help bring about "Better Days."

Writers need time. In getting it, I had the financial support of three generous institutions, which requested nothing in return and waited for years for the results. My gratitude goes to Mark Steinmeyer of the Smith Richardson Foundation and Drew Altman of the Henry J. Kaiser Family Foundation, which awarded me grants, and to Alex Jones of the Joan Shorenstein Center on the Press, Politics and Public Policy at the Kennedy School of Government at Harvard University, where I enjoyed a four-month fellowship in the fall of 2000. Gregg Easterbrook, Lyn Hogan, and Isabel Sawhill encouraged me to apply for the Smith Richardson grant. Judy Feder, dean of the Georgetown Public Policy Institute, put herself out to oversee the grants, as did her administrator, Sandy Fournier. As the hardcover edition was published in 2004, I benefited from another bit of unexpected good fortune—a travel grant from the Annie E. Casey Foundation, which allowed me to expand the book's reach through a series of talks across the country. For Casey's generous support, I am grateful to Doug Nelson, Ralph Smith, Patrick McCarthy, Mike Laracy, and Jane Dinse.

Writers also need readers, especially blunt ones. Nicholas Lemann was a crucial early supporter of this project, as he has been for much of my work; he was also at times a frank critic, who forced me to clarify my thoughts. Jack Rosenthal offered a similar mix of encouragement and critique as I mustered a first draft. Toby Herr and Mark Greenberg win Purple Hearts for reading multiple versions; Toby sometimes saw the story more clearly from a distance than I could up close, and Mark's inexhaustible patience was matched only by his command of the policy details. My father, James DeParle, in reading several drafts, was with me in the trenches, as he has been through every stretch of my life. (My mother, Joan DeParle, contributed to my writing in another way, working long hours to help pay for my education.) Others who helpfully read portions or full drafts include Nancy-Ann DeParle, Elizabeth Fenn, Lory Hough, Gerry Marzorati, Chris Myers, Mary Pattillo, Charles Peters, Nicholas Thompson, and Sam Verhovek. Finally, I'd like to thank Ann Hulbert, who signed on about two thirds of the way through as the book's de facto daily editor and has been improving it ever since. Her enthusiasm brought the effort new inspiration and her exquisite judgment, in matters big and small, gave it a safety net. Every author should be so lucky.

President Bill Clinton took time away from finishing his book to talk with me about mine; for making room on his crowded calendar, I'm grateful to him, Jim Kennedy, and Maggie Williams. Mickey Kaus first suggested I go to Milwaukee and has shared his time and insights over a number of years. Taylor Branch offered unexpected help at an important time. Debbie Bigler of the Milwaukee County Department of Human Services assembled the trio's welfare records and fielded years of follow-up questions with a conscientious good cheer that went well beyond the call of duty. Alex Nguyen, Marc Santora, and Seth Stern offered research assistance. I relied especially heavily on the research of Lory Hough, a tireless sleuth whose contributions touch every chapter. Her skill and enthusiasm allowed me to indulge my curiosity without sacrificing my time and therefore made this a much better book than it otherwise could have been. Charles Peters, my longtime mentor and friend, has contributed to my journalism in ways too numerous to list. His concern for social justice is as deep and informed as any I know, and in urging me to scrub my biases he offered a reporting principle that was particularly useful in tracking a story with so many surprises.

My forays into Mississippi's past were greatly aided by Chris Myers, a PhD candidate at the University of North Carolina–Chapel Hill, who is writing a dissertation about James Eastland; he not only shared early drafts of his thesis but conducted a series of tutorials on southern history. Elizabeth Fenn and Peter Wood of Duke University were two other generous history coaches. In my efforts as an amateur genealogist, I got invaluable assistance from a professional one, Jan Hillegas, who helped uncover pieces of the past in places that wouldn't have occurred to me. Historians Chris Waldrep and Todd Moye shared copies of the contemporaneous news coverage of the Luther Holbert affair. In my research on Chicago, I got help from Chuck Nelson and Marie Pees of the Census Bureau, who supplied the tract-level information on Jeffrey Manor. Conversations with Mary Pattillo helped me make sense of it.

Among those who helped me understand Wisconsin welfare politics, current and past, were John Gurda, Tom Kaplan, John Nichols, Peter Tropman, and Gerald Whitburn. David Riemer offered his time, shared his files, and wrote me a long memo about the events that led the Wisconsin legislature to abolish AFDC. Jason Turner welcomed me as a chronicler of his work, offered many useful introductions in Milwaukee, and spent a great deal of time responding to my questions. Coming to grips with Opal's story required me to learn about the effects of cocaine. I got helpful lessons from Ric Curtis, Francine Feinberg, Jerome Jaffe, Michael Massing, Thomas McLellan, Anne Paczesny, and Pat Tucker. Likewise, to understand the work lives of Angie and Jewell, I needed to know more about nursing homes, and got help from Judy Feder, Robert Friedland, Paul Kleyman, Robyn Stone, and Josh Wiener. I couldn't have told the full Maximus story without the interviews and documents provided by several company employees on the condition of anonymity.

A number of Washington figures involved in the welfare bill agreed to long sets of after-the-fact interviews, which, while quoted sparingly, greatly enhanced my ability to tell the story. My thanks to David Ellwood, Mark Greenberg, Stan Greenberg, Ron Haskins, Paul Offner, Wendell Primus, Robert Rector, Bruce Reed, Donna Shalala, and Melissa Skolfield. Among the social scientists on whose patience I regularly imposed were Greg Acs, Maria Cancian, Sheldon Danziger, Greg Duncan, Donna Pavetti, and especially Christopher Jencks, who guided me on several fronts. My talks with Jared Bernstein were particularly helpful as I thought through the economics of postwelfare life. Yulia Fungard helped me crunch the income numbers for Angie and Jewell. Several friends offered their encouragement and also their understanding when the work caused me to disappear; I drew on the support of Henry Brinton, Patti Cohen, E. J. Flynn, Tim Golden, Jon Rosenblum, and the Katy Varney–Dave Goetz clan. Liza Gorman and especially Allison Curran also did much to keep things on track.

Others to whom I owe thanks include: Jeff Aiken, Peggy Anderson, Ken Apfel, Jose Arteaga, Don Baer, Ruthie Mae Bailey, Hundley Batts, Richard Bavier, Jeremy Ben-Ami, Gordon Berlin, Doug Besharov, Bill Biggs, Helen Blank, Rebecca Blank, Tony Blankley, Andrew Bluth, Mary Bourdette, Heather Boushey, Sheila Burke, Vee Burke, Gary Burtless, Dick Buschmann, Adam Carasso, Felmers Chaney, Lindsay Chase-Lansdale, Henry Cisneros, Richard Cloward, James Cobb, Deborah Colton, Tom Corbett, Wesley Crenshaw, Ellen Dadisman, Kristina Daugirtas, Pat DeLessio, Seth Diamond, Jonah Edelman, Peter Edelman, James Fallows, Lester Feder, Pam Fendt, Don Fierce, Ari Fleischer, Tillie Fowler, Henry Freedman, Bruce Fuller, John Gardner, Keith Garland, Mona Garland, James Gibney, Ed Gillespie, Newt Gingrich, Karen Goldmeier, Marjorie Goldsborough, Linda Gordon, Peter Gottschalk, Bob Greenstein, Mary Gross, Jimmy Hayes, Chris Henick, Kathe Hollingshaus, Harry Holzer, Jack Howard, Paul Jargowsky, Chris Jennings, Julie Kerksick, Nick Kotz, Julie Sorrentino Kresge, Ed Kutler, Rachel Langenohl, Robert Lerman, John Lewis, Pamela Loprest, Ed Lorenzen, Tamara Stanton Luzzatto, Gary Mailman, Bob Matsui, Cindy Mann, Mary Kay Mantho, Jai Marin, Will Marshall, Joyce McFarland, Sara McLanahan, Lawrence Mead, Jan Meyers, Ron Mincy, Robert Moffitt, Kristin Moore, Dick Morris, Daniel Patrick Moynihan, Richard Nathan, Leon Panetta, David J. Pate Jr., John Pawasarat, Frances Fox Piven, Susan Pogodzinksi, LeAnne Redick, Mary Lou Reed, Tara Reed, Grace Reef, Robert Reich, Barbara Reinhold, Lou Richman, Cynthia Rice, Bridgette Ridgeway, Alice Rivlin, Laurie Rubiner, Paul Saeman, Isaac Shapiro, Doug Schoen, Clay Shaw, Ron Skarzenski, Margaret Stapleton, George Stephanopoulos, Gene Steurle, Julie Strawn, Paul Stuiber, James Talent, John Tapogna, Rich Tarplin, Julia Taylor, Barry Toiv, Vicki Turetsky, Jack Tweedie, Stephanie Ventura, Melanne Verveer, Barclay Walsh, John Wancheck, Kent Weaver, Jim Weill,

Marcus White, David Whitman, Julie Wilson, Michael Wiseman, and Wendy Woolcott-Steele.

Along with time and sources, a writer needs a publisher. At Viking, Wendy Wolf's enthusiasm for this project won me over eight years ago, and for her unflagging commitment I've been grateful many times since. A book that juggles dozens of characters across several centuries requires a special set of editing skills, and Wendy, a special editor, kept the narrative train moving. For her patience, and her impatience, I'm equally grateful. To her assistant, Cliff Corcoran, a word of thanks, too. My copy editor, Juli Barbato, gave the manuscript a careful read and saved me from several bad errors. Viking's production editor, Kate Griggs, showed great concern for getting things right, even as my last-minute revisions threw the schedule woefully off-course. For putting me in their good hands and goading me along, I'm grateful to my agent, Chuck Verrill, whose devotion to this book has run deep. Lastly, a special word of thanks to Katy Varney, Andrew Maraniss, and their associates at McNeely Pigott & Fox, for their spirit and skill in giving this book its launch. They give PR a good name.

I started this book on the verge of getting married and ended it as a father of two. My sons, Nicholas and Zachary, have never known a world in which their father wasn't in the room next to theirs, engaged in the mysteriously intense work they've come to call "making the book." They grew faster than it did, and one of the serendipitous rewards of this project was that it kept me nearby, where I could watch their young lives unfold. I can't imagine a writer's garret that offered a happier view. My friend Joe Lelyveld advises authors to eschew spousal encomia in print and indulge them in real life. I'll ignore his advice just long enough to say that Nancy-Ann DeParle is the best thing that ever happened to me.

INDEX